FORD M

FORD MADOX FORD (the na
inally Ford Hermann Hueff
1873. His mother, Catheri
Raphaelite painter Ford Madox Brown. His father, Francis
Hueffer, was a German emigré, a musicologist and music critic for
The Times. Christina and Dante Gabriel Rossetti were his aunt and
uncle by marriage. Ford published his first book, a children's
fairytale, when he was seventeen. He collaborated with Joseph
Conrad from 1898 to 1908, and also befriended many of the best
writers of his time, including Henry James, H.G. Wells, Stephen
Crane, John Galsworthy and Thomas Hardy. He is best known for
his novels, especially *The Fifth Queen* (a trilogy about Henry VII;
1906–8); *The Good Soldier* (1915); and *Parade's End* (his tetralogy
about the First World War). He was also an influential poet and
critic, and a brilliant magazine editor. He founded *The English
Review* in 1908, discovering D.H. Lawrence, Wyndham Lewis, and
Ezra Pound, who became another close friend. Ford served as an
officer in the Welch Regiment 1915–19. After the war he moved
to France. In Paris he founded *The Transatlantic Review*, taking on
Ernest Hemingway as a sub-editor, discovering Jean Rhys and Basil
Bunting, and publishing James Joyce and Gertrude Stein. In the
1920s and 1930s he moved between Paris, New York, and
Provence. He died in Deauville in June 1939. The author of over
eighty books, Ford is a major presence in twentieth-century
writing.

SARA HASLAM is a lecturer in literature at the Open University.
She has published articles on Ford Madox Ford, Henry James and
Modernism, and produced a multi-media CD-ROM on the poetry
of Thomas Hardy. Her book *Fragmenting Modernism: Ford Madox
Ford, the Novel and the Great War* was published by Manchester
University Press in 2002.

Also by Ford Madox Ford from Carcanet

The English Novel
The Ford Reader
The Good Soldier
A History of Our Own Times
Ladies Whose Bright Eyes
No Enemy
Parade's End
The Rash Act
Selected Poems
War Prose

FORD MADOX FORD

···

England and the English

EDITED WITH AN INTRODUCTION BY
SARA HASLAM

CARCANET

This book is dedicated to Paul, a fine companion
in the city and the country

The individual volumes of *England and the English* were first published in
England by Alston Rivers in 1905, 1906 and 1907
The Author's Note was first published in the United States by
McLure, Phillips and Co. in 1907

This edition first published in Great Britain in 2003 by
Carcanet Press Limited
Alliance House
Cross Street
Manchester M2 7AQ

A CIP catalogue record for this book is available from the British Library

ISBN 1 85754 583 4

The publisher acknowledges financial assistance from Arts Council England

Typeset by XL Publishing Services, Tiverton
Printed and bound in England by SRP Ltd, Exeter

Contents

ENGLAND AND THE ENGLISH

The Soul of London

Londoner's disinclination to listen to unlicensed preachers. – The
London Sabbath. – The Sunday papers. – The two Hamlets. – 'The
parades'. – London in the making. – Londoners in decay.

The cloisters of our Valhalla. – The unknown author. – The waste
of individualities. – The pleasantest size for a graveyard. – The
cemetery. – Athens versus Kensington High Street. – The
Londoner. – The impossibility of finding him. – The death of the
Spirit of Place. – The individualist and his neighbours. – At Père-
la-Chaise. – The discussion in the cloisters. – The school boys. –
The disappearance of the great figure. – Spring clouds. – The
forgotten hills. – The stern reformer. – Building improvements. –
'History' ends with the young Pretender. – The beginning of
'movements'. – The ideal city of the reformer. – The end of
furniture. – Utopia. – The alternative. – The end of London. – The
elements. – The charity school. – The garden plots. – The Monastic
reformers. – 'That neurasthenia joke'. – The sick farm labourer. –
A race that will survive. – London from a distance. – The cloud.

The Heart of the Country

The Restaurant. – The Islands of the Blest. – The man from the
Heart of the Country. – The mirage. – The change in our language.
– The permanence of the idea. – Leaving town. – Each man's heart.
– The great view. – The 'note' of the country one of pain. – The
empty room. – The belief in romance. – The watcher by the
bedside. – The country in inverted commas. – The Antæus town.
– The scientists. – The townsman's difficulty in becoming a countryman. – He discovers his ignorance. – The stages of a country
life. – The townsman's induction. – The landowner's point of view.
– The child in the country. – The slum child. – The hopper. – The
railway porter. – Going to a cricket match. – Views. – 'What a lot
a fellow could do if he owned all that'.

ness. – The peasant's print. – The absence of youths in the country.
– The village maiden.

Introduction

Ford Madox Ford published the trilogy of books that make up *England and the English* between 1905 and 1907. Part of a wave of such texts, it investigates England and Englishness[1] with originality, in impressionist style and in ways that provide an excellent introduction to the work of this seminal Modernist writer. Though a work of non-fiction, the trilogy eschews superficially factual history; it shares characteristics with novels of the time – Ford's and others'. The 'when' of Englishness is as stimulating to Ford as the 'where', the 'why' or the 'how' – and we see Ford's nineteenth-century roots here, as well as early examples of the Modernist quest to 'make it new'. Between them, the books form a trilogy of tenses: they gradually peel back layers of the past: Ford conceived of the *Soul of London* as a book celebrating modernity, dedicated to the present and the future; the *Heart of the Country* looked to rural places, older than cities; the *Spirit of the People* travelled further back still. 'For the Country was before the Town', Ford writes in the introduction to the American edition of the trilogy, 'but, before either... was the People itself'.[2]

On publication of the first volume, *The Soul of London*, on 2 May 1905, the *Daily Mail* called it, 'the latest and truest image of London, built up out of a series of negations, that together are more hauntingly near to a composite picture of the city than anything we have seen before'.[3] It devoted a full column to the book, recognising in its interest both something of the zeitgeist and Ford's brilliant, painterly, technique. Such texts were popular at the time, especially

---

1   This is different from 'Britishness'. Ford concentrates on English landscapes, urban and rural, throughout this trilogy.
2   *England and the English: An Interpretation* (New York: McClure, Phillips and Co., 1907), xviii.
3   Quoted by Max Saunders in *Ford Madox Ford: A Dual Life* (Oxford: Oxford University Press, 1996), I, 195.

when they expressed the contemporary fascination with threats to Englishness: notions of urban chaos or flux, degeneration and decline.[4] H.G. Wells' *Tono-Bungay* (1909), one of his most successful novels, is a good example of this trend, and *The Soul of London* also exploits it to a degree. The second two volumes of the trilogy represent the necessary concomitant escape to the country version of Englishness, one which is also a flight into the past. Yet *The Soul of London* is primarily excited about the modern varieties of vibrant Englishness that only the city can provide. London is 'illimitable', 'kaleidoscopic' and resonates with the voices, experiences, memories and aspirations of its countless inhabitants.

The Contemporary Context

Books like Ford's, which debated Englishness, were in vogue for several reasons: perhaps most obviously because of the focus afforded and encouraged by the turn of the century. The act of looking forward also involved looking back. Readers of the 1890s, state Michael Neve and Mike Jay, were 'positively engulfed with imaginative constructions of the next century'.[5] When these included such schemes as the plan for a Channel Tunnel, Englishness was perceived as under threat, and in need of re-evaluation and support. 'Invasion literature' – novels and pamphlets that envisioned the defilement of the island, some of which were linked to the Channel Tunnel project – enjoyed record sales figures from a fascinated and appalled population during the years from 1900 to 1914.[6] In a nice variation on this theme, Ford also sees similar invasive forces at work from within the country, as a result of industry. Such hostile forces inflict a mortal blow on the 'natural' – i.e. what existed there before their incursion. Whereas the 'river is a natural way [...] railroads tunnel through hills [...] and crash through the town itself, boring straight ways into the heart of it with a fine contempt for natural obstacles' (*The Soul of London*, p. 38). The sexual imagery implicit in the Channel Tunnel, and in railway tunnels, is

---

4   In *Haunts of Ancient Peace* (1902), Alfred Austin writes of the city as a place of 'ungraceful hurry and worry, perpetual postmen's knocks, an intermittent shower of telegrams'. The quotation comes from Martin Weiner, *English Culture and the Decline of the Industrial Spirit* (Cambridge: Cambridge University Press, 1981), 45. Late Victorian novels, like Gissing's *New Grub Street* (1891), also provide examples of the widespread theory of urban degeneration.

5   Introduction to *1900: A Fin-de-Siècle Reader* (London: Penguin, 1999), xiii.

6   Samuel Hynes, *The Edwardian Turn of Mind* (Princeton: Princeton University Press, 1968), 66.

significant too: fears of miscegenation went with those of invasion.[7]

The second Boer War (1899–1902) was another important factor in fuelling the debate on Englishness because, as Linda Colley has noted, the construction of national identity depends on an obviously hostile Other, against which it can range and define itself.[8] Reflection on this war, and contemporary notions of a weakening urban workforce – showing the decline from a pastoral English ideal represented by George Eliot's Adam Bede, for example – actually fed into one another, because of the scrutiny under which the (largely male, working-class) fighting population was put. Sir William Taylor, the Surgeon-General, wrote in 1904 of the 'alarming proportion of the young men of this country, more especially among the urban population, who are unfit for military service on account of defective physique' (*1900*, p. 290). If England was to be physically strong, the message seemed to be, that strength would come not from industrial centres, but from rural havens. At the beginning of *The Heart of the Country* (p. 120) Ford mentions reading an 'organ of advanced thought' propagating such theories. Worryingly, he reports that by 1906, in the opinion of this journal, 'country stock' was considered to be too different from the city type and thus, his reader infers, incompatible for regenerative purposes. Even when men were looked for in rural areas for such purposes, however, they were not necessarily there. According to Alun Howkins, the forced migration between the 1870s and the 1890s had worked 'only too well', and he states somewhat dramatically that 'there were no men left on the land'.[9] For the popular conception of Englishness – one reliant on theories of hereditary urban degeneration, or 'physical deterioration' as Ford describes it in *The Soul of London*[10] – to be satisfied, they had to be persuaded to return.

For related and additional reasons, what Weiner calls a 'suspicion of material and technological development and [...] exclusion of

---

7   See my article 'Ford's Training' in Max Saunders and Robert Hampson (eds), *Ford Madox Ford's Modernity* (Amsterdam: Rodopi, 2003) for an analysis of this subject.

8   Linda Colley, *Britons: Forging the Nation 1707–1837* (London: Pimlico, 1994), 5.

9   Alun Howkins, 'The Discovery of Rural England' in Robert Colls and Philip Dodd (eds), *Englishness: Politics and Culture 1880–1920* (London: Croom Helm, 1986), 67.

10 See *The Soul of London*, p. 103. Ford evidently isn't convinced by the validity of this popular notion, turning it into a kind of joke in the text by questioning when it began to strike men down and making it an ancient rather than a modern problem. However, not surprisingly due to the subject matter, he comes closer to accepting some of the parameters of this debate in the later books.

industrialism' in England fomented around the end of the century and encouraged a polarised perception of England as either 'workshop' or 'shire' (recall here the current popularity of Tolkein's *Lord of the Rings*).[11] Ideas of progress associated with the one came up against the nostalgia fundamental to the other. This kind of polarity was popular, and effective, in literature, and not just with those like William Morris who were known for their utopian dream visions. Thomas Hardy, Rudyard Kipling and Edward Thomas had all contributed to its success, and would continue to do so. Writers like Ford, Henry James and Joseph Conrad were more equivocal in their analysis of the polarity of city versus country, as Ford's trilogy bears out. In their representations of rural and urban landscapes, one was not necessarily superior to the other: both could be seen to have their place in the modern literary conception of Englishness.

The Modern Context

In our own time, a second wave of new books questioning English (and sometimes by extension British) identity has provided the best possible context for republication of Ford's contribution to the debate. Examples include Norman Davies' *The Isles*, John Redwood's *The Death of Britain*, Jeremy Paxman's *The English*, Simon Heffer's *Nor Shall my Sword*, Roger Scruton's *England: An Elegy*, and numerous works of fiction, such as those mentioned below. Renewed focus was placed on Englishness as the twentieth century turned into the twenty-first, and it seems as though this occurred for reasons similar to those of a century earlier. In 2000, the Falklands had been the most recent war fought in the interests of British sovereignty, and elements of the media coverage of this event left little doubt as to its catalytic function in relation to ideas of nationhood. Indeed, there were those who claimed that the war was intended to shift energies away from domestic discontent in this way.

In addition, as shipyards, mines and steelworks closed in the last quarter of the twentieth century, difficult questions about technology and industry, and progress, were being asked. Such closures, and other factors such as those mentioned above, helped to create the impression that notions of Englishness were shifting again. Those notions that were foregrounded could easily be mapped onto

---

11 *English Culture and the Decline of the Industrial Spirit*, 5.

ideas from the fin-de-siècle, for, in a final echo of the past, debates
have arranged themselves around the same polarity as those of a
hundred years ago. One reader of Scruton's *Elegy* pointed out the
'absence of urban England, let alone immigrant England' in the
book – which means, curiously enough, that in some ways Ford's
text would read as the more current.[12] (By p. 12 of *The Soul of
London*, Ford is discussing all the nationalities involved in creating
a composite photograph of 'the Londoner', which he also names
'the Modern'.)

In a review of a novel by Christopher Hart called *Harvest*, in June
1999, D.J. Taylor identified a 'new movement in English fiction'.
He describes this new movement (and in a way the adjective seems
hardly to be justified) as 'provincial, if not rural, focused on an older
England outside the urban sprawl, and symptomatic of a revolt
against literary London's gargantuan obsession with the western
postal districts and, ultimately, itself'.[13] Re-vivifying Hardy, *The
Harvest* is set on the borders of contemporary 'Wessex' – this virtual
place still being one of the clearest-ever examples of the literary
contribution to the construction of Englishness. But at this new
turning point, the predictable polarity remains to be contended
with. Martin Amis in *London Fields* (whose dust jacket claims that
in his focus on a richly diverse part of London Amis 'dissects the
nature of a society as it hurtles towards the end of the millennium')
and *The Information*, Peter Ackroyd's biography of London, the
enormous success of Zadie Smith's *White Teeth*, each provide
evidence of a continuing celebration of all that is quintessentially
modern in urban life. Waterstone's Booksellers capitalised on this
mirror image of Taylor's 'new movement' by publishing a *Guide
to London Writing* in 1999. It was advertised with a quotation:
'England is a small island. The world is infinitesimal. But London
is illimitable'. In a tribute to the genre's roots, the quotation came
not from these new millennial writings, but from *The Soul of London*
(p. 15).

Ford's trilogy can profitably be read against this backdrop. City
and country both feature strongly in the record of his impressions
of England and the English. These impressions represent still-felt

---

12 Andy Beckett, in a review of *England: An Elegy*, *The Englishman's Handbook*, by Idries
    Shah, and *Utopian England: Community Experiments 1901–1945*, by Dennis Hardy,
    Guardian, 21 October 2000.
13 D.J. Taylor, in a review of *The Harvest*, *Guardian*, 19 June 1999.

cultural needs regarding the mythologies of the English countryside (the idea that, in Stanley Baldwin's phrase, 'England is the country, and the country is England'[14]). They also challenge them, with kaleidoscopic word-pictures that project aspects of London with a breathless excitement borne of the Modernist project. For these reasons, it is important that each book is read in the light of the others – relatively. Ford's representation of the 'town' is necessary in order for that of the 'country' to be set against it, but it is much too simplistic to see Ford as simply adding to the pile of 'urban degeneration' literature. Publication of these books in one volume helps each to be read more subtly, and more successfully, too.

Biographical Background and Publication of the Trilogy

Ford Madox Ford was born on 17 December 1873, the first child of Catherine Madox Brown's marriage to the German music critic, Francis Hueffer. He didn't actually change his name to Ford until 1919, somewhat unusually *after* fighting in the war (the Madox he had taken earlier as a symbol of the strength of his relationship with his grandfather, the painter Ford Madox Brown). The way in which he constructs, and views, London, 'from a distance', at the outset of the trilogy, may well have something to do with his conception of his own personal and critical distance from the English life and lives he was setting out to record. He describes himself in *The Spirit of the People* as 'a man of no race and few ties – or of many races and many ties' (p. 325). Consciousness of his mainland European heritage and roots infuses his writerly persona in more books than these, and he travelled, partly in order to maintain these roots, from a young age. He lived in some of the great cities of the world, including London, Paris and New York. London was the city that he knew as he began to write the trilogy, however; he had been born on its outskirts, and he had already lived there for periods when he moved there again in January 1904.

Ford's artistic abilities were partly due to the family into which he was born (he was related to Christina and Dante Gabriel Rossetti as well as to Ford Madox Brown). He began to write in 1891, publishing a fairy story written for his sister Juliet, illustrated by Madox Brown. More fairytales followed, and then a biography of

---

14 Jeremy Paxman quotes a substantial chunk of the speech in which this phrase was coined in chapter eight, 'There Always was an England', of his book *The English* (London: Penguin, 1999), 143.

his grandfather, before Edward Garnett brought another outsider to the English literary establishment to call. Ford met the Ukrainian-born, sea-faring writer Joseph Conrad in 1898. This was the beginning of a period of collaboration between the two which resulted in joint novels and, more significantly, in the development of literary impressionism, the technique Ford uses to such brilliant effect in this trilogy. Perhaps as a result of this collaborative stimulation, *The Soul of London* represented Ford's first literary success. (To Alan Hill, this alone is good reason for investigating the book further.[15])

Continuing the organic imagery in the titles of the volumes, *The Heart of the Country* was published the year after *The Soul of London*, on 9 May, and also received good reviews. Dedicated to Henry James, the volume bespeaks Ford's debt to this other companion author who was fascinated by Englishness from the position of outsider. James's essay, 'London', published in 1888, which I discuss below, had also possibly provided more direct inspiration for Ford in his current project. (More immediately, Ford heard that James was planning a book on London as he was writing *The Soul of London*; a letter from James in April 1904 reassures Ford that his project was 'relegated to a dim futurity'.[16]) Max Saunders places the trilogy, from *The Heart of the Country* onwards, in the developing 'Edwardian preoccupation with a folk-culture that was rapidly disappearing'. This may be one reason for the attention paid to its publication by Edward Thomas, C.F.G. Masterman and Edward Garnett, among others.[17] Thomas coined the phrase 'the south country' in a poetry collection published later than Ford's trilogy, in 1908; the phrase recurs in literature of and about the time as a way of encoding the rural vision of Englishness. According to Robert Colls, there was indeed what he calls a 'revival' of interest in 'folk studies' and local archaeology around this time. He puts this down to a sense of social and political unrest, both domestic and international, which caused a flight into the nation's 'racial and rural essence'.[18] As one expression of this flight, chapter 5 in *The Spirit of the People* is called 'Utopias'; rather than being a 'no-place',

---

15 Introduction to the Everyman edition of *The Soul of London* (London: Everyman, 1995), xix. (This is the only volume of the trilogy to have been published by Everyman.)
16 Letter quoted by Max Saunders in *A Dual Life*, I, 165.
17 See Max Saunders, *A Dual Life*, I, 220.
18 Robert Colls, 'Englishness and the Political Culture' in *Englishness: Politics and Culture 1880–1920*, 47.

Ford's initial image of utopia is an agricultural variety that he knows exists.

The Spirit of the People appeared in 1907, and had a less happy birth than the previous two volumes. This was due to a combined failure in Ford's relationship with his agent and his publisher. Unlike the earlier volumes, the book didn't cause a stir, a fact that Ford miserably put down to a lack of effort on behalf of his publishers, Alston Rivers. It was perhaps less easy to market, in terms of the contemporary atmosphere, as the volume is less focused than its partners, and ranges widely in history, psychology, religion and politics. In its analysis of the English character, however, it discusses sexual repression in a way that reveals a germ of the story of Ford's greatest book, *The Good Soldier* (1915).

Technique

Key terms associated with particular techniques appear in the trilogy, some of which relate to Ford's Modernist credentials, and to his collaboration with Conrad, and others to contemporary imagistic fashions. Overall, his style entails a series of 'moments of vision', built up to sections of prose in which Ford makes his case. Often part of this case-making is structured along the lines of 'I know someone who…', 'I met a woman who…'. In an example from *The Heart of the Country*, Ford discusses field labourers he has known, building towards a final image of 'Everyman, this final pillar of the state' who is, for Ford, the 'heart of the heart of the country' (pp. 197–8). This anecdotal style can be distracting, unless one bears in mind that it is an integral part of a philosophy that privileges the ordinary encounter, the individual meeting and sharing of minds, and makes them representative. It is a not uncommon way of constructing 'travel writing', or that devoted to cultural observation. Henry James adopted it in his essay on London, and in many other examples of his travel writing (see *English Hours*). In one of the most famous examples of books about Englishness, H.V. Morton's *In Search of England* (1927), the same technique can be observed. (He meets, for example, the last bowl turner in England, who reveals to him the secrets of his rural trade.)

One of the techniques that Ford practises throughout is alluded to a number of times in the first pages of the text, in the repetition of the word 'impression'. The debate as to the extent of self-consciousness necessary to a writer's professional existence pre-dated Ford (it was particularly associated with Matthew Arnold, amongst others, in the latter half of the nineteenth century) but in the years before the First World War the issue became an essential part of literary life.[19] On one side of the divide were the avowed impressionists, derided by Irving Babbitt as 'the last effete representatives of romanticism'. Michael Levenson characterises impressionism 'as both a precise rendering of objects and an unrepentant subjectivising': as attention to detail, in other words, in what one saw, *and* in what one felt and remembered.[20] Opposed to the impressionists were those, like Babbitt, for whom art was primarily about self-transcendence. Although perhaps most relevant in discussion of fiction, the impressionist debate is played out, as we shall see, in other writing of the period. It is an impressionist approach that Hillaire Belloc describes in 1900 as he begins his book on Paris:

> There comes, I suppose [he writes in the preface], to every one who has felt keenly the modern impression of a place he loves, a desire to know its changing past, the nature and experience that it draws from the centuries, and the platform upon which there can be constructed some little of that future which he will never see... [A man] will end by making a record that is as incomplete and fragmentary... as are the notes and letters we keep to remind ourselves of absent friends [...] This book belongs, then, to that kind of history (if it can be called history at all) which is as superficial and as personal as a traveller's drawing or as the notes of a man's diary.[21]

Ford found himself very much on the side of the impressionists and, with Conrad, developed the style into one for which they would both become known. With grim humour Ford relates the potential cost of their choice: 'Impressionists were considered to be bad people: Atheists, Reds, wearing red ties with which to frighten householders'.[22] Nonetheless, impressionism, which distrusted facts

---

19 Christopher Gillie calls it Hebraism versus Hellenism, or 'conscience' versus 'consciousness', following Matthew Arnold's coinage in *Culture and Anarchy* (1869). Arnold identified two basic attitudes of mind, one moral and practical, the other cultural and aesthetic, to which he gave these names (*Movements in English Literature 1900–1940*, Cambridge, Cambridge University Press, 1975), 4.

20 Michael Levenson, *A Genealogy of Modernism* (Cambridge: Cambridge University Press, 1984), 36.

21 Hillaire Belloc, *Paris* (London: Edward Arnold, 1900), vii.

22 See the extract from Ford's *Joseph Conrad: A Personal Remembrance* quoted in the Norton edition of *The Good Soldier* (New York and London: Norton, 1995), 276.

when it came to representing human experience and instead embraced the multiple truths of how something seemed and looked and felt, was important enough for them both to take the professional risk.

For Ford, impressionism was, above all, about the ability to 'make you see'; it was about using layered perspectives, of time, as well as of space. So Ford isn't interested in facts in his trilogy. He doesn't want to tell us about the '720 firms of hat manufacturers employing 19,000 operatives' (p. 3), he's interested in how those facts are experienced, in showing what things look like and feel like from different angles, through different lenses, with different focal points. It's no coincidence that a favourite image in the trilogy is the 'composite photograph'. By this, Ford means the overlaying of visual images so that each retains its essence but contributes to a multiple whole. (Not so long before, photography had been criticised as a 'democracy of the portrait', a description that perhaps helps to contextualise further Ford's interest in everyday experience.[23]) Sometimes, Ford uses the composite photograph as a way of representing character (see *The Spirit of the People*, p. 270), and sometimes as a means of interweaving past and present time (see *The Spirit of the People*, p. 266).

'Rendering', another key term in the trilogy, is closely related to impressionism. Ford uses it to mean the opposite of making a definitive record. It is associated with impressionism because rendering involves suggesting. The emphasis in artistic terms is on the act of representation, on the approach and re-approach to the experience of the object or event in question. Together, these responses help to indicate Ford's contribution to Modernism – one that is, perhaps, most evident in the first volume of the trilogy, where the chaos and complexity of the city demands such literary treatment.

The visual intent and impact of Ford's technique in this trilogy is closely related to the nature of its imagery. One of the most extraordinary, and bizarre, examples of this is the body of the country, complete with organs, blood, and spiritual dimensions. Country roads and hedgerows, for example, are the vessels which pump the blood from the heart of the country: market days are 'pulse days' (*The Heart of the Country*, pp. 146–8). Most powerfully, though,

---

23 Peter Gay quotes this phrase (which dates from 1867) in *Pleasure Wars* (London: HarperCollins, 1998), 57.

Ford focuses on this body's digestive powers, locating them in the capital city. He uses the phrase 'modern juices' to describe London's ability both to erase the differences between its inhabitants, and to re-define them, on the other side of digestion, as it were (*The Soul of London*, pp. 12–13). Striking as this is, it is not entirely original to Ford. Such organic imagery was popular at the time, and Henry James's famous essay on London (first published in 1888) provides a possible model for the hungry beast that Ford at times depicts in his trilogy.[24] James describes London as 'like a mighty ogress who devours human flesh', needing the nourishment to maintain her levels of vivacity and to do her 'work'.[25] Ford develops this image, however (if he was aware of it). James's is a Darwinian vision, in which it is the weak who are 'gobbled up' as fuel. In *The Soul of London*, it is all of those who go to make up the Modern Spirit who are oozed over, and turned into London's own, before their individual memories and perceptions are allowed to re-assert themselves in Ford's celebration of difference.

The Soul of London

True to Ford's impressionist ethos, this book offers many pictures of the city, some of which seem to contradict each other. The tension between the city as a place that fosters individuality, and one which takes it away, is not resolved. The 'immense crowd' of the city, to which Ford refers from time to time, has much in common with Gustave le Bon's dystopic depiction of the primitiveness and savagery found when large numbers of individuals congregate and agitate, filling the lone watcher with fear.[26] The enormous range of individual sights of one's fellow human beings and their experiences of life, which Ford takes such pains to represent, can be 'nerve-shattering', because there is simply too much to recognise and respond to (*The Soul of London*, p. 90). (One is reminded of the 'roar which lies on the other side of silence' with which George Eliot describes the ability to be 'aware of all ordinary human life', an overwhelming ability because of the frequency of

---

24 Robert Colls and Philip Dodd suggest that 'society-as-organism' analogies were increasingly common in both fiction and non-fiction around 1900: *Englishness: Politics and Culture 1880–1920* (London: Croom Helm, 1986), 7.

25 Henry James, 'London' in Alma Louise Lowe (ed.), *English Hours* (London: Heinemann, 1960), 17.

26 An extract from *The Crowd: A Study of the Popular Mind* (1896) is published in *1900*, 152–3.

ordinary tragedy.[27]) What we are experiencing here is partly the result of Ford's own terrible encounters with agoraphobia and nervous illness (serious episodes of which began in 1904), but in the excitement propagated by the city there is always the fear of chaos if such excitement goes 'too far'.

In general, however, the 'kaleidoscope' of human experiences, to which the city gives the receptive writer access, is to be celebrated as one of the truths of modern existence. Living in the city is comparable to a journey by train, during which one sees a variety of landscapes: geographical, emotional and psychological. All human life is there; the other side of the 'nerve-shattering' plurality is the way in which 'London holds us' – by this Ford means 'fascinates/enthrals' – as she shows us 'many things' (*The Soul of London*, p. 79). The final pages of the book construct an optimistic vision of a 'London of the Future' that continues to preserve the stories of the past.

In terms of contributions to the debate on Englishness, *The Soul of London* and the *Spirit of the People* both provide Ford's perspective on what became known as the 'Great Man cult', part of a debate initiated by the Victorians. In an essay on the rivalry between champions of Wellington and Napoleon (both of whom are mentioned on several occasions in the trilogy), Iain Pears relates the rise of this cult to the 'arrival of the Victorian worship of self-discipline'. In the earlier volume, Ford laments the passing of the Great Figure, attributing it to the way in which the size of the population in London prevents towering figures from asserting themselves (p. 94). In contrast, in *The Spirit of the People*, he develops the theory of the 'Great Man of his type' in a retrospective historical analysis, beginning with Thomas Cromwell (p. 271), whom he credits with 'welding England into a formidable whole'. The Great Man may have retreated in modern life, but he is essential to Ford's historical vision of Englishness.

The Heart of the Country

The utopian theme is strong in the second volume (in which the 'country' is mainly that of Kent). There's no doubt that the country is, above all, intended to be seen as a corrective to city living, a place from which regenerative strength can be drawn when the

---

27 George Eliot, *Middlemarch* (Harmondsworth: Penguin, 1985), 226.

excitement of the city proves too much. Ways into and through the countryside are focal points in this text: web-like structures reveal and create the links between the communities and individuals that make up the rural population. Like bloodlines, they connect the village cottages that compete with the country labourer for Ford's depiction of the 'heart of the heart of the country'. It is the village aspect of the countryside that is often called on elsewhere to illustrate Englishness: H.V. Morton states that 'the village that symbolises England sleeps in the sub-conscious of many a townsman'.[28] George Sturt illustrates the kind of mythical organic community that proliferated in literature, as he laments the loss of Englishness. Unsurprisingly, his focus is 'a village', one 'inhabited by Peasantry: rounded in by its own self-supporting toil, and governed by its own old-world customs'.[29] Ford's text, too, contributes to the belief that country people were tougher than town-dwellers, and, in a manner similar to Hardy, depicts the importance of the relationship between character and place. Divorce from one's roots is impoverishing, and it is the natural base of those roots that provides most strength in the face of a changing world. Ford avoids the temptation towards sentimentality in his depiction of the countryside. Mirroring the structure of the trilogy as a whole, the effects of lack of comfort, poor diet, and ill-education, are shown, as well as the positive aspects of country living.

The many images of the tramp in *The Heart of the Country* are significant in Ford's depiction of Englishness. In Roy Porter's *Myths of the English*, an essay is devoted to the rise of the 'romantic and sentimental tramp of the Edwardians';[30] Henry James is seduced by the 'romantic attractiveness' of the same construct in *English Hours* (p. 100). This primarily literary figure – no one did much sociological research into vagrant life at the time – symbolised the rejection of authority and the 'encroachments of business and city life' (*Myths of the English*, pp. 99, 106). A rural figure in fantasy, the

---

28 H.V. Morton, *In Search of England* (London: Methuen, 1984), 2. (This text was first published in 1927.)

29 This image appears in Sturt's journals, and is quoted by David Gervais in *Literary Englands: Versions of 'Englishness' in Modern Writing* (Cambridge: Cambridge University Press, 1993), 112.

30 M.A. Crowther, 'The Tramp' in Roy Porter (ed.), *Myths of the English* (Cambridge: Polity Press, 1992), 92.

tramp guarded primitive secrets and country codes; Ford's tramps have 'gone back into the heart of the country and become one with the ravens' (p. 135). They inhabit a different world even from those who live in the country, offering a commentary from their perspective as outsiders that is of value to Ford – and other writers of the time – because of what Porter calls their 'innocuous anarchy' (p. 5). They represent the old ways, old knowledge, and can be called up as repositories of Englishness, but they offer no real threat to the status quo. That attribute belongs to the 'Grim Reaper' whom Ford conjures up in 'L'Envoi' – the auctioneer who presides over enforced and painful change due to the death or bankruptcy of local inhabitants. But even he is unable to vanquish the ploughman, with whom Ford leaves us (p. 227), one who seems to walk straight out of Ford and into Hardy's 'In Time of "The Breaking of Nations"' nine years later, without changing at all.

The Spirit of the People

This is the book in which Ford uses the image of the composite photograph to such productive effect. He finds it a useful means to illustrate the merging of times as well as of spaces and objects, as he ranges through history in his discussion of the English character and spirit. Building on the idea of the Great Man cult, Ford develops a theory of the representative type of an age, one that can be compared with other types from other ages in the search for physical and emotional similarities and differences. He refers to a composite photograph that he has had made of some of Holbein's sketches of 'typical Englishmen' of his day (p. 270). Curiously (and humorously) enough, the result reminds him of W.G. Grace. In opposition to this robust portrayal of the English character, Ford explores further the theory of degeneration (p. 265), finding some evidence to support it in both the declining birth-rate and the movement of the population from the countryside to the town. Here, he also assesses the characteristics that make up the typical Englishman. Unsurprisingly, as he tries to impose a narrative, the issues can become confused, especially when he attempts to discuss race and the relationship between 'Englishness' and 'Britishness'. In general, however, the pictures Ford paints are lucid, though perhaps provocative; his forays into Protestantism versus Catholicism, and the law are especially stimulating. Furthermore, the book comes into its own when the theme is repression.

The crowd, as discussed in the *Soul of London*, re-emerges in

Ford's consideration of society here. It is presented less symboli-
cally (and perhaps neurotically) than in the earlier volume, because,
with sociological intent, Ford wants to compare the English crowd
with that of other nations. On the other hand, he displays the same
nervousness at the power of large numbers of people congregated
together – as well as an impressionist style – that we encountered
before. The brutal behaviour of policemen that figures in his
analysis of the crowd, and that Ford acknowledges even as he
dismisses it as uncommon, lends a more distinct flavour to this
volume of the trilogy (pp. 237–8, 244–6).

Finally, as the book draws to a close, Ford takes us back to the
beginning of the trilogy with his celebration of the variety that
makes up the English character. This is the 'type of the future' (p.
232) not in any narrow jingoistic sense, but in the sense that,
throughout its history, this type has been forged by the encounter
with new and different perspectives. Unable to resist the call of
myth in his final sentences, Ford resorts to a beautifully written
passage about the way in which England has made the English. It
is an England that is green and fertile, but one that, nevertheless,
exerts its influence over the city on which it depends for its literary
construction, and for its fame.

A Note on the Text

This edition essentially reproduces the text of the first editions of the three books, published by the London firm Alston Rivers in 1905, 1906 and 1907. I have silently amended typographical errors and some inconsistencies of spelling and punctuation. The trilogy has never been published as one volume in the UK. It has been given the same title as the one-volume edition published by McClure and Phillips in New York in 1907. This one-volume edition retained the same individual book titles (it was divided into Books I, II, and III), and substantially the same chapter titles as the English version. It added sixteen black and white illustrations of urban, mainly identifiably London, scenes (originally intended by Ford, along with others, for the English edition).

I took the decision not to use the American edition as a copytext because of substantial differences between it and its English forerunners. These include the omission of two whole chapters ('Introductory' and 'Utopias', from Book II, *The Heart of the Country*), and different beginnings to many other chapters, particularly in the first two books, which were tailored for an American audience. However, the Author's Note to the American edition is published here as an appendix.

Such that exists of manuscripts for the books (*The Heart of the Country* is most complete) is located at the Cornell University Library. Known as the Lowee Collection, the manuscripts were donated by Stella Bowen's daughter Julia.

With the exception of the editorial notes, which are indicated by asterisks, all notes in the text are Ford's. All ellipses are Ford's.

Acknowledgements

The editor would like to thank Paul Clark, Nick Freeman, Olwen Haslam, Max Saunders and Paul Skinner for information, help and advice in the preparation of this volume. I also owe a debt of thanks to all those who attended the Ford conference in Wisconsin, Madison in 2002 for their enthusiasm for this project.

The Soul of London

A SURVEY OF A MODERN CITY

'A Traveller? By my faith you have good reason to be sad!'

Introductory

MOST of us love places very much as we may love what, for us, are the distinguished men of our social lives. Paying a visit to such a man we give, in one form or another, our impressions to our friends: since it is human to desire to leave some memorial that shall record our view of the man at the stage he has reached. We describe his manners, his shape, his utterances: we moralise a little about his associates, his ethics, the cut of his clothes; we relate gossip about his past before we knew him, or we predict his future when we shall be no more with him. We are, all of us who are Londoners, paying visits of greater or less duration to a Personality that, whether we love it or very cordially hate it, fascinates us all. And, paying my visit, I have desired to give some such record.

I have tried to make it anything rather than encyclopaedic, topographical, or archaeological. To use a phrase of literary slang I have tried to 'get the atmosphere' of modern London — of the town in which I have passed so many days; of the immense place that has been the background for so many momentous happenings to so many of my fellows.

A really ideal book of the kind would not contain 'writing about' a town: it would throw a personal image of the place on to the paper. It would not contain such a sentence as: 'There are in the city of —— 720 firms of hat manufacturers employing 19,000 operatives.' Instead there would be a picture of one, or two, or three hat factories, peopled with human beings, where slow and clinging veils of steam waver over vats and over the warm felt on cutters' slabs. And there would be conveyed the idea that all these human beings melt, as it were, into the tide of humanity as all these vapours melt into the overcast skies.

Similarly, in touching upon moral ideas, a book about places must be passionate in its attempt after truth of rendering; it must be passionless in the deductions that it draws. It must let neither pity for the poor nor liking for established reputations and clean floors, warp its presentations where they bear, say, upon the Housing Question. Its business is to give a picture of the place as its author sees it; its reader must seek in other books, statistics, emotional views, or facts handy for political propaganda.

This author's treatment of historic matters must again be 'presentations'; and he must select only such broad tendencies, or such minute historic characters as bear straight upon some aspect of his subject. The historic facts must illustrate, must cast a light upon modern London, if that is what is being presented. There must be no writing about Dr Johnson's chair in a certain tavern merely because it appeals to the author. The reader will find details of all such things in other books – this author's endeavour should be to make the Past, the sense of all the dead Londons that have gone to the producing of this child of all the ages, like a constant ground-bass beneath the higher notes of the Present. In that way the book might, after a fashion, forecast even the Future and contain prophecies. It should, in fact, be instinct with the historic sense which will afford apt illustrations, rather than the annalist's industry, or the love of the picturesque.

That sense of the picturesque will, however, be both a salvation and a most dangerous stumbling-block. In a turning off an opulent high street, there is a court with the exterior aspect of which I am very familiar. It is close to a large freestone town hall and to a very tall red-brick fire station. It is entered by a square archway through which you get a glimpse of dazzlingly white cottages that, very obviously, were once thatched, but that now have pretty red tiles. It is flagged with very large, old stones. It is as picturesque as you can imagine; it is a 'good thing' for descriptive writing, it might be legitimate to use it. But the trouble is that it is old – and, if the book were all old things, deluding by a love for the picturesque of antiquity, it would give a very false and a very sentimental rendering of London.

But the author might desire to illustrate the tendency of parasitic humanity to lurk in the shadow of wealthy high streets. – This court would be an excellent illustration: it is peopled with 'bad characters', male and female. Or he might desire to illustrate the economic preposition that letting small houses to bad characters is more profitable than selling the land for the erection of flats. Here, again, the court would be an illustration; its extreme cleanliness, neatness and good repair would go to prove how careful that landlord was to prevent the condemnation of his rookery on sanitary grounds.

The author then must be careful not to sentimentalise over the picturesque. His business is to render the actual. His heart may be – it ought to be – torn at the sight of great hoardings, raised for the house-breakers, round narrow courts, old streets, famous houses. He ought to be alive to the glamour of old associations, of all the old associations in all their human aspects. But he ought to be equally inspired with satisfaction because work is being done; because dark spots are being cleared away; because new haunts are being formed for new people around whom will congregate new associations. And he ought to see that these new associations will in their turn grow old, tender, romantic, glamorous enough. He should, in fact, when he presumes to draw morals, be prepared to draw all the morals. – He must not only sniff at the 'suburbs' as a place of small houses and dreary lives; he must remember that in each of these houses dwells a strongly individualised human being with romantic hopes, romantic fears, and at the end, an always tragic death. He must remember that the thatched, mud-hovels that crowded round the Tower of original London, were just as dull, just as ordinary, just as commonplace; that men in them lived lives, according to their scale, just as squalid and just as unromantic – or just as alert and just as tragic. This author – this ideal author – then, must be passionately alive to all aspects of life. What picturesqueness there is in his work must arise from contrasts – but actual contrasts vividly presented. This is what gives interest to a work of art; and such a work must, before all things, be interesting.

It is along these lines that I have tried to work: one falls, no doubt very far short of one's ideal. But, for my own part, if this particular work gives a number of readers pleasure, or that counterpart of pleasure which is pain; if it awakens a Londoner here or there to an interest in the human aspects of his London; or if a man who loves London here and there throughout the world and across many seas is aroused to a bitter sweet remembering of old days, if in fact its note rings true to a section of mankind, I should call myself satisfied.

I should like, if it can be done unobtrusively, to disarm criticism of the title of this book. It appears pretentious; it appears 'soulful'; it does little to indicate the scope of the book. But alas! If the critic will read the Table of Contents, and will then think for a minute or so of what one word will describe this whole hotchpotch, he will, whilst condemning, drop something like a tear for one who has been trying to find a better title, not for a minute or so, but for many months.

F.M.H.

CHAPTER I

From a Distance

THOUGHT of from sufficiently far, London offers to the mind's eye singularly little of a picture. It is essentially 'town', and yet how little of a town, how much of an abstraction. One says, 'He knows his London', yet how little more will he know of London than what is actually 'his'. And, if by chance he were an astronomer, how much better he might know his solar system.

It remains in the end always a matter of approaches. He has entered it – your man who knows his London – in one or other more or less strongly featured quarter; in his Bloomsbury of dismal, decorous, unhappy, glamorous squares; in his Camden Town of grimy box-like houses, yellow gas and perpetual ring of tram-horse hoofs; his eyes have opened to it in his Kensington, his Hoxton, his Mayfair or his Shoreditch. He has been born in it, or he has been drawn into it; he has gone through in it the slow awakening of a childhood. Or, coming an adolescent, his eyes have been opened more or less swiftly, with more or less of a wrench, to that small portion of it that is afterwards to form a 'jumping-off place' into that London that he will make 'his'.

And, with its 'atmosphere' whatever it is, with its 'character' whatever it may be, with the odd touches that go to make up famili-arity and the home-feeling, the shape of its policemen's helmets, the cachet of its shop fronts, effects of light cast by street lamps on the fog, on house fronts, on front garden trees, on park railings, all these little things going towards its atmosphere and character, that jumping-off place will remain for him, as it were, a glass through which he will afterwards view, a standard by which he will after-wards measure, the London that yet remains no one's.

It makes in essentials little enough difference whether he be born in a London quarter, or whether he came, a young provincial, raw and ready to quiver at every sensation, super-sensitised to every emotion. If, as a London child, he has wandered much in the streets, there will remain to him always an odd sensation of being very little, of peering round the corners of grey and gigantic buildings upon greyer vistas of buildings more gigantic – so, with a half touch of awe, we scramble, as relatively little in maturity, round the base of an out-jutting cliff into what may prove a grey cove or what may be a great bay. It is the sense of making discoveries, of a world's opening-up.

In both, at the start, there will be the essential provincialism. The London child, with his unconscious acknowledgement of impersonal vistas, of infinite miles of unmeaning streets, of horizons that are the blur of lamps in fogs, simultaneously acknowledges personalities, local oddities, local celebrities of whom Shepherd's Bush, Highgate or Knightsbridge may be proud. For the provincial adolescent there will be the squire with his long beard and gouty walk, the mayor with his shop in the high street, the doctor with his face screwed up as if he were tasting the full bitterness of one of his own potions. The London child, however, will earlier overcome his awe of personalities. He will wonder at the man, sallow, tiny, wizened and skew-featured, who, with the whispered reputation of a miser able to roll himself in sovereigns, and a hazy identity in a child's mind with, say, Sweeny Todd the Demon Barber, sells him spring-pistols, catapult elastic and alley-taws in the dim and evil light of a small shop with windows obscured by broadsheets and penny dreadfuls. He will attach a certain significance to the grimy stretch of waste ground – it will by now have been, ah, so long since 'built over' – on which he played cricket with meat tins for a wicket, or fought a dismal battle with a big boy from 'another school'. But these local feelings sink very soon into the solid background of memories. He will discover other catapult sellers, he will find playing fields larger and more green, he will have it brought home to him that there are so many of every sort of thing in the world, just as, sooner or later, it will come home to him that there are so very many others of as little import in the scale of things as the catapult seller, the green fields, – and as himself.

For, sooner or later, the sense of the impersonality, of the abstraction that London is, will become one of the most intimate factors of his daily life. And sooner rather than later it will become one for the young provincial.

He will have had his preconceptions: he will have seen photographs of 'bits', of buildings, of bridges. He will have had his vague idea of a bulbous domed St Paul's with a queer fragment of

Ludgate Hill, standing isolated at a corner of the Green Park; of
Nelson's Column and the Monument, of the Houses of Parliament
and Buckingham Palace – all hazily united into one 'view' by a
river Thames that is hazily suggested, green and leafy, by his own
Severn, his own Stour, his own Ouse, or Adur. But this picture
will vanish finally and irrecoverably, like our own preconceived
notions of an individual we have long thought of, whom we meet
at last to find so entirely – and so very obviously – different.

The emotions of his journey to town – and they are emotions
from within so much more than impressions from without – will
last him until he is settled, more or less, for good in his lodgings,
his cellar or his boarding house. They will last him, at least until his
things are unpacked, his credentials presented, his place found – or
until he finds, after how many disillusionments, that he may never
in all probability find any place at all. The point is that, till then, he
will not have any time to 'look about him'.

II

BUT the last thing that, even then, he will get is any picture, any
impression of London as a whole, any idea to carry about with him
– of a city, in a plain, dominated by a great building, bounded by
a horizon, brought into composition by mists, great shadows, great
clouds or a bright and stippled foreground. It is trite enough to say
that the dominant note of his first impression will be that of his own
alone-ness. It is none the less the dominant note of London;
because, unless he is actually alone he will pay no attention to
London itself. He will talk with his companions of his or their own
affairs; he will retain the personal note, shutting out the impersonal,
stalling it off instinctively.

But our young provincial being for his first time cast absolutely
loose will get then his first impression of London – his first tap of
the hammer. He will stand perhaps at a street corner, perhaps at his
own doorstep, for a moment at a loss what to do, where to go,
where to turn. He will not ever have been so alone. If he were
intent upon getting a complete picture of London he might be –
we might imagine him – setting out self-consciously, his eyes closed
during the transit, to climb the heights of Hampstead, the top of
the Monument, the Dome of St Paul's. But he will not.

London, with its sense of immensity that we must hurry through to keep unceasing appointments, with its diffuseness, its gatherings up into innumerable trade-centres, innumerable class districts, becomes by its immensity a place upon which there is no beginning. It is, so to speak, a ragoût of tit-bits so appealing and so innumerable – of Gower's tombs and Botticelli's, of miles of port-wine cellars or of the waxen effigies of distinguished murderers – that your actual born-not-made Londoner passes the whole dish by. He is like the good Scot whose haggis is only eaten by conscientious tourists; like the good North German whose *alt-bier* soup appears at table only for the discomfiture of the English or American cousin. He will not visit his Tower today because there will always remain an eternity in which to see it; he will not, tomorrow, ensue at the Millbank National Gallery a severe headache, because that Gallery will always be there.

Our young provincial, in fact, until he has finished, as a separate entity, his sightseeing, does not become even a potential Londoner. He has to exhaust that as he will have to exhaust the personalities, the localities, that for the time being will make up his 'world'. He must have had squeezed swiftly into him all the impressions that the London child has slowly made his own. He must have asked all the ways that are to carry him to and from his daily work; he must be able to find instinctively his own front-door, his own keyhole, his own string that in a noisome cellar pulls the latch, or his own bundle of rags in the corner of a railway arch. Daily details will have merged, as it were, into his bodily functions, and will have ceased to distract his attention. He will have got over the habit of relying, in these things, upon personal contacts. He will have acquired an alertness of eye that will save him from asking his way. On his 'Underground' he will glance at a board rather than inquire of a porter; on 'bus-routes he will catch instinctively, on the advancing and shapeless mass of colour and trade announcements, the small names of taverns, of Crosses, of what were once outlying hamlets; he will have in his mind a rough sketch map of that plot of London that by right of living in he will make his own. Then he will be the Londoner, and to the measure of the light vouchsafed will know his London. Yet, to the great majority of Londoners whose residence is not an *arrière boutique* London will remain a matter of a central highway, a central tunnel or a central conduit, more or less long; a daily route whose two extremities are a more or less permanent sleeping place, and a more or less permanent workshop – a thing, figured on a map, like the bolas of certain

South Americans, a long cord with balls at the extremities. At the one there will gradually congregate the parts of a home, at the other, the more or less familiar, more or less hypnotising, more or less congenial, surroundings of his daily work. It will be a matter of a daily life passing unnoticed.

III

LONDON itself will become the merest abstraction. He will not moralise upon London. Occasionally a periodical will inform him with notes of exclamation, that London is a very remarkable thing. He will read, 'London more than all else in the scenery of England gives food for thought; this for awe and wonder, not for boasting, is unique' – and he will acquiesce. Nevertheless awe and wonder are the last things he will feel.

London, in fact, is so essentially a background, a matter so much more of masses than of individuals, so much more, as it were, a very immense symphony orchestra than a quartette party with any leader not negligible, that its essential harmony is not to be caught by any human ear. It can only be treated as a ground bass, a drone, on top of which one pipes one's own small individual melody. A human aggregation, it leaves discernible so very little of the human that it is almost as essentially a natural product as any great stretch of alluvial soil. Your marshy delta was brought down in the course of a thousand years or so. Raindrops, born a long way up in the hills, united to run through fissures in the earth, through soil-drains, through runnels in the moss of woods, through channels in the clay of sodden fields, each drop bearing infinitesimal grains of what, towards the sea at the end, becomes alluvial soil – each drop quarried, each drop carried, each drop endured for its moment, and then went hence and was no more seen. It left the grain of loam it had carried. So precisely out of the clouds of the nations, drops have been born. It is that oblivion, that 'being no more seen', that is, in matters human, the note of London. It never misses, it never can miss anyone. It loves nobody, it needs nobody; it tolerates all the types of mankind. It has palaces for the great of the earth, it has crannies for all the earth's vermin. Palace and cranny, vacated for a moment, find new tenants as equably as the hole one makes in a stream – for, as a critic, London is wonderfully open-minded.

On successive days it will welcome its king going to be crowned, its general who has given it a province, its enemies who have fought against it for years, its potentate guest from Teheran – it will welcome each with identically rapturous cheers. This is not so much because of a fickle-mindedness as because since it is so vast it has audiences for all players. It forgets very soon, because it knows so well that, in the scale of things, any human achievement bulks very small.

It cherishes less than any other town the memory of its mighty dead. Its message for humanity is that it is the business of man to keep all on going, not to climb on to pinnacles. Its street names are those of ground-landlords; its commemorative tablets, on house fronts, are no more to be read than any epitaphs in any church-yards. It is one gigantic pantheon of the dead level of democracy; and, in its essentials it is a home neither for the living nor the dead.

If in its tolerance it finds a place for all eccentricities of physiog-nomy, of costume, of cult, it does so because it crushes out and floods over the significance of those eccentricities. It, as it were, lifts an eyelid and turns a hair neither for the blue silk gown of an Asiatic, the white robes of a Moor, the kilts of a Highlander, nor the silk hat, inscribed in gold letters with a prophecy of retribution or salvation, of a religious enthusiast. In its innumerable passages and crannies it swallows up Mormon and Mussulman, Benedictine and Agapemonite, Jew and Malay, Russian and Neapolitan.* It assim-ilates and slowly digests them, converting them, with the most potent of all juices, into the singular and inevitable product that is the Londoner – that is, in fact, the Modern. Its spirit, extraordinary and unfathomable – because it is given to no man to understand the spirit of his own age – spreads, like sepia in water, a tinge of its own over all the world. Its extraordinary and miasmic dialect – the dialect of South Essex – is tinging all the local speeches of England. Deep in the New Forest you will find red brick houses trying to look like London villas; deep in the swamps of coastal Africa you will find lay white men trying to remain Londoners, and religious white men trying to turn negroes into suburban chapel worshippers.

London is the world town, not because of its vastness; it is vast because of its assimilative powers, because it destroys all race char-acteristics, insensibly and, as it were, anaesthetically. A Polish Jew

---

* **Mormon** and **Mussulman**: a member of the American Church of Jesus Christ of Latter-Day Saints, and a Muslim.
Agapemonite: a member of a fanatical revivalist sect dating from 1849.

changes into an English Hebrew and then into a Londoner without any legislative enactments, without knowing anything about it. You may watch, say, a Berlin Junker, arrogant, provincial, unlicked, unbearable to any other German, execrable to anyone not a German, turning after a year or two into a presentable and only just not typical Londoner; subdued, quiet in the matters of collars, ties, coat, voice and backbone, and naturally extracting a 'sir' from a policeman. London will do all this imperceptibly. And, in externals, that is the high-water mark of achievement of the Modern Spirit.

IV

IMMENSE without being immediately impressive, tolerant without any permanent preferences, attracting unceasingly specimens of the best of all earthly things without being susceptible of any perceptible improvement, London, perhaps because of its utter lack of unity, of plan, of the art of feeling, is the final expression of the Present Stage. It owes its being to no one race, to no two, to no three. It is, as it were, the meeting place of all Occidentals and of such of the Easterns as can come, however remotely, into touch with the Western spirit. Essentially unmusical, in it may be found, as it were 'on show', the best of all music. And it has at odd moments 'on show' the best products of the cook, of the painter, of the flower-gardener, of the engineer, of the religious and of the scientists. It does without any architecture, because in essentials it is an assembly of tents beside a river, a perennial Nijni Novgorod bazaar, a permanent world's fair. It is a place in which one exists in order to gain the means of living out of it; an epitome, an abstract of the Christian's world, which he inhabits only to prepare himself for one more bright if less glamorous. Perhaps, for times to come, some individual of today, striking the imagination of posterity, may catch and preserve an entirely individual representation of the London of today. We have our individual presentations of so many vanished Londons. We have the town of a riverside, with steep, serrated warehouselike wharf-dwellings, dominated by a great Gothic cathedral. Through its streets wind improbably gigantic processions of impossibly large mediaeval horsemen. We have a Tudor London merging into the early Jacobean of the dramatists – a small, provincial-minded, crooked-streeted, gabled town, walled, circumscribed, still set in fields whose hedges public-minded citizens of the train-bands delighted to break down. We have the two Londons of the diarists – a London still of crooked streets, of a Gothic cathedral, with an essential stench, a glow of torches round house-ends with red crosses on low doors, a rumble of plague-carts. Then a London rising out of ashes, with streets, heaven knows, crooked enough, but having lost its cathedral and its gabled houses. So, perhaps, for the London of our day.

Some Clerk of the Admiralty is, without doubt, keeping, like Pepys, his diary; some journalist, like Defoe, is writing fraudulent memoirs; some caricaturist now before us, some novelist too much or too little advertised today, will succeed in persuading posterity that his London is the London that we live in but assuredly don't know.

We may take that to be certain. Yet it is not so certain that his London will be as near the real thing as were, in their days, those of Pepys, of Hogarth, or even of Albert Smith. One may hazard that without chanting jeremiads to the art of today. But we may set it down that Pepys going out from Dover to welcome Charles II had somewhere at the back of his head an image of his London – of a town of a few strongly marked features, of a certain characteristic outline, of jagged roofs, of overhanging upper storeys, of a river that was a highway forever clamorous with the cry of 'Oars'.

So, too, had Hogarth when at Calais. Dickens, posting as the Uncommercial Traveller towards France over Denmark Hill, may almost have had an impression of a complete and comparatively circumscribed London. But so many things – as obvious as the enormously increased size, as secondary as the change in our habits of locomotion – militate against our nowadays having an impression, a remembered bird's-eye-view of London as a whole.

The Londoner bites off from his town a piece large enough for his own chewing. We have no symbol of London comparable to the Lutetia of Paris; none to set beside the figure on the reverse of our copper coins. It is comparatively easy to have in the mind the idea of a certain green island familiar in its backward tilt towards the shores of Europe, familiar in its rugged outline, in its setting of silver sea. We may think of it as a bit of coloured marble-facing broken from a palace wall, with counties mottled in green, counties in pink, counties in buff, in blue, in yellow. We may think of it embossed in relief out of a robin's-egg blue sea, with the misty white cliffs of Kent, the slate and marble of Devon, the serpentine of Cornwall, or the half-submerged rafts of the outer Hebrides forming the edges.

It is, in fact, comparatively easy to evoke a picture of England as a whole, still easier, perhaps, to think of this world as a green orange revolving round a candle, or as the pink and blue of a Mercator's projection. One may sail easily round England, or circumnavigate the globe. But not the most enthusiastic geographer – one must of course qualify these generalisations with an 'as a rule' – ever memorised a map of London. Certainly no one ever walks round it. For England is a small island, the world is infinitesimal amongst the planets. But London is illimitable.

V

A BRILLIANT, windswept, sunny day, with the fountains like hay-cocks of prismatic glitter in the shadow of Nelson's Column, with the paving stones almost opalescent, with colour everywhere, the green of the orange trees in tubs along the façade of the National Gallery, the vivid blue of the paper used by flower-sellers to wrap poet's narcissi, the glint of straws blown from horses' feeds, the shimmer of wheel-marks on the wood pavement, the shine of bits of harness, the blaze of gold lettering along the house fronts, the slight quiver of the nerves after a momentarily dangerous crossing accentuating the perception – is that 'London'? Does that rise up in your Londoner's mind's eye, when, in the Boulevard Haussmann, or on the Pyramids, he thinks of his own places?

Or is it the chaotic crowd, like that of baggage wagons huddled together after a great defeat, blocked in the narrow ways of the City, an apparently indissoluble muddle of grey wheel traffic, of hooded carts, of 'buses drawing out of line, of sticky mud, with a pallid church wavering into invisibility towards the steeple in the weeping sky, of grimy upper windows through which appear white faces seen from one's level on a 'bus-top, of half the street up, of the monstrous figure of a horse 'down' – and surely there is no more monstrous apparition than that of a horse down in the sticky streets with its frantic struggles, the glancing off of its hoofs, the roll of eyes, the sudden apparition of great teeth, and then its lying still – is this, with its black knot of faces leaning a little over the kerbstone, with its suggestion of the seashore in the unconcerned, tarpaulin-shrouded figure of the traffic policeman – is this again

'London', the London we see from a distance?

Or do we see it in the glare of kerosene lamps, the diffused blaze of shop fronts, the slowly moving faces revealed for a moment, then as it were, washed out, of the serried, marketing crowds. They will be carrying string bags, carrying paper parcels, carrying unwrapped green stuff, treading on layers of handbills, treading on the white scrolls of orange peels, on small heaps of muddy sawdust, standing in shawled groups round the glare of red joints in butchers' shops, standing in black groups round the carts of nostrum sellers, round the carts of dutch auctioneers; with ears deafened by the cries of vendors of all things meet for a Saturday night, by the incessant whistle of trams looming at a snail's pace through the massed humanity; by the incessant, as if vindictively anvil-like, peals of notes of barrel organs. In a patch of shadow left in a vacant space, you will hardly make out the figure of a forlorn man standing still. With a pendent placard on his chest, announcing one of the ills of the flesh, he offers for sale things that you would think nobody could stop to buy, or indistinguishable quavers of melody that nobody could stay to hear. Is this again the London that comes to one at a distance?

For, almost assuredly, it will be some minute detail of the whole, we seeing things with the eye of a bird that is close to the ground. And with the eye of a bird seeking for minute fragments of seed, minute insects, tiny parasites, we also look for things that to us are the constituents of our mental or visual pabula. The tendency of 'carriage folk' must be to think of the Saturday night market as nothing but the swinging doors of public-houses and of pawnshops, as nothing but the architectural arrangements of translucent gin bottles in pale shop windows. The marketer has his tendency to regard those he sees in carriages as insolent servants conducting people who 'are no better than they should be'. The essential Bohemian must think of those whose sign visual is the aligned brass knockers of suburban streets, as sluggish-minded and intolerable. Thus, humanity not caring to think about what it does not like, the villa resident away from London will see a vision of 'Parks' and 'Gardens', surrounded by uninteresting or repulsive districts of small houses; the working man thinks of high streets, of small streets, of tenement blocks, set down on the fringes of villadom.

The limits of the classes are not of course so crudely definite but that there is an infinity of individual variants. There are the crowds of philanthropists who make swallow flights into slums, the mechanics who dream of their own carriages. There is room for millennialists who strive to create Garden Cities, for socialist prophets who read in the skies signs of an approaching Armageddon after which all men shall be alike in tastes as in habitation. But in the bulk the Londoner is anything rather than tolerant of a class not his own; the unfamiliar is almost inevitably the iniquitous.

We may, among the October partridges, have a sudden vision of a slinking, horribly suggestive pair of figures. We saw them as we walked gaily home from the very best ball of last season, in the pale delicate stillness of dawn, at the mouth of a black court, under the unclean light of a street lamp held out from a dirty wall by a bracket, as if an arm were holding a torch to comment on the blackness of the inwards of this earth. And those figures, slinking back into those shadows, may among the crisp stubble suddenly rise up and stand for London.

Or one may as a child, have crept out of a slum on a summer night, have climbed some area railings in a long street all railings, to peep in at a room where the delicate, tender light of candles shimmering on silver, on the shining shoulders of women, on the shining linen of men, contended with the delicate, tender light of the London sunset. And that picture may rise up for one in the shadows of a black Kentish barn, where in the hopping season straw-thatched hurdles pen off the darkness, and the air is heavy with the odour of hops, of rags, of humanity. But, essentially, the London that from afar the Londoner sees is his own parish, and his own parish is the part he knew in his youth, the human stratum from which he started. A man may have passed right across London in his life; he may have dropped as it were from ledge to ledge; he may have been born in Mayfair to fall in his traces, a sodden beast, outside a public-house of the Tower Hamlets. Or he may have been born in the fifth of a room in a Whitechapel ghetto, to die in a palace of Park Lane. Yet assuredly the London of the one will be, not the purlieus of Bankruptcy Buildings, not the shabby lodgings, not the dismal blind-yard in which sandwich-boards are given out, not any of the intermediate stages, but the west of his youth. He will die thinking himself a gentleman. And – one may hazard the induction – the standard by which the other will appraise the world-centre he has conquered will be the auction for the right to open the tabernacle in the synagogue, the inscriptions in the kosher shops, the grating of the *lingua-hebraica*, the casting of sins at the feast of the New Year into the tidal waters off the parapet of Custom

House Wharf, the feather of the Day of Purification, that were his familiars when a young lad. The middle stages of neither will have counted as, in middle life, the mind lost its impressionability.

Besides which, to see London steadily and see it whole, a man must have certain qualities of temperament so exhaustive as to preclude, on the face of it, the faculties which go to the making – or the marring – of great fortunes. He must, it is true, have his 'opportunities'. But before all things he must have an impression-ability and an impersonality, a single-mindedness to see, and a power of arranging his illustrations cold-bloodedly, an unemotional mind and a great sympathy, a life-long engrossment in his 'subject', and an immense knowledge, for purposes of comparison, of other cities. He must have an avidity and a sobriety of intellect, an untirable physique and a delicately tempered mind. These things are antitheses.

An intelligent foreigner running through a town of strongly marked features may carry away a definite impression of its character and its life, although he will inevitably go astray in point of statistics, of etiquette, or local history. But of London no foreign-ness, which implies an openness to impressions – and no clear intelligence, can, in the lump, make much.

A Paris journalist lamented the gross indecency of London in the matter of the nude. He had taken his first walk in London with a lady friend, near the Serpentine, during the hours when bathing is permitted. An Italian royal Marchioness sighed because there were no birds in England. She had, on the occasion of an international function, spent three November days as a royal guest in Buckingham Palace. A Portuguese diplomatist never travelled in England save armed to the teeth. On his first journey from Dover to London he had been rather roughly handled by cardsharpers. An American commercial magnate speaks of London as the most radiant and friendly place, because his first impression was at a private house, of the white cap and apron, pink cheeks, low voice, and welcoming smiles of a housemaid at the door. I have never been able to persuade a Jesuit Father, a friend of my own, to visit London, because of Bill Sikes and Fagin's academy for thieves.

Away from his town, with no picture of his own in his mind, that is what the Londoner will be brought up against – a Cimmerian*

---

* **Cimmerian**: dense darkness, derived from Cimmerii, an ancient people fabled to live in perpetual darkness.

district where, in a gloom so dense that no bird can see to carry straws to its nest, naked men run pallidly in and out of crowds of cardsharpers, lightened here and there by housemaids, shadowed always by starvation, drink, crime, and the drippings of tallow candles that are to be seen in plates after Cruikshank. He won't, if he has any contact with foreigners, ever get away from it.

Seated at a continental card-table with a 'quite nice', capped and mittened, smiling old lady, he will find the game suddenly suspended. The courteous and restrained smile with which a good Catholic asks a heretic about the outrageous practices of his sect, will beam upon the old lady's face. She will say that she cannot understand how anyone so obviously humane and sympathetic as the particular Londoner before her, can bear to walk the streets of London town, where, at all moments and on all sides, people suddenly drop dead of starvation. She will resume her deal.

Confronted with this particular 'View of London' your Londoner can only gasp. He will realise that his amiable hostess has been reading, in her local paper, a quotation from his Registrar General's returns. And, for purposes of refutation, the trouble is that he knows nothing about the figures. He does not feel assured whether, according to the Return, 75, 750, or 7,500 people died of starvation during the past year. He does not know whether 'cases of death from exposure accelerated by want' are included. He has a hazy notion that no one in London need die of starvation, seeing that there are workhouses. But as a rule he knows nothing of the workings of Poor Law Relief. He knows so little of his London.

He may even, as a result, have added to his particular picture of the place, the dim and disturbing image of a lank-haired, hollow checked, glaring eyed, pale woman, – a Spectre of Starvation with, in the bulge of an old shawl, the suggestion of a naked, frozen baby. He will not have seen them in the Kensington-plus-Cornhill that is his London. But an intangible cloud-like population of white-faced misery, may come suddenly to disturb his ideas of Hoxton or Highgate, of Shoreditch or of Canning Town. Or the comparatively contented mechanician is suddenly confronted with his continental confrère's picture of the luxury, the profusion, the lust, the wantonness, of a foreign view of Hyde Park. In front of the dark eyes, the flashing teeth, the blue blouse, he will grow uncomfortably uncertain whether, outside his own Walthamstow of small pleasant houses, all the valley of the Thames is not Sodom and Gomorrah. Once away from the few facts that he can, as it were, catch hold of with his hands, he knows, your Londoner, so appallingly little of his London. It isn't his business; he has his own affairs. In the gigantic tool-basket of a place he can find pretty well whatever he needs. He will be surprised if others cannot.

VI

LONDON is a great, slipshod, easy-going, good-humoured magnet; those it attracts are much of a muchness with itself. They have not any corporate spirit in particular. And the Londoner when talked to by inhabitants of other considerable towns is apt to be violently confronted with what he hasn't. It is not only that in Essen or Düsseldorf he will learn that he has no factories each employing sixteen skilled chemists continually analysing slag-heaps for by-products; that he has not any secondary schools worth the mention; that his workmen are not efficiently organised, or that his capitalists do not squeeze the last drop of blood out of their men. But nearer home he will learn more severe lessons.

Let him go to one of the larger towns well outside his Home Counties, and he will have it forced in on him that he has no municipal buildings costing well-nigh a million, that he has no ship-canals, that his atmosphere has not half the corrosive properties that it should have to betoken the last word of wealth, of progress, and of commercial energy. He will be told that he has nothing worth having, and that he is infinitely too proud of what he has. Yet as a rule the accusation is unkind. However proud the Londoner may be of his personality, of his wife, of his wine, or of the poultry run in his back garden, the last thing he would think of being proud of is London. His most considerable exhibition of pride will appear in his mild disgust, if he is mistaken for a provincial. He is singularly useless as a Defender of the city's fame. He will know of a Mansion House, but he will probably not know whether it is a municipal place of business or merely the residence of a chief magistrate; he will have a vague idea that something goes on at Spring Gardens. He would not, on the other hand, be certain whether London contained a university, or, tucked away in some corner, a ship canal. He goes through life with the comforting thought that somewhere there are people one might ask, or very good postal directories. In Rhenish-Westphalia he will be assured that London is already as deserted as Bruges. His eyes will have told him that that is not the case today. But, set there in the hideous heart of the German competition he so much dreads, confronted by the blackened landscape, by miles of grey slag mounds, by horizons obscured with rusty cinder heaps, by heaps of sand, by heaps of rust, by clouds of green, of red, of purple, or of black smoke, by dirt of the foulest and labour of the obviously grimmest, he will not be certain of the day-after-tomorrow of London. He will almost certainly not know that, in the marshes round Purfleet, he has factories larger, more modern, better capitalised, more solvent, and a landscape more blackened and more grim.

The Westphalian will say: 'Oh yes, it is all over', and before the Londoner's mental picture of his little bit of the city and suburbs there will rise up a view of the stained and deserted façades of a London like Bruges, with swarms of pauper children tumbling over the doorsteps, and an old grey horse cropping the grass between the flagstones of Threadneedle Street. He will not in the least know what reserves of wealth or of energy his London may have.

VII

ABOVE all his London, his intimate London, will be the little bits of it that witnessed the great moments, the poignant moods of his life; it will be what happened to be the backgrounds of his more intense emotions.

Certain corners of streets, certain angles of buildings, the spray of dishevelled plane-trees, certain cloud-forms, gusts of white smoke, odours, familiar sounds – these, in their remembrance will wring his heart. He will have noticed them, or hardly noticed them, glancing aside in his moments of terror, of perplexity, of passion, of grief. And the remembrance of them, a long way away, will bring up again, tempered by the glamour of memory, by the romance of old days, the reflection of those griefs, of those terrors, of those old piteousnesses.

For London is before all things an incomparable background; it is always in the right note, it is never out of tone. A man may look down out of dim windows upon the slaty, black, wet misery of a squalid street, upon a solitary flickering lamp that wavers a sooty light upon a solitary, hurrying passer's umbrella. He may have received a moment before the first embrace of a woman, or a moment before his doctor may have told him that he is not very long for this world. He will stand looking down; and a sudden consonance with his mood, of overwhelming and hardly comprehensible joy, of overwhelming and hardly fathomable pain, a sudden significance will be there in the black wet street, in the long wavering reflections on the gleaming paving-stones, in the engrossed hurry of the passer-by. It will become, intimately and rightly, the appropriate background for a beginning of, or for a farewell from life – for the glow of a commenced love or for the dull pain of a malady ending only in death. It is that, more than anything, that London has ready for every man.

It can provide a background for everything. With the sympathy of the weeping heavens, or the irony of other men's unconcern, it remains always a background; it never obtrudes. A man may be so soothingly alone – with his joys as with his griefs.

We may hurry across the great stretches and folds of a park, with a glamorous smirched sunset, curling clouds over the distant houses, wisps of mist becoming palpably blue against thorn trees and the call of a closing space and of a closing in day, indescribably mournful and distant. We may hurry to our triumph of love, to our bankruptcy, to our end or our beginning of the world. Or we may be driven behind a slipping, frightened horse through grey empty streets, among whirls of small hard snowflakes, to a house where there are the titter and bustle of a wedding, or where on the stairs there are the heavy footfalls and muffled breathings of men carrying down the coffin of our best friend in the world. The background for either mood will be the right one. It is these things that come back to us at a distance and in odd ways. I have known a man, dying a long way from London, sigh queerly for a sight of the gush of smoke that, on a platform of the Underground, one may see, escaping in great woolly clots up a circular opening, by a grimy, rusted iron shield, into the dim upper light. He wanted to see it again as others have wished to see once more the Bay of Naples, the olive groves of Catania. Another wanted – how very much he wanted! – to see once more the sort of carpet of pigeons on the gravel in front of a certain museum steps; the odd top-hatted unpresentable figure of a battered man, holding a paper of bun crumbs, with pigeons on his shoulders, on his hands, crowding in between his feet and fluttering like an aureole of wings round his head.

London is a thing of these 'bits'. It is seldom that one sees at one time as much of it as one may always see of any country town. It

has nothing, it never had anything, worth talking of as a spectacular expression of humanity, of that incongruous jumble of races
that is in England. It has no Acropolis, no Forum Romanum, no
Champs Elysées; it has not so much as a Capitol or a Nevski
Prospekt. The tombs of its kings, its Valhalla, its Senate, are, relatively to London nowhere in particular. Viewed from a distance it
is a cloud on the horizon. From the dark, further side of the Surrey
hills at night, above the inky sky line of heather, of pine tops, of
elms, one may see on the sky a brooding and sinister glow. That is
London – manifesting itself on the clouds.

CHAPTER II

Roads into London

IS it where the glow on the sky is no longer seen that 'the country' ends and the influence of London begins? I can scarcely tell even where that is. I have heard that it can be seen from near Colchester; from near Maidstone I have seen it myself. But these 'shays' of the larger towns can be caught from very far: I have distinguished that of such a town as Folkestone from nearly thirty miles away.

Speaking a little arbitrarily, we may say that there are three Londons. There is the psychological London, where the London spirit is the note of life, there is the Administrative County, and there is the London of natural causes, the assembly of houses in the basin of the lower Thames.

To where then do the spheres of influence of these three Londons reach out? Frankly, I do not know, and I have asked myself the question many times. The Administrative County includes so little of psychological London. Chislehurst, for instance, psychologically considered, is London; so, in their own ways, are Brighton, Hastings, Southend-on-Sea, parts of the Riviera, and half of the Essex flats.

Highbury, I should say, is London, because the greater part of its inhabitants get their 'supplies' from The Stores, and go for their intellectual stimulants to a place in Oxford Street. Thus the stores and the circulating library make London extend to Jubbulpore and to the married officers' bungalows on the Irawaddy. I heard the other day from an administrator of those parts. He was living in ruined temples, but his clothes, his boots, his whips, his tinned meats, his sauces, his mustard and his wines came from the one institution; he was astonishingly 'well up' in the books of the year, better certainly than most London reviewers, because of the other. He had, too, a phonograph, which supplied him with piano music from St James's Hall and the latest songs of the empire. These ruined temples where he camped for the night became little pieces of London; and we have lately had a Viceroy of India lamenting that Tottenham Court Road has stretched into the zenanas of the native states.

Yet in many places within the Administrative County the tendency is all towards 'localising', or towards remaining separate centres. In Hampstead, for instance, the older residents buy most things of the local tradesmen, and newer families imitate them for sentimental or for social reasons. In poorer neighbourhoods this is much more the case. Old places of entertainment, like the Horns Assembly Rooms, flourish, and large theatres spring up along the tramlines. I think there are no local daily papers, though in the dark heart of the docks knots of men stand round blank walls. On these journalists, having the same relation to those of Fleet Street as the pavement artist has to Academicians, chalk in capital letters details of the last murders, divorces, and wrecks. And the people of the poorer suburbs do their shopping in their own high streets. Where great local emporia have not crushed out altogether the 'local tradesman', shoppers with string bags still nod at the greengrocer and the oilman when passing or when making their purchases.

One cannot, therefore, limit psychological London by the glow on its sky, to the sphere of influence of the stores, or to the Administrative County.

Administrative London, on the other hand, ignores alike the psychological and the natural. It administers in a sensible rule of thumb way South Kensington and Bermondsey, the sewers of slums and great expanses of green land. The natural features of London are obscured, but they underlie the others patiently. They are the hills that made possible the basin of the Thames, the oldest of all the roads into London; they are the old marshes and flat lands on which it was so easy to build. They show still a little in open hilly outlying ring, in odd bits of forest here and there, in level commons, like those near Clapham, where there are still many ponds. No doubt, in the ultimate fullness of time, these hills, forests, and marshes will resume their sway.

But nowadays we may say that London begins where tree trunks commence to be black, otherwise there is very little to distinguish Regent's Park from Penshurst, or Wimbledon from Norwich. This tree-trunk boundary is, however, defective enough; in many parts of Epping the wood is so dense that boughs and boulders are as green, as brown, as mossy or as lichened as at Fontainebleau. The prevailing winds being from the south and from the westwards, again, the zone of blackened trunks extends further than is fair towards the north and the east. But judged by this standard, London, as far as I have been able to observe, is bounded by a line drawn from Leigh, in Essex, halfway through the Epping Forest, to the north of Hendon, to the west of Brentford, the southwest of Barnes, well to the south of Sydenham, well to the east of Bromley, and so up to Leigh again. Other observers will, no doubt, find this tree-trunk limitation a little faulty; but it takes in at least nearly all the looser elements of the sphere of London influence. And, as the invariable and bewildering exception to this, as to all rules, it may as well be set down that the most 'Londony' of all London trees has a bark that is never uniformly black. The plane tree grows best of all in London, because it sheds its bark continually; getting rid of its soot it clears the pores of its skin and flourishes, if I may be allowed an image that appears frivolous but that is sober enough, a perpetual emblem to the city of the morning tub. In the suburbs the plane yields first place to the flowering almond, in the parks to the thorn, but it is the tree of intimate London.

Elms, however, are the trees most noticeable on the roads into London, and their trunks blacken perhaps soonest of all. Nine Elms, Barn Elms, and how many other 'Elms' greet us on the run into town; and the feathery outlines of how many of these trees close the vistas of those new suburban streets that are for ever drilling little pathways into the ancient 'estates' of the Home Counties? To return again to the oldest of all roads into London, elms standing on rising ground have formed familiar landmarks for twenty centuries before there were beacons, lighthouses, buoys, or pilots on the river.

For the 'question' of London, seen from one point of view, resolves itself into that one of highways; and the very origin of London, the first cause of its existence, is that waterway. Nowadays we have discovered, as if in the night, a new secret of rapid communication: with that, as with every previous modification of the kind, the face of London bids fair to change unrecognisably. Whilst the pen is actually on my paper London is spreading itself from Kew towards Hounslow, towards Richmond, and towards Kingston, and on its other bounds towards how many other outlying places? The electric tram is doing all this.

To come into a city by means of one of these new, swift carriages, to come from any distance, say by a motor car, is to fly too fast for any easy recognition of the gradual changes from country to town. There are hedgerows, church towers moving rapidly as if drawn along among clumps of trees, on the horizon; then come brick-fields, inn signs, more signboards, a roadside house, bits of paper on the footpath, then a 'bus, dust whitening hedges, whitening them more, a villa, half a dozen villas, then new shops set one into another without a break, a swift glimpse of a great plain of roofs, grey and without visible limits, a long way below; a swift drop down a slope – a drop that one feels more internally than through the eyes – and one is dodging the close traffic, slowing down, slipping past a dray, boring a hansom in towards the pavement, and it is all over.

We stepped into the thing in our own farmyard; we seem to come to ourselves only in the middle of the familiar things of town, in the light filtering down between the tall buildings, before our own white doorstep, and the outstretched hand, pale in the palm, brown in the fingers, of an urchin who has, or has not, saved the lady's dress from touching the wheel, is before us. We have not been able to differentiate Mill Hill from the Welsh Harp district; Brentford was Chiswick and the Goldhawk Road before one had left the upper river; the Old Kent Road became the Borough High Street after we were hardly out of Maidstone.

It is not so much that the speed is very great, there is always the statutory limit, a sort of nightmare; but the motorist is too low down as a rule, the air presses against the eyes and half closes them; he has a tendency to look forward along the road, to see more of vehicles and of pedestrians than of the actual country or the regiments of buildings. He grows a little aloof, a little out of sympathy; he becomes more intent about keeping a whole skin on himself and on his car than about the outer world.

This is doubtless no more than a matter of time, of 'getting used to it', or of thinking of distances, as it were, in terms of the motor car. One has been accustomed to drive on a 'bus from Kensington to Piccadilly Circus in the half hour. One has seen the tall flats by Sloane Street for some minutes, Apsley House for some more minutes, and one was used to look down on the Green Park from a certain angle for a certain space of leisurely transit. These things have their familiar aspects.

They grow unfamiliar on the motorcar. The motorist is, as I have said, low down, he pulls up before no buildings; narrow streets like the old Kensington High Street present the aspect of tortuous defiles; he dodges in and out as if he were being whirled on a current through the rocky gorge of a river. Hyde Park Corner opens out suddenly like the flat reach below Coblentz on the Rhine. But we shall grow used to that, too.

What the automobile is to the comfortable classes the electric tram is becoming to the poorer. It is a means of getting into town. It does not, however, produce the same psychological effects. For one thing, the speed is not so great, and you have not the least anxiety as to what it may choose to run into; if you want to see things you are at a greater height, your range of sight is much longer. You may pick out upon the pavement any strange object; a tall negro with a blue birds-eye handkerchief round his head, eating, with the motions of a large ape, winkles out of a blue paper bag – or a girl with extremely brilliant red hair. You pick them out from a distance and watch them for a minute or two; you may look down at passing, you may look around. The other day I saw from the top of an electric tram, very far away, above the converging lines in the perspective of a broad highway of new shops, a steam crane at work high in the air on an upper storey. The thin arm stretched out above the street, spidery and black against a mistiness that was half sky, half haze; at the end of a long chain there hung diagonally some baulks of wood, turning slowly in mid-air. They were rising imperceptibly, we approaching imperceptibly. A puff of smoke shot out, writhed very white, melted and vanished between the housefronts. We glided up to and past it. Looking back I could see down the reverse of the long perspective the baulks of timber turning a little closer to the side of the building, the thin extended arm of the crane a little more foreshortened against the haze. Then the outlines grew tremulous, it all vanished with a touch of that pathos like a hunger that attaches to all things of which we see the beginnings or the middle courses without knowing the ends. It was impressive enough – the modern spirit expressing itself in terms not of men but of forces, we gliding by, the timbers swinging up, without any visible human action in either motion. No doubt men were at work in the engine-belly of the crane, just as others were very far away among the dynamos that kept us moving. But they were sweating invisible. That, too, is the Modern Spirit: great organisations run by men as impersonal as the atoms of our own frames, noiseless, and to all appearances infallible.

At night, too, when the broad flat streets out in the suburbs are deserted, these electric trams appear romantic and a little wonderful. Gongs sound at their approach rather plaintively, headlights blaze out upon the black night, the lights within are a tall, mellow flood, a reflection is cast, dim and flying, upon old black houses behind trees and upon the large, blank windows of the tall pink and terra-cotta shops that face them. The great rectangular blaze glides along with a heavy, impersonal groan of sound that is like a new form of silence, the figure of the mechanician in front has a backward rake like that of a man in the bows of a boat; as it passes there is the gleam of a long row of pink faces in the heart of the light. And all these things, the clang of the gongs, the rumble growing and dying away, the strong lights, the momentary and half revealed details of the darkened buildings, the thought of all these people going out a long way to sleep in the blacker darkness, have about them something touching and romantic, something 'characteristic' and foreign.

Of the older methods of communication I suppose the bicycle to come next, but I have always found entering London in this way to be tedious and dispiriting. You have to attend to yourself even more particularly than when you are in a motor-car; you have only half a horizon – the half that is in front of you. You are nearer the dust when there is dust, or nearer the mud. Transition from country to town becomes rather wearisome; you think a good deal in miles. London manifests itself slowly with high-banked and gravelled footpaths, with those same blackened tree trunks, in a certain coarseness of the grass, in houses of call that you feel uninclined to call at. Dogcarts and governess cars begin to look a little out of place, indefinably, you don't know why. And suddenly you meet a 'bus.

I don't know whether it is to me alone that a 'bus running between hedgerows seems forlorn and incongruous. They 'link up' all sorts of outlying villages – Mitcham with Tooting, all sorts of hamlets with Kingston-on-Thames, Islington with I don't quite know where. There is a network of what are called 'bus-routes all over England, but these are mostly carrier's carts. Some have tarpaulin hoods and go at a walk, others look like the station omnibuses of country hotels. Their existence is largely unsuspected, yet it is possible to go from Lewes to York by changing from link to link in market towns, or from Canterbury to Sydenham.

But the just-outside-London 'bus carries no parcels. It is, as a rule, bright green, and has a brilliant orange knifeboard atop. It goes at a good pace, and it is the sign that you have reached the sphere of influence of the very outer suburbs. I at least have never entered London by road without meeting or passing one of them.

They are due to the enterprise of large job masters near the great tram and London omnibus termini; they are the signs of London's reaching out its arms still further; they are really the pioneers. In older days they started from Whitehall, from the Bank, from the Borough, and were called Short Stages. As real London spreads they cease to pay; they travel farther afield, and their place is taken by our municipal services or by those of the larger trusts.

It is a long time since I have come into London on foot, so long that I have forgotten what it feels like. Indeed, I fancy that the proceeding is no longer modern, and is in consequence illegitimate to my purpose. Some tramps do it still, I suppose, and the gipsies who walk beside basket caravans. These, we may say, are as much the country stretching into the suburbs as the 'buses are the town stretching out. It is not very usual to meet them in inner London, though I have seen two or three at a time, with their chimneys smoking, entangled in the centre of the Piccadilly 'buses themselves. They were crossing London thus directly in order to get as soon as possible from some horse fair in Berkshire to another in North Kent – Rochester pleasure fair, I think, because it was towards the end of May. But except when there is some such reason for haste, these caravans rarely cross London. They circle it by the roads just inside the suburbs. Only yesterday, about six miles from Whitehall, I passed twice the mouth of a dingy and sinister passage of small eighteenth-century houses. It was called Angel Court. Fifty years ago it was in the fields, now its entry was between a large modern public house and a large modern pawnshop. I glanced down it, walking outwards; it was empty, silent and sordid. On my return there were in it four or five dark men with heavy, brass-bound whips, eight or nine dark women, and several children with black or red heads. In four or five of the small new streets that ran at right angles to my road there were caravans covered with basket chairs, osier flower-stands, wicker baskets; women were holding these things up in front of the lace curtains of sitting-room windows.

These people are not mere picturesque survivals; their number increases day by day as poorer men find the hurry of modern life too great; but I cannot claim to have entered London in a pikey's cart. I fancy, however, that looking at things through the small square of a back window, being at home in the middle of strange things, the sense too of being very aloof from the rest of the world must make one's point of view rather a special one. One would become more or less of a foreign observer.

That attitude, backed up by that sense of being at home, is the worst that one could assume; it kills even tolerance for the habits of others. It is the reason why the days of most rapid travelling are the days of most frequent misunderstandings between the races of mankind. Your foreigner, reaching his London in a Pullman car, has been during his whole journey in an hotel, very much like one of his own hotels, not very much unlike his own home. He stepped into it in St Petersburg an arrogant Tartar or a wily Slav; he steps down from it in the dim light of Charing Cross. He has gone through none of the processes of travel, none of his edges have been rubbed off, he is not necessarily the best type of Russian. He is quite ready to kick a porter and be cursed for it. He dislikes the place he has come to, and records his hasty impressions in letters home that may become so many international causes of misunderstanding.

In the slower days it was different. He was sent abroad because he was the best type of his race, or he came because he was a fine and adventurous spirit. He came from Moscow on sledges, in travelling carriages, on foot, by ship to Hull, overland to London. He had plenty of preparation, plenty of hardship to rub the angles down, and he was very glad to reach his journey's end. He expected to find savages, he found amiable and civilised white men; he reported well of the place he had reached. If an ambassador, he was polished, cosmopolitan, and pleasing; if an adventurer, he was a fine spirit. He had all sorts of tales to tell of escapes, of strange things seen by the way. He became a delightful person; he was full of deference for local customs, because his life or his livelihood depended on his ability to please. (I am thinking of the evidence given at the trial of Count Königsmarck in London by a crowd of Swedish, Russian, and Bohemian soldiers, stable-boys and hangers on. Or one may evidence Casanova, who was pleased and pleased himself in London; or you may read in Mr Round's *Commune of London* how great a part in the twelfth century foreign merchants, cut off from their own lands, played in exacting from the Angevin kings the liberty of London herself.)

It was the same with those whom London sent out. The few – the gentlemen and the merchant-adventurers – went, say, to the Spice Islands. The hardships of a long voyage, the great mysteries of seas and skies, chastened what of their souls was insular. They went among strange peoples with minds ready to be delighted. They sought, perhaps, nothing more romantic than pepper, but for their lives' sakes they respected local traditions, and were ready to kneel with their faces to the ground when a Soldan went past. They had left their homes so far behind them.

And this, indeed, is the 'defect of the quality' of rapid travel. The Londoner abroad is no longer sought after, fêted, a messenger of the goodness of his race, as were Congreve, Chesterfield, Gibbon, and, in another way, Richardson. Nowadays in the flood of him he has become the tweed-suited, long-toothed being of caricatures. The defect of the quality, because the traveller now, like the gipsy, takes his home and his home-spirit so much with him. And the one and the other are apt to find that every man's hand is against him.

Yet if that be the defect, the product of the quality of rapid transit is London itself. France has its Ministry of Roads and Bridges, and that is probably why Paris is not France: we have none, and London is England. It began by London's settling on the best placed highway in Europe, and England is still very much tied to the Thames. But France is little dependent on the Seine. Her excellent roads have in times past acted as the great decentralisers; Paris has been merely the administrative city. In England administration has remained with fair constancy at Westminster, near enough to the centre of the country. Wealth has always come into England by the Thames at London. At any rate in later centuries, the tendency has been for the Administration to settle near the centres of wealth,[1] and the combined attractions have made the tract of marsh and flat ground in the lower basin of the river the centre of the arts, of the industries, of the recreations and of the moral 'tone', not for England alone but for wider regions of the earth.

The roads into London have always been the crucial matter. They remain both the 'question' and the cause of that question. The first parliament of the twentieth century that might have devoted all its deliberation to the internal affairs of the country

---

1 This tendency was always observable in English history. It became, however, most observable with the eighteenth century. Before then, as in the days of John or during the wars of the Roses, to lose London was not to lose the country. Henry VII indeed held London, but to the end of his reign had practically no administrative power over England at large, and until quite late Henry VIII was powerless, save in the Home Counties. Parliaments, too, were held wherever the kings might happen to be in force. But already with the Stewarts to lose London was to lose England. It was so with Charles I, and so with James II. And the last chance of the Pretender's vanished with the establishment of the National Debt. The Chevalier could get no adherents in England, largely because the wealthy classes feared that he would repudiate. That in fact was the personal influence of London wealth on the country at large. And from that day forth it has seemed more and more impossible that a parliament should be held anywhere but in London.

opened in 1903. The first question it discussed was that of housing in London.

The question is not merely topical to the first years of the twentieth century; it has been the sempiternal question, it will remain unsolved until London and the country begin to fall into decay. It is, in fact, the 'old' question, and just as today the alternative to rapid transit is the erecting of tall buildings, so it was in the old days for ever. The story has been the same down to the minute details.

The Thames was for sixteen centuries the great highway of intercommunication within London walls. London streets were mere footways or bridlepaths between house-walls; when Queen Elizabeth went abroad on land she was carried in a litter by her gentlemen; there were on Thames-side 40,000 watermen, till the middle of the seventeenth century. Then suddenly:

> Fulsome madams and new scurvy squires
> Did jolt the streets in pomp at their desires...
> Drawn by the pampered jades of Belgia...
> That almost all the streets are choked outright
> Whilst watermen want work.

Horse-drawn carriages had been introduced.

The cry is that of Taylor the water poet and a waterman himself. It was that of the stage coachmen when railways came in, it will be that of the cabmen tomorrow, of railway engineers on the day after. That is the detail.

But until the days of Taylor London had been growing year by year more congested. Originally there had been the Tower, a fortress-village with a walled town of mud huts round it, its roads mere footpaths, its space circumscribed enough. As the town grew more important feudal nobles built palaces on the banks of the stream, crowds vast for their day came on foot or horse from the surrounding country or in ships from outer Europe. The houses of London climbed skywards along the narrow lanes – 'Elizabethan' houses, half-timbered, climbing up to six, eight and ten storeys, the upper ones bulging out and almost touching overhead to gain in the air the space that had to be ceded to foot traffic on the ground. Near the river were these houses of the 'comfortable' classes. These palaces of the kings and the great houses of the nobles crowded the face of the river that their owners might keep their private barges and have their own water gates. The others at the public stairs called

'Oars!' as today we call 'Cab'. Then came 'the pampered jades of Belgia'.

Roads were laid down or made up to suit them, then London spread out and the watermen disappeared or starved. (Taylor died a 'victualler' at Oxford.) The poorer classes began to swarm into such of the tall, 'comfortable' houses as the Fire left, the nobles moved their houses on to the larger roads, the comfortable classes built themselves small houses. The riverside palaces became wharfingers' buildings, their gardens and water gates became quays. Exactly the same thing has happened with every subsequent improvement in communications.

Ten years ago tall flats for the comfortable and tall dwellings for workmen seemed to have solved the question. The latter are already discredited, the former have always been disliked, and London is once more sending out bee swarms of small houses. We may consider that the thousands and thousands of small brick, slate-roofed cottages on the flats and low hills of south Essex are the contribution of 'workmen's fares'. These, though still growing, are old-fashioned already, so quickly do we move. The electric tractions are, as it were, spreading layers of the tall flats in villas over new regions of the south and west. London is full of traces of these past stages.

You may find an old water gate at the bottom of Buckingham Street; Somerset House and Whitehall and Westminster palaces remain administrative long after kings and protectors have left the lower river; all over the west central district there are august Georgian houses with panelled rooms and 'ceilings by Adams', inhabited by family upon family of the most entirely poor, or by firm upon firm, in stages one above another, of solicitors, of architects, of money lenders, of journalists.

Varying types of houses are buried in all parts of London in a way that is bewildering and makes classification impossible. They are like the stratifications of pottery and rubble that lie under all large cities, Rome and London alike. But it is as if the layers had been disturbed. It is not necessary to cite such artificially respected fragments as the mediaeval St John's Gate at Clerkenwell, which in any city less prodigal of relics would be a place of pilgrimage for sightseers, or the old houses in Holborn. These are not factors in the life of modern London.

But on certain of the great roads into town you will see the queerest jumble of old terraces, shadowed by old trees, grimed by the soot of generations long dead, jostled by the newest of shops dwelt in by generations as new. You may come into town by the Mitcham 'bus. You find brown, black or red trams waiting for you in a very narrow Square of old, but not ancient, untidy, and probably 'doomed' shops. Rows of the small, red-brick, slate-roofed houses, with bow windows to suggest a certain superiority, run at right angles to the highway. They whirl round and out of sight, as the tram advances, each moving vista ending in the screen of distant trees. Suddenly, on the high-road itself, there is a long block of buildings, white, and with green shutters above, liver-coloured brick below, slate roofed, rather startling and rather impressive. A high paling and a few tall elms still on the road-line, announce that this, too, was, till the other day, an old estate. A large, lettered, black board spells out that here are the County Council's workmen's dwellings and attempt to solve the housing question. What shall be the defects of their qualities, no doubt Time, with the revolution of her wheel, will bring to light. Perhaps the County Council will be forced to play the part of the squire of country villages, to insist that the tenants' floors are washed, and the faces of their children, and that may be an interference with the liberty of the subject. But for the moment these houses, empty still, clean still, and standing on a green field, are stimulating, and, as I have said, impressive. Electric trams are to link this village of so many thousand, let into a district of a million or so, with Westminster, with Blackfriars, and with London Bridge.

There are ancient houses, late Georgian, that peer, as if queru-lously, over the side hoardings. They seem to gloom behind high walls, in the shadow of tall trees, at the end of black gardens. They are painted white, with glass excrescences, observatories, perhaps, on their roofs among the chimneys and boughs. Once they were the considerable houses of an exclusive village. They were built when macadam roads had gradually become practicable for carriages of the leisured and the well off. Now the County Council houses and their trams shall, in the same spot, serve the hurried and the not rich, by right of roads.

Touching these few houses is a short, more modern but still old, double line of shops. The more reputable touch the most jumbled; they have been made by building salerooms out over old gardens, from small ground floors to the line of the pavement – old-curiosity shops, rag and bone shops, the queer, grimy, sometimes astonish-ingly 'old established', sometimes very transitory little odds-and-ends shops (where the servants of the well-off sell old *Times*'s, and kitchen grease, and where workmen buy second-hand tools and old blankets) of the outlying districts. They will disappear, I suppose, soon enough, move further out, and continue their individual, ratlike, and very useful existences.

Almost immediately afterwards there are long 'parades' of shops, stores, emporia, all terracotta, plate glass, soft stone and gilt letters. Crowds move slowly in front of these – it is not possible to hurry even on the broad pavements, and most people move leisurely, with the head a little to one side, looking at the large windows, carrying parcels. Then there are more old houses behind old trees, or behind little terraces, then more new shops. A brand new theatre, immense, domed, suddenly holds aloft, at its very apex, a large allegorical figure that appears on the point to soar over all these buildings and all these people. It is startling, because one does not expect the spectacular; it suggests the domed, statue-crowned brown stone buildings that in Strasburg the Prussians have erected to flaunt in front of the gracious French château of the governor of Alsace-Lorraine.

The effect in London is just as much one of jumble and the incongruous, but there is nothing of the sinister. If it is not an impression of pure happiness it certainly implies a contagious cheerfulness and good humour. In these parts you hardly see a discontented face, and never a morbid one. Right in to the very bottom of the Waterloo Road, and nearly up to Westminster Bridge, old villas, new houses and new shops lie side by side, or stare at one another. They are all mixed together, it is not possible to get any zones to 'synchronise', it is not possible to say 'early Georgian London had reached here, middle Victorian here, the railways produced this district, the short stages this'. They are dropped down in terraces anywhere, nearer Whitehall, or further away. But the general effect is a pleasant one. It is as if the poorer classes had come into the cast-off clothes of the comfortable, and found them roomy, easy and luxurious.

I suppose the speculative builder accounts for this. He found in one generation or the other, bits of waste ground, or rows of smaller buildings; he ran up at one time the fine old houses, at another the terra cotta shops. Probably in each case he was miscalled by the old residents; so does the 'jerry built' terrace of the late Georges become the pathetic old region of today; so no doubt the new shops will, to our children's children, be tenderly reminiscent, quaint, and full of old memories; so does Time assuage all temporal griefs.

The speculative builder's lamentable failures may be traced too. There is an odd terrace in one part of a long main road into London, it contains four immense, thin-walled, pretentious stucco houses, with middle Victorian pinnacles, gables and extravagances. It breaks off in uncompleted doors, uncompleted foundations, and a plot of grimy waste land. Other shops begin again. This place always piques my curiosity. I seem to trace in it a bold speculation's falling to pieces, getting the nickname 'Blank's Folly', growing begrimed, being forgotten.

These great roads into London are pleasant enough, inspiring too and impressive when they are full of people. In the times when one is in the mood, when one is 'looking' – and at such times the top of the horse-drawn tram is the best of all vehicles – one sees glimpses of so many things that it is like sitting before an unending stage procession, only more actual, more pathetic and much more inspiring. The other year I came in by way of the Kennington Road; along Newington Butts, past the Elephant, up London Road our eyes had grown accustomed to a gloom in the upper air. The Obelisk milestone in St George's Circus appeared, pallid under its lamps, pale and grimy, Georgian, grim and surprising; the tall wedge of the Eye Hospital was a deep black among liquid shadows deeper still. All the mysterious and gloomy London of ancient names and ancient lives seemed converging out of those shadows into that dark space. And suddenly, at a swinging round of the tram, there was a long trail of quivering lamps, pink, red, and white, low down on the ground, vanishing in the distance of Waterloo Road.

The road was 'up' for putting down the conduits of the electric system, and these lights guarded the trenches. But there had been no announcement, no expectation of a city rejoicing with illuminations; it was the most gracious of surprises and an unforgettable thing. But that is London.

Yet these great roads are oppressive when they are empty. To enter London in a faint, saffron dawn, along with the market wagons, is to be not awed by an immense humanity but disturbed by entering what seems some realm of the half supernatural. You are coming to Covent Garden, you sit at the shaft-tail beside the driver, he is half invisible in the night, taciturn and half asleep. At last the street lamps appear, at first solitary and brave in the dark, then more frequent and growing palely unnatural before the dawn; the colours of the large horses begin to show, and the innumerable 'pulls up', with their signposts and the yellow paint of the house-facings. Or you may lie softly enough high up on a bed of cabbages.

There used to be at the back of the Camden Town Road a little hay market that I knew well – it may be there still for all I know – and it was far better to come in on top of the hay, half under the tarpaulin, with the sweet scent, the warmth and the half dozing, the pure air of the early dawn. It is purest of all on a Monday, because fewer chimneys have been smoking. One saw the solitary streets for immense distances with, all along the roadways, little heaps that turned out to be cats crouching over garbage or courting; they are the sign visual of London at the dawn, with an air of mystery as of an unsuspected population revealed unawares. But all the empty streets giving out echoes that one never hears during the day, all the vacant blinds, the sinister, the jocular, the lugubriously inquiring, or the lamentable expressions that windows give to houses asleep, all the unsmoking chimneys, the pale skies, and the thought of all these countless thousands lying invisible, with their souls, in sleep, parted from their bodies – all these things give an effect, in its silence, immense, stealthy, and overpowering.

One coffee-stall, grey-hooded and with a pale lamp, does not break the spell, nor twenty; one house of call, nor a hundred. Even the shouts of Covent Garden or the footsteps on the cobbles, and the undertones of the loafers before the tiny black brick houses of the little hay market, seem thin and ghostly without the immense and kindly ground-bass of London awake. And, indeed, all the dawn sounds of London have that quality of thinness – the hoot of locomotives, the thunder peals of shunting trucks, the clatter of cabhorse hoofs, the rhythmical stepping of one's own four great horses. Even the immensely loud awakening of the London birds seems small and circumscribed.

The railways seem to make London commence where the chimney pots begin to be in forests. In comparison with the Thames they are at the other end of the scale. The river is a natural way; roads wind upon hills, descend valleys in zig-zags, make nowadays detours that were once necessary in order to strike fords or to convenience great houses or solitary hamlets. Railroads tunnel through hills, fill up valleys with embankments and crash through the town itself, boring straight ways into the heart of it with a fine contempt for natural obstacles.[1] If we could see the underlying

---

1 Canals have something of this quality, and in them it is of older date. Brindley carried

fineness of these things, the fineness that shall be on the surface when these embankments are as venerable as today the wall of Hadrian, it might make our world more inspiring. There are deep cuttings, coming into London where brick walls, fifty feet high, are black, sombre, and austere. You are in a kind of underworld, savagely impressive enough. The square fronts of houses peep down on you as you run beneath; constant footbridges overhead give to the thin light of day a constant shudder and quiver. We, who are not made for strong impressions, are ourselves inclined to shudder.

Or one may grow bewildered to the point of losing hold of one's identity amid the crash and charge of goods trucks. There are great open spaces all over London where the transfers are made from line to line. At night they are most active. Electric lights glare and seem to drop sparks from very high in the air, blue and mistily; rails glimmer here and there underfoot like marsh pools of water; hooded trucks seem to wander alone and to charge each other in all the black distances. One might be on some primæval plain, watching, in the glare of lightning, to the unceasing crash of thunder, primordial beasts grazing, wandering, or in violent combat. Yet at these things, too, we are apt to shudder, as in his day Horace disliked the Via Flaminia.

Or we cry out: 'These things are bringing in the millennium.' Perhaps they are. To really descend, not in body alone, but with the spirit receptive, into this whirl and crash, to see men running with set faces, at the continual risk of their lives, that they may link up wagons bringing screws from Birmingham, corn from Canada, pine-planks from Norway, pork from the United States, to whirl oneself in the whirl of it, is to be overcome with convictions. We live in spacious times. Humanity is on the march somewhere, tomorrow the ultimate questions shall be solved and the soul of man assuaged. Perhaps it shall. It is possible in the contagion of these

---

the Bridgewater canal over a river by means of an iron bridge in the days when they still wore tie wigs and dress swords. I do not touch on this kind of road into London because it is no longer a very usual one. At one time it was common enough. I remember to have read an account in verse, by a starving and permanently obscure eighteenth-century poet, of a voyage he made from London to Nottingham and back with his entire family, a wife and six children. He was seeking a patron, but finding none he printed this pamphlet and hawked it through the streets. I am familiar enough with several canals. When I was a boy I persuaded a bargee to take me through the tunnel that goes under the Edgware Road and reappears near Regent's Park. The darkness, the plash of waters, the faint stars of light at either end, combined to make a deep impression on me. The bargee and his mate pushed themselves and the barge along by pressing their bare feet against the walls of the tunnel.

things to see the opening up of empires wider of sway than Rome, clearer of sight than Greece, kinder of heart than Carthage, purer in joy than was to be had among the hanging gardens of Babylon. Or is this only rhetoric, or only romance?

For myself, when on a train into London, I feel almost invariably a sense of some pathos and of some poetry. To the building up of this railway, of this landscape of roofs, there went so many human lives, so much of human endeavour, so many human hopes. Small houses, like the ranks of an infinite number of regiments caught in the act of wheeling, march out upon the open country; in the mists of the distance they climb hills, and the serrated roofs look like the jagged outlines of pinewoods with, at the top, the thin spike of a church tower. The roofs come closer together; at last, in their regular furrows, they present the appearance of fields ploughed in slate, in tiles, in lead, with the deeper channels of the streets below. Certain details strike at the eye: parallel lines of white cement set diagonally in the slate courses whirl past, bewilderingly, like snow in a wind; lines of rails shoot suddenly from beneath the embankments; and, rather surprisingly, bits of black field lie in the very heart of it all, with cabbages growing, and a discoloured donkey tethered to a peg. The plain of roof tops broadens out again. Perhaps the comparative quiet fosters one's melancholy. One is behind glass as if one were gazing into the hush of a museum; one hears no street cries, no children's calls. And for me at least it is melancholy to think that hardly one of all these lives, of all these men, will leave any trace in the world. One sees, too, so many little bits of uncompleted life. As the train pauses one looks down into a main street – and all streets are hardly recognisable from a height. A 'bus is before the steps of a church, a ragged child turns a catherine wheel in the road, and holds up her hand to the passengers. Suddenly a blue policeman steps into the roadway. The train moves on.

The other day, too, we were moving rather slowly. I looked down upon black and tiny yards that were like the cells in an electric battery. In one, three children were waving their hands and turning up white faces to the train; in the next, white clothes were drying. A little further on a woman ran suddenly out of a door; she had a white apron and her sleeves were tucked up. A man followed her hastily, he had red hair, and in his hand a long stick. We moved on, and I have not the least idea whether he were going to thrash her, or whether together they were going to beat a carpet. At any rate, the evening papers reported no murder in Southwark.

Incidents even so definite as these are more or less the exception, but the constant succession of much smaller happenings that one sees, and that one never sees completed, gives to looking out of train windows a touch of pathos and of dissatisfaction. It is akin to the sentiment ingrained in humanity of liking a story to have an end. And it is the 'note' of all roads into London.

To indulge in the feeling to any extent would be to add a new morbidity to life. One would, quite literally, never get any for'arder if one stayed to inquire to the end of every tragi-comedy of which, on one's road, one caught a glimpse. And it is unpractical to wish that every bricklayer and mortar carrier who added his wall to the infinite number already existing should be able to sign his work as an artist signs his picture. But that, too, is a universal sentiment and a 'note' of all roads into London, a note of London itself. It arises out of the innate altruism that there is in us all, or out of the universal desire to 'know'.

If one stayed to think, one would like to know what kind of poor wretch set the fifth stone in the third tier of the Pyramid of Cheops.

CHAPTER III

Work in London

THE Thames is the oldest, as it is the most majestic of the roads into London, but its character as a road is obscured, justly enough. Along the others we travel to reach our work, our love, to meet our death. Along the Thames those who travel are working always, the passengers it bears leave it at the very gates of London.

Gravesend, with its high front of piers characteristic in their dark and rigid architecture of piles, is a place of romance to the sailor who comes to London from the deep waters. It is the signal that, after his ninety days of empty sea and empty sky, he has come very near to his harbours. Sailors speak of the place with the remembrance of old and good times, giving a soft look to the eyes, a soft tone to the voice; they are the look and tone of those who think about old emotions, of pleasure, of impatience, of the times when they said 'Only a day more now.' The river front of Gravesend means that.

On the other bank a square, large red hotel faces these pile structures across the broad grey sweep of water and air. It marks the gates of the lowest docks, and here, for the river, psychological London begins. It does not much matter whether the ship turns in there at Tilbury or whether it works up to the docks in Gallions Reach, or to the others in the heart of town itself. Work for them ends there.

It is taken up by the red-sailed barges. They tack in their engrossed manner across and across the wide reaches; they pass under the shadow of dull clouds, of rain squalls, under watery sunlight, the arms of aligned cranes, the smoke from factory chimneys. They linger, going about, in front of bluffs covered with grey buildings and black trees; in exposed stretches of water they are covered, right over the hatches, by the wash from the sea-tarnished sides of steamers so vast, so silent in their motions, so centred in themselves, that as, from the deck of a barge, one looks at their passing, it is hard to realise that they and not the low banks that they obscure and seem to swallow up, are gliding by.

These barges running up from Rotherhithe or from much farther out to sea, pass cement factories, sand works, anchored groups of skiffs where sand is hauled laboriously in buckets from the bottom of the river; they pass petroleum depôts where, side by side, grey retorts are like those of gasworks; they pass candle factories and manure warehouses. They tack about gravely one after another beside a black smallpox hospital that, out in the river, is one half ship and the other a pier with a dingy and mournful resemblance to those of fashionable watering places. They move, these barges, in squadrons in a continual and mazy slant, red sail cutting diagonally across red sail, with here and there a large rent, and here and there a white patch. They give the 'character' to this road into London, to this river of toil. Their only rivals are the sludge boats, a fleet of large steamers owned by the County Council. These are running in a continuous string; they go swiftly down stream, low in the water, and showing all black. They come back empty, so high in the bows that a great streak of red shows from the keel upwards; they swing round in front of one or other of the sewage works, ready to take in another cargo to drop into the sea beyond the Nore as soon as the tide serves. The barges, however, carry coke, carry sand, carry gravel, and a hundred other things. Occasionally one loaded very high with a stack passes them all, looking for all the world like a man buried beneath a haycock; occasionally these, too, are passed by very gaily painted, astonishingly swift, racing barges, that thread the close traffic like brilliant shuttles, and roar and rustle through the water.

So at last, keeping out of the way of the sludge boats, out of the way of powder barges, of great steamers of the famous Lines, of swift fish carriers that raise an enormous wash, and of the Belle steamers that they detest most of all, the small flotillas come to the top of Tipcock Reach. Hitherto the factories have been scarce, mostly unsavoury and solitary. But a beacon rises up beyond the wharf of a powder factory that faces a manure warehouse. This beacon is spindly, tall, of iron lattice work. And all beyond it the river runs as between high walls, shining with a more metallic glitter under smoke and the shadows of groves of masts, crane-arms, chains, cordage. A train of the large steamers lies heavy on the water, hooting signals to agents ashore, waiting at the dock gates for water enough to enter. This is Gallions Reach, and from here upwards London offers a solid black facing to its river. From here, too, the little companies of barges begin to break up. Some stop near the dock gates, some turn into the London canals. Some wait near Waterloo, some go far above the bridges. Here at any rate the river as a road into London ends. It is all the time a grey tide of work, a moving platform of workers.

Workers in London divide themselves, roughly, into those who sell the labour of their bodies and those who sell their attentions. You see men in the streets digging trenches, pulling stout wires out of square holes in pavements, pecking away among greasy vapours at layers of asphalte, scattering shovelfuls of crushed gravel under the hoofs of slipping horses and under the crunching tyres of wheels. If walls would fall out of offices you would see paler men and women adding up the records of money paid to these others. That, with infinite variations, is work in London.

You get the two things united here and there. The other day I was in Tilbury Docks. (It is difficult to get away from this river.) The vast, empty squares of water lay parapeted, arbitrary and dim in their eternal perspectives; the straight lines of the water, the straight lines of the parapets, of the bottoms of the goods sheds, of the tops, of the grey corrugated roofs, all dwindled together into the immense and empty distances. The rows of four-footed, gaunt, inactive cranes, painted a dull rust colour, and the few enormous steamers at the inner ends of the quays – all these things were wetted, fused and confused in their outlines, beneath a weeping sky in which a drapery of clouds had the look of a badly blotted water-colour painting, still wet and inefficient. Knots of stevedores in dim and neutral coloured clothes seemed to be doing nothing perfunctorily in the shadow of the great hulls.

A big, red faced, heavy-moustached man in blue clothes and with cheerfully brass-bound cap and shoulders, hurried out of a tin shed. It was labelled: 'Office of the Steam Navigation Co.' He slipped hastily between the black side of one of the huge sheds and a grey, rusty and sea-fretted liner. Her lower sides gaped in large holes screened with canvas, and from moment to moment obscured by grimy buckets of coal that rose from a lighter; her square, white upper deck cabins were being painted more white by painters in white jackets. He hurried very fast, with a masterful and engrossed step, a cheerful blue figure with pink cheeks, dodging mechanically the pools of greasy water and the fat black mud between the sleepers. He dived into another small office. He was the chief officer of the liner that was coaling and he had a pencil behind his ear.

He was uniting as it were the labours of the men shovelling in the buckets of coal, of the men uttering melancholy wails as they swung-in a white boat, of the men hooking up long planks for the painters to sit on, and of the painters themselves on the upper decks. With that pencil he controlled all their labours, as if he were twisting them into an invisible rope which passed through that tin office and up, far away into town where other pencils and other pens recorded these things on large pages, digested them into summaries and finally read them out to Boards of Directors.

Those invisible ropes – they are strong enough in all conscience – seem to be the only tie between these two classes of workers, between these two great camps set one against another. It is astonishing how different London looks from one or from the other end. Speaking broadly, the man who expresses himself with a pen on paper sees his London from the west. At the worst he hopes to end with that view. His London of breathing space, his West End, extends from say Chiswick to say Portland Place. His dense London is the City as far as Fenchurch Street, his East End ends with what he calls 'Whitechapel'.

The other sees his London of elbow room extend from say Purfleet to say Blackwall. He is conscious of having, as it were at his back, the very green and very black stretches of the Essex marshes dotted with large solitary factories and small solitary farms. His dense London, *his* City, lies along the line from Blackwall to Fenchurch Street. Beyond that, the City proper, the city of the Bank and the Mansion House, is already a place rather of dilettante trifling. Its streets are tidied up, its buildings ornamented and spacious. The end of the West End is for him the Piccadilly Fountain, and this latter quarter of large, almost clean, stone buildings, broad swept streets and a comparative glare of light, is already a foreign land, slightly painful because it is so strange. That, further west, there may be another enormous London never really enters his everyday thoughts. He reads about it sometimes, he hears it spoken of; sometimes perhaps in a holiday frame of mind he goes through it. But it never 'matters' to him, it is never like his familiar, rigid rows of streets all of blackened bricks, windows that are square openings in boxes and plasters of blue and white and begrimed enamelled iron advertisements. These are familiar, these are real life, these are homely, as if warm and alive. The other he does not much want to think about, it would worry him. In just the same way the penworker does not want to think about several dark towns of a million or so east of 'Whitechapel'. It is an unpleasant thought. Given ill-luck, a craving for drink, disease or one or other of the fatal falls of humanity, he too might have to sink into those gloomy and shadowy depths. The other man is vaguely troubled at the idea of the West. There he would have to be tidy, constrained, worried about specks on his clothes, careful of his tongue, less than a man.

These two types, in their mass very human and very comprehensible, are in general very foreign and in general very hostile the one to the other. Yet upon their combined workings the life of London depends. And because there they may work one into another like the teeth of cogwheels revolving antithetically, London attracts them. For the obvious secret of London, its magnetism, is the work that it offers to be done or to be 'organised'. You go there whether you got your training at the tail of a plough in Kent or in Lithuania, with the most salient fact in your experience the knowledge of a pollard willow in which there is always a dog-fox asleep; or whether beside the Isis, on the links of St Andrews, or in the University of Bonn you learnt the sorrows of Achilles, the binomial theorem, or the chemical formulae of all the coal tar by-products. You go there, whether your ideal is to get a wage of fifteen shillings a week more with lighter work and shorter hours, or whether you dream that before 'retiring' you will get yourself turned into a limited company with a capital of six cyphers at the tail of a numeral – you go there to get 'something to do'. That is the grosser view.

But the finer side is the romantic, the adventurous, the dreamer's spirit in mankind to whom work itself in imagination remains the primal curse. In certain cellars here and there in the City, in cellars that have been oil-clothed and tiled, garnished with rows of hat-pegs and with leather seats like planks along the walls, above white marble table-tops that loom like horizontal tombstones through the delicate films of cigarette smoke, contending in the dim atmosphere with the delicate fragrance of coffee – in a City Mecca, in fact – you will see men sit. Their faces of the palest, of the ruddiest, of the blondest, of the most black-avised, will be all united into one serious frown over black and white stones, like smaller tombstones standing or lying prone as if in a disastrously wrecked graveyard. A man will rise in a far corner, pull the lapels of his coat one towards another, shake his umbrella a little, and walk away with a swift step and a half self-conscious air. A young man will look up and lose for a moment his engrossed expression. He will stop his companion's domino in mid air with 'Do you know who that is? Why, Plumly!' – 'What, Plumly of the Dash United?' They will gaze with half awe at the disappearing trouser-ends and boot-heels on the stairs.

'Yes. Plumly was only an auctioneers' clerk in Honiton, where my father is. And now look what he's worth! That was what made me come to town.' The eyes of both young men will have serious and reflective expressions before they resume their game. They will both be thinking, in one way or another, that what man has done man can do.

Or, on the seat before the ferryman's hut in a small harbour you may see a hook-nosed, bearded, begrimed, weather-soiled and wonderfully alert London barge-man. He will wave his tiny pipe at the faces of half-a-dozen young fishermen standing in a circle before him.

'Yes,' he will say, 'you're too young to remember Johnston. But his mother and Mrs Spence, who keeps the "Blue William" here, were first cousins... Bill Johnston of the "Britisher".'

Bill Johnston of the 'stumpy' called 'Britisher' had in his childhood sailed from that port aboard a coaling schooner. Afterwards he had 'been South', he had been in the Cape Mounted Police, then he had returned to London. He had saved a little money and bought a share in his 'stumpy', which is a barge without a topsail: he had carried freight unceasingly from Rotherhithe into the Pool or into the canals; his employers had advanced him money to buy the barge outright; he had carried freights until he had paid them back. 'And now,' his eulogiser comments, 'he sails that there river, Bill Johnston, with his missis for mate and his kid for apprentice; he's in his own home with a cooking range in the cabin and a joint hanging in the hatchway for a larder. He's his own master; he comes when he will and he goes; he draws a steady three quid a week, and he's buying up other barges gradual.'

The young fishermen standing round dive their hands deeper into their russet breeches pockets and gaze out over the rubble of old boats, cork floats, harbour mud and piles. The old man sucks at his pipe, spits, waves a grimy hand wanting a thumb, and says, 'Just such a lad as you be Bill Johnston were,' and a boy moves his hands in his pockets sighing 'Ah!'

You will see scenes just the same besides the Bay of Naples and, *mutatis mutandis*, in Ukrainia and the Levant. For London calls out across the lands to the spirit of Romance, to the spirit of youth and the spirit of adventure – to the Finer Spirits.

There are such glorious plums. And the thought of them eventually fills alike those City Meccas and the square, blackened brick, balconied dock-dwellings; it fills the bare rooms in Whitechapel, where darn and hook-nosed men sit amid the stench of humanity, their mouths filled with small brass nails, silent amid the rattling clatter of hammers on boot soles. It fills, too, the behind-counters of large drapers, the very sewers with large neutral-coloured scavengers, and the great Offices in Whitehall. In the whitewashed and grimy courts of Saffron Hill splendid-limbed, half-nude children tumble, dark eyed, like the cherubs of Cinquecento pictures, round the feet of dark men puffing cigarette smoke, and fair Venetian girls lean back, smiling and chattering, in bright head-cloths, bright neck-cloths, bright bodices and bright petticoats against brilliant barrows. Hook-nosed, saturnine and imperturbable old men mix, with the air of sorcerers, flour, vanilla, cochineal, and condensed milk in pewter freezing pots like infernal machines. The Finer Spirit… because, today as always and for ever, the streets of London are paved with gold.

I remember reading somewhere a long time ago an ingenious article pronouncing boldly that this splendid figure of speech, this myth shining down the ages, was literally true. I remember the bare existence of the article, but I cannot remember its arguments. It was, perhaps, because the ground in front of the Mansion House is worth its area in sovereigns set on edge. Or it may have been that, according to the writer, the mud trodden underfoot was, for some profound chemical reason, worth its weight in gold. In either case a favoured few do undoubtedly possess the secret of alchemy, in that everything they touch – mud, too, no doubt – turns to gold. And the number of that favoured few is very great, because in London there are so many things to touch. Hence the immensity of London's silent appeal. She calls to all the world.

'In the old days', there were, say, the Holy Land, the 'Wars' where thousands of mercenaries cut by turns the throats of Ferrarese, of Bolognese, of French, of Burgundians, of Kaiserliks and of each other. There were afterwards the Indies, Peru, Mexico, the Spanish Main; then more Wars of Seven, of Thirty Years' duration – then the opening up of the silent East, then goldfields. These things called to the adventurous of succeeding generations for ten centuries. But these appeals were limited. They called only to those who felt able to handle a sword, fire a thatch, cut the rings off a woman's hand, set a sail, shoot in a wood, march a thousand miles or come out of a death of thirst. They were for the valorous alone who could work with their hands.

The appeal of London is far wider. She has seemed for the last century or so to stand on high, offering, like the figure on the Duke of York's column, laurel wreaths to all the world. She seems to hold them for bank clerks and for bargees, for charlatans and the Founders of Faiths, to poets and to privates in the Foot Guards, to actors as to all sorts of robbers with violence. But the appeal is on the whole a modern one: it was not until the wider world of woods and seas was nearly all exploited that the Occidental peoples 'discovered' London. To enter minutely into this movement would be impracticable. It would take one very deep into that odd psychology of statistics that is called Political Economy.

But it had its rise, this modern appeal of London, at about the time of the triumphing principle of Free Trade;[1] it had its beginning at about the time when the world evolved the equally triumphant principles of Limited Liability, Specialism in Labour and the freedom of knowledge.

It was probably foreshadowed in the opening years of last century by the triumphant figure of Napoleon I. He more than anyone stands for that other triumphant principle: What man has done man can do. He raised the standard of the adventurer not only towards respectability but towards apotheosis.

---

1 I have, however, just read the book of a well received Political Economist who asserts that it did not. The modern spirit is by him attributed to the 'consistent, unrelenting, true-sighted policy of five centuries of English governmental action to a protective system which, in fact, was only relaxed when the supremacy had been reached.' It isn't, of course, my business to assert the one or the other dogma. The supremacy of London's particular attraction came at about the time of Free Trade. But Free Trade itself may have come because just then London had become supreme owing to five centuries of Protection. Or the reverse may have been the case.

Both are possible enough, because in the arena of Triumphant Principle pendulums swing backwards and forwards: the undisputed right of today becoming the open question of tomorrow; and the unquestioned wrong of the immediate future. That is a platitude because it is one of the indisputable verities. In the country they say that large clocks when they tick solemnly and slowly, thud out the words: 'Alive – Dead; Alive – Dead' – because in this world at every second a child is born, a man dies. But, in London, a listener to the larger clock which ticks off the spirits of successive ages, seems to hear above the roar of the traffic, the slow reverberation: 'Never – Again; Never – Again,' as principles rise and die, and rise and die again. For in London that fact forces itself upon the ear and upon the eye; it is a part of the very dust. It is, perhaps, the final lesson of the great, human place. Arts rise and die again, systems rise and die again, faiths are born only to die and to rise once more, the only thing constant and undying is the human crowd.

Before his day the great London adventurers were, actively, the Drakes and the Raleighs; passively, Casanovas and Cagliostros. Roderick Random's idea of 'making a career' after the Wars had failed him, was to pretend in London to be a man of fashion, to victimise an heiress, or in some miraculous way to pick up a 'patron' with influence. There was not in those days any other career in the Town. Macshanes, O'Creegans, an occasional Colonel Evans, perhaps a French barber spying in the service of the Pretender, a few poets like Thomson of the 'Seasons' and a few bastards like Tom Jones – all these people were obsessed by these two ideas. They sat in their best clothes toying with their snuff-boxes or ostentatiously winding up jewelled watches in boxes at the Opera; they panted to attract the attention of an heiress or they wrote dedications and fee'd the footmen of peers.

It would be fanciful to make Buonaparte too responsible for the Modern Type; but he, upon the whole, was the discoverer of the principle: apply yourself to gain the affection of the immense crowd. After his day the mere heiress and the patron as ends of a career vanish. They remain merely as stepping stones.

But the immense crowd is still the indubitable end. If hardly any of us aspire to its suffrage in its entirety, we have, in London at least, discovered the possibilities of capturing its custom in its smallest trifles. To make a corner in collar studs would be rather American: the method in London is to invent, or to buy up the invention of, a collar stud that will appeal straight to the heart of the million, a collar stud that will be not only in all the street vendors' trays, but in all the barbers', all the hosiers', all the drapers' windows. It ought to be very cheap, very picturesquely 'put on the market', and just perishable enough to make a constant supply desirable. The man who did put it on the market would immediately become the Napoleon of the Collar Stud.

There are already so many of these: there is at least one, I am not sure that there are not several, of the Press; Napoleons of the Lower Finance find their Waterloos every few years. There is a Napoleon of Pharmacy, one of the Tea Trade, one of Grocery, one of Underclothing. This is not a mere figure of speech on my part: the words are used month by month by each of these Trade Journals. There is very obviously one of politics, but that 'career', as things are in London of today, has become comparatively decorative – a hobby for Napoleons in retirement. What one would sigh for is no longer the making of a people's laws or of a people's songs, but of a people's socks. With that behind one, one may die Chancellor of the Exchequer and a peer of the realm.

This obviously is desirable enough; we sigh very reasonably for business men in our cabinets. It is picturesque too, and inspiring, it brings about kaleidoscopic changes, and the wildest of contrasts. It makes life more worth living, because it makes life more interesting, and more amusing. The trouble, the defect of this particular Quality, is that the work suffers. The workers and their immediate dependents suffer perhaps still more.

The two clerks in that City Mecca – I happened to be watching them – saw that particular millionaire cross through the cigarette smoke and disappear. He, too, was a Napoleon of a particular financial order, and those two young men, when they rose from their dominos, pulled together their coats, shook their umbrellas a very little, and set their hats on at a particular angle. They were imitating almost gesture for gesture their hero.

I have no means of knowing how much further in the real mysteries of his craft they imitated him. I do not know whether they possessed his tremendous energy, his industry, his nerve, his knowledge of the market – whether they possessed even a shade of his temperament. It is obvious, however, that the great majority do not, that the chance against any average young man is a 'thousand to one'. I used to know rather intimately a talented and in that sense romantic young man, whom I will call X. X. had several irons in the fire: that meant that he had several Napoleons he could imitate. He had a very reasonable competence: he invested it in a certain wholesale business, of which he knew little more than that fortunes were rapidly made in it. He occupied certain offices which looked down on Aldgate Pump.

The rooms appealed to his romanticism: he found it extremely picturesque to see women, actually with pails, in London, in the twentieth century, really fetching water. It was interesting, too, to look at the Trade Papers, and his office had lockers all round it. They were meant to contain samples of the raw material he traded in. I happened once to open one; it revealed rather astonishingly the tinfoil necks of champagne bottles.

X. sanguinely and amiably explained. Strauss, an awfully sharp man, the Napoleon of the… Trade, had his lockered office just round the corner: he always offered his clients – perhaps 'suitors' would be the right word – that particular brand of wine. He kept it in just such a receptacle.

That part of the business X. attended to with amiability and success: he had also an idea that the banks were advancing his partner money on some sort of 'cover system'; the crop somewhere in the East was going to fail: his partner – X. financed this partner – had taken care to be early in the market: as soon as the season commenced they would be making a profit of £90 a week, and with a few more such lucky specs, X. would be able to clear out with £50,000.

He attended at his office thus amiably, he wrote an occasional letter on his typewriter, which was rather fun, he looked out of window at the Pump, he counter-signed cheques, and genially acknowledged that the… Trade was full of rogues, from ten until four.

Then he hurried westwards to his large white and ormolu house, and sat down to a rosewood Chippendale bureau. He had there another Napoleon before his eyes.

This was a celebrated novelist, who made £7,000 a year, by dictating topical novels into a phonograph. X. accordingly dictated topical novels – when the war broke out, a romance of South Africa; during the Chinese Massacres, a Chinese novel.

He displayed an astonishing industry over this speculation, and, having devoted his two or three hours a day to it, he 'dressed', and with his wife, either dined out, or 'dined' other amiable and fashionable persons. That, too, was part of the game, because to get on in either the Book or the other Trade, you have to 'know people'. Sometimes after returning from the opera X. would sit down and write a topical critique and sketch – he had a talent for sketching – the dresses and the *mise en scène*. This was because he knew a journalist – a Napoleon of the Paragraph – who said he made £4,000 a year at similar odd moments

But I never heard X. attach any importance to knowing how to 'write', or to learning the ins and outs of the… Trade. He had his irons, however, in these fires. His partner might scoop the market with Bosnians when the Honduras crop failed, or X. himself might make a hit with a novel. Either would mean a swift and easy affluence.

There is nothing inherently impossible in X.'s ideals, just as there is nothing criminal or mean. He represents, rather diffusely, the Modern Spirit. For, speaking largely, we in London today see life as a great gamble, London as a vast Monte Carlo, or, if you will, an immense Hamburg lottery. We put in a quite small stake, we may win a six figure lot. That is why London attracts us so supremely. If we do not at once win, we put in another small stake, and we continue until either we win, or our capital, our energy, our health, our youth, or our taste for gambling, come to an end.[1] This tendency is, in fact, a trade custom, like any other: it is a vast frame of mind, that one may not like, but that one has not any valid ethical reason for condemning.

But the pity for X., as for so many other amiable and gallant young men, is that even in this modern market, the essentially old-fashioned must be to be found at the bottom of the sack. What work we do must still in one way or another be good in the sense of being attractive. You must still lay a good coin of some realm or other on the green cloth.

I know, for instance, another young man not so dilettante – neither indeed so charming nor so amiable as X. – but almost more romantic. I will call him P. He had inherited a business of a specially old-established, a specially trustworthy, a specially eminent kind – one of those houses as reliable and as 'placed', as is Childs' in the banking, or Twinings' in the tea trade. When P. came into it, it was already beginning to feel the touch of competition from Stores. It had relied upon old-fashioned 'good' customers; it had never advertised.

P. not only advertised generally and lavishly, but he put on the market cheap and attractively packed 'specialities'. He tried in fact to corner London's collar studs. What his business lost immediately in caste, he tried to make up at home. He devoted his leisure time to a species of scientific investigation connected with his trade, which along with Napoleons of Specialities, has room for disinterested and abstruse investigators with great names and no money – famous 'benefactors of their kind'. P., in fact, was making a large and romantic bid: he sacrificed the particular aroma of respectability of his business to a kind of large altruism: he sacrificed his great name in his trade organs, to the chance of gaining in the wider papers a considerable and undying fame. And this is very charac-

---

1 I do not of course mean that steady work is no longer to he found in the town of London. The industrious apprentice still climbs as he did in the time of Hogarth. But the essential 'note' of those who stand out among workers in modern London, appears on the surface to be that of gambling. That, in fact, is the most striking note of work in modern London, it is in that that it differs from work in all past Londons, and it is that which is the pre-eminent attractiveness of London itself. There is obviously mere work enough, sober and uninviting, to keep men in the country districts all over Europe.

teristic of the conditions of modern work in London. Our poets
have to gain a daily bread in the public offices, our scientists in
electric light works. We may all know an admirable critic of *belles
lettres:* he gives eight hours of his day to checking the issue and
return of dog licences at Somerset House, and there are many
religious enthusiasts of the type of Swedenborg who spend even
longer hours in measuring and selling cheap ribbons. They are
doing it in order on Sundays to preach in the parks.

London, in fact, if it make men eminently materialist in their
working hours (and that is the great cry of all idealists against the
great place), makes them by reaction astonishingly idealist in their
interior souls. I know a railway signalman. He spends dreadfully
long hours, high up in a sort of cage of wood and glass, above the
innumerable lines of shimmering rails just outside the dim cave of
a London terminus. He works himself dog-tired, pulling levers that
are constantly bright with the friction of his hands; he listens to the
drilling sounds of little bells, straining his eyes to catch the red and
white placards on the breasts of distant engines. At night in a cottage
'down the line' he spends more hours, making out of pith and
coloured paper little models, like stalactite work, of the English
cathedrals. His small holidays go in making trips to Bath, to Exeter,
to Durham, and his small savings are spent on architectural drawings
and photographs of details. His ambition is to make a model of
every cathedral in this country, and, if life holds out, of those at
Rouen, Amiens, and Notre Dame de Paris.

This is an ideal: his eyes grow hazy and romantically soft at the
thought of finally having in his working shed all those small white
objects. But he does not in the least care about architecture. I once
met by accident a man of forty, a cashier of a London 'bus company.
He rather disliked the country, but his ambition was to cover, on
his bicycle, every road of the United Kingdom. He inked over on
his ordnance map each road that he travelled on, and he saw, in
imagination, as a glorious finale like a dream, one of the sixpenny
papers publishing a half-tone block representing this map with all
its coach roads inked and distinct like the filaments of a skeleton
leaf.

Collectors and connoisseurs there have been, no doubt, in all the
ages since Nero carried off his five hundred bronzes from Delphi.
But the recreations of this signalman and this 'bus-cashier are simply
mental anodynes: if they were not necessary for self-preservation
they would be imbecile. The conditions of modern labour make

them almost more than necessary. A man who retires from any routine work at all strenuous, signs nowadays his own death warrant if he have no hobby.

And all work in modern London is almost of necessity routine work: the tendency to specialise in small articles, in small parts of a whole, insures that. It becomes daily more difficult to find a watch operative who can make a timepiece, from escapement to case. One man as a rule renders true little cogwheels that have been made by machine, another polishes tiny pinion screws, another puts all these pieces together, another adjusts them. In just the same way one woman machines together trousers that have been roughly cut out by machine, another buttonholes them, another finishes them. And in just the same way in offices, a partner mentions the drift of a letter to a clerk, he dictates it to a shorthand-typewriter, she writes and addresses it, a boy posts it. And the clerk, the typewriter and the boy go on doing the same thing from the beginning of the working day to the end without interest and without thought.

In the minds of these workers, work itself becomes an endless monotony; there is no call at all made upon the special craftsman's intellect that is in all the human race. It is a ceaseless strain upon the nerves and upon the muscles. It crushes out the individuality, and thus leisure time ceases to be a season of rest, of simple lying still and doing nothing. One needs, on the contrary, to assert one's individuality, and to still the cry of one's nerves. This leads to these hobbies which, psychologically considered, are a form of new work making some appeal to our special temperaments. In men this means, as a rule, some sport in which they have a chance of asserting an individual superiority, and women workers find their vent in personal adornments or housework.

But women workers, at any rate of the very poor, have not even this solace. I call to mind one in particular, and this was her life. She was married – or perhaps she was not married – to a waterside labourer who, when he could work, made fair money. As a rule he suffered from chronic rheumatism, and was next door to a cripple. She had four children under nine. She was a dark, untidy-haired woman with a face much pitted by small pox, and she had a horribly foul tongue. The room looked out upon a boxlike square of livid brick yards, a table was under a window, a sugar box held coals. Another, nailed above the mantel, held bits of bread, a screw of tea in white paper, a screw of sugar in blue, and a gobbet of margarine in a saucer. When her man was in work or bad enough to be in hospital, when, at any rate, he was out of the house, there would be no coal in the one box because he was not crouching over the fire, and a bit of bacon in the other because there was no fuel to pay for. What he made went for the rent. There was nothing else in the room except a mattress and, on a damp and discoloured wall, a coloured mezzotint of Perdita, the mistress of George IV. I do not know how she had come to be pasted up there.

Till the school bell rang the children worked at her side. I don't think they were ever either dressed for school or given breakfasts by her. She made matchboxes at 2¾d the 144, and it was wonderful to watch her working – engrossed, expressionless, without a word, her fingers moved deftly and unerringly, the light very dim, the air full of the faint sickly smell of paste and of the slight crackling of thin wood, and the slight slop-slopping of the pastebrush. Sometimes she would sigh, not sorrowfully, but to draw a deeper breath. It was the only sound that was at all arbitrary, the only variation in the monotony of her life, the only thing that distinguished her from a wonderfully perfect machine. Now and then a piece of the thin wood cracked along the line of a knot, but she showed no sign of exasperation.

Her husband, as a rule, sat in front of the fire; his right hand had lost two fingers, his others were too swollen to be able to catch hold of a paste-brush, he sucked silently at the end of an empty pipe. To me, however – I used to stand in the doorway and watch – what was appalling was not the poverty. It was not the wretchedness, because, on the whole, neither the man or the woman were anything other than contented. But it was the dire speed at which she worked. It was like watching all the time some feat of desperate and breathless skill. It made one hold one's own breath.

In face of it any idea of 'problems', of solutions, of raising the submerged, or of the glorious destinies of humanity, vanished. The mode of life became, as it were, august and settled. You could not pity her because she was so obviously and wonderfully equipped for her particular struggle: you could not wish to 'raise' her, for what could she do in any other light, in any other air? Here at least she was strong, heroic, settled and beyond any condemnation.

As for ideals… Looking at the matter from a broad field which includes Theocritus, Nietzsche, the Eastern question, or a general election, she had not even ideas. She was an engrossed and admirable machine. But if you gave her 2¾d, the price of a gross of boxes – if you gave her time literally, she would utter long bursts of language that was a mixture of meaningless obscenities and of an old fashioned and formal English. She did not see why the Irish were allowed in Southwark, and she would shoot forth a monologue of grievances against her husband's mates, shouldering the poor old chap out of a job, and stealing his 'bacca, and him next door to a cripple; she had stuck the carving knife through the arm of a drunken man because he had tried to come into her room one night when her man was in hospital. She laughed hoarsely at the idea, and made feints with her hands.

These topics seemed to come out of her as words come out of certain machines, unnatural and disturbing. She had not much desire to talk, her hands and eyes were continually going back to her paste-brush. But as for ideals! She wanted to keep off the rates; she wanted the Charity Organisation people, 'them enquiry blokes', to keep away. She wanted her children to get their schooling done and easy things up a bit, helping her with the pasting. Above all she wanted the two lads to keep out of bad ways, and the two gals not to be bad gals with these here shiny top boots. She wanted them to stop indoors and paste match boxes. Sooner than see them on the streets she would use the carving knife to them; she had a sister a flower hand, making artificial flowers, who had 'fallen'.

Those were her ideals. If you translate them into terms of greater material prosperity you find them identical with anyone else's. One desires for the later years of one's life a little ease. She would have it when the law permitted her children to aid her. One desires privacy when one suffers, she would have it if the enquiry blokes would keep away. One desires that one's children should grow in virtue.

I should say that she was as contented and as cheerful as myself; she probably knew better than people more enlightened and with higher ambitions, the truth of the saying that was constantly on her lips, 'We can't b... well all have everything.' And, as I have said, to be in her presence was to find all 'problems'. Police court missionaries, societies, and sisters of the poor grow dim and childish along with the Modern Spirit itself. It was like interviewing the bedrock of human existence in a cavern deep in the earth. 'Influences' on the surface, busy about raising her seemed to become mere whispers a long way above. She supported them all.

As you went upstairs to her room you were presented with an astonishing picture. (I was at the time looking for an investment, and this house had been offered to me as producing a highly desirable rental.) It had once been a model dwelling; the stairs were of stone, but the railings, the banisters, the panels of nearly all the doors, and sometimes the very doorposts, every cupboard and every shelf, had been chopped down for firewood. As I went up past all these open doors and ragged door holes, in absolutely every room there were women, sometimes several, sometimes several children, bending over tables or over old sugar cases, silently and with great swiftness making matchboxes, making umbrella tassels, running together cheap coats, making artificial flowers – the very poor.

The thought – or rather it was a sensation so irresistible as to be an obsession – that in all that district all the houses were as similar inside as their outsides were unvarying, the thought was more than overwhelming. To look at London from that grim warren was to have a foreground like an untidy and uninspired battle field in which the background of broad streets and fine grey buildings vanished to almost nothing. No cathedral spires and the turrets of no museums peeped over those serrated roofs.

That problem that is no problem – the matter of the very poor workers – becomes there the only question of London. It is not, unfortunately perhaps, one that we can write or think about with any amiable cocksureness. It is not, unfortunately, one that any one man, any ten, or any two hundred can even touch from the outside. All these districts are honeycombed with missions, brotherhoods, and organisations. But the solution must come from within, and, inside there, there is no movement and only work. It is, in fact, a problem to all human intents insoluble, precisely because this particular class of worker is composed of individuals who, through heredity, through 'type', through temperament, for a hundred predestined and tragic reasons, are absolutely incapable of creating Movements.

Their whole nerve force, and nearly all their thoughts are given to their work. They are the dust filtered down from all the succeeding dominant types, they are the *caput mortuum* precisely because they are hopelessly old fashioned. They cannot combine, they have not any thoughts left for it; they could not strike because they have no means of communication; they are inarticulate.

They are forming, and they have been forming for years, an hereditary class. Education hardly touches their children. It means that for ten or eleven years the poor little things are made acquainted with facts, and are underfed, and that when they are fourteen they fall again to their parents. They learn no trade, they go apprentices to no craft. After a year or two of matchbox making the 'facts' of their instruction are worn down out of their minds.

And that very virtue of their mothers, that fierce determination to keep the little things 'respectable', means tying them more and more to their rooms. That particular striving, a fierce craze for keeping the children straight, is an almost universal 'note', a dominant passion among the mothers of the very poor.

These, then, are the obverse and the reverse of the medal of work in London that appears to be so much of a gamble, that is really so fierce and so logical a struggle. For if we take X. as paying too little attention to his actual work, we must think of this woman as paying too much.

Work in London today, if it have become in all its branches less of craft, depends more and more, if its worker is to make any individual success, on 'temperament'. Temperament in that particular sense we must take to mean the quality of inspiring confidence in one's employer or in one's customer. It is something akin to the artist's temperament, it is something akin to the charlatan's power to hypnotise mobs. The worker, if he is to rise out of the ruck, must impose his private personality upon a greater, or upon a lesser, public.

This tendency is most observable in the periodical press, that most enormous and most modern of industries. Here upon the whole the aesthetically intrinsic quality of the work offered by a young man does not matter much. The employer sits as it were in an office chair between the great public and the men who besiege him. It is not, obviously, his business to secure men whose work will remain, he wants stuff that will 'go'. He will select for his permanent favours men who inspire him with confidence, men who have not any nonsense about them. Nonsense in this case is impracticable ideas of one kind or another.

X. will drive down to an editorial office in a nice dogcart and during an interview, interrupted by frequent calls at a telephone, will fidget towards a window overlooking the street in order to call pointed attention to the fact that his horse will not stand. In that case he may demonstrate that there is not any nonsense about him, that he is not dreamily poetic, but up to date and practical. He makes, perhaps, a chance for himself, but he might have done still better by studying his market, by acquiring a knowledge of the characteristics, the tone and the scope of the journal he has designs on. The editor, on the other hand, merely wants to get at whether X. will appeal to his own particular 'crowd'.

This tendency of dependence on the tastes of the great crowd is most handily demonstrable in the case of the Press; but it underlies every other industry. I happen to have followed the career of a man who is now still young and a very flourishing cabinet maker. He was the son of a widow in domestic service, Huguenot by descent, merry, dark and handsome whilst a young boy, but not otherwise strikingly intelligent.

The master of his mother got him apprenticed to a working carpenter, and he developed what was practically a passion for fret-sawing. He rather lost his looks and his clothes were always dusted with the little particles of wood that fall away from the teeth of fretsaws. As soon as he was out of his time he set up for himself as a jobbing cabinet maker, in a small Walthamstow shop; he continued to pay serious attention to fretwork. Eventually he evolved what was practically a style: he made small hexagonal coffee tables, of the sort one sees now in the smoking divans of seaside hotels. These things had a kind of pierced screen, Oriental in inspiration, between each pair of legs and were painted a dead white. He made perhaps a dozen of these, with more than a dozen little stools, and some over-mantels and settees to match, all in white, with quasi-Moorish perforations.

About this time W. saw an announcement in his trade paper: a certain large linoleum seller was giving one of his windows to bamboo furniture. W. set off at once with a specimen coffee table under his arm; he managed to see the proprietor of this shop – it was in a well-frequented thoroughfare. The latter consented to 'stock' the rest of W.'s white things, which were ludicrously inexpensive. He arranged in his window an alcove in which a white coffee table, some white stools, and a white settee stood, or supported cheap Oriental trays and vases full of peacock's feathers. There was not a day to wait for the things to 'take on'.

In a few days W. was turning out scores of white tables and over-mantels. His ingenuity ended by no means at quasi-Oriental nick-nacks, he had in him an astonishing faculty for knowing what the public – in this case mostly young marrying couples – could be induced to 'want'. He turned out cheap Chippendales, cheap Louis XIVs, cheap farmhouse styles; he went with his customer, the former linoleum seller, to Arts and Crafts Exhibitions. Whatever there appeared to them as a 'line' in tables, chairs, beds or whatnots he could modify very slightly, cheapen very substantially, and turn out in large quantities, and W. is rapidly growing rich.

This, of course, is a *Roman d'un Jeune Homme Pauvre,* but it is something more because it casts a strong light upon the characteristics of work in modern London. For of the worker nowadays there is demanded more than the old-fashioned attention to work. Unless you wish to live for posterity you cannot any more put out good work, work that is solid and lasting, leaving it alone to push its way in the world and to bring you customers paying a goodly price. You must obviously produce work that is good in the sense of being attractive for the moment; that is the one essential. But also, as I have said, you must have temperament – the temperament that brings luck, because it makes you take the right step instinctively and at the right moment. And you must have that sympathy with the humanity around you that will let you know just what modification of your product will for the time hold the sympathy of the crowd. This essential holds as good for the company promoter as for the cabinet maker. And you must have the qualities of inspiring confidence and of knowing instinctively whom you can trust.

This personal element tends to become, paradoxically perhaps, of more and more importance as the spirit of combinations spreads. And it is spreading into the most personal of the industries of today. There died in March of 1903 a sufficiently remarkable woman, a Mrs Russell of Southwark. She was shrewd and eccentric, she had a passion for displaying her fingers in an armour of gold rings, and her breast in a mail of gold chains, and it was a certain fortune for a costermonger to get on her soft side. For she had achieved nothing less than a 'combine' of coster barrows in Southwark.

The tendency in all things is either towards the trustification of all activities or towards State and Municipal trading.[1] Into either

---

1 I do not wish to imply that the prospect pleases or displeases me. But the strong feeling against say Municipal Trading must disappear as soon as Trusts become universal. The Trusts may simply become the State as is the tendency in America. Or in the more likely alternative they may grow so oppressive that an outcry for State Trading will arise. In either case the individual trader will have disappeared, and with him the opposition to State Trading. The individual's sons and daughters will be simply the employees of the Trusts, and will view with indifference or with more probable favour their absorption by the State or the city in which they are interested. The third issue, the triumph of the co-operative system, will be so precisely the same in its effects on the individual worker that it may for my purposes be classed with either.

The broad fact remains that the individual worker for the time being is doomed. He has been so for a long time, in London at least. This again is most strikingly observable in the periodical press. Upon the whole that of literature makes of all the pursuits the

the personal factor must enter very largely. We may suppose the grocery trade to be taken over by the State. There will be no scope at all for individual brilliancy; counter clerks will take orders with about the same capabilities, and what 'rises' there may be will go either by routine or by the recommendations of foremen. These latter, as today they do, will recommend juniors who appeal to them for one reason or another. The same thing will happen if the grocery trade in the alternative becomes one vast Trust.

This tendency is as observable in a London bank as in a London cement factory. The bank manager watches and considers the personal characteristics of his clerks with an anxious solicitude. He notes the particulars of his clerk's dress and the details of his home life. A subordinate, who hopes for promotion must be careful never to be seen wheeling a perambulator for his wife; it would, if he happened to become manager of a suburban branch, damage the standing of the bank in the eyes of the customers, excellent accountant though he may be. On the other hand he must be an excellent accountant, and he must impress his superior with his knowledge of human nature. He must be able to gauge, both with his intuition and by the skilful utilisation of local gossip, what customers it is safe to trust with those overdrafts that are the life of suburban trade.

It is very much the same in cement or kindred works. A hand must commence by being a good and an industrious workman, but he must also, if he is to rise, give the impression of being very much alive and very much interested in his work. I am thinking of a case in point in some rather small works of the sort. Here there is a managing foreman whom I will call Stanley. He is perhaps twenty-nine. These works were started to work a new process about twelve years ago, and Stanley, at the time a boy, helped in making the bed of the first engine. He was particularly alert, and entered into the spirit of the thing. This at the time was not very obvious, the engine being set down on the slope of a green hill into which it has since

---

most call for individuality. Yet ever since Cave let Johnson dine behind his screen, ever since those two started the *Gentleman's Magazine* it has become more and more essential to men of letters to live in London. And today it is impossible for the many of them to exist, or for the very few to grow rich without the aid of journalism in one or other of its manifestations. This means their becoming the employees of small or of very large combines. All the learned professions have for centuries now been combined with their headquarters in London. They have been empowered with charters to become administrative, examining, or penal bodies, of solicitors, barristers, surgeons, doctors and even pharmacists, – to become close corporations.

tunnelled and cut until an arena of sand, of rubble and of chalk, opens an immense face to the lower Thames. It shelters alike on its flat surface a huge cement factory, sand works, and a large brick-field. Immense chimney shafts like thin pencils pierce up into the lower clouds; the ground is sticky and white under foot, channelled with open conduits of hot water, a maze of small lines on which run tiny locomotives, a maze of the little black shelters that cover drying bricks.

In the midst of these grey and monstrous apparitions, in the faint and sickly odour of steam, under the drops that condense and fall from the eaves of engine sheds, clambering through small holes, dressed in dull clothes, clean shaven and with sparkling eyes, Stanley moves like a spirit of romance. If he chances upon a visitor he becomes almost a spirit in ecstasy. He slaps the bed of the engine that he helped to set there, he bids workmen run the wet sand through trap doors, he explains how these three industries, set there together in that hollow, work one into another so that nothing is lost. The hot water from the boilers of the cement works runs in those open conduits to separate in the sand works the sand from the loam; the separated loam makes the bricks in the brick works. He waves his hands and shouts in the immense roar of pebble-crushing machines to explain how what appears to be a lot of old ploughshares tied together with rope is really a nice device of his own for regulating the pressure on the crushing rollers. These things are the great, the romantic facts of his world. Because they are so, his managing director has advanced him very quickly from being a shovel boy, paddling in the warm and sandy water, to be superin-tendent of the whole works.

But it is almost more important that the hands all like him. His director can go home and sleep, or leave the place for days on end, confident that Stanley has the knack of infusing into his men some of his own interest in the work itself, and that he will not by petty tyrannies bring on a strike. That particular human quality, the particular sort of artistic delight in his work which brings to birth an *esprit de corps*, is almost the most precious quality that a man can offer in these days of organisation. Without at least a share of it Stanley could never have risen from the ranks; with as much as he has there is no limit to his possibilities.

At the same time, as a defect of this particular quality of work in London, the making of Stanley has meant throwing out of work of a whole small industry. It has caused to disappear almost the last of the old small flotillas of barges that used to dredge sand by hand from the bottom of the river. (Thames sand is indispensable in the London building trade; it is stipulated for in all the contracts for honest mortar.)

Travelling through all that eastern London of toil, no thought is more oppressive than that: a little way away or at a great distance people are unceasingly working to mature new processes that will ruin any one of the works that the eye rests on. Nothing can well be more tragic than such an announcement as this, which one may read any day in a trade paper: 'Owing to the competition of the new D—— process of Messrs W——, the D—— Co. of Plumstead have been forced to close that branch of their works. Two thousand workmen have been discharged this week. Messrs T., of Erith, have notified their ability to take over fifty mechanics at once and fifty-nine more later on. If other firms requiring men will communicate with the secretary of the D—— workers' Union they will assist in mitigating the local distress.'

I must confess to finding that thought the most exciting and the most sinister that can come into one's head in those parts of the vast city. They are grim, they are overhung with perpetual miasma, they lie low in damp marshes. Square and stumpy chimneys rise every-where in clusters like the columns of ruined temples overhung with smirchings of vapour. Great fields are covered with scraps of rusty iron and heaps of fluttering rags; dismal pools of water reflect on black waste grounds the dim skies. But all these things, if one is in the mood, one may find stimulating, because they tell of human toil, of human endeavour towards some end with some ideal at that end. But the other thing is sinister, since the other influences are working invisible, like malign and conscious fates, below the horizon.

To assist at the obsequies of one of these great works is more suggestive than to have seen the corpses in the snow of the retreat from Moscow. It is more horrible because the sufferers have fought in a fight much more blind and suffer inarticulately in the midst of their suffering children and in the face of their desolate homes. They suffer for no apparent principle, for no faith, for no fame, for no nation, for no glory; they suffer the shame of poverty without the compensating glory of defeat. They have not ever seen their Napoleon ride slowly along their cheering lines.

For London, if it attracts men from a distance with a glamour like that of a great and green gaming table, shows, when they are close to it, the indecipherable face of a desperate battle field, without ranks, without order, without pity and with very little of discoverable purpose. Yet those that it has attracted it holds for ever, because in its want of logic it is so very human.

CHAPTER IV

London at Leisure

I WAS talking some time ago to a timekeeper in one of the 'bus yards in the west of London. In a sort of very clean square of stables horses stood patiently in couples with their traces hooked over their backs, the chains jingling a little, and yardmen with their braces about their loins bent over pails of water into which they stirred a powder of coarse oatmeal. A big man in painfully clean-washed corduroys came furtively and hesitatingly under the square entrance arch. His eyes wandered round, resting with a look of acquaintance and friendship upon the small litters of straw that lay outside each of the house doors. He began fumbling in an inner pocket painfully for his testimonials, his 'character'. The timekeeper said, 'No, mate, no job here,' and the man, after staring again at the straw, turned away without a word spoken, painfully shy, tired, and mutely disappointed, slowly as if he had all the time of the world upon his hands. They had had five men like him already in the yard that same morning.

This particular man appealed to me – and upon the whole you cannot hope to find in London anything much more pathetic, in a small way, than the peculiar 'action' of a genuine labourer seeking work, his slow and heavy movements, his vacant and undecided air, his evident not knowing what to do with his hands, and all the signs that go to tell of a hungry and undesired leisure, and the fact that, as a rule, you cannot do anything in the world really to help him. This man was one of a great many employees in a soap factory that the vagaries of one of our Napoleons of Finance had lately caused to 'shut down'. It was a hopeless bankruptcy at a time when trade was too slow to make it feasible for the debenture-holders to carry on the work. All the hands had been thrown as if out of a barrow to find other holes somewhere in London. This man had been for a fortnight without a job, and he said it seemed precious likely he wouldn't get one for a good bit.

He had walked that morning from East Ham way right across to Hammersmith but his case was not a particularly poignant one. He had a missis but no kids, and his missis did a bit of charing for a Mrs North and a Mrs Williamson. He had been, as a boy, a wagoner's mate – one of those boys who walk with a brass-bound whip beside a team either in the cart or in the plough – in Lincolnshire. But things had seemed a bit slow down there and he had come up to London to find shorter hours, lighter jobs, better pay, and the chance to save a bit – to find, in fact, these streets paved with gold.

'Mart's well be back there,' he said, with a humorous smile, as if the idea were absurd. For London, if its work, even from the outside, have the mysterious and magnetic attraction of an immense gambling table, may, and inevitably does, rob those it attracts of that tremulous and romantic idea. The gambling becomes a hard and almost unceasing struggle, with the pay proportionately worse, with the hours really longer because the work is so much more strenuous. But London itself and for itself takes a hold of the hearts of men; along with disillusionments grows up a hunger, like a new sense, for London only. These men in the mass never go back. When I offered to this particular man to write to a farmer who I knew was in want of a hand he looked at me as if I must be joking. He groped in his mind for a reason. 'The missis would never *hear* of it,' he said. 'Besides –' His power of invention seemed to break down till he got out: 'Oh, London's the place!' His eyes roved along the sides of a cab that was passing and up the front of an establishment called, I think, the West London Stores. 'London's the place,' he repeated. I objected that he could not see much of London inside a soap factory. He considered for a moment and said: 'No, but it's the Saturday afternoons and Sundays.' He paused. 'It's when ye hahve your leisure.' He continued with the air of one trying to explain something difficult to a stupid person or a child: 'It's the dinner hour with your mates and the snacks of talk between whiles loading barrows. Don't you see?' He paused again for a long time and then added: 'London's the place.' He could not think of going back.

Thus what London attracts with the mirage of its work shining across the counties and the countries, London holds with the glamour of its leisure. We never go back, never really and absolutely: London for those who have once, for however short a space, been Londoners, is always on the cards, is always just beyond the horizon. We may 'go back' to the country for our health's sake, for our children's health's sake, if we can. We may 'go back' in a sense to the Colonies because we are not fitted for life or for work in London. But all the time London is calling; it calls in the middle of our work, it calls at odd moments like the fever of spring that stirs each year in the blood. It seems to offer romantically, not streets paved with gold but streets filled with leisure, streets where we shall saunter, things for the eye to rest on in a grey and glamorous light, books to read, men to be idle with, women to love.

If the idea of the 'working classes' seems to call up a picture of the black plains of the East End, the picture when the 'leisured classes' are in consideration is that of a circumscribed parallelogram of rows of tall buildings. It is a square block like a fortress that we all, more or less, are besieging – the little plot of ground bounded on the south by Piccadilly, on the west by the railings of Hyde Park, on the north by Oxford Street and on the east by Bond Street. It stands fairly well for where we should all live if we were 'really rich', it represents, as far as London is concerned, our castles in the air whether we should be contented with a small, bright house in one of the angles of Mayfair, with a suite of rooms in the P——— that overlooks the Green Park, or whether we should be contented with nothing less than one of the palaces in Park Lane.

These streets are quiet, for London, and bright and well swept and almost joyous. From their exclusiveness one steps out so easily into Rotten Row, which stands for the high-water mark of out-of-doors laziness in the modern world; and, if the clubs from which, as from an opera-box, one looks out across the parks towards Buckingham Palace – if those clubs are not, for social traditions, for standing, for gravity, or for place, 'in it' with the older clubs near Pall Mall or about Whitehall, they are at least more pagan in the sense of being more humanly enjoyable to the uninitiated. A man can, in these places, lounge so utterly and entirely.

And that, in essentials, is the charm of social life in London. There are not any really rigid barriers; one has so immense a choice within the limits of any purse. There are in London institutions that are rigidly exclusive, but these are so rare as to be merely the spice of the large dish. This, of course, is only the case comparatively with the other capitals of the world.

It is, for instance, impossible for a French outsider to 'get into' the real society of the Faubourg St Germain; a relatively great number of quarterings are needed, a certain tradition, a certain habit of mind, a certain, let us say, inanity. It is also relatively impossible in Berlin to 'get into' the military, or the blood aristocracies. Money cannot do it, or personal charm, or immense talents. It is absolutely impossible in Vienna where society is ruled by a Court, and that Court absolutely insists on quarterings as a social qualification. It is, I should say, with certain modifications the same in St Petersburg and in Rome. It is almost more markedly so in Madrid and Lisbon. In all these places a man is 'placed'; he knows his place and it is known for him.

But in London, comparatively speaking, a man stands pretty well by what he is or by what he has. He cannot, of course, occupy the throne but, given the temperament or the wealth he can sit in almost any other chair. Essentially, the other capitals ask a man to be something; London society asks him to give something – whether dinners or personal charm, whether financial tips or a soothing personal effacement.

It is probably this last characteristic that is the most essential, or, at least, the most attainable. It is that that, as it were, gives every man his chance. Paradoxically enough the reason for it is that London society is made up of such intensely individual types that the comparatively characterless man is absolutely essential. He fills up holes, he tones down dinner parties, he may be relied on not to jar, not to shine – not to worry one's nerves. In a society which is made up very much of strong individualities more or less constantly at war, self-effacement has a charm; the listener grows very precious.

And, upon the whole, in the other capitals of the world the thing is very exactly the other way round. In societies where the essential quality is birth, individuals are rare. In those closed ranks men are very much alike, and women – in character, in point of view, in gesture, in speech. In consequence an individuality tells. It is not, as in London, questioned, doubted and mistrusted; it is, if the individual belongs to the society, welcomed as a rather pleasant relief from the dead level.

The fascination of life in London is essentially its freedom. In society of the one type you may do very much what you like short of eating peas with a knife, wearing a felt hat with a frock coat, or a coloured tie with evening dress. You may, in the realm of ideas, be as heterodox as you please; you may 'pass' being a Roman Catholic, a Buddhist, even a Jew or Mohammedan. (Obviously it is not good form to intrude your personal views in mixed company, but you are allowed your freedom of private thought.) But in, say, Catholic circles in France, entry is barred to a man suspected of being a Protestant or a Republican.

But if, on the one hand, private freedom of views is permissible in London, the rule that you must not express in Society any views at all is so rigid, that any infringement of it causes a shudder. It is a want of tact. Examined into minutely, you will find again, as the basis of this characteristic, the individual unit. There is not any London type. London is a meeting place of all sorts of incongruous types, and, if you must not utter your views, it is simply because you run so sure a risk of hurting the feelings of every individual near you. In Catholic circles abroad you may talk freely of the Deity, the Virgin, the Saviour, or the Saints, because what is thought about these divinities is rigidly defined. In London society you may be – it is considered commendable to be – devout in private, but it is a shuddering offence to mention the Deity in company. Similarly all metaphysical topics, all political matters going below the surface or likely to cause heat, the consideration of sexual questions, the mention of the poor or the suffering, are avoided. This is, in origin, because your neighbour at dinner has his or her private views, and has a right to them. You do not enquire into them, you do not know them, and you cannot air your own views because they will probably give offence.

The net result is to make London conversations singularly colourless; but they become singularly unexhausting. No call is made upon your brain or your individuality; it is precisely not 'good form' to make any kind of display. You may be yourself as much as you please, but it must be yourself in a state of quiescence. No strain at all is put upon you, because it is the height of good manners to have no manners at all.

This of course is most noticeable abroad, where the Londoner is celebrated for his atrociously bad manners. He does not bow over his hat on entering a room; he sits down on any chair, he has no gesticulations of pleasure, he stops short at being well groomed and undemonstrative. There is not, in fact, any etiquette in London, there is only a general rule against obtruding your personality – a general rule against animation in society. 'Die verstaendigste und geistreichste aller europaeischen Nationen hat sogar die Regel, "never interrupt", das elfte Gebot genannt,' says Schopenhauer.[1] But obviously if you never interrupt you must have schooled

---

1 'The most understanding and most spiritual of all the European nations (the English) has named the rule "never interrupt", the eleventh commandment.' – Parerga und Paralipomena. 'Über Lärm und Geräusch', p. 679.

yourself to care little for the discussion you have in hand, or you must avoid the discussion of subjects you care for.

Essentially we may say that the other great societies of Europe prescribe rigid codes of manners, and a member of society attains to self-respect by his knowledge of these codes. He tries in fact to do something. London society has no code, it prescribes an attitude of mind. You do not enter a London drawing-room with one, three or six bows; you do not kiss your hostess's hand. But you lounge in and get through that ceremonial contact as best suits you. You try to show no impressment at all. For it may be said that, in London, the mark of the leisured class is to be without restraint. One may go even further: to be conscious of any restraint is to be guilty of bad manners.

For supposing a severe moralist frown, at a dinner, because the guests, being all intimate, calling each other by familiar nicknames, sit unbracing genially, ladies and all, with their feet on the table. The frown will – and, after all, quite rightly – be set down as a piece of 'unsoundness'. For, in the first place, what does a moralist – a man with an occupation or a mission – seek in this particular galley? It is – this particular leisured class – circumscribed and walled in; it circumscribes itself, too. It is, as it were, a deer park within London; a Zoological Gardens within the ring of a Regent's Park.

If we may call the very poor – the sweated workers – a *caput mortuum* of the body politic, beyond hope of being raised, beyond hope of being moralised upon because they are always at work: so, in the London of Leisure we may call this other class above hope of being touched, above hope of being moralised upon – because they are always at leisure. It is unprofitable for the moralists to worry about them: they have reverted to savagery, really. Having no work they must needs disport themselves – and the occupation of the idle must necessarily tend towards display. Emulation in display tends, humanity being poor humanity, towards barbarism. (Not towards primitive barbarism, be it said, for that devotes all its energies towards the straitening of its tribal laws, of its moral and ceremonial observances. It veils its women; prescribes fasts; enjoins hygienic ablutions, abstinence from certain meats, usuries, fornications, and the depicting of actual objects.)

But this other barbarism, which comes after a race, a society, or a family, has passed upwards through the painful strata of observances and of tribal laws, is a breaking of all bonds. It is humanity drawing a deep breath, 'going fanti',★ running amuck through the laws of public opinion. It is the man that is in all of us breaking loose and seeking to wallow. It may not go further than putting our feet on the dining table, than pouring champagne cup upon our host's head, or, as an amiable bishop put it the other day, 'neighing after our neighbours' wives',★★ but, having arrived at that stage, these 'sets' begin again to evolve their tribal laws, so that not to put up our feet, not to pour champagne cup, or not to 'neigh' is to be an enemy to that particular republic. This phenomenon does not matter, it is past banning and past curing. You cannot learn any moral lesson from a Malay running amuck – and, as the Chinese proverb has it, 'It would be hypocrisy to seek for the person of the Sacred Emperor in a low tea house.' Thus it is really much better for the moralist not to think about them. If, in the guise of a Savonarola, he fill them with fear for their immortal souls, it will not mean any more than a hysterical revival. In the body politic they do not 'count', they are a shade more hopeless than the very poor, they will run their course towards ruin, physical decay, or towards that period of life when ginger being no longer hot in a mouth that has lost all savours, they will become aged devotees and perhaps make for edification.

No doubt to the passionate reformer, of whatever code, the idea of so many individuals living the life of beasts is horribly disturbing. (I know, indeed, one reformer who was driven to fits of rage at the waste of time in a family of the leisured class. They had lived at this particular reformer's house in the country, and apparently washed themselves ten times a day.) But no doubt, too, this phenomenon makes for good to the body politic.

Work is the original curse of mankind because it is the original medicine. We may go on working till we drop, occupying our minds, keeping our bodies sound – but the moment we drop work our minds decay, our bodies atrophy, it is all over with us in this world. As with individuals so with the Body Politic, or with London, the modern World Town.

Whilst, in essentials, it is a Town of Work it keeps all on going; it sweats out at the top these atrophied individuals, or it sweats them

---

★   **going fanti** (also 'fantee'): to go native, from the name of a tribe in Ghana.
★★ **neighing after our neighbours' wives**: a critical phrase echoed in the later Ford novel *A Good Soldier* (1915). As the narrator of this novel adapts the phrase, he is considering which kind of man has 'the right to existence' (see p. 15 of the Norton edition (1995)).

out at the bottom (they hang round the street posts and make books outside the doors of public-houses); and thus Work, the medicine, purges the unhealthy corpuscles of the blood or revenges itself of the too healthy. For if we may call the poor loafer the unhealthy, we must call the rich leisured class the too healthy. In one way or another their ancestors, their family, their *gens*, have worked too much for them: they are left without the need to labour. If, then, these families, these 'sets', could preserve a stolid middle course, if they could live for ever within their incomes, restrict their families, and remain leisured for ever, the end of London would indeed be near. But human nature steps in.

So whilst there is emulation there is hope. We shall, it is to be trusted, go on 'cutting dashes' until we drop out, until our children sink down to rise up again fighting, or until we die out, childless and forgotten, unhealthy corpuscles, purged and got rid of. There would be a greater danger to London if this Leisured Class were to spread very far; but that, for a city so vast, must mean an accumulation of wealth inconceivable, and in these latter days practically impossible. Rome decayed because, being mistress of the world, she robbed the whole world and lived profusely, rioting for centuries upon the spoils of primeval empires. But there is no such hope any longer for London; she has her too urgent competitors, and the primeval empires have been by now too often gutted to leave any very substantial pickings. So that the wealth of London has to be gained by work, and this fortress of the leisured class remains as a lure, as a sort of Islands of the Blest, glamorous in the haze above Park Lane and Mayfair, an incentive to health because wealth means leisure; wealth means work, and work health. A nobler incentive would of course be nobler, and no doubt it might be more valuable when attained. But perhaps an all-seeing Providence arranges the world in the best way for the child that is man, for the child that will train, harden itself, strive and race – upon no matter what cinder track – for a prize cup that is of no intrinsic value, for a championship that carries nothing with it but the privilege to struggle and retain the honour, or to rest, grow fat, and decay.

So, save for the very few whom the reformers influence, and save for the very few whom philosophy really makes wise, and the very few whose wings have been singed – for all the really healthy and not self-conscious humanity of the world that is London, this mirage of the Leisured Class, hanging above the smoke of the roofs, appearing in the glamour of the morning dreams, gilding how many castles, in how many airs, is the incentive to life in London.

'It takes a good deal out of you,' this leisured life of display. You rush more or less feverishly, gathering scalps of one sort or another; being 'seen' in the record number of places where anyone who is anyone can be seen; you pack your days with drives on coaches, fencing matches, luncheons, afternoons, dressings and re-dressings, dinners, the founding of new religions in drawing rooms, polo matches, cricket matches, standing against walls at dances, neighing perhaps after your friends' wives, seeking heaven knows what at operas, theatres, music halls, dashing out into the Home Counties and back, or really and sensuously enjoying the music of a good concert. At any rate you live very full and laborious days, seeking excitements – until finally excitement leaves you altogether. If you are really in luck, if you are really someone, each of these events of your day is 'something'. Each concert is something portentous and, in the world of music perhaps, makes history. Each religion that you see founded is to the sociologist something really significant, each cricket match a real 'event' in which the best muscle and the best brain of the day is striving, delivering beautiful balls and making deft and beautiful strokes. But each of these things sinks back into the mere background of your you. You are, on the relentless current of your life, whirled past them as, in a train, you are whirled past a succession of beautiful landscapes. You have 'seen' such and such a social event as you have seen, say, Damascus, from a saloon window.

You carry away from it a vague kaleidoscope picture – lights in clusters, the bare shoulders of women, white flannel on green turf in the sunlight, darkened drawing rooms with nasal voices chanting parodies of prayers, the up and down strokes of fiddle bows, the flicker of fifty couples whirling round before you as with a touch of headache you stood in a doorway, a vague recollection of a brilliant anecdote, the fag end of a conversation beneath the palms of a dimmed conservatory, and a fatigue and a feverish idea that if you had missed any one of these unimportant things you would have missed life.

But, if you had been a beanfeaster who missed a beanfeast, or if you had been a Saturday footballer who missed one match, you might have missed so much more of your life. And, indeed, since life is no more than a bundle of memories, your life is so much shorter, since you remember seasons, not events. It is with you:

'The season when good old Hinds had his place in Cadogan Square'; or, 'The year, don't you remember? when we used to drink barley water', or, 'Hermit's year'. But the Saturday footballer remembers so many glorious Saturdays relieved by so many blank weeks. He remembers the splendid crowded journeys back – 'The time when Old Tommy sang "Soldiers of the Queen" – 'The time when we had the cask of beer on the luggage rack coming back from playing Barnes' – 'The time when Black and Moses stuck the ticket collector under the seat and kept him there till Waterloo'.

So the life of seasons and years is shorter, swifter, more regretful, less filled. And, the breaks being less marked, the life itself is the more laborious and less of a life. For it is in the breaks, in the marking time, that the course of a life becomes visible and sensible. You realise it only in leisures within that laborious leisure; you realise it, in fact, best when, with your hands deep in your trousers pockets, or listless on your watch-chain, you stand, unthinking, speculating on nothing, looking down on the unceasing, hushed, and constantly changing defile of traffic below your club windows. The vaguest thoughts flit through your brain: the knot on a whip, the cockade on a coachman's hat, the sprawl of a large woman in a victoria, the windshield in front of an automobile. You live only with your eyes, and they lull you. So Time becomes manifest like a slow pulse, the world stands still; a four-wheeler takes as it were two years to crawl from one lamp-post to another, and the rustle of newspapers behind your back in the dark recesses of the room might be a tide chafing upon the pebbles. That is your deep and blessed leisure: the pause in the beat of the clock that comes now and then to make life seem worth going on with. Without that there would be an end of us.

For, whether we are of the leisured class, whether we are laundry-women, agricultural labourers, dock labourers, or bank clerks, it is that third state that makes us live. Brahmins would call it contemplation; the French might use the word, *assoupissement*. It would be incorrect to call it reverie since it is merely a suspension of the intellectual faculties; it is a bathing in the visible world: it is a third state between work and amusement – perhaps it is the real Leisure.

It is not obviously a product of London alone. For your agricultural labourer who hangs over a gate at dusk, just gently swinging a foot and gazing, wrapt unthinking and voluptuous, at black and white, at speckled, at bright red and flame-plumaged poultry on the green below him, tastes it very well along with the flavour of the straw in his mouth – and the women who, after their hard days, stand above the half doors of cottages and gaze at nothing. But with them it is not a third state, since it takes the place of amusement as well as rest. Your London dock labourer really has this third state, since along with his hard physical work he has his sing-songs, his club nights, his visits to music halls, his nights when he takes his 'missus' to the theatre. I knew one very good fellow, a plasterer's labourer, hardworking, making good money, and as regular as a church clock. His hobby was chaffinches. In the mornings before work and in the evenings he gave a certain amount of time to teaching his birds to pipe. At nightfalls he would go to his public house for a couple of pints of ale and a few pipes. On a Saturday afternoon he was shaved and went to a club where there were singing and debates. He always came home sober enough to put beside his bed – he was a bachelor – a pailful of treacle beer that he had brewed himself, and an india-rubber tube.

And there on a Sunday he would lie nearly through the day sucking up the treacle beer through the tube and gazing at the ceiling, thinking nothing at all, letting his eyes follow the cracks in the plaster from one wall to another, backward and forward for ever. Late in the afternoon he would get up, dress himself carefully in his best; wrap his chaffinch cages in old handkerchiefs, and, carrying them, saunter along Petticoat Lane, look restfully at the cages of birds exposed for sale, meditating a purchase for next year, passing the time of day with a Jew or two, and losing himself, stolid, quiet, and observant, in the thick crowd. He would come to a greengrocer's shop, the door open, the interior a black and odorous darkness, where you trod upon cabbage leaves and orange paper. Behind this was another dark room, in the centre of which a ladder stood up going into an upper loft through a trap-door. This loft was the 'Cave of Harmony' where, in the light of brilliant gas jets were held the contests of the piping chaffinches. There, taking the gas jets for a fiercer sun, the little birds sang shrilly and furiously one against another, the attentive crowd of faces around them, thrown into deep shadows and strong lights, hard featured and intense, with every eye fixed upon the small and straining singer, fingers ticking off turns in the song and a silence broken by no shuffling of feet and no clearing of throats.

So, having scored his 'marks', our friend would go slowly and soberly home; set another pailful of treacle beer to brew against next Sunday morning, and put himself quietly to bed.

Thus his life was perfectly regular and calm; hard muscular work giving place to sober amusement, dashed once a week with that intense leisure of lying still, looking at the ceiling and thinking nothing. On off days, bank holidays and the like, he would take his cages, wrapped up, under his arm, out into Epping Forest. For these chaffinch fanciers have a notion – no doubt it is a true one – that unless their captive birds refresh their memory of the wild song by chanting against free chaffinches in the woods or parks, they will lose the brilliance of their note, and finally mope and die. There are in London many thousands of men like this.

Chaffinches, bullfinches, prize bantams, prize rabbits, whippets, bull terriers, canaries, and even pigs occupy their leisure moments, and are regarded with pride by their wives, and awe by their young children. These breeders and fanciers are mostly country born, deliberate, gentle, sober, with a pipe generally in the corner of the mouth, from which come rare jets of smoke accompanying words as rare and as slow. And their 'fancies' provide them with that companionship of animals that is such a necessity to the country-bred Englishman. It gives them a chance to get rid of some of the stores of tenderness towards small living things which, for lack of words, they cannot so well lavish on their wives and children. I have known a carter who did not apparently trouble himself in the least about illnesses in his own house, driven to a state of distraction because one of his old companions, a draught-horse, was on the point of death.

They give him, too, these 'fancyings', not only the chance to gaze ineffably, like the agricultural labourer, at the motions of animals, but the chance of emulation, the chance, if you will, of sharing in a sport. That, as it were, is what London supplies, and what makes London in a way both attractive and salutary. For we may say that the man who ceases to compete ceases to be a perfect man, and, in the actual stages of heavy manual work there is no room for emulation. It is true that in the country you have ploughing matches, but they touch only the very few; you have cottage garden prizes, but those are artificially fostered 'from above', and, indeed, they call for efforts too like those of the everyday work to afford much of an occupation for a man's leisure. So that, as a rule, these prizes flourish most in the neighbourhood of the small towns, and fall to railway signalmen, cobblers and the non-agricultural. Starling and sparrow shoots are, of course, mere bank holiday carouses, not the hobbies that are necessary for the everyday life of a man. Thus the country districts are depleted.

And, inasmuch as the arts are matters of association, we, loving a picture, a melody, a verse, because for obscure reasons it calls up in us forgotten memories of times when we were young, in love or happy, so these 'fancies' which are Arts, call up in the hearts of these countrymen become town-labourers, moods like those they felt in forgotten green fields. I know a man who breeds pheasants in the green enclosure of a City churchyard, and when, towards October in the early black mornings of that tiny and shut-in square, roofed in from the sky by plane leaves high up near the steeple, overlooked by the gleaming plate-glass windows of merchants' offices, these noble birds utter their shrill, prolonged and wild crockettings, like peals of defiant laughter, their owner says rhapsodically: 'Doesn't it make you think of Norfolk?' It makes me think of covert rides in Kent, dripping with dew, and of the clack of the beaters' sticks and their shrill cries; but all the same it makes that City caretaker have all the sensuous delight of the green fields of his youth.

Nevertheless, he comments; 'It's better here nor there. – Down there it meant forty shillings if the keeper caught you so much as smelling a pheasant's neck feather.' – Here he needed no gun licence, and they paid him ten times over for their keep, and kept his hands nicely full.

So the birds with their delicate gait, high and dainty spurred steps, and peering, brilliant necks, seek unceasingly for issues from the closed railings of the churchyard, and contribute all that, in London, is needed to keep their owner there for ever. I knew a Rye fisherman, a lazy, humorous scoundrel, who never went to sea when he had the price of a pint in his pocket. He grew tired of that life and became a doorkeeper in some Southwark chemical works. He spends his leisure time with his hands in his pockets, leaning over the river wall, spitting into the eddies of the water and commenting on the ineptitude of the men on the dumb barges. Their sweeps dip up and down, to all appearances senselessly and futilely, and H—— comments that ne'er a one of them ever seems to know that twenty yards in shore there's a current that would take them down three miles an hour faster. H—— will scull you down to Greenwich for a pipe of tobacco just for the fun of the thing; whereas five shillings, in the old days, would not have induced him to scull you down from Rye to the harbour mouth, a matter of two miles. Sails, he used to say, were his business, oars being against nature. – But London has changed that, making of former toils present leisure.

Your London 'bus-driver takes his days off sitting on the front seat of an omnibus with his head close to that of the driver at work, just as the sailor lounges round harbours, glances along ropes with quietened but still professional eyes. – He gets in this way the feeling of leisure 'rubbed in' and, without anxieties, his mind is kept employed by the things he best understands. And it is because in London there are so many things to see, so many anecdotes to be retailed, such a constant passing of material and human objects, that London holds us.

I do not know that it really sharpens our wits: I fancy that it merely gives us more accidental matters on which to display them, more occurrences to which to attach morals that have been for years crystallised in our minds. – I was listening to the observations of two such 'bus drivers. They were like this: of a red-nosed fourwheel driver: 'Now then old danger signal!' To a driver of a very magnificent state carriage: 'Where are you going with that glass hearse?' Of a very small man conducting a very tall lady across the road: 'I reckon he wants a step ladder when he kisses her goodnight!'

Whereupon the driver who hadn't made the remark muttered: 'Just what I was going to say, Bill. You took the very words out of my mouth.' – Thus these famous witticisms of the London streets are largely traditional and common property. No doubt London breeds a certain cast of mind by applying men's thoughts to a similar class of occurrences, but the actual comments float in the air in class and class. In the classes that are as a rule recruited from the country, the type of mind is slower, more given to generalisation, less topical, more idealising. It is broader, in fact, because it has two experiences of life, and depends less upon the daily papers.

The children of these countrymen are quite different. The power of generalisation has left them altogether, with their town breeding; their conversation is a collection of town topics, their allusions are gathered from the interests of daily papers, they have international nicknames for the food in cheap eating houses and for common objects. – Thus whiskers become 'Krugers'; slices of German sausage are 'Kaiser's telegrams'; macaroni is called 'A.J.B.' out of a fancied resemblance to the entwined legs of the Prime Minister of a certain epoch. Thus for the Londoner the 'facts' of the daily and weekly press take the place of any broad generalisations upon life.

It takes, too, for at least the poorer classes, the place of animal 'fancies'; it dictates, the daily and weekly press, their very hobbies. For to a man with an individuality and the countryman has a strong and knotted one as a rule – his hobby is his mental anodyne. To the real Londoner the press is that. You get the distinction strongly in this way. My Lincolnshire waggoner become a soapmaker's hand, has his bit of cold steak wrapped up in a fragment of newspaper six weeks old. At lunch time he spells out from this, laboriously, a report of the trial of a solicitor for embezzling £40,000. He says slowly: 'Well, well: why *do* the Law always breed rogues and ruin fools?' – a general speculation. He reads the report of a wife unfaithful to her husband who has been fighting in South Africa, and he says: 'You can't trust a woman out of your sight… Reckon he didn't beat her oft enow… A spaniel, a woman, and a walnut tree, the offer you beat 'em the faithfuller they be' – and many more speculations of a general kind.

But his son, an office boy, his overseer, a smart London born workman, the clerks in his office, his general manager, the directors of the company he serves; these sit morning after morning in their city-going trains, with the sheets held up before them, swallowing 'news' as they swallow quick lunches later on. These things pass through their quiescent minds as under the eyes of the clubman that string of vehicles: 'The Play that Failed; A Chat with the Manager' – 'Varieties in Weather' – 'Scorned Woman's Vengeance' – '"Objected to Fireguards"' – 'Comedy in the County Court' – 'Slavery to Drugs; Alarming Growth of the Opium Habit' – 'Country's Loneliness, Mental Isolation of the Cultured' – 'Infant Motorists; The Automobile as an Adjunct to the Nursery' – 'Home Rule for Egypt; Khedive's interest in an Organised Agitation' – 'Married to a Scoundrel' – 'Batch of Stabbing Cases'. All these things flicker through the dazed and quiescent minds without leaving a trace, forgotten as soon as the first step is made upon the platform at Mark Lane or the Mansion House Stations – as much forgotten as any telegraph pole that flickered past the train window out towards the suburbs. Very salient and very characteristic figures may make a certain mark upon the mind – the German Emperor is, for some reason or another, particularly impressive to the lower order of Londoner – 'Kaiser's telegrams' is an evidence of it. He will evoke some such comment as 'Willie's a bit dotty', but practically never such trite general reflections as that immense power, immense isolation, or immense conspicuousness, will drive a man to eccentricities of speech and action. And indeed, anyone who made such an observation aloud, would run the risk of being silenced with: 'Oh, don't talk like a book here.' Or: 'When we want to hear a preacher, we go to the City Temple.' In a country cottage, on the other hand, the remark would be considered, accepted, and even commented on. This dislike for generalisations is as a rule set down as an English trait. An English trait it is not: but *the* London habit of mind it is. Probably, too, it is what has made conversation in London a lost art. It gives one something of a shock to read in Emerson: 'English stories, *bon mots,* and table talk are as good as the best of the French. In America we are apt scholars, but have not yet attained to the same perfection: for the range of nations from which London draws, and the steep contrasts of conditions create the picturesque in society, as a broken country makes picturesque landscape, whilst our prevailing equality makes a prairie tameness: and secondly, because dressing for dinner every day at dark has a tendency to hive and produce to advantage everything good. *Much attrition has worn every sentence to a bullet.'*

An American writing that passage today would be accused of irony, since we no longer utter sentences at dinners. Yet when we consider the ages of Johnson, of the Prince Regent, even when we think of the Table Talk of Shirley, we must remember – and we must wonder what has become of that mighty stream. And we must wonder why we will no longer listen to talkers: why a talker is something we resent; why, in fact, a conversational artist strikes us nowadays as 'a bounder'.

The really good raconteurs of the Brummel type did survive in London, as very old men, into the late 'eighties: the mild, splendid, whiskered creatures of the Crimea still talked; the mild, splendid and bearded creatures of the 'seventies still told anecdotes '*à propos* of some general idea or other; nowadays we tell a 'good story' with diffidence, being afraid of being taken for a sort of Theodore Hook or professional diner out. But, as a general rule, London limits itself to: 'Did you see that extraordinary case in the So-and-so today?...' or 'Have you read Such-and-such a novel? Seen such a play? Or such a picture show?' and it comments: 'Rotten, *I* think,' without reason given for the condemnation.

Partly, no doubt, it is because we have become so 'democratic', as Emerson puts it, that society resents any monopolist of talk. Perhaps, too, the Englishman never did really enjoy being talked to or 'entertained'. (Indeed an American hostess has put it on record that an English guest commented to her the other day 'But, we don't *want* to be entertained.') But, undoubtedly, conversation began to go out of fashion when the phrase: 'He speaks like a book' was first used invidiously. It marked the bifurcation of the English language: the distinction between our spoken and our written tongue. For this the periodical press must be held responsible.

London was always press-ridden. In the days of Johnson – who invented the magazine – the newspapers would make a prodigious fuss; they could drive a lady so sensible as Mrs Thrale-Piozzi almost to distraction, with comments upon her debated marriage, and supply the Town with Talk – as opposed to Conversation – about such a matter as that Piozzi marriage, for days, months and years on end. And earlier, even Defoe, who was the first of the journalists, made Town Talk out of solid facts, unsolid fiction, or practical projects. But books still monopolised the airy realms of philosophical speculations; preachers still retained the sole right to lecture upon divinity – and books and preachers entered intimately into the lives of men and women. People read *Clarissa* by the year, and debated, at dinner tables, as to the abstract proprieties of the case of Pamela. The Generalisation flourished, Conversation in consequence was possible.

But, with the coming of the modern newspaper, the book has been deposed from its intimate position in the hearts of men. You cannot in London read a book from day to day, because you must know the news, in order to be a fit companion for your fellow Londoner. Connected thinking has become nearly impossible, because it is nearly impossible to find any general idea that will connect into one train of thought: 'Home Rule for Egypt', 'A Batch of Stabbing Cases', and 'Infant Motorists'. It is hardly worth while to trace the evolution of this process. In the 'seventies and 'eighties the Londoner was still said to get his General Ideas from the leader writers of his favourite paper. Nowadays even the leader is dying out.

So that, in general, the Londoner has lost all power of connected conversation, and nearly all power of connected thought. But if his dinner-table has become democratised, and he will not suffer a connected talker among his friends, he still retains some liking for duly licensed preachers, some respect for the official talker or moralist. Generally speaking, he sets apart one day in seven for this individual, and, generally speaking, that one day is the Sabbath.

The stolid London of squares and clean streets, to the westward, still retains something of its Sunday morning hush: the pavements are empty, and as if whitened, and where there are the large detached houses, with bits of garden, and large old trees, the town still has its air of being a vast cemetery of large mausoleums, that no one ever visits. Then indeed that third state, the deep leisure, settles upon the middle London of the professional and merchant classes. There is a stillness, a hush. Breakfast is half-an-hour or an hour later than on other days, the perfume of coffee, the savour of bacon, of fish, of sausages, floats on a softer and stiller air. The interminable rumble of all the commissariat wagons, of butchers', of greengrocers', of stores' carts, all that unending procession that on week days rattles and reverberates throughout the morning, is stilled. In the unaccustomed quiet you can hear the decent hiss of the kettle on its tripod, you can hear the rustle of stiff petticoats coming down from the second floor, you can hear even the voices of the servants in the kitchen, just suggested, as if down there an interminable monologue were being carried on.

And beside the breakfast dishes there lie, still, the Sunday papers. As a rule there are two of these, strips of white, and strips of buff, like supplementary table-napkins. The more venerable contain practically no news; they are glanced at to see the 'Prices' of the day before. But the arms that support these sheets are not the nervous, hurried arms of the week day; the glances meander down the columns. There is time, there is plenty of time – as if the reader in that hush and pause, realised and felt, just for once, that he is after all a creature of Eternity, with All Time before him. There is an opulence, a luxury of minutes to be bathed in, as it were, in that sort of London Sunday, that makes one understand very well why that part of London is so loth to part with its Sabbath.

The Sunday paper is now, I should say, a much more general feature than it used to be. It invades the most Sabbatarian breakfast tables. But I remember that, as a boy, I used to have to walk – in Kensington – nearly two miles to procure an *Observer* for my father, every Sunday morning. (It was considered that the exercise was good for me, lacking my daily walk to school.) And the paper-shop was a dirty, obscure and hidden little place that during the week carried on the sale, mostly, of clandestine and objectionable broad sheets directed against the Papists. The Sunday paper, in fact, was shunned by all respectable newsagents – and, in consequence the Sunday breakfast table was a much less restful thing, since no book of sermons beside the plate could equal that respectable anodyne.

All over the town these sheets, as if they were white petals bearing oblivion, settle down, restful and beneficent, like so many doses of poppy seed. In the backyards of small cottages, separated one from another by breast-high modern palings you find by the hundreds of thousands (it is certified by accountants) ——'s *Weekly News*; ——'s *Weekly Paper*; ——'s *News of the Week*; and, on each back doorstep, in his shirt sleeves, in his best trousers and waistcoat, voluptuously, soberly and restfully, that good fellow, the London mechanic, sits down to read the paper.

And, in general, those Sunday and weekly papers preach to a considerable extent. One middle-class favourite contains at least six different headings under which can be found reflections on social subjects, on sporting subjects, on religious subjects, even on subjects purely jocular and on such abstruse matters as 'Are Clever Women Popular?' And the mechanics' weeklies have sturdy 'tones' of their own; they fulminate against the vices, meannesses and hypocrisies of the wealthy; they unveil the secrets of Courts; they preach patri- otism or the love of God. So that, even if he no longer go to church or chapel, the Londoner on Sunday mornings, before his Sunday dinner, gets as a rule his dose of general reflections. And it is char- acteristic of him that, although he cannot bear preaching that he might have to answer – conversational preaching – he dearly loves the preacher who is beyond his reach. He will listen to sermons, to funeral orations, to public speeches, to lectures; he loves no novel that has not a moral basis of one kind or another, that has not some purpose or other, that does not preach *some* sermon; upon the stage he likes most of all moralising old men and heroic generalisations in favour of one virtue or another. But it is characteristic of the strong lines that he draws between life and the arts, that although he is never tired of seeing a Hamlet upon the stage he will call a Hamlet of private life morbid, dangerous, unhealthy and insup- portable.

Thus, in the London of leisure, any social intercourse between men and women is now-a-days become almost impossible. For no man can be himself without sooner or later proclaiming whatever may be the particular moral that he draws from life. He could not really utter his thoughts without revealing the fact that he loves virtue, or does not; or that he considers there is such a thing as virtue, or is not. He is therefore driven, the social Londoner at his leisure, to action instead of to speech. He puts his feet on the dinner table; beguiles his after dinners with cards, with recitations, with mechanical pianos, with the theatres, with moonlight automobile drives or with watching skating competitions on artificial ice. He plays golf; he witnesses cricket matches, football matches, billiard matches; he goes to twopenny gaffs in Mile End or parades in dense and inarticulate crowds of young men and young girls, for hours of an evening, in front of the shops of the great highways.

And these paradings are, for the million or so of the young people of this huge world that is London, the great delight, the great feature of a life otherwise featureless enough. In externals one parade is like another, but the small gradations are infinite. Thus in one parade there will be a great number of sets each of the same social level; each set with its gossip, its chaff, its manner of accost, its etiquette, its language. You get, as it were, an impression of entering one vast family party amid the rustle of feet, of dresses, the clitter-clatter of canes, the subdued shrieks of laughter, the hushed personal remarks. As a rule in all these parades, in the Fleet Street 'Monkey Walk' as at Shepherd's Bush; in Islington as in Mile End Road; the youths early in the evening stand in knots, cloth caps not consorting with bowler hats and straw-yards with neither. They talk with a certain ostentation and a certain affectation of swagger, boasting, or acting as chorus in praise of one another. The girls parade up and down arm in arm, white aprons being shunned by stuff dresses, and feather hats shunning the straws perched forward over the eyes. Heads steal round swiftly over shoulders as line of girls passes knot of youths, and at these electric moments the voices grow higher and little shoves and nudges pass like waves in a field of corn. There is not any psychical moment for pairing off, but the process begins as the kindly dusk falls. A youth slips away from a knot, a girl hangs back from a line, till little by little the knots dwindle away altogether and there are no more lines.

The ceremonials of the actual greeting are astonishingly various and more rigidly observed than the etiquette of the Court of Spain. In Westbourne Grove the young shop assistant raises his bowler, drawls 'How are you, Miss?' for all the world as they do in Rotten Row. In the Mile End Road and in Shepherd's Bush the factory girls slap likely youths violently upon the back and are as violently poked in the side for answer, both girl and young man uttering obscenities positively astounding, without any obscene intention in the world. And then commences, mysterious and ceremonial, the walking out, the period of probation, the golden age. For, after all, it is a golden age, an age of vague emotions, of words uttered, insignificant, but fraught with more meaning in each absurd syllable than in all the tirades of Romeo to the moon: 'Do you like fringes?' 'Um! – ah! – um! – Well ———.' 'There, you *are* a one ———.' 'I dote on blue eyes.'

So that, by nine o'clock, the parades are full of couples, orderly, quiet, moving unceasingly up and down, with conversation utterly exhausted, with the glamorous fall of light and shade, with titillating emotions, with inscrutable excitements, rustling, supremely alive and supremely happy, with here and there a violent heartache, and here and there a great loneliness. And here for the good democrat is the best sight – the really good sight – of London at leisure, since here is London, the great London of the future, the London that matters to the democrat, in the making. This is London really young, really pagan, really idyllic, really moral, really promising a future to the race, really holding its population by the spell that nothing will ever break, the spell of contagious humanity and of infinite human contacts. These are the Londoners who will never go back.

So by her leisure moments London holds us. And if you desire a sight, equally impressive, of London at leisure, go down Piccadilly to Hyde Park Corner on a pleasant summer day. On the right of you you have all those clubs with all those lounging and luxuriating men. On the left there is a stretch of green park, hidden and rendered hideous by recumbent forms. They lie like corpses, or like soldiers in a stealthy attack, a great multitude of broken men and women, they, too, eternally at leisure. They lie, soles of boots to crowns of heads, just out of arm's reach one from the other for fear of being rifled by their couch-mates. They lie motionless, duncoloured, pitiful and horrible, bathing in leisure that will never end. There, indeed, is your London at leisure; the two ends of the scale offered violently for inspection, confronting and ignoring steadily the one the other. For, in the mass, the men in the windows never look down; the men in the park never look up.

In those two opposed sights you have your London, your great tree, in its leisure, making for itself new sap and new fibre, holding aloft its vigorous leaves, shedding its decayed wood, strewing on the ground its rotten twigs and stuff for graveyards.

CHAPTER V

Rest in London

IN the black and dismal cloisters of our Valhalla – for still for London's heroes it is 'Victory or Westminster Abbey', though Nelson, who uttered the words, is buried under all the stones of St Paul's – there is a small, pale mural tablet. 'In memory of Elizabeth, Dear Child', it reads, and sets us thinking of all sorts of dead children, dear in their day, and now how utterly unremembered, as wavelets are forgotten! And recumbent before it is a blackened paving stone, smoothed with the attrition of thousands of the feet of Londoners, of American tourists, of Members of Parliament, of prostitutes, of school boys. It states that here lie the remains of so and so many monks who died of the plague so and so many centuries ago.

When I was last in that dim place a man with a quick, agitated step hurried up and down the cloisters like a dog nosing out a rabbit in a hedge. He had a penetrating eye, a sharp nose, and high, thin cheekbones. He caught my glance and suddenly stretched out a hand. His voice was sonorous and rather pompous, with the *ore rotundo* in which Victorian poets used to read their own poems to one another. He uttered:

And I said:
Happy are they that do slumber and take their solace here For they cease from their labours and have known the worst.

He added, confidentially and confidently that: into this fane his corpse would be translated by his thousand votaries of the day to come. His name was one that posterity would not willingly let die.

His name was Tockson; he was by trade a cobbler, and he was rather a good poet. I really believe that posterity might be none the worse if it ever come to read some of the verses that, with his own hands, he printed at odd moments on grocers' bag-paper and stored in the back of his shop. He troubled no reigning sovereign and no

established poet with his verses; he never sent them to papers;
sometimes he wrapped up repaired boots in an odd sheet, and he
was not in the least discontented or in the least mad, unless it be a
madness to trust in the literary judgment of posterity and to take
'Marlowe's mighty line' (the words were for ever on his lips) as a
model.

He liked these cloisters, he said, because he could 'contemplate
the memorials' of forgotten monks, legislators, children and philanthropists freezing in the cold and soot outside the walls, whilst it
was his destiny to be 'translated' from Kensal Green Cemetery into
the inner warmth of the 'fane'. And it pleased him to recite his
verses there, because there, it seemed to him, they sounded better
than in Clerkenwell.

He came to see me once or twice, then I lost touch with him,
and going down to Clerkenwell, found that his little shop had
another tenant. He had been run over by a brewer's dray. His verses
– half a hundredweight of them – had been removed by a medical
student from the hospital to which he had been taken. There were
vague ideas in Clerkenwell that they were going to be made into
a book, so that posterity may still benefit, and his dust, which duly
lies in Kensal Green, may still ensue 'translation'. London is full of
such men – poets, generals, framers of laws, men of great mechanical talents, of great strength of will, of lofty intellects. They get
called 'characters' because they never have the chance, or have not
the luck, the knack of self-advertisement, the opening to use their
talents, their wills, their intellects. And this is the heaviest indictment that can be brought against a city or a world – that it finds no
employment for its talents, that it uses them merely to form layers,
as it were, of fallen leaves, that it blunts our sense of individualities.

This London does more than any other place in the world. As a
city, it seems, as has been said, not only to turn Parsees into
Londoners but to make us, who are Londoners, absolutely indif-
ferent to the Parsees, the Kaffirs, the pickpockets or the men of
genius we may pass in its streets. It blunts, by its vastness, their pecu-
liarities, and our interest it dulls. So that it seems to be a city formed,
not for you and me, not for single men, but for bands of
Encyclopaedists, Corporations, Societies. Speaking roughly, we
may say that the pleasantest size for a graveyard – and what is
London but a vast graveyard of stilled hopes in which the thin gnat-
swarm of the present population dances its short day above the daily
growing, indisturbable detritus of all the past at rest? – the pleasan-

test size for a graveyard is one in which each man and woman at
rest could rise up and proclaim: 'In my day I played a part. I had
an influence upon the whole community here. Who is here that
does not know my virtues and my vices? I planted the chestnut that
gives all that shade on the green.' But imagine the great London
'cemeteries' – for they are graveyards no longer – those vast
stretches of heavy clay land, desecrated with all manner of hideous
and futile excrescences that no passer-by will be caught to look at,
appealing like piteous beggars in endless rows for the charity of your
glance; the trees that appear half unreal in the mistiness because they
are such that no one would place anywhere but in a 'cemetery'; the
iron railings that are grotesque because they serve to keep nothing
within a space that no living mortal is anxious to enter. But no
doubt it is the penalty of being dead that one's memorial should be
grotesque: the penalty of fighting against oblivion which is irresistible and pitiless. And, no doubt, it is with the sense of the fitness
of things that London, the city of oblivion, consigns her dead to
the distance of dim and grim suburbs.

At any rate, there they take their rest and grow forgotten. For it
is impossible to imagine the ghost of, say, Macadam, if Macadam
be buried in a London cemetery – rising up at the end of some
dreary and immense vista, and calling to its fellows: 'I made my
mark in my day: I influenced you all.' That unfamiliar voice would
arouse no other spirit; late comers would answer sleepily: 'Oh, our
roads are all wood and asphalte now. Who are you?'

And, if that for all units be the pleasantest for our resting-places,
it is also the most human of units for those still labouring on this
earth. For, as soon as a city becomes a mass of Corporations, individualities die out and are wasted of necessity. We may consider
Athens, which was a city not more vast than is Kensington High
Street: probably its inhabitants were not really more cultured or
more wise, but certainly they had, each one of them, better chances
of influencing *all* their fellow inhabitants. And that for humanity
would seem, in the individualist's eyes, to be the best of social units.
Only the most hardened of democrats, seeing humanity not as poor
individuals but as parts of a theory, as negligible cog-wheels of a
passionless machine, would deny that, from a human point of view
Athens was better than Kensington High Street, or than
Westminster itself. So London casts oblivion upon her dead and
clouds out the individualities of her living.

We talk of the Londoner and we firmly believe there *is* a

Londoner: but there is none. If, in walking along the streets we open our eyes, if we search for him, we never meet him. We see men like Jews, men like Arviragus, men with a touch of the negro, costermongers with the heads of Julius Caesars, but the Londoner we never see – and the search is painful. An awakened sense of observation is in London bewildering and nerve-shattering, because there are so many things to see and because these things flicker by so quickly. We drop the search very soon. And these great crowds chill out of us the spirit of altruism itself, or make of that spirit a curse to us. Living in a small community we know each member of it. We can hope to help, or to be interested in, each man and woman that we meet on the roads, or we can at least pay to each one the tribute of a dislike. But that, in London, is hopeless. The most we can do is to like or dislike bodies of men. If we read the *Morning* —— we have a contempt for the readers of the *Daily* ——, although we know personally no such reader. If we take so much interest in our town as to be moderates – or the reverse – we may dislike our opponents. If we be working men we despise the professional classes and distrust all others. But the individual factor has gone and the power of the individual over the mass.

What prophet shall make London listen to him? Where is London's 'distinguished fellow citizen'? These things are here unknown, and humanity, as the individual, suffers. Economically the city gains. Social reformers, those prophets who see humanity as the grey matter of a theory, would make our corporations more vast, our nations still more boundless, for the sake of fiscal efficiency, for the avoidance of overlapping, in order to make our electric light more cheap or our tram services more adequate. The London County Council should control all South England from the North Foreland to the Land's End. But what we gain thus in the rates we must inevitably lose in our human consciousness and in our civic interests. Londoners, says the Individualist, take no interest in their municipal affairs because the spirit of place has gone. A certain vestry inscribes its dustcarts 'R.B.K.' – the Royal Borough – but the proud title was gained not by any wish of the inhabitants of the Court suburb, but because of some energetic mayor or borough alderman struggling to gain for himself an infinitesimal moment of royal attention. What Socrates of London would commence a discourse, 'Oh, men of London!' – 'ὅτι ὑμεῖς, ὁ ἄνδρες Ἀθηναιοι...'

What Londoner, asks the Individualist, cares about Westminster?

Nelson did at sea, and some people in Minneapolis, Minnesota,
USA, are thinking about this cradle of the spirit of their race, this
old heart of England. But, for the Londoner, there is a convenient
station on the Underground, and the name occurs frequently in the
endless patter of many 'bus conductors. So Westminster, as an architectural whole, as a place with strong features, a great history, a
place of countless anecdotes whispering from every stone,
Westminster is wasted on London. Yet it is the heart of England;
the cradle of its laws, of its empire, of its, on the whole, beneficent
influence upon the comity of nations. So London extinguishes
thoughts about places.

   There is in each man of us an Individualist strain more or less
strong, and in each, a more or less strong flavour of the Theorist
who sees mankind only in the bulk. I imagine the Individualist-half
of a man musing like this: 'I inhabit a large, pompous, gloomy
London house whose atrocious architecture, in any other spot on
the globe, would preclude any idea of my ever countenancing it to
the extent of becoming its tenant. Two doors off there lives the
greatest violinist in the world, next door an old lady who sat on the
knee of George IV; her mind is alive with the most vivid of
anecdotes of a century or so – and next door on the other side is a
girl with a face as beautiful as that of Helen of Troy, a delicate and
tremulous walk, a proud neck, a radiant costume. Yet, here, I care
nothing about any one of them. They are "the people next door".
For here in London we have no more any neighbours.

   'In a smaller community I should choose my house carefully; I
should talk to and admire the violinist, listen to and rave about the
old lady, and no doubt fall in love with the girl like Helen of Troy.
But here, her face will launch no ships; the old lady will find no
Boswell to record her table talk; the violinist will die and, after his
name has filled a decently small space in the obituary columns, will
go to his rest in some cemetery – and will ensue oblivion. Had he
been born in Argos, in a golden age, he would be now the twin of
Apollo – or his name would have been one of the attributes of that
composite mystery. So London has dulled my love of the arts, my
taste for human gossip – my very manhood.'

   'Vous rappelez-vous, dit-il, une réflexion d'Auguste Comte:
   (L'humanité est composée de morts et de vivants. Les morts sont
   de beaucoup le plus nombreux)? Certes, les morts vent de
   beaucoup les plus nombreux. Par leur multitude et la grandeur

du travail accompli, ils vent les plus puissants. Ce sont eux qui gouvernent; nous leur obéissons. Nos maîtres sont sous ces pierres. Voici le législateur qui a fait la loi que je subis aujourd'hui, l'architecte qui a bâti ma maison, le poète qui a créé les illusions qui nous troublent encore, l'orateur qui nous a persuades avant notre naissance... Qu'est-ce qu'une génération de vivants, en comparaison des générations innombrables des morts? Qu'est-ce que notre volonté d'un jour, devant leur volonté mille fois séculaire?... Nous révolter contre eux, le pouvons-nous? Nous n'avons pas seulement le temps de leur désobéir!'

'Enfin, vous y venez, docteur Socrate!' s'ecria Constantin Marc; 'vous renoncez au progrès, à la justice nouvelle, à la paix du monde, à la fibre pensée, vous soumettez à la tradition...'[1]

This, of course, was written of Paris where, indeed, those at rest are more remembered, since there Parisians hold once each year a tremendous festival of the dead. But it might stand at least as well, in those Westminster cloisters, for the shadows that are for ever flying over this London of ours. It epitomises the two habits of mind. For the Individualist, the humanist, sees his dead and his living as human beings: law givers, architects, poets who trouble us still with their Illusions, orators who provided the catch-words that still influence us and our minds. He may stand, that Individualist, for the London that is eternally passing and past. He sees figures in that mist. But the words of his opponent, the man of the future; 'Progress', the 'New Spirit of Justice', the 'World's Peace', are always abstractions. Looking forward, looking into the mists of the future, the future whose men are unborn, he sees no figures. And looking at Westminster Abbey he thinks of Building Enactments.

---

1 "'Do you remember, he said, a reflection of Auguste Comte: (Humanity is composed of the dead and of the living. The dead are much the more numerous)? Certainly the dead are much the more numerous. By their multitude, and on account of the greatness of the work they have accomplished, they are the more powerful. It is they who govern: we obey them. Our masters are beneath these stones. Here lie the legislator who made the law I submit to today, the architect who built my house, the poet who created the illusions that trouble us still, the orator who influenced our minds before we were born... What is one generation of the living compared to the innumerable generations of the dead? What is our will, dating only from today, before their wills that are a thousand centuries old? Revolt against them? Are we strong enough? We have not even time to disobey them." "There you are then, Doctor Socrates," cried Constantin Marc; "you renounce Progress, the New Justice, the World's Peace, Free Thought; you submit yourself to Tradition.'"

And there, where the great towers rise up, grim and black, where the memorials cower at the base of walls grim and black, where fountains stand in the weeping light of obscure and useless cloisters that suggest the gaunt and blackened skeletons of obsolete faiths, obsolete pursuits, obsolete hopes and obsolete despairs; where there are all sorts of courts and alleys of old houses that seem to whisper of faded virtues, faded vices, faded pleasures, dead crimes – that seem to whisper of all the past, and that are being swept away along with all their 'character', all their romance, by Building Improvement Schemes – in that Westminster, where suddenly you come upon boys' figures, flickering in white jerseys, playing football in a small square, the very heart of England, there the old Individualist and the man whose eyes look forward may very well confute each other unanswerably. For, says the Theorist that is in all of us, in that abbey and in that cloister, how many legislators will not be found, venial, selfish, treacherous, legislators who inflicted upon us laws under which we still groan? How many poets who wrote ignoble verse from which the art of poetry still suffers? How many orators who started ignoble, base, and harmful catch-words that still sway our mobs, that still govern our corporate lives?

And, looking at those school boys playing football, your Individualist will retort: 'Observe that redheaded boy with a squint, with the low forehead, the bad skull; observe that good, honest, stupid looking muscular boy by the goal posts; observe that dark, shifty, clever little rat of a chap dodging like a weasel with the ball: what will your Corporations of the future be like when those are the units, when you have swept away the love of place with your improvement schemes, when you have swept away all fear of public opinion by weakening our every individual tie? Do you imagine, really, that "Tomorrow will be like today but much more sweet?" Do you imagine that poor humanity will ever be other than poor humanity?'

So the shadow passes over their argument – the shadow of the Passing that seems, in that heart of the nation, to be for ever on the point of overwhelming those old things. Yet, as a matter of fact, it never really overwhelms them until the new things have already grown old. For all of old Westminster will not be swept away, there will still remain a fragment of the ancient monastery wall, pieces of the cloisters, old Georgian courts, when already the improved buildings of today will be found to be inadequate, insanitary, smoke-begrimed for certain, picturesque probably, possibly glamorous, and surely very old. For once a building rests upon the soil of London, it seems to grapple to the earth as if with hooks far stronger than steel; just as once a man is at rest upon his bier he is so strong that it needs four others to take him to his resting place. And, upon the whole, the Philosopher in us, the part which observes passionlessly, will be upon the side of the friend of the future.

Poor humanity, which works out its own destinies, has given its vote unconsciously against the Individualist. Catch-words, the illusions of the poets, the streets paved with gold, have drawn these great bodies into this great city. And, inasmuch as the Philosopher is a person who accepts the accomplished things, he must accept along with it the Corporations, the gradual death of altruisms, of creeds, of humanities and of the individual as a factor of public life. The great figures of the last century – like the Ruskins, the Bismarcks, the Napoleons, the Tennysons, the Gladstones – have passed away, because no man can now appeal largely enough to affect the immense public. What single great figure is there in the world of whom it could be said that the noise of his death being cried in a suburban street of liver-coloured brick boxes would cause half a dozen blinds to be pulled down, or half a dozen figures to come to the doors to hear the news? There is no such name.[1]

So it seems as if the Great Figure as a human factor has gone, and it seems as if London will never again know another Dr Johnson, although at a hundred street corners you might meet men as wise, as mordant, as dogmatic, as unhappy, as vivacious, as great figures.

This, however, is not an indictment of London. It is rather the mere statement of losses in a great balance sheet. We have lost great figures, old buildings, all touch with history, much of Christian kindness, much of our fear of public opinion, much of our capacity for interest in our fellow men, much of our powers of abstract reasoning, much of our old faiths.

We have gained a certain amount of public efficiency, the avoidance of much 'overlapping', a dim sort of idea of how the world may be carried forward, a comfortable indifference to many

---

1 This of course is an exaggeration on the part of the Philosopher, who looking too closely at the present forgets that one of his young friends – or he himself – may stand revealed to Posterity as a great figure. But, except, perhaps, for a single politician, it is difficult to find one man whose name today would be familiar in every street of this London.

sham observances, class distinctions, and personal infringements of the social codes; and gradually we are evolving a practical means of living together in the great city. If the profit side of the account sheet seems unsubstantial, that is only because of poor humanity's innate inability to see, to understand, the good of its own day – because of the sentimentality of poor humanity that will continue to think an old faith more attractive than an efficient system of local government. We are, after all, still troubled by the illusions of our dead poets. So speaks the Philosopher, who stands midway between the Individualist and the Theorist...

Outside in the woods it is spring, and Nature is preparing for her tremendous waste of individual leaves, birds, gnats, and small and great beasts. There may be sun there, and certainly the sap is stirring, or there may be cloud shapes to be seen, and there is always a sky. But I stand in my window and look down the long perspective of a street. It vanishes, dwindles, grows uncertain, and fades into a black and uniform opacity. There is no sky, or the sky has descended upon earth like a grey pall. There is no colour visible anywhere but grey save for the red of a letter box that seems to float, blotted, in vapour, and the white triangular tops of the lamp-posts. Through the gloom hail falls steadily and close, like fine rain, and behind it everything is flat, dim, as if the house fronts, the garden walls, the pavements, were cloudy forms printed in grey upon a large cloth.

Suddenly space exists: it is as if a red torch were shaken in the air and quenched. That is lightning, a reminder of the outside world that we have half forgotten. A broad shaft of sunlight reddens for an instant, in the distance, the white square face of a house whose dark windows seem to peer back like gloomy eyes: it fades, and the eye is drawn upwards to an immense and sullen glow, the edge of a heavy cloud that towers perpendicularly on high. The vast pall of vapour that overspreads London, becomes for that moment visible and manifest on account of that rift in its surface. It joins again, the blackness descends once more, the hail, the colourlessness of all the world. The houses once more look like clouds.

And indeed it is impossible, without an effort, to dissociate in our minds the idea of London from the idea of a vast cloud beneath a cloud as vast. The memory cannot otherwise conceive of all these grey buildings, of all these grey people. You do not, for instance, call up in your mind all the houses you would pass between Charing Cross and Knightsbridge: they fade into one mass, and because that mass is one you will never touch and finger, it seems cloudlike enough. But all the limitless stretches of roofs that you have never seen, the streets that you will never travel, the miles and miles of buildings, the myriads of plane-trees, of almonds, of elms – all these appalling regions of London that to every individual of us must remain unknown and untraversed – all those things fuse in our minds into one cloud. And the Corporations, the Water Boards, the Dock Boards, the Railway Organisations, the bodies of men who keep the parks in order, the armies who sweep in the streets – all these are cloudlike too. They seem unnatural, all these things, and London itself is at times apt to seem unreal. So that when we come across a park with sharp folds in the land, sharp dips, sudden rises, it is almost astonishing that anything so natural and so real should remain in the heart of this cloud beneath a cloud. For, little by little, the Londoner comes to forget that his London is built upon real earth: he forgets that under the pavements there are hills, forgotten water courses, springs and marshland.

And beneath and amongst all those clouds – thunder clouds, the cloud of buildings, the clouds of corporations – there hurries still the great swarm of tiny men and women, each one hugging desperately his own soul, his own hopes, his own passions, his own individuality. To destroy these individualities is impossible. I am acquainted with a reformer, however, whose ideal of impersonality is so close, so stern, and so unflinching that he would abolish all names of persons, substituting numbers. He would have all men and women who perform any public functions, all candidates for State examinations, go masked and dressed in cloaks that should destroy all distinction of figure and limbs. Physical beauty must be concealed, physical defects must be 'levelled up'; personality must go.

This, of course, is *la justice nouvelle* – the new justice; and it is obvious that these impersonal corporations of the future cannot work ideally without some such precautions against favouritism, or against the 'personal magnetism' that gives sway over crowds. But, in the meantime, those days seem far enough off. Our street-corner Johnsons if they cannot any longer get the ear of the world are none the less Johnsons; our unpublished poets are none the less poets. It is only the audience that is unreachable, and perhaps it is only the world that is the loser. But, after all, no doubt it matters little. What is of importance is whether the sum of human happiness be affected in this great town.

Westminster Building Improvements sweep away whole crowds of human associations: they run up barracks that apparently are distinguished by no single merit. But those Georgian houses that are disappearing, swept away in their day houses older, streets narrower, halls where still greater history was made. Those Georgian streets, courts, culs-de-sac stood mostly for brocaded coats, for powdered wigs, for brilliant talkers, great gamblers, women very dissolute and men very coarse; they stood, in fact, rather for still-life gossip than for national actions, rather for Memoirs than for 'History'. But the older streets that they displaced stood for kings, great nobles, great churchmen. Westminster Hall – which has given place to that great ugly box with its futile tracery of misplaced ornaments – Westminster Hall saw History. The times then were less spacious, and, London, being so much smaller, the really insignificant acts of kings, nobles, and churchmen 'counted' to an extent that no single act of any one man could today count.

And that tendency is inevitable as the world grows broader, as the cities stretch out. 'History' becomes impossible. It was already, as far as London was concerned, over and done with when the young Pretender failed in the '45. Had he taken London, sacked the City, crowned himself in Westminster, misruled, caused new revolutions to foment, new deeds of blood and rapine to set the stones of the Court whispering, history might have continued to be made until near our own day. Nay, even London itself might have been checked for a century or two of its growth, since turbulence and the civil wars inevitable to the Stuarts would have delayed the coming of Arkwrights and Kays, have put back the clock of our industrial developments, have influenced the fate of the whole world. But history of that type ended with Culloden.

The Chronicler had to turn his pen to the accounts of the great impersonal movements, as: 'It was then that cotton spinning was established'; 'It was then that, great depression having overtaken the agricultural districts, immense bodies of the rural populations moved into the great towns.' The race of memoir writers began to discover the witty, the sensible, the profusely dressed, or the profligate Great Figures. Now those, too, are done with, since, as the background grows, the figure dwindles in proportion and loses its importance amongst the vaster crowds upon the canvas. We have no longer, as it were, pictures of Sir Thomas Gresham, M., burning in the presence of the King the King's IOU's to a fabulous amount. Instead, in the historic picture of today, it is 'the Sovereign' (who is now much less a human being than the representative of a political theory) 'attending service at St Paul's, met by the Lord Mayor' (whose name nine-tenths of London ignores), 'the Sheriffs and the Corporation of the City of London'. The City itself has no longer any visible bounds, walls, or demarcations; it is a postal district, 'EC', an abstraction still playing at being an individuality. On our new chronicle-canvas the Lord Mayor is a tiny speck that Sir Thomas Gresham, M., of the older picture could swallow; the sovereign is not much larger; the spectators make a large bulk, and the major part of the composition is filled up with London, the impersonal buildings, the columns, pilasters, the shop fronts, the advertisement posters – the cloud.

The man with an eye to the future may even wonder whether those heavy buildings – that cloud pressing so heavily upon the hills and the marshes of the ancient river mouth – may not be little more than an obsolete incubus, or at least an obsolescent one. The point is whether the 'old building', the heavy permanent mass of stone, timber, and brick is not a mere survival of the worship of the spirit of the hearth. The point is whether, except for that sentimental reason, portable buildings of corrugated iron, of woven wire – even for the summer, of paper – might not be more sanitary, more in keeping with the spirit of the age, less of a tie to the people of the future, our children; for as London weakens the human ties, so it weakens the spirit of the family and the spirit of hospitality. I knew, for instance, an old gentleman who would never quarrel with anyone in his own house, because of his respect for his own roof; he would quarrel with no one under a friend's roof out of respect for his friend's. He would not even write an unfriendly letter in his own or a friend's house. Consequently if he wanted to 'have it out with' a man he had to invite him to some public place, or, if he wanted to write to *The Times*, denouncing some public 'job', he would retire to the nearest hotel and call for a pint of claret, pens and paper. He would himself acknowledge that these proceedings were rather exaggerated, but his instinctive feelings in the matter were so strong that not even the necessity of a bath chair in extreme old age could prevent his going to that hotel for that purpose.

That feeling, I fancy, has died out, or is dying, in London. We have slackened all these ties, and the sanguine reformer foresees also a gradual decay of respect for family portraits. It is, after all, to house heirlooms, he says, that we build great houses or inhabit them. We collect our grandfather's old, too heavy, insect-infected chairs and

chiffoniers, punch bowls, spoons or bedsteads. These things are full
of cobwebs, dirt, microbes; and the old houses, that are largely our
ideals still, are still more insanitary and demoralising. We have even
a London proverb: 'Three moves are worse than a fire'; that is
because we have too much of this unwieldy bric-a-brac. Really,
says this reformer, we ought in the interests of hygiene to cultivate
an extreme cleanliness, and that is only possible with a minimum
of furniture. We should promote, as far as possible, portability in
our houses, because ground that has been dwelt upon too long loses
its resilience, its power of assimilating human debris.

Thus we must pull down our London; burn our ancestral
furniture; melt down our punch bowls; recognise that our associations as far as they are ancestral, are so many cobwebs; and send
the best of old family portraits into the museums. – These last will
soon – says the Reformer, seeing his dream as a reality of tomorrow
– be the sole heavy buildings to raise lofty roofs and turrets above
the plateau of small houses – houses of aluminium, of woven wire,
of corrugated iron, of paper pulp; small houses containing only a
mat or two, a vase for flowers, a cooking stove; houses that we shall
pack on to motor cars when the fit moves us to go out into the
fields for a month or two, or when business becomes slack in
London itself, or when we desire to 'air' our camping site.

The obsolete system of land tenure would facilitate this; the
growing restlessness of the people; the desire for change of scene;
the dearth of domestic labour; and, above all, according to this
Reformer, the fact that no house *ought* to be more than twenty
years old.

I suppose that such a London with its portable houses, its masked
and numbered inhabitants (perhaps we should arrive at such a pitch
of impersonality that a child would recognise its mother, like a
sheep, by the sense of smell) – this London would be sane, sanitary,
and beneficent to the human race. Most of us, being poor humanity,
a prey to the illusions of dead poets, will shudder at what is raw and
naked in this idea. But what is the alternative London that is offered
us by the man who upholds the past?

It is a vast stretch of mounds, a gigantic quagmire with here and
there a pillar of a mediaeval church serving as a perch for a hawk's
nest, and here and there a clump of trees, descendants of those in
our parks, in whose shadow foxes and badgers shall herd, on whose
tops the herons shall nest. The praiser of Times Past will tell us that
the breed is deteriorating physically: it is growing hopelessly neuras-

thenic; it is losing its business energy. It has sapped all the blood from the counties; it is closing its doors to emigrants from the countries. It is breaking with the old social conventions: it is running blindly to perdition.

And indeed this picture of an immense town, shut off from the rest of the world, black, walled in, peopled by gibbering neurasthenics, a prey to hysterias, useless for work, getting no pleasures from horrible self indulgences – this image of a City of Dreadful Night is appalling enough. And its logical end would be that wide desolation, those mounds, those quagmires.

For, supposing that physical deterioration to exist, we must lose our business capacities; a sound mind going with a healthy body, London must lose her trade. The small houses on the outskirts would first lose their populations. Imagine then all those horrible little hutches that have spread out over Essex. – Slates will come loose, rain trickle in, frosts split asunder the walls, naked rafters clutch at the skies, until at last all that great uninhabited region of damp ground will have its thin plastering of rubble, of rubbish, levelled on the ground and making small mounds for the couch grass to cover with its thick tangle. And, as trade ebbs and ebbs from this city of neurasthenics, the Vestries, the Corporations, the Conservancies, will lack the money with which to fight the Thames, that great friend that made London, that great enemy that ultimately shall overwhelm it. A very little want of attention to the sewers, the embankments and the up-river locks would swamp at each tide all the City and all London. The sliding sands would get into motion beneath St Paul's; all the hidden streams and rivulets that London has forgotten would swell, burst their bonds, and beneath the ground eat into the foundations of the houses. (I know, for instance, a London dwelling where a spring has suddenly and invincibly burst its way through the kitchen stairs so that the house has had to be abandoned.)

We who walk about the streets forget the elements; we hardly ever realise by what minute and meticulous patching up the great city is rendered water-tight and air-tight – with tiny slates on the roofs and tiny tiles in the sewers, or with what constant filling up of fresh materials the roadway of the Victoria Embankment is kept from becoming a mere swamp. But you may realise this last if you go, in heavy weather upon any kind of vehicle, along this the worst of London's great roads that flaunts itself against the remorseless forces of nature.

And who, says the praiser of Times Past, would live in London if it did not pay him? London has become a mere bazaar, a mere market. Its associations have gone; its humanity has gone; it is uninhabitable for its atmosphere, for its inhuman solitude, for its indifference to architecture, for its pulling down of old courts.

So, in this image, London, an immense galleon, drifts down the tideway of the ages, threatened imminently by those black and sulphurous clouds, Neurasthenia, Decay, and the waters of the Earth. So, in the other image, it will – humanity being redeemable – become a gigantic, bright, sanitary and sane congeries of little white houses that can be folded up and carried off in the night. On the one hand there will at last be rest in London; on the other – humanity being redeemable – there will never be rest at all, but the great city will go staggering along through a series of changes in the nature of man.

But the contemplative portion of our psychologies seems to reply to these extremists that there is never any change in the nature of man. Furniture is, it is true, getting lighter and more flimsy, but the natural man will go on accumulating as much of it as he can, or as much as his servants or his wife can dust. And his grandson will go on – with variations dictated by the fashions of his day – treasuring such of his grandfather's heavier and more costly pieces as he imagines will do credit to the family. There passes one's window every morning a Charity School: a hundred and twenty girls, each in grey skirts, grey cloaks, heavy boots, and straw hats. They have been drilled to adopt as nearly as possible a stereotyped walk, an odd sort of swing from the hips, and shuffle of the toes on the ground. They have eaten the same food, slept in the same long dormitories. – Turning off one's street there is a long narrow road of small houses, each precisely alike in dingy and indistinguishable architecture, each the same in rent, in chimneys, in window space. – Here, then, are stereotyped citizens and stereotyped houses.

Yet, in spite of the efforts of the good nuns to sap the individual spark in each of those girls, each has a different swing of the hips, cock of the shoulder, glance from the eye. And, in spite of the effort of the architect or jobbing builder to render each of those houseboxes indistinguishable from the other, each has an entirely different atmosphere. Here a door has been painted green, here a handle has been polished till it shines like gold, here the curtains are clean, here a window has been broken and replaced with gummed paper. So that from each of those houses a soul seems to peep forth, differing from each other soul. My bedroom window being very high, I look down into innumerable tiny garden plots when I dress. In the first the tenant is out every morning directing his gardener to put in bulbs, to roll a tiny shell-path, to re-arrange a rockery, to stick up little boxes for the starlings to nest in. In the next the tenant has had the whole space tiled and reddened to save the trouble of attending to it. In the next there is nothing but blackened and sodden grass. Thus, in these stereotyped pocket-handkerchief squares of a quarter where one would imagine the solid middle class to be most uniform and alike, individualities stamp themselves upon the very waste ground.

So that, to those who love their fellow-men, it seems unnecessary to fear much. Even in the Utopia London of masks, dominoes, and, in place of names, numbers, it seems unlikely that one pair of eyes will not gleam more brightly through the eyelets, one domino be worn more jauntily, or one voice be the more thrilling. And the range being less wide, the minute differences will be all the more apparent. Even today class and class of us go seeking appointments in uniforms that, if individuality could be blotted out, would surely do it. We go to offices in high hats, frock coats, trousers cut alike, or in bowlers, broadcloth, or corduroys. But there is difference enough between wearer and wearer of these uniforms.

Tall blocks of office buildings are crushing out the associations of the Westminster courts, alleys, and squares. We see terracotta ornamental excrescences, meaning nothing to us; heavy masses that, to those of us who care about architectural proportions, are repulsive, because, for us, they have no associations. The Memoirists have not yet written them up. But to our great grand-children these excrescences will have meanings and associations, these heavinesses will be suggestive, because we, their ancestors, lived amongst these things our pathetic, petty, and futile lives.

When Westminster was still an ecclesiastical islet with a draw-bridge, odd roads and quaint figures, there were men who grumbled because apple orchards had taken the place of swamps where the wild geese cried all night. And there were monks who rejoiced that new stone salting houses had taken the place of the old, rotting wooden curing huts. They thought their houses looked better, just as nearly all London thinks the office buildings look better than the eighteenth-century rabbit-warrens of small houses. And there were others who foresaw gigantic and impersonal futures for the Church, the Minster, or for Mankind. And your Abbot

Samson found his Jocelynd of Brakelond to be a Boswell for him.

Even the Great Figure still lives: for humanity craves for admiration to give and to take. In the streets you will still hear: 'Oh, such a one: he's a *one-er*', in the Clubs they still say: 'So and so is rather a good man, isn't he?' whether So and So be a surgeon, an admiral, or the administrator of a province in Upper Burma. So the populations of the many towns that form London jog along together towards their inevitable rest. The associations that are forming around our street improvements are none the less poignant, because they are less historic in the large. For the poignancy of these things comes from the man, without regard to the object to which it attaches.

These sayings without doubt are so many platitudes: but if we consider Rest in London, we have to consider the Future, and to consider the Future, we must deal in generalisations, which are brave platitudes. There remains then the question of physical deterioration. 'That Neurasthenia joke,' said a modern doctor, a man looking half Jew, half negroid, but young and alert with beady eyes behind large spectacles, 'It's as old as the hills. Jezebel was Neurasthenic; so was Lot's wife when she looked back; so was the writer of the book of Job. So was Edward II; so was Shakespeare, or whoever wrote *Timon of Athens*. If we've deteriorated physically, when did the deterioration begin?' He paced up and down his consulting-room smiling, and tapped his patient on the shoulder with a stethoscope. 'We've improved: we're improving. Why, my dear sir, what was old age in the mediaeval centuries? A man – a king – was worn out, crippled with rheumatism, too heavy-bellied to mount his horse before he was forty-five. As to the common people, they died like flies: they had no stamina, no power of resisting disease. Town life isn't unhealthy: the art of sanitation did not begin until the towns grew large. Did you ever see an old farmhouse? Where did they build them? Always in hollows, in muddy, airless bottoms, to be near water – you understand: near water – and they drained into that water – and they were plague houses all of them.

'Did you ever have to do with a sick farm labourer? Those fellows! Why, they fold their hands and die for a touch of liver. Their life doesn't hold them because it contains no interest. Half their healthy hours are spent in mooning and brooding: they all suffer from dyspepsia because of their abominable diet of cheese and tea. Why, I'd rather attend fifty London street rats with half a

lung apiece than one great hulking farm bailiff. Those are the
fellows, after all, the London scaramouches, for getting over an
illness.

'Don't you see, my dear sir, your problem is to breed disease-
resisting men, and you won't do it from men who mope about
fields and hedges. No! modern life is a question of towns. Purify
them if you can: get rid of smoke and foul air if you can. But breed
a race fitted to inhabit them in any case.'

That indeed is the problem which is set before London – the
apotheosis of modern life. For there is no ignoring the fact that
mankind elects to live in crowds. If London can evolve a town type
London will be justified of its existence. In these great movements
of mortality the preacher and the moralist are powerless. If a fitted
race can be bred, a race will survive, multiply and carry on vast
cities. If no such race arrive the city must die. For, sooner or later,
the drain upon the counties must cease: there will no fresh blood
to infuse. If it be possible, in these great rule of thumb congeries,
'sanitary conditions' must be enforced; rookeries must be cleared
out; so many cubic feet of air must be ensured for each individual.
(And it must be remembered that, for the Christian era, this is a
new problem. No Occidental cities, great in the modern sense, have
existed, none have begun to exist until the beginning of the
Commercial Ages. The problem is so very young that we have only
just begun to turn our attention to it.)

But, if the rest that comes with extinction is not to be the ultimate
lot of London, the problem must solve itself either here or there –
in the evolution either of a healthy city or of a race with a strong
hold upon life. We know that equatorial swamps have evolved
tribes, short legged, web-footed, fitted to live in damp, in filth, in
perpetual miasmas. There is no reason therefore why London
should not do as much for her children. That would indeed be her
justification, the apology for her existence.

The creatures of the future will come only when our London
indeed is at rest. And, be they large-headed, short legged, narrow-
chested, and, by our standards, hideous and miserable, no doubt
they will find among themselves women to wive with, men to love
and dispute for, joys, sorrows, associations, Great Figures, histories
– a London of their own, graves of their own, and rest. Our
standards will no longer prevail, our loves will be dead; it will
scarcely matter much to us whether Westminster Abbey stand or
be pulled down: it will scarcely matter to us whether the portraits

of our loves be jeered at as we jeer at the portraits of the loves, wives, mistresses and concubines of Henry VIII. Some of us seek to govern the Future: may their work prosper in their hands; some of us seek to revive, to bathe in, the spirit of the Past: surely great London will still, during their lives, hold old courts, old stones, old stories, old memories. Some of us seek relief from our cares in looking upon the present of our times. We may be sure that to these unambitious, to these humble, to these natural men, who sustain their own lives through the joys, the sorrows, and the personalities of the mortal creatures that pass them in the street, wait upon them at table, deliver their morning bread, stand next to them in public-house bars – to these London with its vastness that will last their day, will grant the solace of unceasing mortals to be interested in.

In the end we must all leave London; for all of us it must be again London from a distance, whether it be a distance of six feet underground, or whether we go to rest somewhere on the other side of the hills that ring in this great river basin. For us, at least, London, its problems, its past, its future, will be at rest. At nights the great blaze will shine up at the clouds; on the sky there will still be that brooding and enigmatic glow, as if London with a great ambition strove to grasp at Heaven with arms that are shafts of light. That is London writing its name upon the clouds.

And in the hearts of its children it will still be something like a cloud – a cloud of little experiences, of little personal impressions, of small, futile things that, seen in moments of stress and anguish, have significances so tremendous and meanings so poignant. A cloud – as it were of the dust of men's lives.

The End

The Heart of the Country

Author's Advertisement

THE present volume forms the second of three small projections of a View of Modern Life; it is a natural sequel to a former work, the *Soul of London*. Its author has attempted to do in this volume just as much as in the former one he attempted to do for a modern city. As the *Soul of London* was made up of a series of illustrations to a point of view, so the *Heart of the Country* is a series of illustrations to country moods. The subject of the 'Country' being so vast a one the limits of the attempt must be obvious. Every man, in fact, has a sort of ideal countryside – perhaps it is a Utopian vision that he conjures up at will within his own brain, perhaps it is no more than as it were a mental 'composite photograph' of all the countrysides that he knows more or less well. It is this latter vision of his own, this survey of several countrysides that he knows more or less intimately, and, of many countrysides that he has passed through or visited for longer or shorter periods – it is some such mental 'composite photograph' that the author of such a book must attempt to render upon paper. In this book the writer has followed implicitly the rule laid down for himself in the former volume, and the rule that he has laid down for himself for the forthcoming volume of this trilogy; that is to say, that though for many years he has read many works, returns, or pamphlets dealing with rural questions, and though these may have tinged his views and coloured his outlook, he has attempted here to do no more and no less than to depict – that is the exact word – his personal view of his personal countryside. This particular countryside limits itself strictly to that portion of the British Isles that is most psychologically English. It leaves out the greater portion of Yorkshire, which is, in most of its conditions, a part of Lowland Scotland; on the west it runs no further north than Carlisle; it neglects Wales. Within these limits it gives, as well as the powers of depiction of its projector have allowed, a rendering of a rural cosmogony. If the attempt appear somewhat megalomaniac, it has been undertaken nevertheless in a spirit of true humility by a person who, having spent the greater number of his years in one or other Heart of the Country, has a very wholesome fear of awakening all the sleeping dogs of controversies most heated and most bewildering. At the same time it leaves unsaid nothing that its author wished dispassionately to record. It preaches no particular sermon; it announces no particular message; it is practically no more than a number of impressions arranged after a certain pattern and in a certain order. (What that order is may be seen if the reader who is interested in the matter will refer to the paragraph that occupies the greater part of page 122.)

F.M.H.

WINCHELSEA, April, 1906.

NOTE. A number of extracts, selected from the completed book by the Editor, have appeared in the columns of the *Tribune*: the book itself was written without any eye to such a form of publication.

The Country of the Townsman

IN the cigarette smoke, breathing the rich odours of ragouts that cloy the hunger, of verveine, of patchouli, beneath tall steely-blue mirrors, over crumpled napkins of an after-lunch in a French place of refection, an eloquent and persuasive friend with wide gestures was discoursing upon some plan that was to make for the rest of the company fame, fortune, rest, appetite, and the where-withal to supply it – an engrossing plan that would render the Islands of the Blest territory habitable for them almost as soon as they could reach the 'next street', which, in most of our minds, is the Future. Their heads came close together across the table; outside in the narrow street carts rattled; all round them was that atmosphere of luxuries of a sort, with an orchestral accompaniment of knives thrown down; of orders shouted in French, in Italian, in Spanish; words in broken English, words in tones of command, of anger, of cynical passion, of furtive enjoyment – a sort of surf-sound, contin-uous, rising and falling, but utterly beyond analysis. And, as if it were a compartment that shut them in from all the world, beneath the shelter of this Babel they discussed their Eldorado of the day after tomorrow – their dim Cyclades of the next street.

Those names, those myths shining so graciously down the ages, have still for humanity a great fascination. In one or the other of them each soul of us finds his account. Dim Cyclades, Eldorados, Insulæ Beatæ, Happy Hunting Grounds, Lands flowing with Milk and Honey, Avalons, or mere Tom Tiddler's Grounds – somewhere, between the range of dim islands of a purple west, or that field where we shall pick up gold and silver – somewhere in that vast region is the spot that each of us hopes to reach, to which all our strivings tend, towards which all our roads lead. The more close and airless the chamber from which we set out the more glorious, no doubt, the mirage; the longer the road, the more, no doubt, we shall prize the inn at the end – the inn that we shall never reach; the inn that is our goal precisely because we never can reach it by any possible means. But in bands, in companies, in twos or threes or singly – in labourers' cottages, in omnibuses, in tall offices, we discuss each plan that shall bring us one step nearer, or in the dark silences of our own hearts we cherish a passion so fierce and so solitary that no single soul else in all the universe has a hint of our madness, our presumption, our glorious ambition, or our baseness.

Thus in that dubious place of refection the one friend could well enough discourse to his companions upon their common Eldorado that should, the gods being good, give them fame – and rest. It held them, the idea, among all the clatter; it made glorious with its glamour the foul atmosphere. It was, as the slang phrase has it, a master idea. Suddenly, pushing out from behind the door, came a long, grey, bronzed man.

Bewilderment at being torn from their train of thought, surprise, recognition, were the steps towards immense pleasure.

'You!' slipped from all their lips at once. He dropped his great length into a small chair placed askew at the corner of the table, and began to talk about the country.

He had just come up from the Heart of the Country! He was a man always very wonderful for them, as to most of us in our childhood the people are who have a command over beasts and birds, who live in the rustle of woodlands, and commune with ringdoves as with spiders. We credit them with powers not our own, with a subtle magic, a magnetism more delicate than that which gives power over crowds of men – with keener eyesight, quicker hearing, and a velvety touch that can caress small creatures. They have something faun-like, something primeval, something that lets us think that, in touch with them, we are carried back into touch with an earlier world before cities were, and before the nations of men had boundaries. There are naturalists – but these men are not naturalists; they come out of no studies; in museums they shudder and are disquieted, just as gipsies are vaguely unrestful when you ask them to enter your house. In the towns these men will see things that we never see; they will note the fall of sparrows, or, sailing through the air a mile above the cross of St Paul's, a sea-hawk will be visible to them. Into the towns they will bring a touch of sweetness and of magic – because they come from the Heart of the Country.

He was all in grey, so that against an old stone wall you would hardly have seen him, or on a downside no bird would startle at passing him. It happened that he mentioned the precise green valley that for one of those men was the Heart of the Country. It nestles beneath a steep, low cliff, in the heart of an upland plain as vast and as purple, as wavering and as shadeless as the sea itself. But the green valley runs along a bottom, a little winterbourne directing its snake's course; trees fill it and overshadow old stone houses, and it is alive with birds driven to it for water from the plains above.

So that, green and sinuous, a mirage seemed to dazzle and hang in air in the middle of the cigarette smoke, making a pattern of its own, vivid and thirst-inspiring, across the steely-blue of the restaurant mirrors. It seemed to waver right above, and to extinguish the luminous idea – to extinguish the very light of their Eldorado. They talked of place after place, pursuing the valley along its course, of a great beacon here, a monolith there, of millponds and villages that run one into another, boasting each one a name more pleasant in the ear, or a tuft of elms higher and more umbrageous. For if each man have (and each of us has) his own Heart of the Country, to each assuredly that typical nook, that green mirage that now and then shines between him and his workaday world, will be his particular Island of the Blest, his island of perpetual youth, his closed garden, which as the years go on will more and more appear to contain the Fountain of Youth. And as time goes on, too, life will assume more and more an air of contest between the two strains of idealism in the man – a contest between the Tom Tiddler's Ground of the Town and Islands of the Blest that lie somewhere in the Heart of the Country.

These metaphors, this ideal of an island smoothness in Hyperborean seas, are not the less true because they are not part of our present vernacular. Our necessities, our modes of travel, our very speech, have changed; the necessity for that ideal remains. Whilst, indeed, our speech was forming itself, they wrote books with titles like *Joyful Newes from the West Over Seas*, and still in the tangible unknown West, they could hope to find Happy Valleys. Now with a mapped-out world we can no longer have that hope. We travel still with that ideal, but the hope has grown intangible.

On the one hand the world has become very small, since we may have it all in a book, in pink, in green, in yellow squares. We can reach any portion of it so easily, we may have so easily pictures of it all, that it is hardly worth the seeking. Intellectually, we have learned that there is no Island of the Blest; in our inmost selves, automatically, we never acknowledge it. We have brought our island nearer home, it lies beyond the horizon, but only just beyond. In a sense we may even hope to reach it by the most commonplace of methods. For the mere taking of a pill there may be ours health, which is the fountain of youth; for the mere pulling the ropes of a machine, for just waving our arms in certain magical postures before dressing in the morning, there shall — so the advertisements say — be ours a day of vigorous and unclouded brain, a day that shall see us, unhandicapped by any bodily ill, descend to do our battles in the marketplace — a day in the land of Eldorado. Thus do the clamant charlatans of the beyond in the pale columns of our journals attempt to play upon strings that three thousand or three hundred years ago were rendered sweet by the melodies of those other charlatans who were once living poets.

These things we only half believe in, even in this England, which for the rest of the world is the 'Land of Pills'. But observe the face of your interlocutor when you tell him that you are going into the country. Observe the half envy, half yearning, the mixture of reminiscence and of forecasting plans that will waver across his face, and mark all the shades of expression in his 'Lucky you!'

Round the flat, dark, toilsome town there is the vast green ring, the remembrance of which so many men carry nowadays in their hearts. Put it, if you will, that its attraction is simply that of the reverse of the medal, that it is a thing they love merely because it is not theirs'.

Its real pull is felt, the rope is cast off, when, in his club, on his mantelpiece at home or at his suburban post office, the townsman leaves directions for his letters to be forwarded. At that blessed moment he loses touch with the world, casts off his identity, heaves a sigh as if a great weight had fallen from his shoulders, or even moves his limbs purposelessly in order to realise to the fullest how a free man feels. He has shaken off his identity. For as long as the mood lasts he cannot be traced, he cannot be recalled to earth. And supposing he never went to the spot to which his letters are to be addressed — supposing that, instead of taking a train to that flyfisher's inn, to that moorland farm, or to that friend's manor house, he went afoot to the shore of a Devonshire sea, he might never be found again. He might shake off all responsibilities; he might form ties lighter to bear than the lightest snaffle that ever horse submitted to. He might find a threshold over which, when he stepped in the morning, his feet would go lightly, his eyes glance confidently over fields, seas, and skies of a fabulous brightness.

He never does it – at least he has never done it since here the townsman is and here, in whatever particular town of life he has an abiding place – here he is likely to remain. Some no doubt break the chain. It has been asked, as we know well enough, 'What's become of Waring since he gave us all the slip?' But they never know, they who form the 'us all' of the line. Waring has disappeared – gone; he no longer exists; the Heart of the Country has swallowed him up. He was a weak man who broke; those remaining are the strong, who shiver a little sometimes at the thought that they may do as Waring did.

The mood may last him for an hour or two; it obsesses him a little as he leans back in his train – the fact is still there; his letters are being forwarded to a place that he has not yet reached. For a little time he is still in the grey of the town; its magazines, its papers, its advertisements hold his eyes immediately. Gradually through the glass that encages us he sees the green flicker through the grey of the outskirts, as through the ragged drab skirts of a child you may catch the flash of her knee when she runs. The cloak spread over the ground becomes a covering less and less efficient; then it is all green, and amongst a geometrical whirl of corded posts turning-slowly right away to the horizon he shall see the figures of women with blue handkerchiefs over their heads kneeling down and tying the hops.

But that is still all remote, all shadowy. His lungs are quite literally filled with the air of his town. It is only when he steps out at his junction where he 'changes' that he is conscious of some strange and subtle difference. On his forehead he feels a sudden coolness, his foot falls more lightly, he draws a deeper breath. It is because he is breathing the breath of a free wind.

So he crosses the platform, and in the gloaming gets into the smaller, dirtier, stuffier and darker, and how infinitely more romantic, boxes that will carry him through a fast darkening land into his particular Heart of the Country.

★ ★ ★

Each man of us has his own particular Heart, even as each one has his own particular woman. And the allegiance that he pays to it is very similar. He has his time of passionate longing, of enjoyment, of palling perhaps, or of a continually growing passion that is a fervour of jealousy much such as a man may feel for his wife. He has his love of the past, or he has been whirled past places that later he will hope to make his; he has, and always, his ideal.

This he will never attain to. Put him upon a great hill. Below him there will stretch plains almost infinite; down into them the slopes on which he stands wave and modulate indefinitely. Above his head is the real blue infinity; on his left hand the purple sea, with just a touch of the pink shore of another land that may carry the mind to distances yet more vast. At his back there are grey silences; before his face, miles and miles away in the heart of the sunset, there are dim purplish hills, like a lion couchant, stretched out in a measureless ease. To this height he may have attained with great labour; until he reached it it had represented his ideal. But after the first intaking of free air into the lungs he will see those dim and glamorous hills. And just beyond them once more his ideal will lie hidden. A moment later, too, he will remember that in the valley that he crossed to reach this height there were an old mill with a great pond in which swallows dipped, an old wheel revolving in a dripping tracery of green weeds, a stream running down a valley all aflame with kingcups. This old mill that he passed nonchalantly enough may, he remembers when he stands upon the height, contain his ideal chamber; or if he had followed the slow stream through the marsh marigolds that would brush against his knees he might find the particular Herb Oblivion that he seeks; or, lying down within sound of that old wheel, he might by its incessant plash be lulled into slumbers how easy!

Thus along with him he will carry always those two small fardels, regret for neglected loves, longing for the unattainable. No doubt at times he will drop them. We differ much in these things. Some men will feel all burdens drop from them for a time when they buffet an immense wind; others, again, are lulled into a pleasant doze in the immense heat and haze of sheep-downs at noon; upon some an immense placidity is shed when in the late twilight they step across the threshold of their inn into the mistiness of a village street, when they hang over the stones of a bridge and see waving in the eddies of a trout-stream the reflection of rosy cottage windows.

These moods are rare enough; yet they give for us the 'note' of the country, and certain of them stand out for us through all our lives. Thus I remember, years ago, running down through veiled moonlight, between hedges that were a shimmering blade of cow-parsley, upon a bicycle that by some miracle of chance ran so smoothly that I was unconscious of it as of myself. And the gentle slope was five miles long. It was one of those sensations that are never forgotten; it was one that may hardly be recaptured, unless, indeed, the hereafter be one long lying on the tides of the winds.

For many – perhaps, if one knew the secrets of all hearts, one would say for all humanity that is really tied to the towns – the 'note' of the country is one of pain. This not because the country herself is sad – she is only passionless – but because she is the confidante of so many sorrows. The townsmen tear themselves to pieces among the spines that abound where men dwell. Their friends, their vocations, their taxes, their rail service, their mistresses, their children, their homes, all the creaking doors and monotonous wallpapers – all these things grow wearisome, grow nauseous, grow at last terrible even, and so they take to the country for consolation. Sometimes they find it. Sometimes the country, like a jealous wife, will say, 'No, you bring yourself to me only in your worst moods. Find another consoler.' That, however, happens seldom, and, as a rule, we discover eventually that she has acted for the best in one way or another.

I know, for instance, a man whose Heart of the Country is a certain empty room in a labourer's stone cottage in the backwater of a tiny inland village. He remembers it always as it was at night, with all the doors and windows open in a breathless June, and two candles burning motionlessly above white paper. The peculiar whimper of sheep bells comes always down the hill through the myriad little noises of the night. In the rare moments when the bells cease there comes the mournful and burdensome cry of the peewits on the uplands. If this too is silent there is the metallic little tinkle of a brook on pebbles, the flutter of night moths beating against the walls and ceiling of the lit room. The room itself contains nothing save a table, a chair, a shaving-glass and a razor, a pen and a little ink in an egg-cup; and the black night, magical and gleaming, peers through the open windows and the open door. It was like, so my friend tells me, being hidden in a little lighted chamber of an immense cavern – a place deep down in the eternal blackness of the earth's centre.

And, according to his view, no man in the world was ever more terribly burdened with griefs of a hundred kinds. The inflictions that Fate can bestow upon a man are ingenious and endless; he may have, say, the temperament of a poet, a hopeless passion, a neglected genius, the disclosure of hidden basenesses in himself, the consciousness of personal failure, the ingratitude of friends; or at given moments the whole circle of his life may seem to crumble away and leave him naked beneath the pitiless stars. Let us say that all these calamities had overwhelmed this particular Waring. In that solitude and blackness he fought, unavailingly enough, against these devils; he tried to people that room with figures of his own imagination, so that still in remembrance he seems to see a whole galanty-show* of kings and queens in mediaeval garnitures passing dimly from door to door. At times the razor that lay on the shelf behind his back had the fascination of a lodestone, and on a hot, blazing moonlight night he would rush out from his room and wander, appalled and shaken, to the middle of the white silent village, with the thatches on the wall-tops silver, and the shadows vertical beneath the moon. And then from the little village bakery there came always the constant and unchanging thrill of a single cricket – a monotonous sound that seems to be shaken out upon the air as a powder may be shaken from a box with a pierced lid.

Thus that cave-like, cool room, those hot nights and that thrill of the cricket, those shadows and that fascination of an instrument that should bring a swift and utter change, the slumbrous cottage faces, the imagined and shadowy pageants, the creaking cry of the peewits and the clamorous whimper of sheep-bells – all these things, fusing together and forming a little fold in space and time, go to make what remains for my friend his Heart of the Country. He did not in that solitude find any alleviation, but, perhaps because his particular cross drew him away from the real contemplation of material objects, that spot remains to him something glamorous, something mysterious. Probably on account of those woeful associations he will never go back to that spot, and so it will remain for him to all time remote and wonderful.

Thus that glamour and mystery are what he gained from that stay; and that subtle witch, the Country, if she gave with one hand neither composure nor good health, those illusions that are our daily bread, gave with the other hand that other illusion, blessed in its way – the belief that the earth holds valleys filled with romance and mystery.

---

* **galanty show**: a shadow pantomime, created by throwing shadows of miniature figures against a wall or screen. This is a recurring image in the later Ford novel *The Marsden Case* (1923).

The powers of the country, its powers over our moods, are not illimitable. At times hills, great skies, bright hedgerows, or barns the thatch of which is a network of mosses and flowers – at times all these things are mockeries upon whose surface the very sunlight lies like a blight. But at times, again, she achieves the impossible, and serene twilights, the chorus of birds at dawn, the sound of children's voices from deep woods or the blue floors of coppices in May, some immensely vivid sight or some indefinitely complicated sound, some overwhelming odour or the feel of the wind on the forehead, some blessed touch from the material world will pierce through the cloud of gloom that besets poor humanity at its lower ebbs. And it is these things that are unforgettable, it is these things that keep us going.

Other men will remember having watched by a sick bed for several days and nights in succession, in a house full of sickness, waiting all the time for a temperature to fall. The drag of such nights and days becomes terrible towards four in the morning. A man sits in a twilight too dim to read by, he fears to move lest the tinkle of medicine bottles awaken the sleeper. He dare not sleep, he dare hardly think for fear that sleep will overcome him. He remembers, on the third or fourth of these nights, a feeling like breaking, a tightening of the screw until it seems that something must burst, so that without more deliberation it is a necessity to be out of doors for a second, for a minute, for however tiny a space of change.

Out of doors there is coolness, the merest shimmer of grey above the distant sea, the slow shaking out of rays from a lighthouse that seems to be lessening its pace out of weariness and because the dawn is at hand; flowers and leaves appear indistinct and visionary, the air is absolutely motionless. And suddenly there comes a waft of light right across the sky; a rook caws from the trees high overhead – then the voices of the whole colony, soothing and multitudinous; a breeze stirs a spray of hops. The corner is turned, the night is over. It does, perhaps, consecrate the memory that, going back to the close room, one may find that at last the temperature of the sufferer has fallen, but the unforgettable psychological relief comes with that stir of the dawn breeze, and that sudden motion of the hop tendrils is the acknowledgment that we are no longer alone in a dead world.

★ ★ ★

All this is no doubt about 'the country', in inverted commas – about the land from the outside. It is one of the anomalies of our present civilisation that the majority of self-conscious humanity – the majority, at least, of those who read books – should regard unbuilt-upon land from that outside. It is a fact physically more remarkable in its way than the earliest systems of cosmogonies. That the earth should contain the universe was thinkable enough. That the cities should contain 'the country' is one of those unthinkable things that have passed into the subconsciousness of a great section of mankind.

Hitherto, through the course of history the country has seemed to triumph inevitably. The image of the struggle has been not so much a moving of the pendulum between town and country, but a kind of Antæus-town giant has gained its strength only by touching the ground; or, if you will, the image is that of a bird that may soar but must come back to earth. The country has 'had the pull' because in their origins all foods and all the necessaries of life came from seeds of one kind or another, the chain going always through the carnivore and the cotton mills to end eventually in vegetation.

But modern scientific thinkers proclaim that this chain is broken. Foods exquisite and nourishing are to be made from mineral oils and acids; raiment of glorious dye and skin-caressing texture is to be had from all sorts of coal-tar products. The necessity for the Nature of green fields is at an end, according to the New Millennialists. These scientists adopt towards that particular Mother Nature an angry and querulous tone; they accuse her of producing a slow-witted race of men, of hindering social progress, of fostering an anti-human malady, the desire for solitude. And indeed today I read in an organ of advanced thought that 'the country stock, which some reformers have been demanding as an invigorating and necessary renewal of the city race, is likely to prove positively harmful, as adding an element not adjusted to city conditions'. The city, in fact, is said to have bred its own type.

And once outside the country habit of mind the townsman finds a considerable difficulty in getting back to a more psychological possession of a country life. He may buy land, he may even take to rearing stock, which is supposed to be the surest passport to some sort of social standing in the country; his face may become bronzed, his raiment approximate to that of the half-golfer, half-horse-coper, which is nowadays the country's undress livery; but he will not, save thus externally, get very much nearer to being a countryman.

It may appear paradoxical, but it is as a matter of fact a truism that country life is in all its branches a singularly complicated matter. In a month or so a man may get to know a town sufficiently for all practical purposes. Generalised, all bricks and mortar are much the same; all town streets fall under wide headings, and town societies are easily classed within comfortable limits.

But your clever man of the world set down in the country is, as soon as he opens his eyes, confronted with an ignorance of his own that will at first render him infuriated with the ignorance that he meets all round him.

It will end, if his eyes remain open, in a modest disbelief in his own mental powers. He will discover the bewildering idiosyn-crasies of each component factor of the social life of villages and small towns; he will discover that it is possible to make Montague–Capulet quarrels out of grounds incredibly unimpor-tant in his point of view; he will discover that, broad-minded and aloof as he may be, he himself, if in any sense he 'lives' in the place, will become involved over head and ears in these small feuds; and a little later he will discover himself— himself as an entity cast inward upon itself for intellectual support, for interest, for employment, and for life.

It is, perhaps, then only that he will discover that he knows nothing and probably never will know anything appreciable of what in the cant of the day is called Nature; and to the measure of his humanity and of his thirst for knowledge he will be irritated or saddened by the amount of time that he will think he has lost in the cities. The amassing of his fortune such as it is will seem a small thing compared with the fact that in amassing it he has so spoilt his quickness of apprehension that he can never hope to distinguish the flight of a redshank from that of a sandpiper. And the longer he lives, or the longer his interest remains alive, the deeper will his thoughts penetrate. He will discover that he knows nothing about wild flowers, nothing about ploughed fields. He will be startled by such questions as, 'How many sheep will an acre of marsh-land carry all the year round?' and that most bewildering of problems, 'In the profit and loss balance-sheet of a fatted bullock what should a farmer charge himself for the straw off his own farm; and what should he pay himself when in the form of manure that straw is put upon his own fields?'

The farmer as an entity or as a problem will begin to exist for him, and the farm labourer as a 'problem' perhaps still more than

as an entity; and all the problems of the country – of game
preserving, of wild bird protection, of the introduction of new
crops, of the proper form for education, of smallholdings, of the
amenities of life and scenery, of the question of small houses, of the
influence of surface drainage upon trout streams, and of the destinies
of the country child – all these things will give to his broad green
horizon hundreds of new significances, so that it will teem with a
life more complicated in its interworkings than any of which he
had before conceived.

These things differ very much in different men, but as a broad
general plan the induction of a man into a countryside runs upon
these lines, and by these steps he seems to descend further and
further into the bowels of the country. He views the country from
a distance; coming into it he studies the means of communication,
and makes nodding acquaintance with the men he meets between
the hedgerows; next, crossing the fields by short cuts that he has
discovered, passing through little lanes and coppices, or hopping
laboriously from ridge to ridge of a ploughed-up footpath, he comes
across wild birds, or watches yellow sheep gasping in the washing-
troughs; he hears, pattering like a little shower of rain, the sound
of the turnip-flea at its devastations; he penetrates next into the
farms and cottages and makes acquaintance with all sorts of slow,
browned creatures of his own species. Then he will begin, to the
measure of the light vouchsafed him, to speculate upon how the
lots of these men may be ameliorated, and, after he has speculated
as long as time is granted to him, after he has essayed his own
seedings and garnered his own crops; he will die, and his 'things'
will be sold, another pressing to occupy his accustomed place. It is
then, under these main headings, with a hope of attaining to such
a gradual deepening of interest, that I have undertaken this projection of the rustic cosmogony as it presents itself to me.

Speaking very broadly – and to a writer of generalisations a very
great latitude of speech may be allowed – this 'Country' in inverted
commas, this peculiar Island of the Blest may be said to exist only
for a more or less lettered, more or less educated, more or less easily
circumstanced town class. Owing to the social convention of land-
holding the most easily circumstanced of our body politic belong
to the landed class, and such attractions as the green earth possesses
for them is very much part of their daily life. They are born among
green fields; they went bird's-nesting, they rode their ponies over
spring wheat, they were, however artificially, part of the landscape

itself. For them, the associations of the country will be the associations of youth and of high spirits, accidental matters personal to
themselves. The peculiar decorative line of a pollard-willow-tree
will appeal to them in after-life, not because willow-trees were
things of which their youth was starved, but because in the small
hole of the pollard top of one particular willow-tree they used, say,
to leave small packets of chocolates for a particular keeper's
daughter, or because in another hole of another tree they made, in
company with a good-humoured red-haired boy, their first
gunpowder mine. Thus in after years willow-trees will have
romantic associations for them as they sit over the table full of corre-
spondence of a room in the Foreign Office.

And the poorer town classes do not, as a rule, regard the country
as a place in which they shall regain health, or as a place of glamorous
associations; for, on the one hand, their purses, their whole
arrangement of a yearly budget will not allow them to contemplate
as part of the year's programme a definite month in a farmhouse or
beside the sea. And as a general rule, if the industrial or shop assistant
townsman began life in the country, his particular beginning of life
was neither romantic nor glamorous. He felt himself too near the
earth, he was too conscious of the social obligation to touch his hat
to people in more shining raiment, while he himself was ungra-
ciously clad, as a rule insufficiently fed, and almost invariably
miserably lacking in the more poignant interests of life.

For it is undoubtedly one of the great defects of life in the country
that really contagious occupations for the leisure times of any one
not a child are wanting, and the hobbledehoy must pass his unoc-
cupied moments in long, aching hours at the corners of village
streets. Up to a certain age there are many pleasures to be had;
bird's-nesting, with its peering into cracks and crannies of old
masonry and into the mysterious half-lights and distances of thorn
bushes, offers at once a sport and a collector's hobby; whilst to the
ordinary seasonal games, to the marbles, tip-cat, hoop-driving and
leg-wicket of the town child, the country child can add the slightly
perilous delights of trout-tickling, tree-climbing, and the robbing
of apple orchards.

Thus upon the whole the child of whatever degree does prefer
a real country life to the life of the streets. He does not, of course,
attach romantic values to natural objects, but he finds in them
enough of interest to 'keep him going', to tide him over the periods
of terrible monotony that fall upon the lives of all children. I have

questioned and closely observed a number of children who had the opportunities of an amphibious existence, who had practically only to ask to be allowed to go either from town to country or from country to town. Once the pleasures of gazing into shop windows had been exhausted for the year – and this passion is as natural in children as is that for marbles and bull's-eye lanthorns – once this passion had been exhausted for the year, the children invariably preferred to be in the country; they loved it for the freedom to be out-of-doors roughly dressed, for the roads that they can run across without being confined to the rigidly straight line of destination; and they loved it above all for its profusion.

To the real slum child, the child brought up in a grey atmosphere, the sole window into any sort of delight is an infinitesimal copper coin; without an unattainable number of half-pennies this child can never really handle any number of any kind of objects; and only those who can remember their own childhood can realise what that means. For in stone-paved courts and asphalted streets there are not even little stones to be picked up; there is nothing to be made believe with, and sharp-eyed rag-pickers seize upon even the old tins that with a bit of string a child might turn into a representation of a railway train. So that almost the only things that the slum child sees in any numbers are trouser buttons that he gets from Heaven knows where, by Heaven knows what process of gambling. The only other profusion which he ever sees is sealed from him by glass windows or barred to him by the invisible barrier of Property that erects itself even before the greengrocer's stalls on the pavements.

So that, set down in front of the tremendous waste of plant life, the ownerless blades of grass, the enormous spread of fields, the scampering profusion of wild rabbits, or the innumerable and uncontrolled sheep, the slum child, the poor town child is rendered absolutely breathless. He is for the time being like a lifelong prisoner to whom has been given the key of an unneeded street.

I came last hopping season upon a London child raptly contemplating a little brook that ran close to the golden straw wigwam in which her mother was cooking bacon over a chip fire. They had arrived only that afternoon, and their untidy bundles of sackcloth gave a dilapidated look even to a very radiant corner of a valley. The child, in a misty black skirt that did not close at the back and wearing a battered sailor-hat below which her curls hung limply, turned a sharp little face suddenly to me and remarked, as if it were a profound truth that had shaken her whole world –

'There don't appear to be no turncocks here! And there's more water than when the main burst opposite Mrs Taylor's.' The nut-trees arched over her head and, standing rubbing one foot upon the instep of the other, she pulled a leaf that she let drop into the water. It appeared to bring into her mind another profound and wonderful truth – the fact that here, in an every-day world, was a region in which there were almost no 'coppers' to cut and run from. She had 'often heered tell of the country', she said...

I was never able to trace what further mental revolutions took place in her, for almost immediately afterwards typhoid fever broke out in that kraal of hoppers and it grew expedient to avoid their corner of the long sunny hop valley; but that 'note' of the country has been the dominant one for any slum child with whom I have ever spoken, and if, sooner or later, the 'copper' does become manifest vaguely, and laws of property, even in hazel twigs, do finally assert themselves, profusion remains for most of the poorer townsmen the master 'note'. I drove yesterday nine or ten miles along a hog's-back ridge to a cricket match in company with a railway porter who was just one of those slum children grown up. He had entered the service of the railway in a London suburban station (he had been born in one of the worst rookeries in Hammersmith), and he had to be 'shifted' on account of his health to one of the smallest of wayside stations. Here for several years he led a curious existence, in, but not of, the country, passing his daylight hours in the station, but having his home in the nearest large town – one of those towns which are practically slices of London arranged along the face of the sea.

We drove for some time down the valley, broad, vividly green and tumultuous with thorn bushes in flower. The railway man talked of the morning's frost which had filled all that bottom land. 'Warm the night was in H——,' he said; 'but when I came out here first train – cor – ' he paused. 'White – .' He paused again, seeking for a simile, but finding none he repeated, 'All white.' The rest of the eleven who came from up the hill had nothing to say. 'Farmers say in the papers that there hasn't been no such frost since '92. Bad for the station-master's "taters", I hear. Fruit too. Say, Jimmy, what does frost do to French beans?' 'Kills 'em, reckon,' a farmer muttered.

So the Cockney went on repeating 'Cor! 'and 'White! You should 'a' seen!' and gaining horticultural information with a swiftness of speech and intentness that compared with the taciturn acceptance of nature by the farmers as the eagerness of a terrier before a rat-hole compares with the stoicism of a great cane. We jogged between the hedgerows till, just as the road began to mount, the fisherman who was driving the waggonette pulled the pipe out of his mouth, and remarked that he was born in Martello Tower No. 42 in the year '57. The Cockney suddenly burst on us with –

'I hear we sh'll see views from the top of this hill!' The farmers said, 'Ay, views! The finest views in England.' Their voices were phlegmatic and nonchalant by comparison, as if they had a local pride in the view, but carried the enthusiasm no further than that. But the Cockney said again, 'Views! I've often wanted to see them views. I've often thought of walking up the hill to see them views.' And he repeated with an interminable variety of accentuation the fact that he had often thought of 'them views'.

We reached the top of the hill, and from far below the crepitation of a train met his ear. He pulled out his watch, exclaimed, 'The 1.27 not more'n ten minutes late', then turned and caught the trail of smoke that appeared like a plume being blown swiftly across immensity. It was as if the whole of the world opened out to him between the gaps of the hedgerows. There were plains, woods, fields like pieces of a pattern, two glimpses of sea between shoulders of purple hill, innumerable churches, innumerable villages, all the foreground an immense valley, bright with vivid sunlight, dotted with white thorn trees, like solid and soft substances moulded by careless fingers, casting shadows vivid and sparkling; and all the background fading into those almost incredible mysteries of haze that give to our distances so pathetic and so romantic a beauty, that so wonderfully allure the eye to travel deeper and deeper, or to rest itself in shades always more and more soft.

As he turned his head to speak his words were stopped by the other broader view that swept up to the horizon on the northern side of the ridge. Here there were fields smaller, hillocks more abrupt, and always more and more and more woodlands of every shadow and shade of colour, until at last the whole surface was like an unbroken carpet, a purple lawn with swelling cushions to the indistinguishable distances.

We drove for many miles between these two views, always along that upland hog's-back. I do not know just when the railway man delivered himself of *his* profound truth, but it was, 'Cor! What a lot a fellow could do if he had all *that*!'

The farmers uttered deep 'Ahs', not in reference to his sentiment, but in the fashion of proprietors, as if before his eyes and to impress him they had unrolled that tremendous panorama which I believe hardly two of them had twice before seen; for the real countryman travels very little beyond his own valley, and except for the road to the nearest market towns is little of a guide in his country.

And, as I stood fielding through a long and sleepy afternoon, in a rough outfield whose grass was above the ankles, over a shoulder of hill below which was spread just such another panorama, it ran through my head: 'What a lot a fellow *could* do if he owned all that!'

What sermons he could preach in the primeval church whose weathercock flashed sudden scintillations through miles of space; how, with the love of his heart, he might for ever hide himself in one of the white thatched cottages that fit into their hidden valleys as children's toys fit into their boxes; what straight and joyous blows his axe might deliver through the saplings of those shaves and coppices (and surely in all life there is no sensation more satisfying than that of a truly delivered, truly swung axe-stroke as it sinks into and through a young tree as thick as your leg!); or what Utopias he might, a benevolent despot, set up somewhere on hill or dale, between the grass that gives him foothold and the last hill that his eye can reach!

These thoughts are no doubt anthropomorphic, but I think that they are inherent in poor humanity, to whom the high places of the green earth seem for a time to communicate a feeling of having the height of a giant and the powers of a godhead. In one of the infinite variations to which human thought lends itself this feeling of oversight, of control over one's own destiny, or over the destinies of an immense number – whether of human beings or of blades of grass – some species of supernatural endowment is the 'note' of the promise that the country makes to us, whether in the rushings of its winds, in the tumultuous lines of the parti-coloured mantle thrown down all across its surface, or in the mighty chorus with which, from dark flanks of a wooded hill, the birds sing down the sun in May.

In some subtle and mysterious way the country seems to offer us the chance, the mirage of attaining, each one of us, to his ideal. And for that reason each one of us, at the different times of the year when the *malaise* seizes him, itches to set forth in some sort of knapsack, and on horse, a-foot, in swift carriages or in the sheltered sloth of his own veranda, between the hedgerows, across the fields, by the sands of the sea, or through the interstices of his own thoughts whilst his eyes follow sinuous lines of greenery, he will attempt to track down that master-thought of his existence, that mysterious white fawn that lies couched beside some fountain, in some valley, in some Fortunate Island.

CHAPTER I

Between the Hedgerows

EACH road has its own particular individuality, nay more, each has its own moral character, its ethics as it were, since what are ethics and morals but the effects of one's attitude upon the beings who come in contact with us? Roads will soothe us, tire us, exhilarate us, fill us with thoughts or excite our minds with pictures of the whole hosts of history that have passed along them.

Some of us love best the turnpikes — and I love them very well — broad, white, smooth, with generous curves, with carpets of turf along the sides enough to make lawns, with gentle rises and with great skies above them.

How many centurions, how many Roman missionaries, how many sweating bearers of tin ore, how many earls, how many kings, how many royal brides, or how many forsaken women have passed over these still, long stretches! How many feet have danced gaily along, how many have ached in the dust!

When men go along such a road it is as if they went amid a crowd of invisible phantoms, hearing a continuous rustle of inaudible whispers. Here is the spot where a king drank, at the top of the rise. Here is where the five robbers lay in wait in the coppice. Here is the milestone on which, on a moonlight night, there sat the ghost of a bride whom a peasant woman saw raise a white face to hers...

There are solitary roads that look over the corners of great uplands and seem to be peopled by no ghosts; only above the not distant barrows or the many-tiered fortifications of grass slopes one imagines that there peep the shaggy tousled heads of the ancient and forgotten inhabitants of the land.

There are roads that climb the sides of hills, aslant, so that from a distance they seem to be white sashes of honour; and from distances, too, one may see, high on the downs, white fragments of roads, like plumes or like bill-hooks, hanging from the skies. One hardly imagines that one will ever climb them; if one does so, the road assumes so new an aspect that it loses for the time the identity that it had for us upon the lower steps.

But the essential road of 'the country' is one that runs between hedgerows – nay more, the essential first note of 'the country' is the hedgerow itself. For, as far as I have been able to discover, the tendency of the town dweller is to circumscribe 'the country', to restrict it within comparatively narrow limits. Thus, to go out of town may be to go to the Riviera, to Cape Coast Castle, or to the Broads. But to go to any one of these, to the sea-shore, or to the Yorkshire moors, is not to go into the country. If the townsman were taking a summer holiday at Lynmouth, he would be at the seaside; if from thence he went inland towards Barnstaple, that would be going into the country. But if his course led him Brendon way, he would be going, not into the country, but on to the moor.

Land, in fact, that has any very distinctive features – moors, hills, peaks, downs, marshes or fens – such land is not the country. It is only where the hedgerows journey beside the turnpikes, close in the sunken lanes, or from a height are seen, like the meshes of an ill-made net, to lie lightly upon hills and dales, to parcel off irregular squares of vivid green from jagged rhomboids of brown, of yellow, or of purple – it is only where the hedgerow has its agricultural use that the country of the townsman is. No doubt this is a splitting of philological hairs, but by minutely enquiring into philology one comes upon historic truths; and this hedgerow definition leads us to see that the word indicates not mere land that stretches beneath the free sky – otherwise the country would take in the continent or the habitable globe itself – but it indicated in the old days simply and solely the agricultural land of England, the land that in the slow revolution of the centuries has been agricultural, pastoral, and agricultural again, and now again pastoral. It is a vague stretch of territory, with unknown villages, unknown fields, brooks, plough-lands, smithies, ricks, hop-oasts, tithe-barns, dovecotes, manors – but always the hedgerow shuts in the horizon, so that to go into the country is, as it were, to lose oneself in a maze; whereas to go, say, on to Lobden moorside, is to expose oneself nakedly to the skies.

The hedgerow, indeed, is so much the mark of the country that it conducts a man there from the towns and conducts him once more home again, since, where the quicken hedges of the railways take command of the lines, there the country begins. There are few hedges so beautiful as those that we see flitting past us, green, solid, sinuous, with here and there a touch of blossom and here and there a trimmed peacock. And there are few surfaces pleasanter for the eye to rest upon than their slight mosaic of spiny stem and green leaf.

There are, however, not many such hedges stretched across the countryside, and perhaps in one's everyday mood one may be glad. For a land where all hedges were perfect quicksets would be a land fat and prosperous, but a land slightly soulless. It is true that one has one's other frame of mind, the frame in which one longs for the good piece of work, well executed for the work's sake – the frame of mind in which one prefers a newly-tiled barn to the broadest, most moss-begrown and sparrow and rat-tunnelled thatched surface; in which a new, white, five-barred gate is as a soothing and beneficent rest for eyes tired and depressed by age-green wattles straddled across the gate gaps of an ill-tenanted homestead.

But before one will have reached to that frame of mind, one will have travelled between many hedgerows riotous with dog-rose, odorous with elder in blossom, along which the nefarious but beloved bramble will carry the delighted eye from briony to briony. And journeying between these hedgerows, the townsman who loves the country will pass through several phases until he arrives at one or the other of the two stages of country thought, until he arrives in one or the other of the two camps that are set over against each other. Loosely put, because the point is one that must come to be elaborated later, these two schools, these two hostile camps are that of the farmer who likes to farm as his fathers did because the life is goodly where farms are gracious, and that of the man who clears away all picturesque lumber because business is business. With both combatants a really proper man will find himself at one time or the other in sympathy, but the less-thinking of us enlist for good under one banner or the other. And, loosely put again, we may say that the townsman who really 'takes up' farming becomes a 'business man', whilst the townsman who merely lives in the country because he loves it will groan at each new strand of barbed wire and each new cement pigsty.

I have walked over many countrysides with many different men – with an American Jesuit, who wanted to see the most beautiful village of my own county 'tidied up', stripped of creepers and of ivy, painted, and lit with electric light; with a tramp, who was lividly indignant because the local countess had cut down some timber and spoilt a whole stretch of park land; with a lawyer, to whom the

first bit of dusty fallow with barbed wire round it was already
Arcadia; with sailors ashore, who wanted to see always more barns
and more barns round the homesteads, to indicate endless
profusion; with a peasant poet in a smock frock and with aged,
faded blue eyes, who declared that God did not love steam-ploughs;
as well as with a steam-plough and traction-engine proprietor, who
declared that his great hulks of iron, standing, like enormous
toys dragged by some godhead, askew upon the hillside, dragging
from side to side across the furrows giant insects all of iron – his
devouring monsters were sending up those pillars of smoke that
should lead the Chosen People back to the Land. But always,
subconsciously enough, they divided themselves into these two
strains – they wanted hedgerows because they sheltered birds,
yielded flowers, or had existed in the days of their fathers; or they
wanted iron fences and barbed wire because these give no shade
upon the crops, harbour neither birds nor insects, and indicate that
the right type of man, the economist, is in charge of land that shall
be rejuvenated.

My tramp, with his rain-beaten clothes, his jovial, peak-bearded
face, his luxurious sprawl along the roadside, like a Roman emperor
on his couch at a long table – my tramp was probably the most
disinterested, or the most interested, of them all. Tramps are, after
all, first to be considered as users of the highways or the hidden
lanes, since they, along with sparrows, weasels, traveller's-joy and
young lovers, really live their lives between the hedgerows. The
gipsy, with his caravan or his withy-supported wigwam, is by
comparison an indoor dweller. The individualities of these travellers are infinite, but the good tramp, the real thing of his kind, is
precisely the one who lies by the highway, banquetting with his
eyes. He is the artist – the man who loves the road for its own sake:
he has not any other ambitions than shade from the sun, long grass,
and eternal autumn weather.

It puzzled me for many years to know what castles in Spain a
tramp built – what was *his* particular Island of the Blest; and after
getting over the first shyness of accosting these slightly repellent
bundles of clothes (for it is, after all, the clothes that repel us), I
pursued this ideal with some diligence. It was Carew, the tramp of
whom I have spoken, who got me most easily over my shyness. He
was a man of no particular book-learning, though he said that hardly
a day passed without his picking up a paper. He was the son of a
Guardsman and a prostitute, and his professional tale had it that he

had been bred up as a tooth-comb maker; machines had destroyed *that* occupation. He carried a comb in his pocket; but I fancy that he delighted to comb his long golden beard, and had the comb for that purpose, inventing the profession to fit the implement. I have met him in Regent's Park, on the Sussex Downs, in Cornwall, and in the Strand; but he always carried his boots under his arm – I never knew quite why. I fancy it was on account of some superstition: he did not like boots, but a sort of luck, I imagine, clung to this particular pair. An odd mixture of sardonic candour and savage reticence, he would admit to having been in every gaol in the South of England, but he would never reveal what he was afraid of on the roads at night. He always crept into the shelter of some house at nightfall, and he had once, he told me, been arrested for following a young lady five miles across Salisbury Plain in the moonlight – with no other evil purpose than the desire to keep a human being in sight.

In spite of the comb, he said he had never done a day's work in his life, and never meant to. He lay by the roadside, and sometimes he had been so magnificently lazy that he had gone without food for two days rather than beg. 'You get sick of people's faces at times,' he said.

But Carew, as far as I can discover, built no castles in Spain. He supposed that pneumonia would carry him off one of these days, probably in China, as he styled Lewes gaol. He called the various prisons by the names of countries, and nicknamed workhouses after the great cities of the world. Thus Eachend Hill Union was Paris with him, and Bodmin, Rome; though this caused confusion, because, of course, London itself is Rome in the lingo of the hedgerows. His crimes, as far as I know, were limited to sleeping out; in this flagrant offence he was very frequently taken because of the nervous tendency which made him sleep in stackyards near cattle, or in farm stables near horses, for the sake of company. He exhibited with pride a small sheaf of newspaper cuttings which recorded his convictions, and his insolent retorts to magistrates. He was delighted with these; but he seemed to have no further ambitions. He was as contented with a 'bob' as with a 'quid' if I gave it him, and apparently contented with a 'brown'. He let life roll by in front of him, and took from it as little as he gave.

If you stay for any time at an inn looking down on one of the great tramp highways, you will see the same faces, the same clothes, the same battered hats, the same splay feet, pass and repass your window at intervals of a day or two; for many of these tramps, having found a string of two or three comfortable wards, will spend, like summer ghosts, the whole of the warm season haunting the same countryside. Congenital lack of candour, the desire to please their interlocutor, sheer muzziness of brain, or sheer ferocity, make it difficult to discover what may be the ideal of this brown flotsam. Their universal and official shibboleth has it that if they could only get a steady job and a nice little cottage they would settle down with the missus and kids and live respectable under the parson for evermore. The more candid of the men, when they were assured that their reply would make no difference in the number of coppers destined for them, confessed almost without exception that their ideal was to have a pension like a soldier. This appeared to be, as it were, the good establishment that every middle-class man wishes for his daughter. As a matter of fact, a very considerable percentage of the innumerable old soldiers who solicit alms along the road do have such pensions, and for perhaps three glorious nights out of the month are kings of the earth – kings over draggled and carneying subjects, as aware as their monarch himself of when pay-day comes round, and where the floodgates of oblivion will be let loose.

One very hot day last month, on a high-road broad and parched, stretching out level and without end beneath an empty sky, on a day so hot that the very larks were silent, and the twittering duologue of the linnets sounded as if it came from dusty little throats, I sat down in the long grass under the hedge by the side of a very inviting and swarthy tramp. He suddenly brought out in a rich soft voice, without any inquiry of mine –

'Lord! I'd like to be a workhouse master. By —— I'd like to be the master of a workhouse! Wouldn't I give the casuals champagne and porter-house steaks one day, and wouldn't I wollup them the next!'

A little time before I had walked along the same road in a drenching rain with a German tramp, tiny, wizened, ferret-faced, and with the extravagant gestures of an actor. With his right hand he held firmly to my sleeve, and from a great scroll of manuscript in his left he read passages from a poem about the beauties of nature abounding in the forest near the town of Carlsruhe in Baden. His whole being was engrossed in his work, he saw neither road, sky, nor sea; only from time to time he broke off to exclaim, 'This is very pleasant, you will like this very much!' His life-history, varied and unromantic as it was, would occupy too much space in the telling, but *his* consoling thought was that Wagner had been too poor to possess an overcoat whilst he was writing his music drama of *Rienzi*; and hope, ardour, confidence and romance were in his eyes and voice when, at saying farewell to me, he uttered the words: 'There is a Russian author, I forget his name, who has just bought an estate on the Volga for 700,000 marks; once he was only a tramp like me.' He was quite illiterate and his poem was atrocious, but he said that people on the road were very kind to him; one gentleman at Brighton had given him board and lodging for three nights.

Thus between the fragrant hedgerows the townsman newly come into his heart of the country will see this vast body of dun-coloured units driven backwards and forwards like ghosts upon the tides of the winds. For him, indeed, they must remain ghosts; as a rule he will feel the repulsion that we must all feel for those who are outside our world, outside our life, outside our praise, outside our banning or our cursing.

They are as much outside pity or regret as are the innumerable dead; they have gone back into the heart of the country and have become one with the ravens, the crows, the weasels, and the robins, picking up the things that we have no use for, from such small parcels of ground as we have not enclosed.

To the really inveterate townsman every weatherbeaten man or woman that he passes along the road is a tramp. It is as difficult for him to distinguish a genuine waggoner from a fraudulent tooth-comb maker as to tell rye grass from permanent pasture, or the mistle from the song-thrush. But gradually as he sinks deeper into the life of the country, passes during weeks and months between hedgerows and begins to note differences between the songs of birds, he will acquire a sort of instinctive knack of distinguishing between one sort and the other. The differences lie in minute things, in the poise of the head, the way of setting down the foot, the glance of the eye in passing. The townsman may make experiments in reclaiming the tramp – like Hercules he will wrestle with death for possession of one soul – but once the man is really dead there is no recalling him. He may set him up and endow him with tools, clothes, a place to live in and all the fair simulacra of our corporate life; he may keep him propped up for a day, for a week, for a month, for a year, but sooner or later the body will collapse and the soul once more be at one with the Maker of the hedgerow. To try preventing the real tramp from following out his life is like attempting to stifle the words of a poet or the sighs of a miserable lover. But if he ever come to examine meticulously, the townsman will discover that amongst these ghosts there whirl past some that still cling to life, that claim our pity and need such helping hands as the gods will let us give. Once, when I lived on a hillside below a common, I came home in the evening down through the furze and saw a faded old man and a faded old woman, with the usual perambulator of the traveller, encamped in a small sandpit. They were both painfully clean, and beneath an arbour of gorse bushes had an odd air of being Philemon and Baucis cast upon an unsympathetic world, where the very twilight of the gods had passed away. But what struck me most and most disagreeably was to see my own favourite yellow Orpington cock dancing up and down in front of the old man full a quarter-of-a-mile away from my gate. I imagined that he was one of those people who can whisper poultry out of a field, just as gipsies are said to do with stallions. But on reaching home I saw my cock contentedly dusting himself in an ash-heap, and when I went a couple of hours later to the post, passing the old people's settlement, I saw that the yellow cock had been reinforced by a gigantic lop-eared rabbit, an aged tortoise-shell cat and a battered accordion. These were the Lares and Penates of this ancient couple, the signs that, evil days having fallen upon them and the hatred of the workhouse having forced them to take the road, they still clung desperately to as much as they could carry in a perambulator of their former householder's dignity; they still clung desperately to life, the old man still hoping for fruit trees to prune, the old woman still cherishing her ideal of many beehives to look after.

Such cases as this – of people whom it would be possible to help – are, of course, innumerable, perhaps less to be numbered between the hedgerows and across the fields than even in the towns; for so slender in the country is the margin between keeping on going and folding one's hands that the real wonder is not that the poor are always with us. The high-road at one bend or another, or climbing to the skyline, will inevitably take our townsman past a great and gaunt building – the inevitable last earthly home of how many! – and the sight of aged forms in a uniform brown, sitting as if they were part of the patterns of a dado along the bottom of the tall blank wall, must almost as inevitably give our traveller pause. Here are more of the dead, more men outside the world, withdrawn into a mysterious state which is neither work nor leisure, neither rest nor anything but merely waiting; and waiting for what? I have often wondered what castles in the air these particular poor mortals could find it in them to build; perhaps the territory upon which these edifices are to arise will only be found on the other side of the last stream of all. I have never had the heart to enquire. But perhaps the real speculation in most of their minds is as to how many currants will be contained in the piece of 'spotted dick' that will form their Sabbath pudding.

When I think of all the remarkable men I have known who have finished their careers in these last resting-places and of all the august women, I am filled for the moment with a sense of my own extravagant unworthiness or with a fear for my own future. The country, I think, breeds individualities stronger, more vigorous, precisely more remarkable than are bred in those stretches of territory where the cotton shuttles fly in millions or trains burrow under the ground. Or perhaps it is only I who have been fortunate enough to come into contact with no man true to type and no women who have not achieved much or suffered greatly. I think, for instance, of Ned Post, a wizened, blear-eyed, boastful, melodramatic old ruffian, who was the last of a family of great mole catchers – a man with an inherited gift in its line as great as that of Bach's. I think of Swaffer, who had year after year taken prizes as the best ploughman of his country, who had crossed the Atlantic in the sixties to take the prize as the best ploughman in the State of Pennsylvania. I think of old Mark Swain, who founded a poetic and remarkable religion of his own; and I think of old Mrs Sylvester who had for thirty years kept going a small four-acre holding, out of which she supported a bedridden husband and two dissolute sons. And all these remarkable people died in the same workhouse in the same winter week. These things, of course, cannot be helped; and perhaps it is merely the touch of genius, or of that immense patience which is so good a substitute for genius, which each of these people possessed; perhaps it was only that indefinable touch in men that, making them care more for their work than for its profits, dropped them down those steps of this world which have only one lowest stage.

But it has often occurred to me to wonder how their particular villages, hamlets or homesteads get on without them. For sooner or later the townsman in the country will discover how delicately balanced is the human economy of the village even in these days of distributed resources. In each community there is, as a rule, only one of a trade, and, if that one drop out, go into the Union, or, what is worst, if he become incensed against our particular townsman, the result will be hindrances most disastrous, most disturbing for the customer's daily life.

Turning out of the byways and lanes that run from each of the villages round a market centre, there will come hooded vehicles drawn by old and gaunt horses. On the big roads these will seem to our townsman quaint or merely negligible. But each will be driven by an autocrat, grim, jovial, loquacious or saturnine – an autocrat having indispensably that gift which is said to be inborn among the dwellers on thrones, the gift of memory. Before the gate of each cottage on the way to market the cart will draw up, and from the doors will issue suppliant women with their petitions, to which, all being well, the tyrant will give his gracious assent.

The image is by no means so very far-fetched, for should the carrier, as the phrase is, 'get his knife into' any particular household upon his route, he can cause its inhabitants nearly as much personal inconvenience as any form of bad government. And the results are almost as far-spreading if he fall ill or die. I lived at one time in a farmhouse some ten miles from a cathedral and market city, and the stackyard was used by a carrier whose tattered old vans and dilapidated horses, with ankles fringed like those of a Cochin China fowl, occupied the tumbled-down barns and leaking sheds. It gave one a very good opportunity of studying means of communications in the backwaters of the very heart of the country. And indeed the carrier's route to D——— was an artery.

Towards eight o'clock of a morning there was a sort of informal gathering in our yard. Children came with notes from outlying farms; the baker brought empty sacks, women patterns to be matched; the clergyman's wife her books to be changed at the circulating library; gamekeepers came from afar with rabbits by the hundred slung before and behind them like fur garments. The dismal and dingy old cushions were fitted on to the seats, and up a shaky ladder climbed the market women in their best clothes, with great baskets on their arms, ready for the three-hours' drive, with their feet on the dead rabbits, stifling in the smell of paraffin, of sugar, of stable hartshorn, of road dust and of humanity. Slowly jolting out of the yard, so that all the heads jerked one way and all back together, beneath the great elms and down towards the highway the swaying caravan set forth, with the tongues already going.

No man of the world of towns would believe what those tongues utter; to listen is to have the pleasant country rides converted into something blighted. In the thatched cottages there dwell covetousness, drink, theft, incest – Heaven knows what! In the great farmhouses there are covetousness, drink, theft, land-grabbing, sheep-stealing, swindling of the illiterate – God knows what! And Heaven knows what of truth there may dwell beneath the cloud of witness that goes up from that swaying machine with the drooping horse and drooping whip-lash. That something of truth is there we may well concede; the carrier's cart hides amongst its other microbes no microbe of imagination or substantial invention. I am inclined to believe that almost every 'scandal' that one hears in the carrier's cart is true to fact, and only as to motive exaggerated. What is wanted is the remembrance that poor humanity is poor humanity, that there are in the world pitfalls, gins, temptations – works of the devil, as they had it in the old days.

And the townsman between the hedgerows must remember that the countryman has a prodigiously long memory. There was a farmer I knew well, an aged, apple-checked, hook-nosed, blue-eyed creature, with just a suggestion of frailness to add charm to his personality and to the fringe of white hair that fell below his old weather-green hat. He had not as far as one could tell a vice. He was popular with his hands, all of whom he had retained for many years; he was cheerfully obeyed by his sons; he was up every morning at daybreak, and he brewed his own ale. One day he had a stroke, and there was an end of his activities.

'Well, and that's a judgment on old F——!' a peasant woman said to me. F—— was then seventy-two. At the age of eighteen he had committed some fault – no doubt with a girl, but I have forgotten. So the paralysis was a judgment on him for *that*. The countryside could not set any other sin to his account; but it had a memory casting back over the half of a century. Assuredly it is not here, but rather in the streets of the towns, that there grows the Herb Oblivion.

And inasmuch as there is not one of us without his secret that under the searching eyes and ever-waiting ears of small communities eventually comes to be disclosed – inasmuch as there is no man without covetousness, hardness of heart, intemperance, or whatever may be the seven deadly sins, the catalogue of remembered crimes will seem to fall like a blight across the bright countryside and for a time at least dim its greenness for our townsman. But gradually the problem will readjust itself, and that particular aspect over the hedgerows will become, as it is to the carrier himself, part of the day's journey.

Arrived at his market-town, that autocrat will stable his horse at the 'Leg of Mutton'; will leave his cart in the inn-yard for parcels to be thrown into it, and will set about ordering chicken-meal, butcher's meat, No. 50 cottons, paraffin casks, volumes of poems, bedding-out plants, branding irons and sheep-bells. And towards nightfall in summer, or long after dark in the winter, my friend Grant would be once more in the yard – with a pleasant smell of hot dust, or a romantic gleam of lamps under the great thatched eaves of the barns – and we should fall upon him for our joints, our weekly papers, our candles, and our bodily food, our physical and spiritual illuminants.

One evening a wild, prolonged and incomprehensible drumming penetrated into our house; it brought all the white aprons of the village to the doors, and finally to the banks of our small stream. In a turmoil of foam, its neck wildly elevated, its eyes starting, its hoofs kicking up the very pebbles from the bottom of the brook, the carrier's horse lay, pinned down into the water beneath the van itself. Left alone for a minute whilst the carrier was taking lemonade in our kitchen – the day was terribly hot – the horse had wandered to drink at its accustomed spot; the van, tilting over upon the bank, had done the rest.

The result was desolation in the village and in many outlying homesteads. To be left with one's three-days' provisions at the bottom of the brook is, in places where shops are ten miles apart, as much of a hardship as would be entailed, say, by having for that space of time the bailiffs in the house for rates. And what more can a tyrant do than that? The whole current of one's domestic life – a thing with which, in the country, one's peace of mind is very much bound up – is disturbed and rendered distressing. One is forced to ask all sorts of favours, and to stand cap in hand before peasants whose rigidity of soul one discovers, enhanced by one's own physical emptiness. Mr Cary, the sexton, may have a fowl or two to spare, and Mrs Hood certainly has carrots. The point is whether Cary, who has never – one remembers at this instant – touched his hat or received twopence from us, can be brought by softness of voice or praise of his walking-stick to part with one of his chickens; and how in the world is one to soften the heart of Mrs Hood, who married a gentleman's coachman, and has in consequence a rigid back and a great personal dignity?

Such treatment of the subject may appear humorous, but it is sober enough when one needs must undergo these humiliations. It is customary to regard the rustic as servile in his habits and his mind; but one of the first things that the townsman journeying between the hedgerows will discover is how very little he counts, how very little he is 'placed' amongst the real peasants. His clothes, his air of command, his glance of the eye, will secure for him in the towns ready touchings of the cap and profuse 'Sirs' spicing the speech of inferiors. And as long as he keeps to the railway stations and inns of the country he will as likely as not receive the same courtesies. But once between the hedgerows, he will be conscious of a struggle. He may be, our townsman, eminent in the tea or upholstery trade, in the world of letters or of horse-breeding; it is all one to the peasant. The other day, in my own village, I heard a wealthy lady lamenting that the little girls did not curtsey to her: she had been in the place six months. Yet I know residents who for many years have paid their way, who in the outer world are celebrated, who occupy fine houses and dress simply but well – who, in short, are 'good' people – and the only man who touches his cap to them is the policeman. The townsman, in fact, will be struck at first by the sense of being appallingly alone and unplaced so far as his inferiors go. He may be 'called on', may drive in a carriage and pair, and may distribute blankets and brandy; but the backs of the hedgers will remain obstinately towards him when he passes, and sheep-shearers will keep their eyes down upon the fleeces falling between their legs. It will be impossible to engage in conversation with the better farm hands. Respect may be purchased from some sort of men in stained corduroys, at hedge-alehouses, for pints of beer; but the men and women who have a stake in the village, who are 'old-standers', will remain for long years wonderfully stiff in the back and arms. And the stages by which recognition will come will be curious and definite. The hat-touching test is, after all, the most convenient standard, and, looked into carefully, after allowance has been made for differences in different localities, the process will be much as follows. After six months or a year in the heart of the country the townsman will find himself invited to become, say, vice-president of a quoits club; he will find himself at the club dinner the neighbour of the jobbing gardener of the village and of the permanent road-mender. He will offer them cigarettes at the end of the meal. After that, perfunctorily and when no one is looking, these two will touch their caps to him. But in the publicity of the village street, or if they happen to be walking with other men, they will still turn away their heads, or look with a stony and unrecognising gaze.

The countryman is, in fact, extremely loth to come to subjection; something does force him to acknowledge the existence of the Quality, something indefinite that he obeys involuntarily and with dislike; and he is more than loth to pay cap-service to any newcomer, since he aspires always to shake off the yoke. The touch of the cap in secret places is due perhaps as much to shyness as to anything else – an involuntary action of muscles that know nothing else to do. Backed up by other men, however, and unwilling to let the others know that he has come to heel at all, the countryman will face the matter out with as brave a heart as he can. So that at a certain stage the townsman in a winter dusk may pass six men going home from work together, and every one of them may be personally known to him, yet not one of them in his dun-coloured clothes, with his rush basket over his back, will move an eyelid in recognition. But, after many years of paying his way and of being got used to, for no earthly reason and at no given signal, passing the corner of the churchyard on a Sunday evening, when all men conscious of their best clothes are at their stiffest and least amenable, the townsman will find himself greeted by a whole chorus of 'Fine evenings!' Then indeed he has received his accolade and has found his place and welcome home.

It is almost necessary to write of the return to the land thus from the standpoint of the comparatively well-to-do. For the poor and the working classes of the towns never really go back. One in five hundred may be attracted by a 'good job', but perhaps not one in a hundred goes seeking, however unconsciously, a country spirit. As a rule, town life weakens the fibres of the muscles, more particularly the muscles of the leg, so that a dock labourer however robust is apt to break down hopelessly when put to a job of hay-making. I knew, indeed, one very fine figure of a Covent Garden porter. He had a face that, seen under a high tier of fruit baskets, appeared like a sun trying to burst out from under a pillar of fog, and, at the side of the Opera, he could run backwards and forwards across the pavement from dawn to noon without perspiring. Some odd whim sent him down, in his own words, 'to see where things bloomin' well growed', and he took kindly and good-humouredly to a piece of charlock weeding in an immense wheatfield, in which even his considerable bulk was as the tiniest of specks in a whole downside of mustard-yellow. He liked the work very well; but ten days sent him into the infirmary, and, after going on tramp for a month or so, doing a hand's turn here and there, he returned to the piazza and work that he could do. He was the only really competent London workman that I have come across between the hedgerows, and except for the fact that beneath a Wiltshire sun you could get such a thirst that even somebody's blooming patent lemonade tasted good – except for that, I extracted from him no sign of any mental revelation that had come to him in the silent places of the great hills. He had had the patent lemonade served out to him amongst the other haymakers of a temperance farmer, and the fact that it was poured out of beer jars gave a touch of savage and rueful indignation to his voice.

He, as I have said, was a really competent man, in the sense that he had work in a town and could do it efficiently. But most of the rural immigrants that I have met have been men, for one reason or another, disqualified or disabled. Thus I have found employed or seeking employment a trick diver and swimming master, whose eyes had failed owing to the pressure of water beneath the surface, a Drury Lane super who had lost his voice, a metropolitan policeman who had been treated once too often by a publican, and several city clerks whose health had failed. But, as far as my own observation goes, I should say that good men in good work never do go back to the land. How should they indeed?

Towards Michaelmas or near Lady-Day* – in any of the seasons of the quarters – you will see beneath the highway elms or over the white roads of the downs, crossing bridges, at elbow-like little angles of sunken lanes, tall waggons covered with tarpaulins that bulge in ways that the eye, accustomed to the rounded lumps of corn sacks or of bales of wool, must needs deem barbarous and strange, with the inverted leg of a chair sticking out of a fold or the handle of a saucepan through an eyelet hole of the tarpaulin – you will see high-poled waggons ponderously blocking the road, creeping onward with a great gravity as if in pensive thought. Perched on the shafts will be a child with a cat in her arms, and hanging to one of the side-boards a wicker cage, through whose

---

* **Michaelmas and Lady-Day**: Michaelmas is 29 September, the Festival of St Michael and all Angels; Lady-Day is the Annunciation, 25 March. Ford's Catholicism is evident in this way of dividing and defining the year. Quarter Days are traditionally when rents are due and magistrates are chosen. The other two days are 24 June and 25 December.

interstices there dazzle the orange bill and coaly feathers of a blackbird. Here is the countryman on the move – a whole family, a whole unit of the human race in suspension betwixt failure and new hope, betwixt the worse and the better or the worse and the worse. Suddenly the farm waggon, from being the dull transporter of dusty bags and fat sheep covered in with nets, is transformed into a ponderous machine of fate; suddenly a family, fixed and immovable, tied down to the ground with all the weights of imped-imenta as a balloon is tethered by heavy bags of sand – suddenly this family has become nomadic. Its tables are woefully inverted beneath the sky; its memorial cards, these milestones of life that are the most precious decorations of all cottage walls, are packed away in some obscure corner of the creaking car.

But just because these flittings are so ponderous and so slow, they are very costly. I have seen blue farm-carts with red wheels in the courtyard of the British Museum, and only yesterday in the New Road a cart with the inscription, *So and So: Carrier, Crowborough, Frant and Tunbridge Wells to the Spur Inn, Borough High Street*, was loading up the furniture of a tinsmith who was migrating to the town of the Pantiles. But this flit would cost five pounds: the tinsmith had come into money and had bought a little business of his own. He was not in any case going into the country, but pursuing a fragment of London across the Weald of Kent. How then, lacking State-subsidised pantechnicons or something of the sort, or municipal moving loans or something of the sort, is the town mechanic without legacy or windfall to transport his goods, his wife, his children or himself back to the land? The people moving from the austere government building were of course seeking the idyllic; but they too no doubt had some means, and could possibly work as well in their cottage as in Bloomsbury. They did not at least pass from a big wage to a low, and incur a great expense at a time of transition when there is inevitably least in the purse. The town mechanic might indeed be willing to move into the country, but how is he to get there?

It is difficult enough for the countryman to 'move' sometimes. In a remote down-land district there was a farmer I knew rather well who was noted for keeping his hands for very long periods. He was envied, moreover, because he managed to pay them less than any farmer of those parts. He still paid on the scale of the now nearly obsolete great hundred – six score instead of five – for any piecework, a once universal custom that education of the farm hands has nearly killed in the land. On one of his down roads I once met a waggoner I knew. The man was notoriously good with horses, steady, sober, and ready to sit up all night for a week with a sick mare. Now his whip drooped, his feet dragged in the cart ruts – and he was sobbing.

It was because he simply could not get away from his master. It was a physical impossibility. Other farmers were ready to take him – but he could not 'move'. He had six children; he earned fourteen shillings a week. How in the world was he to get away? He could not save; his master jeered at the idea of advancing him money to move with, or of lending him a waggon. There he was – there, it seemed, he must simply remain. And this, I discovered, was the secret of my friend keeping his hands so long. Taxed with it, he merely chuckled. He had selected all his men for their large families; he lent them his waggons to move in with over the heartbreaking downland roads. And they never got away.

This, naturally, is an extreme case; but I seldom meet a Michaelmas move without thinking of that successful farmer's chuckle. They never get away. And it is much the same with the labourers in the great towns of the South.

In parts of the North it is different. Round about Middlesbrough, for instance, you may judge fairly well of the state of farming by the attendance on the second day of the annual statute fairs. If things are well with the country, the farmer can offer attractive terms to the extra hands that it is always the farmer's first luxury to indulge in, and the men are ready to be hired. But if the terms are not sufficiently good, the farm hand will simply go back to the furnaces – for a year, for two, or for three, and, iron work being heavy, the muscles do not deteriorate as in so many other trades. Thus in these particular parts there is a constant flux between slag-heap and moorland.

But as a general rule town is town, and country country; and it is only in special districts that along the high-roads you will meet with strong-armed men passing from one to the other; and, except for the automobiles, which as yet have done little to change the face of the country, the great roads are singularly deserted. Tramps, carriers, postmen, farm-waggons, farmers' gigs, governess carts, flocks of sheep with their pungent odour, droves of cattle with their piercing and mild eyes, cyclists passing in whisps – all these do not contrive to make a population for highways that were meant to reverberate every quarter of an hour beneath the heavy wheels of stage coaches. (And, indeed, the hard surface which Macadam invented first began to render the horse obsolescent, since no hoof can really stand much fast work upon the iron of our great roads.)

Level, white and engrossed beneath the sky, as if they too had purposes, as if they too sought some sort of lovers' meeting of their own, where they intersect at the journey's end, the great highways run across the green islands.

The small by-roads, the sunken lanes, all the network of little veins that bring, as it were, tributary drops of blood, go off from side to side as if they were the individuals of a marching body dropping out to do sentry duty in hamlets off the line of march. They have about them an air of secrecy, as if between their hedgerows rather than on the great roads we may learn what is at the heart of the country. Upon them the townsman will meet more often little children going upon the tiny errands that make up the home-life of the countryman; carts will be few, and the tramp will be a rare visitor. But even in the sunken lanes the note of the country road is one of solitude, and if one desires privacy one will find it there almost more certainly than in the fields themselves. Foot passengers take the footpaths in all but the worst weather, and the by-roads are little enough used save by an occasional grocer's cart or the parson's son upon his bicycle with his tennis-racket across the handle-bars.

Seen from a height, a countryside may appear extraordinarily populated; thatched roof may almost touch thatched roof, and garden-tree twine its branches into the apple boughs of the next orchard; but the real countryman travels so little that, save where there are many 'residents', the population of both high-road and lane is extravagantly small. He works, the countryman, in his nearest fields; his wife stays indoors and mends things; it is only the fringe, the hangers-on, the *dilettanti*, the children going to or from school, and the distributors of the means of existence, who make use of the roads of either class. They are used, the roads, by all sorts of inhabitants of fields and thickets; the hedgerow birds have a tameness, an unconcern that they would show in no coppice, where the presence of an intruder will be heralded by all sorts of warning notes, sibilant and rancorous, or by the wild flutter of arising wood-pigeons. I remember once having fallen into a sort of reverie upon a road, and come to a halt unconsciously. I do not know what was in my mind, something pleasant and engrossing, I think, because the day was hot, the hedgerows sweet and umbrageous, and the long high-road sloped down into the distant blue of the Devonshire sea. Suddenly, many yards away, a strange little beast with a fantastic gait appeared to be covering the ground with tiny bounds. Seen from the front it was impossible to recognise it; it had the amble of no creature that one is familiar with. I stood still, and it advanced, paying no manner of attention to me. It assumed a reddish hue, its progress took the aspect of a series of tiny bounds, its tail in fore-shortening lengthened out. It was a squirrel – and it passed right over my foot.

The episode was disagreeable to me, because in my part of the country they say that when the woodland beasts no longer regard you, you are 'fey' – as good as a ghost. But it gave the measure of the solitude of that particular highway that so shy a beast as a squirrel could use a road for its passage upon any errand. And it travelled with an engrossed certitude, as if it were very assured of no danger or interruption. And indeed I had met no one for the last half-hour, and I met no one else till I got to Kingsbridge, a matter of three miles. Yet this was a main coast road leading to a market town, the metropolis of that peninsula.

Even on market-days, when once a week the highways assume the air of processional routes, it is only a small fraction of the country populations that shows itself. There will be farmers in their gigs; if the day be fine their wives will be with them too, and the hearts of the shopkeepers will be rejoiced. (I use the word 'gig' generi-cally for the farmer's conveyance. It is very largely a matter of fashion or of roads. Thus, round Canterbury the farmer almost invariably uses some kind of dogcart, whilst in Devonshire and Cumberland he goes to market mostly on horseback, and round Salisbury the roads are filled with enormous and dusty versions of the familiar governess car.) Farmers, stock-breeders, veterinary surgeons, horse dealers, a small army of cattle drovers and succes-sive companies of sheep, cattle, pigs, and even turkeys at times, will on these market-days pass in a pageant, out in the morning, home in the afternoon when the hour of the ordinary is passed. For an hour or two of the day the shops will be filled, the streets be impass-able, the stairs of the inns be thronged with men falling over each other's legs, in a fine atmosphere of malt liquors and a fine babel of prices and the merits of foodstuffs. But before nightfall each partic-ular little heart of the country will once more have discharged its rustic blood as with one great weekly pulse; the dust or the mud of the highways will bear the impress of the innumerable feet of sheep, and silence and solitude will once more descend between the hedgerows, along which the white forms of owls will beat without sound. And so it will be all round the year.

But even the pulse-tide of market-days will not dislodge from their crannies and pockets the great populations of the country. The real labourer will go on working over his furrows, whether wheat fall below starvation price, or wool rise from fivepence to tenpence halfpenny. So that upon the roads the townsman come into the country will not make any intimate acquaintance even with the outward aspects of the whole body politic of the country. He will learn, first, how little he or his great town matters; and, lastly, how closely knit is the organisation of great stretches of territory that at first he will regard as so many miles of inhabited country occupied at haphazard by men having little organisation and less connection the one with the other. What will have swayed his particular town will in the country matter nothing. What will matter will be the price of things in the nearest marketplace or cathedral city. Once out of his particular London the townsman will find himself come into the spheres of influence of innumerable places of small magnitude. 'Going to town' will not be taking a railway journey to any great city; it will mean a short jaunt to Ashford, to Shrewton, to Kendal – or it may mean hardly more than going to the single shop of the next village. And going to town for the inhabitants of the small centres will mean going to centres only relatively more important – to Exeter, to Leicester, to Devizes, to Manchester, or to Carlisle. And in each of these places the townsman will discover new trade-marks, new puddings, new newspapers, new specifics, new celebrities, new names to honour. His own standards will not any more count; his best known will be the utterly ignored; and he will discover that in coming to his particular heart of the country, in searching for his Islands of the Blest, his fountain of youth, he will have gone through a sort of purification. He will have lost, along with his old landmarks, his very identity. And only very, very gradually will he take to himself a new form, a new power of influence for good or evil, a new knowledge, and even a new appel-lation. For quite assuredly some nickname will be assigned to him.

He will grow wise in time; he will get to know all the highways and lanes, and having exhausted their aspects and their lore, will take to the field paths. But even there – and there more than ever – he will have driven in upon him that fact of the extraordinary solidity and solidarity, the extraordinarily close grain of life in the heart of the country. It will depend upon himself whether or no he will ever force a way somewhere beneath its close-textured skin; whether he will take, as it were, real roots in the soil, or still for his social and mental support will call in aids from outside. He will have come to the heart of the country for rest; he will, if he is to be at one with it, find himself engaged only in a new struggle.

CHAPTER II

Across the Fields

THE wheat, the pastures, the slow beasts, birds, flowers and the little foot-bridges from which we may look into the dark waters of clear brooks, the hum of insects and the dewdrops that form a halo round our shadows when we walk across the fields in the moon-light or at dawn – all these parts of what we call Nature must of necessity take the second place, fill up the second phase of a country life. Being men, we must first settle our human contacts; then we may step over the stiles or pass between the kissing-gates. We must have found our *pied-à-terre*, our jumping-off place; we must set up our tripod before, as it were, we can take our photographs. We must have studied our maps, have asked our ways, have got the 'lie of the land'.

This is no more than saying that we must have taken our bed at the inn, or have furnished our cottage and discovered where the nearest butcher has his shop; we must have 'settled down' either in body or in spirit. Reversing the course of history, we must learn the highways which were built last before we can master the oldest ways of all – the field-paths. How long the first stage may be in its passing through is a matter that each man settles with his soul; it is essentially a matter of how much interest he can take in the practical side of his settling down. There are men so happily made that their pleasant lives are spent in doing little tasks in their rockeries or passing the time of day at tennis in walled gardens. They find, as it were, freedom in prisons; whilst others breathe only when they have the turf beneath their feet and are out of sight and sound of the roadside hedgerows.

I do not know that these latter penetrate more deeply, really, into the life of the country, but I am certain that they draw the deeper breaths. They take, as it were, the short cuts across life and, avoiding their fellow-men who present the more harrowing problems to the mind, they float along a stream of minute facts that afford solace, distraction or rest. There is, after all, nothing so soothing as to watch the growth of grasses, and no man to be envied so much as he who can keep his mind for so long tranquil. If the high-roads might lead us to some palace of human truth, somewhere along the footpaths, between a wood track and an oak-bole, we might find Nirvana and the Herb Oblivion.

We may find, too, the country in its undress, since the footpaths lead us to back doors or through stackyards, whilst to the high-roads farms and cottages turn their lace-curtained windows and their decorous drives. I had an equestrian friend who had passed during a number of years on a main road a square, stuccoed, dull box that was known as New Place. He visited it during several croquet seasons, and, entering it always through the front door, saw no reason to think that it was other than just a new place like any other. But one day, being afoot on the dull highway, he saw a kissing-gate in the hedge and a track that led across a broad bend of the wood. He passed outside a stone-walled stackyard, and at a pleasant distance there raised itself a charming, mellowed structure of red brick with six gables that offered to the rolling fields a glance, a yellow of lichens and a tracery of wall-pears it had taken three centuries to attain to. He could not fix the place in his mind; he could not find a name for it; it seemed miraculous that in a land he knew so well there could have been such a house unknown to him. Then he realised that it was the back of New Place. The front had been stuccoed and squared to suit the tastes of the 'fifties. It offered that view to the new high-road; but the ancient path, that had been there before any house at all had stood, had led him to the other and the lovelier aspect.

The footpath, indeed, much more than doubles the attraction of the countryside, since the tracks, leading mostly from cottage to cottage, are almost innumerable. It is one of those things to which one hardly ever gets used – it is one of those things that change alike the aspect of countrysides and of the men who work upon them. I had walked a certain road for many days; I had seen for many days a certain labourer, not on the face of him estimable, slouching at night towards his beer-house. Suddenly, one evening, I saw this man, his rush basket slung across his back, with a bundle of rabbit-parsley tucked into the thongs; he was descending, so slowly that he appeared to hang in air, an ungracious Ganymede in fustian, over a hurdle that had appeared merely to close a gap in a hedge. Behind him, in the grass there ran the sinuous snake of a pathway, wavering as if for companionship beside a coppice or a little straw. And it was a relief – a clearing of the air. For the man will appear no longer a loafer, sustained from hour to hour through the day by the thought of beer, or kept in suspense, as it were, by the cankerous artistry of self-indulgence. Here he was dropping into the road with limbs rendered heavy by work; he has become part of the body politic, one of those slow Titans who like wood-props keep up the inordinately weighty fabric of the State. He has gained dignity, and, since the number of inhabitants of my village is small, the whole village has gained dignity, and the whole world of which that village is the part with which I am best acquainted.

And with the discovery of a new footpath the countryside gains, to more than the extent of one new way, a feeling of liberty. The road you have traversed is less a begrudged piece of dust running between imprisoning hedges. You yourself are more free, since, if the wish moved you, here you could step aside; the fields on each side of the bridge seem more accessible, more your own and your neighbour's, less the property of an intangible landowner. For I think that it is inborn in humanity to resent another man's ownership in land. Those of us who belong to the land-owning class resent trespass on our acres; but the minute we become travellers beyond our own ring-fence we desire, even unreasonably, to make short cuts. There was once a Midland squire whose acquaintance I had made actually through trespassing upon his home paddock. He had then been irate so that his grey whiskers trembled. It seemed that he had just lost a right-of-way action and he thought I was part of a 'put up job', to flaunt his loss of the right-of-way case in his face. I had pleaded my ignorance of the neighbourhood, the greater freedom of our parts of the country in such matters; and I succeeded in convincing him so well of my innocence that he conducted me across his own kitchen-garden very amiably towards the high-road from which I never ought to have strayed.

I met this same gentleman later at an inn in a foreign countryside more or less my own; we took a walk together, after he had good-humouredly recognised me as the 'fellow who trespassed' – and I was horrified at the short cuts that he proposed to take to reach a certain church. We went over peasants' fields of tobacco, across the corner of a protected stag park, through a vineyard, and right into the door of the priest's cowshed before we emerged in the churchyard. My friend had made a bee-line, and it was only in the miraculous absence of a *garde champêtre* that we escaped a fine, since the squire actually plucked an apple from a wayside tree, tasted it, and swore it was like wood compared with a Ribston pippin. Outside his own circle of landed responsibilities he felt himself, in fact, to be a free Briton.

In a sense we are all that. The average Briton does indeed tremble at the thought of 'trespassing'. He trembles even unreasonably, since, except for the obviously poor, no penalty attaches to the offence. But he has a sort of shyness; it is hardly so much respect for the laws; he would dislike being turned off land, perhaps because it would mean a sort of 'setting down' for him. Yet the one of us most shy about trespassing will the most violently resent being impeded on a footpath once he is assured that it is a footpath. He will break down fences or furiously harangue gamekeepers; he will go his way – he will, more than any Hampden, assert his rights.

And because we are all lovers of our rights, we rejoice at the discovery of new paths. Here is a strip of land a foot wide, but inalienably the property of ourselves and our neighbours – a space of breathing-ground and of escape, where, as it were, we may remain within the letter of the law and yet cheat its spirit. Of course, if we are poor men, the path will have its dangers; a keeper, intent on preserving the privacy of his partridge nests, *may* lay a dead rabbit beside the path and, walking after us with a mate, swear it lay there just after we had passed. Then probably we shall be fined ten shillings. (I have known a footpath closed to all the cottagers of a village by this dread.) But essentially the footpath is a place on which we may all snap our fingers at Authority; so for that alone it is beloved.

And the paths, in most of England, are innumerable. I know whole tracts of country, forty miles long, in which there is hardly a field that one may not walk across or skirt. Thus, for instance, from Aldington Knoll you may pass under the nut boughs and oaken underwood of the Weald, thirty-seven miles, by wood paths, only going out of the shadow to cross a road, or where the timber has been newly felled. There are, of course, tracts of the Home Counties and the Midlands where, in the presence of the landowning spirit and the absence of a spirit of resistance, miles of fat fields shaded by elms are closed to the wayward foot. And there are immense moors and downs where the pedestrian may choose his own way by a compass across heather and ling or sheep turf and wild thyme, where the footpath ceases on account of so great a freedom of direction. But the country of parks and millionaires is not the country, but a sort of arid pleasure tract, and moors and plains are unhallowed by the work of the slow countrymen. For certainly, wherever he is busied about the hedgerows or in the wheat, there his lines of communication will be found. Their real cause for existence is to help him the more quickly to and from his work; and the farmer is not yet born so foolish as to hinder his own hours of labour.

Thus here, as in the print that is common in our hedge alehouses, and more common still in France, the man who works in the fields bears the brunt of the fray. It is true that you may trace – mostly on hill-tops – the old ways of communication, pilgrim ways that pass the remains of tiny chapels-of-ease and make, like the rays of a spider's net, either to the shrine of St Thomas or towards the ports from which men set sail for Compostella; there are broad soft roads across plains; there are bridlepaths that climb immense downs and in the softer bottoms are paved, still, with great flag-stones, and there are pack-tracks that have been abandoned for ever by the feet of mules. In the North of England, in the folded valleys and scars of the solitary hills, you may still, as it were, see the hoof-marks of the pack-horses the last of which made its last journey not twenty years ago. And the survivals of all those tracks do still add to the number of ways by which a man may travel across the fields. But they remain mere survivals; the reason for their existence having gone, they are seldom travelled; fences are being run across them more and more as the years go on. It is no one's business to keep them alive; so they are dying out.

Thus the footpath of the heart of the country tends to become more and more a means of access to work. And indeed it is there that we seem to feel the real heart-beats. On the roads the touch of the cities is still to be felt. Miles and miles away from any town one may be, nevertheless the road is a filament, a vein, running from one to another. The real footpath is the telephone, steering merely between countryman and countryman. It is true that in the vicinity of the house-congeries we may find footpaths that are degraded into cinder tracks. Broad and black – that colour for which the Nature of the fields seems to have so great an antipathy – they are bordered with fringes of grass so green that it appears, like the brilliant hues of aniline dyes, to be a coal-tar product. These tracks let the foot sink into them with a faint suggestion of being quick-sands. They pass cement cottages; dusty palings separate them from the sordid bits of spaded earth that always in the vicinity of a town seems to have a dun colour, a clay consistency, and a top-dressing of bluish meat tins. Reaching in his walk these antiseptic footways, the lovers of the country or the town lover feel an antipathy, heave perhaps a sigh, and, making for the nearest street, look out for a cab.

It is not that they will necessarily hate the town; what they will hate is the hybrid thing that is neither town nor country – that is, a product as it were of city fathers trying to bring themselves into a bucolic state of mind. 'Let us have either town or country unadulterated; let us have paths in which we shall meet humanity in undress or citizens decently clad!' he will exclaim. On these ways he will meet mechanics in broadcloth or the club-doctor of mean streets in clothes that are neither here nor there. Then he will seek swiftly either the shop-fronts, the artificial stone façades, the electric light standards and the faint smell of horse-dung and dust of the centre of a town; or he will return upon his tracks to where the path ran beneath nut bushes in the heart of a wood.

The false idlers of the country, the young ladies picking flowers, the retired solicitors, admirals, bankers, and racing touts, the village clergyman who thinks that his real sphere is, say, a smart West End parish, and who in consequence wears a querulous fold near the ends of his pursed lips, or that most townish of all inhabitants of the country, the student of nature – these, occasionally, with their infinite variations, are the most exotic products that one will meet on the footpaths. They have dropped, as it were, over the hedges, out of motor cars or desirable residences. They pass us like foreigners, and have haughty and challenging glints in their eyes. And I am almost tempted to say that the lovers of nature, the self-conscious students of birds or flowers – the modern Whites of Selborne – are themselves town products. The real countryman does not know much about these things. He accepts them, and would perhaps miss them; but it is hardly part of his nature to 'name' them. It would probably be disturbing to him to enquire too closely into the history, say, of the oil-beetle, that lustrous inactive creature that he crushes with his heavy foot in the hot dust of the roads.

It would disquiet him, it would disturb the simple and large outlines of his conception of life, just as to conceive of eternity, of infinity, or of the indefinite immortality of the soul would be disturbing to most of humanity. We live, poor creatures of a day that we no doubt are, in the midst of these mysteries, much as the countryman lives among beasts, fowls, and insects, one more mysterious than the other; but the consideration of these shivering abstractions humanity leaves to the priests, the metaphysician, and all the other soul doctors whom it agrees to regard as slightly extra-human. In the same spirit the countryman leaves Nature to the stranger who lives in the field. We crush with a careless foot a creature impeded by the dust. But supposing we knew that from egg to lustrous wing this beetle had made a journey more perilous and more miraculous than any Odyssey of Ulysses – that it had survived a chance of a million to one against its survival? Some such life-history as this is to be told of how many small creatures of the grasses and the brooks? It is laid, as an egg, anywhere in the earth; it must, when it comes forth, find a certain plant. Say a million eggs are laid; say a hundred thousand tiny creatures reach the plant. It must then ascend the stalk of that certain plant; it must reach the stamens of the flower, a dizzy journey in the course of which ninety thousand succumb to rain, to predatory insects, to birds, to the Will of God manifested in one way or another; there remain ten thousand in these flowers. There they must stay until a certain bee comes to gather honey: one thousand are able to hold to life till then. When the bee comes they must grapple to a certain spot of the bee's hairy thigh; they must be carried by the bee home to its cell: one hundred may reach the bee's cell. There, at the precise moment that the bee lays its egg, the beetle larvae must drop into the egg: maybe ten will do that; and maybe one, after having fattened on the life juices of the bee-grub, will come forth to the air a beetle – one survivor of a million! And it has gone through these perils, it has endured the fatigues, the hair-breadth escapes, the miraculous chances of this great journey, to be crushed by a hob-nailed boot before it has travelled one yard on the face of the earth. To what end?

For assuredly the countryman would ask, 'To what end?' The nature student has essentially a concrete mind. He observes, he registers. He sees little yellow birds with jerking tails gliding over the surface of a water-plant, searching in the hot sunlight meticu-lously for tiny insects. He notes the fact, and it is sufficient for him. But the countryman is either nearer God or nearer the necessities of life, put it in which way you will. He desires to know 'what is the good of the thing?' How much weight of seed-corn will so much nitrate-fertiliser add to the yield of his acre? – What is the good of an oil-beetle? he would ask, if it came into his head to consider.

Perhaps it is fortunate that he never does. For, surrounded as he is, overwhelmed as he is by the tremendous profusion, the inexplicable, seeming waste of Nature, he would inevitably come to ask that question which is the end of human effort.

I know a farmer – rather a good farmer – who came from Lincolnshire into Kent, and was in consequence called 'Linky' in our marsh parish. He became, perhaps on account of the change in the soil, singularly loquacious and singularly full of ideas. Things went wrong with him, and he began, as the saying is, to hear the grass growing.

Tall, gnarled, bony, with enormous joints all over his frame, he stopped me one day on a high-road and began to put all sorts of questions as to the good of things. What was the good of charlock? Why had God made bindweed and the turnip-flea? Why was a man to feel as if he were overlooked – bewitched? His old horse, who was cropping the hedge, nearly overturned the cart that contained a dilapidated turning-lathe; Linky had just bought it at a sale, not that he needed it, but because once, years before, it had come into his head that a turning-lathe might be a thing to possess. He caught the horse's rein furiously, pulled the beast into the road, and then, with a sudden, dispirited motion of his hand, let go the rein, and pointed over the ridge inland. 'The Union's there,' he said; 'and I feel it's calling me! I feel it.' He turned on me: 'Now, I ask you, sir, what's the good of all this? What's the good?'

He was not exactly dejected – in fact, his eyes, sunk beneath a grotesquely-bumped forehead, were remotely humorous. He looked over the plains on both sides of the ridge. There were things agrowing all over there, he said. All sorts of things. They scratched up fields and tried to make corn come; but weeds came with the blessing of God – weeds didn't need no help. Same with vermin as took his poultry; same with mildew as turned his dumplings sour in the larder. Well, now, what were all those things? What did it all mean? If so be the weeds had a right to be there, they were of some account. God looked after them and the vermin. Then where did *he* come in – he, Linky? Perhaps he wasn't of no more account than weeds or vermin. Then what was the good of going on?

Linky, of course, had been drinking a little. But, as far as I have been able to discover, it was that sort of thought that had made him take to drink. And, as a rule, so stern is the fight that Nature wages with the countryman that, once he begins to think that kind of thought, he *must* take to drink or one of the devils of the flesh. In consequence, the survivors, the men who keep to the land, are precisely those who do not look around them, and who do not name the beasts and the plants. Weeds are weeds, and vermin vermin. You kill them one with another, and there's an end of it. You must have a very firm belief that the fields are made for crops, the pastures for grass, and yourself the instrument of God's administering the earth, or you will very soon slacken in your struggle.

Man does not 'name' his fellow-strugglers, partly from indifference, no doubt, but also because he is afraid. I remember seeing a whole downside in central England white with a flower that I did not recognise. It was something like a bleached campanula, but square-stemmed and sweetly scented. There were several village children, with long black hair, big black eyelashes, and blue eyes – a type as unfamiliar as the flower – kneeling down and plucking the white blossoms, their hair sweeping the tops of the long grasses. I asked one the name of the flower. None of them knew, but they were picking them to put on the coffin of little Charley, who had been drowned in the mill-dam down the hill last Saturday night.

A sudden and violent death of a child is a thing so outstanding in country districts, that, up there in the white light of the sun, on the green of the grass, very high, the news seemed to make one see beneath the shadows of the massive trees far down in the hollow a deeper shadow. But no one in that countryside seemed to know a name for those flowers – neither the children nor the clergyman, nor even the schoolmistress. They were flowers that were used for putting on coffins – simply 'flowers' as we say, 'Let us get some flowers for the table'. And indeed such things are generally sorted roughly into broad categories – thus, most green things lacking flowers or odours are 'weeds', most gay-coloured blossoms not known to be poisonous are 'flowers', – and most white flowers are omens of death, since they are used to deck biers, and at such times alone are carried home. I always remember the tone of weary contentment with which an old lady, suffering much pain, received a gift of snowdrops brought in ignorance of the meaning attached to them. 'You're letting me go,' she said. 'I've wanted to go for a long time; now I shall.' And very shortly afterwards she died. No one else of her friends or family would have brought white flowers into her home.

White hawthorn, Madonna lilies, the white owls that screech, so it is said, outside lighted windows, white insects that sometimes fly in at the casement, in certain districts even daisies and marguerites and Scotch roses – all these things are ominous of death if they enter the house. I have even heard it said that certain feathery, and delicate moths that come very rarely to flutter round one's lamp at night, are the souls of the dead coming to summon away the living. The emblems of life are rarer; but in a Lancashire cottage I heard a sick girl say, when a friend brought her the first pink dog-rose of the season, 'Now I shall get well since I've lived so far round the year.' And to see the first swallow is, in certain parts, regarded as an assurance of life until these travellers return again over the seas.

In the same large way owls, hawks, jays, shrikes, and cuckoos are classified as vermin; swallows, robins, and sometimes wrens are given their names and regarded as sacred; edible birds, from pheasants to jacksnipes, are called game or wild fowl; and most song birds and such others as have brownish plumage are called, and hated as, sparrows. An American naturalist who covered half the globe and a portion of England in the forlorn hope of hearing a nightingale sing, had the fortune to hear Philomela herself called 'a sparrer'.

But this large acceptance of the pleasures afforded by nature implies no lack of appreciation. Upon the whole, I think the real countryman enjoys the sights, the sounds, the heat of the sun, and the odour that the earth gives off after rain – he enjoys them as much as and perhaps with a more pagan enjoyment than any of the townsmen, who get much of their pleasure out of books. A townsman will read pages of such passages –

'A linnet warbles, a bee drops over the hedge, the tips of the hawthorn petals commence to become brown, the odour of bean flowers is wafted from the neighbouring field' – a whole catalogue of rural sights and sounds, that will as it were 'waft an odour' of the country into the atmosphere of fog and gaslight. In the same spirit ladies who never cook will read old-world recipes, and 'book lovers' who have no still-room will smack their lips in imagination over cordials the concoction of which went out before stage-coaches died from the roads.

And coming into the country, the townsman will find that some of the glamour that he felt in his room attaches for him to the monotonous chaffinch as, with its shimmer of rose, purplish-brown and grey-white it drops, crying 'Pink, pink', from an elm bough into the long grass beside the footpath.

In the same way a person with a very good cook of her own will dredge flour into boiling milk, scorch her face above a wood fire, prepare passably, and eat and enjoy hasty pudding or frumity – things not unpleasant to the palate, though, save for the associations of their names, not really worth scorching one's face for. And I have known a sober friend seriously endanger his equilibrium by drinking my own mead on a summer day, rather because of the sound of the name than because the liquor is really delightful.

The countryman, of course, never eats hasty pudding save when some accident has taken his missus unprepared; frumity, even in Dorsetshire, he will no longer look at; mead he might drink in winter to keep off a cold when he cannot get hot rum with a lump of butter in it; but he will certainly not read 'Nature books', and he will certainly never get into the frame of mind that will make him transfer the thoughts of any book into his attitude *vis-à-vis* of Nature herself. He has a general phrase that he applies to all these things. 'It does you good…' It does you good to see the wheat go rippling in great waves up a twenty-acre field; it does you good to smell rain coming up on the south-west wind, to hear church-bells chiming melodiously across smooth grass, to hear the birds singing in the dawn, to watch hounds break covert, to stand gazing at a great sunset, to hear the jingle of harness as the horses come back from the hayfields in the moonlight.

Labourers, farmers or their womenfolk develop tastes in such matters. One man loves a frosty dawn, with the roads as hard as iron in the ruts; another likes the feel of the north wind on his hands. Another loves the coolness that comes with the sea wind only after immense heat in a long day; another, the peculiar tang of odour that rises with mist from the salt marshes. What may influence these tastes you never learn. The man I spoke of as loving a frosty dawn, told me (I met him at such a moment – a gnarled shepherd, a 'looker', as they call them, not much higher than my shoulders, with whiskers glistening with rime and his black clay pipe sending forth the tiniest wisps of smoke in the face of a blood-red sun) that on such a morning as that he was first breeched. No doubt, the pride of that transition from babyhood to boyhood sanctified such frosty mornings for ever in his mind. Perhaps association has most to do with it – perhaps the mere sensation of physical well-being. Who can tell?

But certain shadows and lights, certain winds that quicken the blood in the veins, certain cloud forms, the songs of certain birds, or certain views at certain times of day – one each of one or other of these things will undoubtedly give a 'moment' – the moment of the year – to every countryman. And these things hold him in a country that is every day losing its other attractions.

I know a country solicitor, a grave, unsentimental, taciturn man, who repressed with sternness any tendency towards imagination in his children or his clerks. He was offered an exceedingly lucrative partnership in London, and he refused it because of a sunset. It was a long valley that wound away between spurs right into the west, and there the sun always went down with an incredible glory, sending its light level along the bottoms, mirroring itself on flat stretches of mist or glistening in winding channels. At the eastward end a hill rose, and standing by a windmill the solicitor was accustomed to look at this sunset every Sunday evening. He had seen it for years and he could not leave it. And, indeed, this particular sunset view – it was seen between tall stone pines – attracted all the little town on Sundays. You met, on the path to the mill, the blacksmith, the grocers, the hotel-keeper's wife, the village lovers from hamlets all round, the squire's cook, and the Wesleyan minister. These people would gaze and gaze and go away without saying anything. No doubt for the blacksmith it sublimated the thoughts of the price of shoeing iron, and for the others, too, it put a fine or a tranquil glory into that moment of their existence. One rather inarticulate person once told me that the conflagration of the descended sun and the lights whirled heavenwards from the mists and pools reminded him of the Plains of Heaven. I fancy that he was thinking of Martin's picture of that name. On the other hand, a man of great taste, who had savoured, as a connoisseur does his wine, many famous views the world over, regarded such a sunset and remarked that it was very suburban.

That is the connoisseur, speaking from the outside; but the real peasant, the real pagan, loves nature and the earth inarticulately. After we have worked for long hours of long days in the years that beneath the sky are so long in turning, we get, even the most inarticulate of us, moments of sensuous delight from merely being in the place in which we are. The woodman, working alone in the thick woods, will at noon in the winter sunshine stand still and lean on his axe. In his small clearing he will feel as if he were in a church. (I have heard a man say so.) The sunlight will be warm, the silence absolute all round him, and the very sound of the other axes in the distance will be deliberate, reflective, as if sacred. Or the farmer, lying on his stomach in the dewy grass at twilight along the edge of a black coppice, waiting with his gun for the rabbits to enter dimly out of the burrows – in the shadows and the silence, beneath the brush of the owl's wing as it skims over him, he will feel the indefinite fear of the supernatural steal over him, a curious sense of mournful ominousness different altogether in kind from the dread that will beset him in any haunted house or churchyard.

One gets, if one be at all sensitive, odd little shocks and emotions in the fields. I have myself dug very late in a potato patch, after many hours in a hot day. There comes a time when one cannot leave work; one goes on as long as light holds, even if it be only the light of the stars. The whitened apple trunks stand out like the pillars of an aisle down by the hedge; the glow of the supper fire dances visible in reflection on the cottage ceiling, the sound of the brook becomes important in a windless dusk. And the air having grown cool after the sun had set, I have thrust my hand into the earth to feel for potatoes, and found it flesh-warm. After all the heat seemed to have departed from the world it was like suddenly coming in contact with a living being. I am, perhaps, over fanciful, but to me it has always seemed like finding the breast of a woman – as if Nature herself had taken a body and the heat of life.

But, indeed, in the intense solitude of field work the mind exhausts its material topics. And of material topics there are few enough in the country and its cottages; so that the mind of the man who is much employed along the hedgerows turns inwards very often and exhausts itself in metaphysical speculations. This is more particularly so at dusk, when not only is there little to think about but less to see. In the countryman's mind there arise superstitions about beasts and birds, theories of life and of the universe, even new religions. He will be extraordinarily callous in the face of death; but he will be wonderful in his speculations as to what will happen after death.

I knew very well a labourer of the rather better class. Small, very brown, with the clear enunciation that still in places survives the blurred cockney of the school-teacher's work, with little eyes that twinkled in a clear-cut face, he was much sought after in the village as a sick nurse during nights, when the wife of a man needed rest. Certain men have the gift of being asked, the soothing voice and the willingness to perform these last functions – and my friend must have seen the death of many men. Quietly, but without any abating of the twinkle in his eyes, he would tell you how So-and-So died 'sweering dreadful'; So-and-So went off sudden like the bottom falling out of a bucket of water; whilst it was more than he could do to hold down old Sam, the hop-dryer, who had the delirium tremens, so he died on the floor. And at an inquest I have seen Mark go up to the corpse that we were viewing and, catching hold of the hand, say, 'Reckon that won't ever lift no more pots; 'tis main still for you now, old Quarts.' 'Quarts' was the sobriquet of the dead man, and he had died of the cold.

There, in the rough barn where we stood huddling together for warmth, Mark was brave enough, and he was brave enough in a death-chamber. Indeed it is hardly braveness, just as it is hardly callousness so much as a survival of the early temper of men accustomed to the ending of lives – of the temper that has given us the 'Dance of Death' or the Gravedigger of Hamlet. A dead man is to the countryman of hardly more account than a dead mole or the dry tufts of feathers that January leaves underneath all the bushes. It is a frame of mind repulsive or grotesque to the townsman, who never sees a dead thing save on butchers' and fishmongers' slabs, where indeed he sees more than enough. In the countryman it is merely part of that large innocence that allows him to accept as so many of the natural processes of life things that are always hidden in towns behind the serried walls of house-fronts. He sees more of life, and of necessity more of death.

But this same Mark had his own private conception of what would happen to *him*. He was not in the least mad, but he had – who knows how? – gathered it out of the Scriptures that he would never die, but be carried up to heaven in a chariot of fire. His eyes twinkled humorously when he said so, but you would put him into a fury if you expressed a doubt. He was a hedger and ditcher by trade, and, if he heard a rustling of some invisible object in the dusk or in the woods at night, he was tranquilly convinced that it was one of the Beasts of the Revelation. Being unmarried and living by himself in a tiny, disused toll-house, he was more solitary than most, and had more time to think. And it is astonishing how many countrymen have bizarre beliefs of this kind. I have come across them in tenant farmers, in veterinary surgeons, in water-bailiffs, and even in rural policemen – who, indeed, are the most solitary of all the users of high-roads and footpaths. The fact is that to be alone much in the country is to find oneself giving to hills, rows of trees or the coping-stones of bridges – to anything that one likes or dislikes for the obscure reasons that sway us – personal identities. One measures the world, after all, in human terms, and two foxes' earths on a knoll will take after a time a semblance of eyes in a green forehead, just as houses have grim or jovial or lugubrious personalities expressed in their window blinds. And thus, for reasons obscure to us, certain portions of the familiar country influence us. There are hills that we ascend without weariness and downward slopes that we vaguely dislike; there are sheltered spots that for no known reason we find lugubrious, and bleak downs where some mysterious presence seems to temper to us the most dreary of winds. In that way a countryside comes to have the value of a personality; and so we speak of the Spirit of Place.

Standing on certain hills it is impossible not to feel a conviction that the green earth waving away on each side into illimitable space is a vast entity, living in the growth of its grasses, and in the voice of its birds, the little tunnels of subterranean beasts and insects forming its veins and, whatever be the colour principle of its surfaces, being the blood of its complexion. But the feeling is arrived at only after a sufficient familiarity – a familiarity the length of which will differ with each individual, since there are some of us who will fall in love with a certain corner of the earth, even as with a certain woman, at the first glance. And just in the same way there are featureless stretches of land in which we feel at once at home, whilst blue regions of alps, of woods and mirroring lakes tire us as we may be tired by a brilliant talker.

For myself, no landscape is restful unless it contains many hedges and woods, and unless the horizon is somewhere broken into by the line of the sea – unless at least I feel that, from the top of a hill near at hand, that still, blue line might be seen. Far inland I seem to be beneath an impalpable weight, and on an absolutely naked down I am conscious of glancing round, in search of at least a clump of trees in which I might take refuge from the great gaze of the sky. But I have one friend who cannot live at peace out of sight of heather, and another who hates hedgerows because they interrupt the journey of his eye over the contours of the ground. I knew a farmer who moved from the marsh into the uplands; and he was forced to rent a cottage on the level again, because he missed the stagnant dykes and could not bear the sound of running water in the beck beneath the bedroom window of his farm in the hills.

In the stage of intimacy to which a man reaches as soon as he masters the field ways of his countryside he thus begins to make acquaintance with the mysteries of the earth; he begins, according to the light vouchsafed to him, to frame his own reading of the

green kingdoms. He does it, no doubt, in the search for intellectual solace; it is part of his journey in quest of the Fortunate Islands.
In a sense and to a certain degree other things will turn him aside.
He will find refuge from himself in making toys for his children,
in sleep by his fireside, in the slow talk of the ale bench, in the
hunting-field, or over a book. No doubt the book is the best of all
the things with which a man may stave off introspection, if the
gossip of the alehouse be not better. And no doubt next to these
we may place the saddle. Books and small-talk bring us in contact
with the minds of our fellows; we may revel or idle in them without
emulation and without effort. In hunting we are taken out-of-doors
and brought into contact with beasts wrought up to their highest
pitch, and with the animal in ourselves wrought up, that too to its
highest vitality.

To the man who can feel it there is no sensation in life comparable to the waiting, on a frosty morning, by a woodside for the
hounds to break cover. All the senses are keenly alive; each tuft of
grass is of importance in the mist: the nostrils are filled with the
faint twang of the morning and of the frost; the ears catch minute
sounds — the crackle of underwood beneath the feet of the silent
and distant hounds, the clink of stirrup against stirrup, the hard
breathing of a horse. And one's whole body, all the sensation of
feeling that one possesses, is instinct with the shiver and breath of
the beast that one bestrides. There is no waiting quite like it, since
there is nowhere else just this union of nerves in two beasts so
widely dissimilar the one from the other.

With the first whimper of the hounds on the scent, with the note
of the horn, the cry of 'Gone Away!' or the crash of the hounds
breaking covert, this particular psychological 'moment' ends.
Contests have their place and emulation is aroused in horse even
more than in rider. It isn't — that particular tremour of waiting —
recaptured at any check, though perhaps no theatrical performance
is half so engrossing as the watching from one's saddle of the
hounds, with their noses to the ground, making a wide circle to
recover the scent. But of course one has moments of another sort.
One remembers putting one's right arm over the eyes in rushing
through a bullfinch. And I have a memory that I do not know
whether I would or would not willingly dispense with, of lying
helpless on my back on the further side of a sunken Devon hedge,
with high above my face the silhouette against the sky of a horse's
fore-legs and a rider's boot-tips. It seemed for a moment a curious

and interesting spectacle, since it is seldom that one sees from below into the very shoes of a horse.

Thus in this as in all field sports, man, according to his sympathies, finds solace, oblivion, animal excitement, the means of passing the weary hours. They have their 'moments', and afterwards we can say that there is nothing like them. There is nothing like casting the last salmon flies of the day at dusk into a still and almost invisible water; there is nothing like the old and forgotten shooting with a trained dog in the thigh-high stubble of October wheat-fields; there is, for boys, nothing like the laying of a trail of paper across the trembling tufts of a bog at noon; there is nothing like… But what is there anywhere like any one of these things that beneath the sky and across the green acres will keep the mind from working in the treadmill of its proper thought? And what, after all, will arouse a rough fellowship between man and man so well as the tumble and scurry in a stackyard where the rats are bolting and squeaking among men and terriers, sheep-dogs, spaniels and broom-handles?

And in a sense the field naturalist pursues a similar sport. With his eyes or his field-glasses he shoots the events of little creatures' lives. To give himself moments, he is seeking to nail down to his consciousness the 'moments' of their existences. Peering along the hedgerows, if he has seen a rabbit run fascinatedly around the uplifted head of a stoat, he will have bagged his event; or if he could see a cuckoo drop its egg into the nest of a chaffinch, the adder swallow its young alive, or the night-jar carry its children in its claws. He is building up his little house of observations; he is filling in the chinks of the wattle-wall that shuts out for him the monotony of his life. And the lines of the trees, the smell of the grass crushed beneath his feet, the sound of wind in the river reeds, the bow of the sky, the forms of clouds, or the great stillnesses of noon – all these things soothe his mind and make sacred these hours of his.

That in its way is the best gift that the Nature of the fields offers to man – a memory of oblivion tempered with a sensation that is hardly a memory of times passed with the cool airs on the cheek, with the eye unconsciously deluded and filled by the lines of a world drawing all its hues from the air, the soil and the vapours that hang as it were in a third space between air and soil. I have said that the most engrossing of pastimes are the gossip of the alehouse and the reading of men's thoughts. And in a sense these are the things that keep us going nowadays through the between-beats of the clock.

But there are times of break-down when neither of these human emanations has power to hold the mind, or, to put it more justly, when the mind has no longer the power to hold to them. After long periods of illness, of mourning, of mental distress, no news of the outside world and no ecstasy of verse will hold the mind; events and thoughts pass through the tired consciousness leaving no trace, as the smoke of orchard fires passes through apple boughs. Then Nature may assert a sway of her own.

I remember seeing a countryman recovering from a long illness with his bed-head set towards the window. He seemed to be in a state of coma, but from time to time he asked for a looking-glass. Because his appearance after his illness was rather terribly emaciated, the glass was for long refused to him. At last he fell to weeping weakly, and some one found a hand-mirror for him. He held it high up, never looking at himself, but turning the face of the glass to the window. He had been longing to see the green of the grassy hill that rose up before his cottage, and although his brain had been too weak to say that he wished his bed turned round he had imagined that stratagem of bringing greenness into his confining room. It was a longing, he said afterwards, such as women are said to feel before the birth of children; and no satisfaction ever equalled that of this poor man who had imagined himself doomed to die without again seeing sunlight on the grass.

The country, in fact, the country of the fields and of the footpaths, gives most freely to those who bring something with them, whether it be the labour of their hands or of their brains, whether it be an interest, a hobby, a pursuit, a tranquillity or merely an exhaustion. To those whose minds are simply empty, or to those whose thoughts centre upon themselves, the country is a back cloth, a flat surface portraying an aching pageantry of hills, of fields, of woods, a concrete frame for a dull listlessness, or an intolerable prison. But to those who love her as a support, as an addition to a self-sacrifice, as a frame to a passion, to those who work and those who love, she is a beneficent personality. Ask indeed the lovers who wander along the little footpaths or shelter in the ways and nooks of woodlands what the country is to them. They might not answer in words, but they feel that hers is a beneficent presence, auspicious, soothing and sheltering, a presence that finds words for their dumbness, that lends them patience in their suspenses. So that when a lover says, 'How sweet the May do smell!' he voices an unrest and praises at once the perfume of the flowers and the being of his mistress who has quickened his senses. And the worker with his mind who comes out of his door to stand gazing across level fields to the horizon, he too finds his thoughts purified and supported, set as they are in relief, so that his ideas themselves appear to be the pattern upon a groundwork of flat green. That indeed is the mission, the vocation of the fields that we cross – to be a groundwork for the thoughts of poor humanity that in its journey through life needs so many supports, so many solaces.

CHAPTER III

In the Cottages

A T the end of a closed field, in a hollow of the woods, so deep and so moist that it was twilight there even at high noon, there stood a thatched mud cottage – a two-dwelling house – the door-sill of which I never crossed without anticipations of pleasure such as I have known on the sills of few houses. There lived at one end of the hovel an aged man for whom I had no respect, and in the low dark rooms, hung with clothes upon lines that kept away the draughts of the gaping walls, Meary.

I met her first at dusk, scrambling over the high stile of a path that, running between squatters' hovels on a common, was one of a maze of similar paved footways. In a purplish linsey-woolsey, as broad as the back of a cow, her face hidden in a black sun-bonnet that suggested the hood of a hop-oast, she was burdened with two immense baskets, from which protruded the square blue, white, and lead-coloured packages of the village grocer up on the ridge from which we had both descended. I offered to carry her burdens as far as we might be going together, and she said, without the least touch of embarrassment or of over-recognition –

'Why, thank ye, mister. I'll do as much for you when ye come to be my age.'

Her face was round and brown, her forehead broad and brown, and her brown eyes were alert and reposeful as if she were conscious of a reserve of strength sufficient to help her over all the stiles that are to be found in this life. They had, her eyes, the sort of master-fulness that you will see in those of a bull that gazes across the meadows and reflects.

I think I cared for her more than for any friend I have made before or since, and now that she has been dead for a year or so her memory seems to make sacred and to typify all those patient and good-humoured toilers of the fields that, for me, are the heart of the country. If you saw her at work in the hop-fields, with her hands and arms stained walnut-green to the elbows; in her own potato-patch stooping, in immense boots, to drop the seed potatoes into the rows; striding through the dewy grass of the fields to do a job of monthly nursing; or standing with one hand over her eyes in the doorway that she fitted so exactly that her thin hair was brushed by the four-foot thatch, she had one unfailing form of words, one unfailing smile upon her lips – 'Ah keep all on gooing!' And that was at once her philosophy and her reason for existence.

And to keep all on going until you drop – as she did, poor soul, until within three days of the appearance of her illness – that is the philosophy and the *apologia pro vitâ* of the countryside. Your ambition is simply that: health, so that you may keep getting about; strength, so that you may, to the end, do your bits of jobs and have a moment to do a job or two for a bedridden neighbour; and, in old age, a sufficient remainder of your faculties to pass censure on the doings of the neighbour you have helped. To have accepted helping hands enough to let you feel that you too are part of the body politic, and to have retained independence enough to let you refuse benefits when the spirit moves you – these are the undefined aspirations that keep occupied the weather-beaten cottages at the corners of fields, the two dwelling-houses with roofs green from the drip of orchard trees, and the quiet and solitary graveyards of the scattered hamlets.

This particular Meary, being just a month younger than the Queen (there is still only one Queen in the cottages), had lived just the life of every other countrywoman, and in her conversation, *à propos* of whatever topic might occur, fragments of her past life came constantly to the surface. If you spoke of the drought being bad for root crops, she would say –

'Ah! I lost my two toes after a bit of turnip-peel when I was four, jumping down into a ditch for it.'

In those days the children searched the dry ditches for such things. Or, before the A——d draper's window, she would give a quaint little idea of herself in a yellow nankin dress, cut so tight to save stuff that she could not move her tiny arms. You knew you had 'innards' most days of the week, she said, when she was a child. Once, out of mischief, she had handed her mother, who was at the kneading-trough, a paper of snuff instead of one of allspice, and the whole week's baking came yellow and evil-tasting. But they had had to eat it. She had never eaten baker's bread till she was twelve, nor butcher's meat till she was twenty; sometimes they had had a bit of tug mutton, which comes from a sheep found drowned in a dyke. Her stepfather had a bit of bacon once a week, and then the children had the crock water it was boiled in.

After a time – 'I was a pretty girl then, I'd have you to know,' she used to say – she had been attracted by a travelling basket-maker. When he was about their village she used to slip out and put a pinch of tea into the kettle over his fire in the dingle. She was sent away into service to preserve her from an infatuation for the 'pikey', who was not regarded as respectable, though he earned better money than two agricultural labourers. At nights, lying in the servants' bedroom of Lady Knatchbull's (the great house had as many windows as there were days in the year), the girls were accustomed to tell each other folk-stories – of queens who went wandering over the earth, having been turned out-of-doors for inscrutable reasons, whose hands were cut off for reasons more inscrutable, or who were reconciled to their kingly husbands or princely sons at the price of a pound of salt. Or the dark room would be peopled with witches, or dismal songs sung of the murder of trusting girls – with obvious morals for the girls of the servants' room. There were twelve slept together there. They taught each other to read, but no one knew how to write, and Meary never learned. They were sent to church of a Sunday, filling a great square pew for all the world like a cattle truck, but they never learned anything of religion. Nevertheless, at times Meary dreamed of Jesus Christ preaching in a green field from a waggon, and telling the women again not to trust the men, but to be good to each other and to small children. Once while Jesus was preaching Meary's mother, who had died years before, came to her, dressed all in white, and told her to be a good girl.

But eventually the pikey came to mend baskets at the Hall, and she went away with him. She did not see any use in being married; she reckoned it was something for the Quality. If he was your man, he was your man, and there was an end of it. If he wanted to leave you, he'd leave you, married or not; it was all one. Once her man did leave her, and she walked right from Paddock Wood to St Martin's Cliff in twenty-eight hours to find him again. It was on that journey that she saw the ghost. It was sitting on a milestone, dressed like a bride in a coalscuttle bonnet. She thought it was just a woman, and said, 'Hullo, missus!' three times, to it. Then it raised its head, and she saw that there was no face in the bonnet.

'Oh, well, poor thing,' says Meary, 'reckon I never hurt you and you've no call to hurt me.' So she went on her way along that long Dover road.

Eventually her man grew too weak or too lazy to keep the roads. He was much older than she, having already in 1815 been condemned to be hung for stealing oats when he was a waggoner's mate, and having been reprieved on consenting to serve in the Navy during the Hundred Days. They settled down in a cottage by the canal at B——, and there for years Meary kept herself and him. She had a certain original genius, such as that which prompted her to keep fowls for profit at a time when no labourers had ever thought of such a thing; but for the rest she worked at stone-picking on the uplands, at tying hops, at potato-planting, at pea-sticking, at one of the hundred things by which the rural economy is maintained, and in addition she did her monthly nursing, her sick-tending, her laying-out corpses, and her weekly job of charing at the rectory. It was to secure this last that she eventually consented to be married to her man. Shortly afterwards he was stung in the leg by an adder, and, blood-poisoning setting in, he became more useless than ever. Then she fell, broke her leg, and lay for long weeks in hospital, using up all her savings of hen-money, until one day, being seized with a presentiment, she rose, dressed herself, and, crawling in one way or another painfully home, she found her man dead. She retained a lame leg for the rest of her life.

And for the rest of her life she worked. She kept 'all on gooing'. Eventually, as I have said, she died very suddenly of cancer at the age of seventy-four. But even then she showed no signs of decay. You might have taken her for a hard-worked woman of forty; she was as solid and as brown as a clod of earth. She died, of course, in the workhouse infirmary, and of course, too, the chaplain, or the surgeon, or the man who drove her there, or possibly even myself, since I was known to have seen much of her, were suspected of having in some way got hold of 'her money'. For the poor, who ought in all conscience to know how hard it is to amass the smallest of sums, are exceedingly credulous as to the hoardings of old creatures living in the most sordid of hovels. I have seldom known an old woman die without some such legend attaching itself to her corsets, as that they crackled with bank-notes, or were as weighty as so much lead with a lining of sovereigns. In the French country, it is said that such old women have a very uncertain tenure of life, but the fact that such stories do not much attach to English coun-trysides should be evidence that the English peasant is more law-abiding in his imagination.

I was standing, I mean, in the doorway of a low French *estaminet* when there came in an exceedingly old, toothless, and bowed woman, with a broken basket slung over her back. She began to talk in a happy gibberish of a *beau marin* who was to marry her next Thursday. She groped under the table with a pointed stick for a crust of bread that by a miracle lay on the sanded floor, and dropping it over her back into her basket, went her way, a hopping figure like a little old goblin, under the thin poplars of the immensely long and dusty road. 'What a life!' said one man at a table.

'Why no,' retorted the benignant-thinking hostess. 'Is she not as happy as we others? When she finds such a crust of bread is it not to her as great a pleasure as to us when we add forty sous to our savings?'

Life is like that, after all! And if every new Thursday no *beau marin* comes to marry her, would it not be every next Thursday that he would marry her?

'Such a man,' retorted a waggoner, sitting with his head between his hands – 'such-and-such a man was seen on the thatch of her hut, listening at the chimney last week. One Thursday will come when, not the *beau marin*, but the excellent *sergents* will find her with her throat cut and her rooms stripped bare.'

'You are a fool,' the hostess blinked.

'Ah!' the waggoner answered, 'don't we all know that M. Un Tel dropped old Marie Thérèse down the draw-well? They say she fell. But why did she go who had no cause to use water? And why was no money found?'

It is not that sort of story that one hears on the alehouse bench in England, and it is not the fear of the law of libel that prevents it. It is simply that the English imagination does not run in that groove. Or perhaps it is only that the English peasant is more patient, for in his stories the thief always waits for the old woman to die before going through her stays.

And indeed the fact that the only reward for a life of toil should be the empty reputation of stays quilted with bank-notes, or, for an old man, the legend of a baccy-box filled with golden sovereigns – that fact seems to be a proof of a wonderful patience in these tribes of the fields. For all the rest of humanity – for the humanity who read or write books, cast up ledgers, minister behind counters, bars or the grilles of banks – for all of us who do not walk behind the plough, draw furrows for potatoes, tie hops, or tend pigs, for all of us who are not down upon the earth itself, there is always a vision of a modest competence at our day's decline. But here there is nothing.

There is not in the country even a day-dream of anything. Upon the whole my Meary was the wisest person I have ever met. Broad-minded, temperate, benevolent, cheerful and cynical, she could confront every hap and mishap of life, whether her own, her neighbour's, or the state's, with a proper fortitude or a sane sympathy. She had experienced more vicissitudes in her own scale of things than had most people; she had covered more miles of country and gone through more hours of toil. Yet her philosophy of life was simply that, that you 'keep all on gooing'. And even that you could only do if you were most fortunate, if you had that greatest of all gifts, health, which alone makes possible the pedestrian existence. Without that your 'gooing' ends in the workhouse.

Perhaps that peasant imagination, the stays quilted with notes, is, as it were, a rudimentary trace of our ideal of retiring. It is the nearest approach to a castle in the air, a faint mirage of our impossible Island of the Blest. It is the peasant's acknowledgment that a modest competence is at least thinkable for one of his number; and, oddly enough, it is always to the weakest, the oldest and the least competent that he credits the possession. Not even Meary herself ever thought of 'saving'; whereas you will observe that to the French field labourer – as to my hostess of the *Estaminet de l'Espérance*, who in her turn was the wisest French person I have ever spoken with – the first idea of the sou which he so sedulously hunts for in his sandier soil, is that of a thing to be 'saved'. It is the basis of some sort of investment in *Rentes*, *viagères* or otherwise, or it is the commencement of the purchase of some tiny patch of land, of a new cow or a first goat.

But short of a pig, which only too often does not pay its way, English 'Meary' has no machinery of lucrative banking; she has only her stays or her stocking up the chimney, just as her husband has only his baccy-box or the loose brick in the hearth floor. And improvements in the conditions of living have of late centuries limited themselves almost entirely to a cheapening of commodity in the case of the field labourer. He gets his food, which is now largely tinned or packet stuff, cheaper than he did, and for smaller sums he buys his comparatively shoddy garments; but his wages and his housing remain practically the same.

No doubt my Meary and her neighbours are improvident: the

cottages contain children and beer is drunk in the houses of all, and if men and women did without these two luxuries they might have reasonable sums in the savings-bank or nest-eggs that would fall to them from benefit societies when they reached the ages of fifty-five. It is no doubt appalling to think that whereas the average earning per agricultural family in England is fifteen shillings per week, the average expenditure upon beer (the figures are those of temperance reformers) should be eleven pence per family. Exactly reckoned out this means that, if it lived at so proportionately appalling a rate of expenditure, a family existing upon £1,000 per annum would spend £61 2s 2¾ upon its pleasures – its clubs for the heads of the family, its wines, spirits, liqueurs, mineral waters for itself and its guests. For it must be remembered that the alehouse is the club, the only place of meeting save the corner of the church-yard, the only possibility that the field labourer has of enjoying any kind of social life at all in almost every English village.

No doubt this 6¹/₉ per cent of unnecessary expenditure upon enjoyment would be impossibly high in any other English class; and of course, when we add to it the necessary expenditure upon the children that the field labourer so lavishly indulges in, we do attain to a picture of improvidence that is eminently disturbing to many people. But the fact seems to me to be that when a man has so little opportunity for pleasure or for rational investment as has the English field labourer, it is almost hypocritical to expect him to be only a little less abstemious than the angels of God or very much more than a man.

I have pondered a good deal upon this problem of the absence of earthly castles in the air; they are simply not to be found in the scheme of life of my good Meary and her neighbours. They do not seem to hope for any kind of Island of the Blest, and are agreeably surprised and a little ashamed if, when old age reaches them, their children support them. But a period of real rest or retiring is not for them. It does not come, at least, within their scheme of things. Of course, scattered over the countryside, we find old couples enjoying a modest leisure. But these are almost invariably people who have come across some unwonted stroke of luck. In a parish that I know very well, for instance, there were three such couples. But one pair had been gentlemen's servants, and made a way for themselves by keeping a cow and drawing small pensions. Another pair had good children earning good money in several towns. The third had inherited a little money from a not very creditable source, and lived a hidden, odd life in the shadow of the deep boughs of a wooded hill in the midst of a random collection of squatters' huts that somehow they had come to own. In one they lived, in another they kept their pigs, in another they had a great number of bees. The whole little encampment was shut in by a very high quicken hedge, so that they seemed to pass all their days in a mysterious shadow, not very willing even to part with their honey as far as one could discover, for their garden gate was almost always padlocked, so that to knock at their front door it was necessary to find a hop-pole and to prod it from a distance. Then an upper window would open and a small wizened face look out.

It finally came to light, in the mysterious way in which these things will out in the London papers, that the little old man was the son of an informer. His father had betrayed a whole neigh-bouring village of smugglers seventy years before, and these, his descendants, a brother and sister, still lived on the blood-money. Where they had been in the interval before they came to B——, or why they should hide their heads in a country where the sons of notorious criminals flourish and are honoured, is a little of a mystery still; but there they did live and there they enjoyed such rest as is vouchsafed to anyone here. And it will be observed that all these three resting couples were the exceptions of the country-side.

The other one or two old people who there lived at home and in a measure of ease had parish relief. I have never come across a man or woman who had saved enough to live on when they grew too old to work, and I have never come across one who seriously thought of such a thing.

They take, the country people, their rests between work in snatches so intense that perhaps they scarcely rouse themselves to think of any longer spaces of doing nothing, for I know of no object, no symbol so absolutely typical of relaxation as the attitude of one of our field labourers after a hard day. If you will think of him sitting beside his tea-table, his head hanging a little, his legs wide apart as if to balance himself on a thing so fragile as a cottage chair, his hands, above all, open, immense and at rest, as if, having grasped many and heavy things, they would never again close upon a plough-handle or use-pole – if you will make a mental image, refining a little and idealising a little, you will be thinking of mankind utterly at rest. You will be thinking, too, of the mankind who does not consider either the future or the past – of the man whose nights are the walls between concrete periods of the mere present, whose days are each one a cell, shut off and unconnected, having no relation to the day which went before, and none to that which shall ensue after the black oblivion of the coming night. For in which of those days, dominated by a real sun, overshadowed by real clouds, or swept by real and vast winds, shall they find leisure to formulate a scheme of life to provide against that figurative rainy day that the rest of the world so continually dreads? There is no time between bed and bed, and at night no lying awake. That, after all, is the improvidence of nature. For the ideas of making a career, of putting by against the decline of life, of retiring – these ideas are of a very modern, an artificial, growth. I am almost tempted to say that they have sprung up only with the growth of the Anglo-Saxon-Teutonic-industrial-commercialism that is Modernity. That is, naturally, a side-speculation; but what has always seemed to me an astonishing, an even astounding feature of most social comities is, not that the peasant should now be leaving the land, but that he should have been content to remain for so long the mere substratum of the body politic. For here we have a whole body of men control-ling the one thing that is absolutely necessary to all other estates, controlling absolutely the one thing without which human lives cannot be lived.

'They must then,' a philosopher from another planet and another plane of thought would say, – 'they must necessarily be the lords of the world. All other trades, professions, avocations, guilds, castes, crafts, or followings must come to them, suing upon bended knees for the mere stuff to keep their ribs from sticking through their sides. They control, your field-workers, the food supply of your world; then they *must* control your world.' And, indeed, it is odd to think that from the days of Pharaoh to the days when the rulers of Rome kept themselves in place and power by supplying bread *et circenses* to a town populace, from then to mediaeval days, and from those days to these of transatlantic market manipulations, through all the mists of time to which annals and chronicles supply dimmed charts and landmarks, there has never been a wheat-corner of one kind or another that has been 'engineered' or had its origin with the actual peasant – with the actual field-worker. There have, of course, been wars for the fixing of labourers' wages, as there was in England, and there have been Peasant Wars, as in Germany, but there has never been a case in which the peasant has shown himself aware of his actual power – his power to withhold food. Such class wars as he has waged – and in England there has only been the one – have been wars in which he used the weapons of the other classes, swords, billhooks, and whatever other primitive implements of steel he could lay hands to. But he has never used the most terrible weapon of all – he has never simply stayed his hand.

It is not, of course, very wonderful, though it is appalling to consider what would be the results of a universal peasants' 'strike'. But the peasant has hardly ever had a corporate self-consciousness; he has certainly never 'organised', it is much, even, if he have so much as thought of his rather wretched circumstances. You get, for instance, his philosophy of keeping on going expressed in *Piers Plowman* – how many centuries ago – and in addition to it a consciousness of the bitterness of life; and in addition to that a belief that Providence, on the Last Day and for ever, shall give material recompense to those who suffered so long and so inarticulately:

> There the poor dare plead
> And prove by pure reason
> To have allowance of his lord
> By the law, he it claimeth.

And, joy that never joy had, he asketh of the rightful Judge. Since to the birds, beasts, and wild worms of the green wood that suffer grievously in winter, God sends summer that is their sovereign joy, assuredly and of pure reason God shall give to the poor toilers of the field, after their long winter of this world, an eternal summer. Something of this bitterness, tempered with the idea of retribution hereafter, may have remained to the peasant throughout the ages; but how different it is from the corporate consciousness of the other nearly indispensable crafts. How different it is from the spirit of the blacksmith's motto:

> By hammer and hand
> All Art doth stand.

It was, I imagine, during the French Revolution that some idea of this sort began to permeate the field labourer. But even then it was more a matter of individuals than of a body corporate. The print to which I have referred already is not, at any rate, in any form discoverable earlier than in a French version of 1782. It shows a man bearing upon his back many others: a king on the top, then, in a bunch, a soldier, a priest, a lawyer, a doctor, a merchant. Those who form the burden bear scrolls: 'I govern all', 'I fight for all', 'I pray for all', 'I cure all', 'I sell for all', and the figure with its bowed head, like Atlas groaning beneath the weight of a world, exhibits the legend: 'I work for all'. I have seen versions of this print, redesigned with different attributes in wood engraving, in steel engravings, in chromolithograph or even copied by hand, all over Europe – in *estaminets* in La Vendée, in inns in Herefordshire, in farms in Kent, and in the *Kotten* of Westphalia. If it is not the charter, it is, this print, at least the claim to recognition of the worker on the soil. It was probably first designed in the France of 1782. Yet even in the England of a century and a quarter later the field labourer has not found any corporate or articulate means of inter-communication; he has not imagined any method of revenging himself on the classes above him. He has not, I mean, waged any war, claimed the land, or so much as 'struck' in any vast numbers. What he *has* done has been simply to go over to the enemy. For, with the spread of education, with the increase of communication, there has come not the determination to better the conditions of life in the country, but the simple abandonment of the land. It is, I think, a truism to anyone who knows the country, though I have found townsmen to deny it, that there are whole stretches of territory in England where a really full-witted or alert youth of between sixteen and thirty will absolutely not be found. I visited lately eighteen farms of my own neighbourhood, covering a space of about four miles by two miles, and on this amount of ground only five boys found employment. Four of these were below the average intelligence, and had at school not passed the fourth standard; the fifth was so 'stupid' that he could not be trusted to do more than drive the milk-cart to and from the station. And of all the farm-labourers' families that I know well – some forty-six in number – only two have youths at home, and one of these has 'something the matter with his legs'. Of one hundred and twelve of other families that I know in a nodding way, not more than five have boys at work in the fields. Making a rough calculation of the figures as they have presented themselves to me, I find that just over five per cent of the country-born boys I have known have stayed of their own free choice on the land. The public statistics for the whole of England are somewhat higher in this particular; but in the purely agricultural Midlands the standard of intelligence is somewhat lower, and in the North of England the living-in system still prevails, and does for various reasons keep the young men in their places.

The figure among the girls is probably even more striking. A girl of moderately good looks or of an intelligence at all alert is almost unknown in many, many villages of England. I was much struck by the statement of a friend of mine the other day. A man of much intelligence and of unrivalled knowledge of country life, he had been spending a month watching the birds and small beasts of a certain countryside. He had covered a good deal of ground in that time, and at last he saw a pleasant and bright-looking girl. He had grown so weary of seeing only worn, stupid or dazed faces that he got off his cycle and remarked to her that he was glad to see that she at least was stopping in her own village.

'I!' she said with an accent of scorn; 'I wouldn't stop in such a dull old hole if you gave me £10 a day! I'm visiting my parents for three days.'

Yet the village in question was almost world-famous for its beauty, and her father's wages were rather high.

I do not for the moment want to extract any other meaning from this striking rural exodus than may attach to my own astonishment. But it *does* seem to me astonishing that this really downtrodden class should have given just this form to its protest. There has not, I mean, been any discoverable attempt worth the mention to fight the battle as a battle. You do not anywhere find that the field labourer has attempted to raise the price that he receives from his employer,[1] nor do you find that the young people of the country-sides have ever made any attempt to brighten or to enhance the intellectual colourings of their lives. You do not find anywhere spelling bees, newspaper clubs, debating societies, or subscription dances. Yet there is no reason in the world why these things should not have been attempted. Nay more, all the old seasonal excitements of the country are dying out: the fairs, the May-day celebrations, the sparrow shoots, the bonfire clubs, even the very cricket clubs, which are subsidised, as a rule, 'from above' – all the

---

1   You will find this most strikingly exemplified in the case of such temporary industries as that of hop-picking, where a whole village turns out together, and where, if anywhere, some sort of stand for better money might be made. 'Strikes' do, of course, occur where there are many 'foreigners' employed, but practically never where all the pickers are village people. The cottagers accept uncomplainingly the grower's wage, which is based upon his computation of what the price of hops may be expected to prove; of course, when I say the peasant has never struck, I do not forget the name of Mr Joseph Arch. But from his day back to that of John Ball agitators and stack-burnings have been so comparatively rare that 'never' remains a word sufficiently accurate for the uses of impressionism.

old merriments and 'merryneets' of the country have almost gone. In the course of the last four years I have seen the custom of May Barns and the village waits abandoned in a place where they have existed since its first houses were built. But no trace of any attempt to amuse themselves is to be found amongst the peasants of this countryside. The whole population of field workers is simply throwing down its tools; it is making no struggle for existence; it is simply going away in silence, without a protest and without a trace of listening to outward persuasions. And I know very well that if I live to be as old as my old Meary there will be no one like her to lift my basket over the stile.

And when I think of her, standing dun-coloured, smiling and square in the dusk of that sunken footpath, I am rather saddened. For, following her footsteps into the shadowy land that is the past, all the generation for whom she stood is going, now so fast.

There will be none to take their places. If any remain they will be the slow-witted: whilst she and those she stood for were merely unlettered, a thing very different. Yet, perhaps, we do wrong to regret that there should no longer be a whole world of our fellow-creatures pulled out of their natural shapes, stunted in their minds and leading lives dull and unlovely so that we may have certain æsthetic feelings gratified. No doubt in the scale of things the young shop-assistant, with her preserved figure, her gayer laugh, her brighter complexion, her courtships, her ideals and her aspiration for a villa in a row, with a brass knocker and an illustrated Bible on the parlour table – no doubt the young shop-assistant is a better product of humanity than Meary, with her broad face, her great mouth, great hands, and cow-like heave of the shoulders. Nevertheless, I suppose that we must needs regret this passing. For, after all, it is a stage of the youth of the world that is passing away along with our own youth. It is the real heart of the country that is growing a little colder as our own hearts grow colder. It is one of the many things that our children – that our very adolescent nephews and nieces – will never know.

CHAPTER IV

Toilers of the Field

I DO not know why in particular, and at this particular moment, there should come up in my memory a very rainy day. I was with three other men, driven in from work by the weather. We were idly watching the heavy showers that slanted across the triangular farmyard, driving down from the grey hollows and grey slopes of the downs behind, until the water dropped like curtains of beads from the eaves of the waggon lodge beneath which we sheltered.

I had been making a new strawberry bed, and a Falstaffian, shiny, shaven-faced scamp, by-named Sunshine because of his appearance, had been helping me. The shepherd, or, as we styled it, the looker, was flaying a sheep that hung from one of the tie beams of the open shed, and Hunt, a retired soldier, who also did a job of lookering on the farm, lank, ill-shaven and sallow, leant back against a mowing machine, and looked with red and malignant eyes across the slants of rain. He rubbed his wet nose with the back of his hand and snarled out, 'Now if I had my rights I shouldn't be here wet and sick feeling.'

The shepherd – who had been a shepherd all his life on the one farm – made a slight incision with his knife, and drew the skin a shade lower on the red carcase.

'If we all had, we shouldn't none of us be,' he said, with a laconic air.

Sunshine, who had run away from his wife in the next county, grunted merrily.

He himself would be sitting in Brock Castle drawing-room, and all the lands below the hill would be his, Hunt drawled viciously.

'And I'd have a tidy bit of land of my own, too,' the shepherd said.

An aunt of his had died with property in the Chancery, Sunshine laughed, and, as luck would have it, I could make a similar claim.

'Reckon no one would have to work if it wasn't for they lawyers,' Hunt snarled; and the shepherd said that if a man in a black coat came along questioning him he kept very whist and quiet.

'Might be a parson, now,' Sunshine argued.

Well, parsons and lawyers pig together, too, the shepherd answered. More than once he had taken a note to the vicarage, and seen parson and lawyer Hick having tea together. No – take his advice, and do not speak to a man with a white collar and a black coat.

He was of opinion that your own quality was as much as you could deal with: 'Never you have no truck with strangers, or as like as not you'd sign away rights of yours you'd never heard of – and before you could say Jack Ploughman.'

The retired soldier had been born on the wrong side of the blanket, I believe, for I could not otherwise make much of his wrongs, and a large liver, gained in India, seemed to sour him. But both Sunshine and the looker were of most contented kinds. Yet they told remarkable stories of the wrongs that they, their relations, or A., B. and C. of that countryside, had suffered at the hands of the local Quality. The shepherd's father, for instance, had owned a mud cottage and a good orchard – probably squatted land. One day, when he was about sixty-six, Squire C——k had come along and said, 'Look here, old looker; I'll build you a brick cottage and let you live in it till you die, roomy and comfortable, if so be when you die you will engage it comes to me.' The old looker had consented; and all the other squatters on the common had taken similar offers. But the old looker had died before the new cottage had been built two months, and out the old woman and her kids had had to turn.

'That was how the C——'s came into all the C——n property,' the looker said.

Sunshine beamingly told the story of how his aunt had signed away her land in Chancery to a lawyer come all the way from the shires to get her name to a paper when none of her nephews were by. And the shepherd capped it with the tale of old Jacky Banks, who had worked all his life on that very farm. He had had fifteen pounds a-year for forty years, never spent a penny of it except for baccy, and had it under his bed when he died, along with his watch. Well, he lived in, on the farm, and died in what was now the drawing-room. Old missus, who was a powerful old woman, lugging buckets about the stackyard and doing a man's work till she died, had taken all old Jacky's money from under his bed before his eyes were properly glazed, and his relations never saw a penny of it, nor the watch and chain neither.

I have frequently thought that the reputation for stupidity, for slowness of brain, for grossness of manner that the townsman accords to the field labourer must really arise from mere suspiciousness. The shepherd's advice to his friends to keep a shut head to people wearing black coats is very generally followed in the cottages. It must be remembered that the labourer cannot see any reason why his betters should want to talk with him. The only motive that he can accord to them is that of desiring to 'get something out' of him. He has heard of land-grabbing, of land in Chancery; he has known of cases innumerable in which the small tenant-farmer, the three-hundred-acre man, has over-reached his labourers. His cottage doors are beset by pedlars of sorts – watch pedlars, pension tea pedlars, illustrated Bible pedlars, and the agents of foreign lotteries. All these people wear black coats and speak with specious and silky accents of gentility. I remember, too, walking along a dark road from the station with a youngish girl of the scullery-maid type. She chatted amiably as long as I was invisible, but when the light of a carriage fell upon me she looked at me with startled eyes, uttered, 'Why, you're a *gentleman*!' and took to her heels. For in the eyes of the cottage mothers there is only one reason why a gentleman should wish to talk to a cottage girl.

And the speculation has sometimes occurred to me, too, what impression the voice, the accent and the language of the more instructed class must make upon the ears accustomed to broader and harsher sounds. I remember discussing a certain rather charming lady with an old labourer, and he said –

'Why, she was very nice in her ways, but she'd a pernicketty way of speaking that *ah* couldn't stomach much.'

If, in fact, brogues, dialects and dropped 'h's' affect the educated ear disagreeably, must not soft and delicate inflections of vowel sounds cause a vague or a very definite feeling of unrest? I do not imagine that a labourer can ever feel really at ease with that particular kind of foreignness. It cannot be home-like. Most country speech nowadays is tinged and coarsened by the horrible sounds of the cockney language, but it was not always so. I remember, years ago, going to order a waggon at a new dismal-looking villa residence, the property of a self-made man. The man himself came to the door. He was over ninety, tall, straight, with faded blue eyes, very white hair and trembling hands; but his voice and accent were charming and flute-like. He said, for instance –

'De harses beien't home from plovin' most deas till nün.'

The words look grotesque in print, but all the sounds were very clear and precise. And indeed with the very old people of all countrysides it is generally the same. They give the impression of speaking, very correctly and with great self-respect, a dead language.

So that for these and many reasons the person of quality, the strange squire, the Bible pedlar, the parson, or the dog-licence man, are suspect. All these wearers of clothes not weather-beaten and soil-stained, all these speakers with unhomely voices, all these people who have too ready a flow of words to be easily trusted – all these English foreigners, in fact, are individuals to whom it is wisest to keep a 'shet hed'. You can gain nothing from them, they may be after some vague property of yours. I think, really, that the attitude of the field-labourer towards his betters is that of, say, a Dutch colonial farmer towards the early diamond prospectors. There may be diamonds, gold, petroleum, or Heaven knows what upon his property; who knows what these strangers might make out of the unknown mysterious possibilities?

I heard, for instance, the other day of a quite authentic Chancery case. Here an old labourer, who had served with distinction in the Army, was really the heir to some property. His children had employed lawyers, but the old man obstinately refused to give them any assistance. Once he went to the solicitor's office with his medals and birth certificate as means of identification, but having surrendered them he sat all night upon the doorstep for fear they should be taken out of the office and sold. Now, having recovered them, he sits upon them continually in his hooded chair, he absolutely refuses to swear any affidavit or to give any testimony in any court of law. And there the case remains at a standstill. This, of course, is an extreme instance, but it is as it were a symptom of a very widespread disease.

For it must be remembered that the field labourer has not *any* reason for courting the society of his betters. He cannot by any possible means rise in the social scale. A successful draper will become a knight and build a manor-house, but there is no kind of 'success' open to the usual farm labourer. Hence he has no reason for snobbishness and 'knows his place'. A lady of my acquaintance once invited her wood-reeve to sit down to tea with her. He gave as a reason for refusing that –

'You don't put a toad in your waistcoat pocket.'

Perhaps for that very reason the field labourer has as a rule much

less of class hatred than his town cousin. You do not hear, beside
the alehouse ingle, the same diatribes against the rich that you will
in a workman's train; you will not, if you are one of the rich, have
such approaches as you may make met with an ostentatious
defiance. I *have* been met in the country by 'shut heads', but have
never been harangued for my lewdness or luxurious habits as has
time and again happened to me at the hands of town labourers. The
nearest I have come to it in the country was once when I asked my
way of a statuesque old woman in a lilac sun-bonnet. She misdi-
rected me, and when, returning an hour later, I saw her and
reproached her, she said –

'Well, you idle chaps has nothing better to do than to waste time.
How did *I* know ye really wanted to go to L——?'

The feeling expressed in the lines I have quoted from *Piers
Plowman* does undoubtedly still exist. Once I took one end of the
table at an underwood sale dinner in an inn barn. The churchwar-
dens had been brought in; I had made the best of ladling out rum
punch with a ladle that had a George II guinea inlaid in its bowl
(and you have no idea how difficult it is to ladle punch into thirty
tumblers without spilling a quantity. The quill-like silver stem
quivers in your hand and you feel that sixty or a hundred eyes are
fixed upon your fingers). The smoke from the pipes ascended to
the rough rafters of the barn; repletion mellowed the talk of cants,
of ash-saplings and of chestnut wattlegates; we had eaten roast goose
and plum pudding with brandy sauce; we were a matter of ninety
buyers, all labourers, except for three farmers, the auctioneer and
myself. Then songs were called for; ten or a dozen men set themselves to press one of the farmers for *Old Joe's Wedding Day*. The
farmer, a man who worked himself, fat, hard, bullet-headed and
inscrutable, sat with twinkling eyes, sunk deep in his chair as if he
heard and saw nothing of his persuaders. Suddenly in the midst of
their clamour a high, clear, thin sound thrilled through the air.
Coming as it did from his lips which hardly appeared to move, it
produced a most extraordinary impression, as if a bull had spoken
with the voice of a canary.

But the next favourite, or perhaps the real favourite, since Farmer
Files had a kind of official position, was a fanatical-looking man
called Hood, whom I had never seen before. He rose without any
pressing. Tall, scraggy, long-necked, bearded, and with flashing
eyes, he reminded me of some furious Hebrew prophet or of some
Solomon Eagle. He had impassioned gestures of claw-like hands

when the whites of his eyes would show. He recited a piece of verse called, I think, 'Christmas Day'. It was full of the miseries rather than the wrongs of the poor. Because he had a real dramatic gift the piece was moving to listen to.

The rate-collector harassed a poor family – Hood glared round the room; a keeper unjustly accused the house-father of stealing goose eggs – he thundered with one hand on the trestle table and a glass fell to the floor; finally the bailiff came in for rent whilst the thaw drip was trickling through the thatch – and the man's lowered voice and gloomy eyes seemed to cast a real shadow of tragedy on the faces of his hearers.

For me at least the rest of the poem spoiled the effect, since a long-lost son from Australia came back at that very moment, and after having taken the oppressed family to the inn for a square Christmas meal, he bought the house of the oppressive landlord and settled his parents in it. That, of course, was the retributive joy of the *Piers Plowman* poem. Joy that never joy had, had come into more than his own even on earth, and whatever one's regret for the spoilt art of the piece (the agony really *had* been skilfully piled up), one would not grudge the hard-faced peasant listeners their touch of idealism and softening. The wood sale is the great event of the year in these parts.

But the reciter evidently had *his* feelings, his grim humour. For as he sat down amidst violent sounds of feet and of hands on the table, he said –

'I reckon, tho', when *they* got into their big house, they'd send chaps for three months to Maidstone along of a turnip, just the same as if they'd never been poor.'

It was not, I mean, in his mind a song against the rich, but merely one against the bitterness of things. He seemed to be uttering in his own sardonic way those inimitable French words, '*Cela vous donne une fière idée de l'homme.*' But, indeed, it has always seemed to me that the countryman is more of a man of the world than his offshoot in the towns. He has a far greater knowledge of life.

The faces of town houses are inscrutable masks; class and class pass each other's streets but never penetrate the rooms. The town labourer relies for his knowledge of his social superiors upon the relatively vile gossip of the Press. The superior townsman has even less opportunity for really observing the lives of the poorer of the working classes.

In the country the social barriers are more rigid, but the peasant really does know something of what goes on in the great houses and may comment upon them after his lights; and after *his* light the country gentleman may know and comment upon the lives of his upholders. Life in the country has, in short, a great solidarity and a great interdependence, and with this greater knowledge comes, as a rule, a greater tolerance. This must, indeed, be the case where one's ideas of life are founded upon a knowledge of that life.

But, of course, along with the easy tolerance of the man of the world there goes a larger morality. I know a Cabinet Minister whom in town one would never suspect of robbing the public funds, yet when he had a part of his park re-fenced he calmly caused the palings, where they abutted on the high-road, to be set five feet further out upon the roadside turf. Thus he stole one acre-and-a-half of public land; and the local peasantry rather applauded the act. It was, they said, part of what one expected of the gentry.

I was talking, too, to a village carpenter the other day about a notorious financier who had made a notorious failure. He had bought the local estate from Lord A. and had employed this carpenter to the tune of £150. Of this the carpenter had received 2s 0d in the pound. Said the red-bearded, pleasant carpenter –

'Well, Mr P. was a gentleman. Only he got among these great folks and they led him wrong.' A rough diamond but a gentleman. Why, Lord A. used to give only five pounds to the school fund and five pounds to the club. Mr P. he gave fifteen to each. He was a gentleman.

When I objected that he had made £135 out of the carpenter to give thirty to these charities, he only answered –

'Oh, you expects *that*! But Mr P. was a gentleman. He gave fifteen pounds where Lord A. only gave five!'

If you are a countryman you do indeed 'expect that', because you are a man of the world. But for the same reason you are not strictly honest yourself, you repay yourself in kind. At one time I lived two miles away from a pillar-box, and on my daily journeys to the post I used to make a halfway house of a certain lonely one-floored damp cottage. There dwelt in it an aged couple. The man had had eleven children by a former wife, and the woman twelve by a first husband; they had married at the ages of seventy-nine and seventy, because two blankets are warmer on one bed than one a-piece on two. The old woman was intensely active, an indefatigable maker of mushroom catsup, which she carried up hill and down dale to sell, and a most lugubrious and whining beggar. But old S.

was the most venerable person I have ever seen. He had a high bald head, from which there flowed silky white locks, an aquiline nose, a full voice and a sort of quaver that would have done credit to any ecclesiastic. Seated in his chair beside his duck's-nest grate in the low room, the walls of which were covered with black-and-white memorial cards and glass rolling pins as thickly as is the side wall of a cathedral with votive tablets, he would mouth out noble sentiments such as 'Honesty is the best policy', and stretch a quivering hand across the square opening of the fireplace. He appeared then like one of those venerable patriarchs that one sees in woodcuts illustrating the *Cottar's Saturday Night* or early Victorian pietistic works. And indeed he was a fine old fellow.

Yet when I gave him a job of picking up potatoes for me and overpaid him handsomely because his appearance was so venerable, he would beg me to tell the neighbours that he only did it out of friendship, since he was 'on his club'; or he would relate some such anecdote as the following:

'I was a-gooing up the Knoll Hill one evening when what does I see leein' in the roadway but a golden guinea and a broken stick with some drops of blood on it. "Hullo, my fine fellow," says I, "theer's been some bad work here, so up you comes into my baccy-box." And off I goes into the woods as quick as quick, for why, if the owner had come back, he might have claimed it of me.'

I do not mean to say that these instances of dishonesty are striking or even singular. Naturally there might be cited numbers of cases of sharp practices that would bring the hearts of countrysides up to a level in these matters with the bars of the towns where the confidence trick flourishes; but old S—— was a little above the average of his fellows in the precepts, the appearance and even the practice of morality. Yet here we find him swindling his club – which is the meanest of crimes really, since it tells against one's fellows in poverty – and we find him taking advantage of what he supposed to be a crime. He told the anecdote with a twinkle of the eye and that fine preaching inflection of the voice which goes with the statement that honesty is the best policy, that upright and manly inflection of the voice which so amply conveys the idea that Providence is on the side of the speaker.

Upon the whole the most honest person that I have ever really known in the country was W——n. He was a man of about forty, grizzled, brown, grey-eyed and altogether pleasant in the face. He had an air of pathetic weariness too, and I really liked him very much, and have spent many hours talking to him whilst he worked for me. In a rough-and-ready way he could do anything from managing a steam-plough to indoor painting and glazier's work. He has thatched a stable for me, planted an asparagus bed, made my book-shelves, and, though he can neither write nor cypher, he has managed my coverts of underwood and kept the accounts to the last farthing. He is extraordinarily hard-working.

Once when I was making alterations in an old farmhouse, piercing a door through an outside wall and opening up an ingle, I carried W———n from his own village and set him to these tasks. I went to bed myself one night thoroughly worn out and offered W———n a bed too. He preferred to get on with his job, and I left him crouching by the hearth, his hand half up the chimney and one candle burning on a brick in the desolate dining-room. All through the night I could hear, when I woke, W———n's cold chisel hammered against the hard mortar or the rumble of bricks as they fell in the chimney. And when I went down in the morning to get him a cup of tea, there was W———n, the ingle completely opened out, the man with his head on one side, the chisel in one hand and the mallet in the other, sitting on a pile of old bricks, reddened from hair to boot soles with brick-dust, and fallen into a light sleep, so that when I stumbled over a brick his hammer as if automatically struck the cold chisel and knocked away a flake of mortar.

He did not make the least fuss about his hard night, and did not even ask for overtime pay. It was all in his day's work. And upon the whole, thinking of the way he must have kept on going through the hours that to me would have been intolerably long and solitary, I felt proportionately ashamed of myself and respectful to W———n. I mean that I felt that he was a better man at his work than I at mine.

I would trust him with untold gold, and indeed I do still trust him with sums of money that for him must be very considerable. But I am quite certain that, though he will fight for my interest with all sorts of builders, seed-chandlers or market-gardeners, he will pick up inconsiderable trifles about my house, little things that I shall not miss, cracked boots, old caps from cupboards under the stairs – all sorts of things that I would give him with all the joy in the world. And he tolerated the fact that his 'missus', who used to do our washing, would fail to return an occasional handkerchief or baby's petticoat (W———n like all his improvident brethren has an immense family of tiny children). 'Women *are* like that,' he would

say between puffs of his pipe. His grey eyes would twinkle pleasantly when he recounted the small peculations of his mates, the
larger dishonesties of the builders whom he knew very well, or the
land-grabbing of the Cabinet Minister of whom I have spoken.
That was his world as he saw it, and W——n was a man of the
world.

He had been a waggoner's mate as a boy, he had been a plough
hand when the marsh took more acres of seed turnips than now,
alas, are to be seen in all England. When the plough failed as a
profession he had migrated to Margate, which was in the throes of
building a new suburb, and he had worked as bricklayer, plasterer,
paper-hanger, painter, plumber and layer-down of lawn grass in a
whole estate of new villas. When the 'slump' in the building trade
came he returned to B——n. He worked for the farmers at
hedging, at lookering, at hop-tending, at haying when work was
plentiful in the summer. In the winter he would take a contract for
dykeing from the War Office or would make rather good money
by working in his own covert of wood, which he bought each year
at the Michaelmas wood sales. He kept a pig or two and a few fowls,
and did upon the whole fairly well.

Here is, in short, a very proper man, an all-round one, and one
fairly well contented. He did not want to return to town life, where
the fact that he was illiterate hampered him a little. In a vague way
he was conscious that there was no kind of career open to him at
all. He would have liked to have got a small bit of land, and it
worried him a little that this was absolutely impossible. Or he would
have liked to have been able to work all the year round in the
woods. And indeed W——n is the best worker in the underwood
that I have ever come across, and had a way of making the best
penny out of the fourteen different kinds of poles and withies and
wattles – a way that when I did employ him in the woods I found
singularly lucrative. He had, in fact, a certain administrative gift,
and although absolutely without resources he could always manage
to raise the fifteen or twenty pounds that were needed for his
Michaelmas transaction.

W——n was a good man; perhaps he was the best of his district,
or perhaps it was only because of his handsome, saddish, brown face
that I took to him. But if I had not chosen him I could have had
twenty or fifty others in that part nearly as good workmen, practically as hard-working and practically as honest and with practically
as much resourcefulness and business ability. It is probably the

underwood that keeps this goodish type of worker in these parts, since wood-work calls for a large amount of intelligence, handiness with tools and ability to keep out of debt over the year-end, though you must needs be in debt for nine months out of the year. But given these characteristics it pays well and, upon the whole, surely.

For these reasons I liked W——n's countryside better than any other I have known before or since, and indeed, with its deep folds of the hills, its little jewel-green, dark and misty fields between tangled coppices, with its small cottages, its aged farms and its high and deep woods covering the ground like a mantle for further than the eye could reach from any height; with its good, nourishing, greasy mud, its high hedgerows and its spreading neglected small orchards, it remains for me my particular heart of the country. The cottager there is of a good type; the cottages are old, rat-ridden, clay-floored, but the fires are well tended, the wood-smoke pleasant, the furniture old and substantial as a rule, the bread heavy, the butter good, the pork fat, the tea strong, the cheese stings the tongue.

These things mean a good deal in the psychology of a people, and the people there, having been much left to themselves, and having come of a riotous, smuggling, harum-scarum stock, were independent, resenting intrusions, and willing only to take you at their own particular valuation. What was curious to me were the 'bad' villages of the neighbourhood. There were two of these, C—— Street and the Freight, set at each end of the united villages of A——n and B——n. It was difficult indeed to say why these were 'bad'; but in each of them the people were darker-browed, squalider, more furtive-eyed. A family resemblance ran from cottage to cottage; drunkenness was certainly unusually frequent and various other forms of vice were said to characterise them. I do not know about that, but certainly no decent family, however pressed for housing, would willingly move into either C—— Street or the Freight. Thus their populations were constantly recruited, whenever a cottage fell vacant, by families lacking in self-respect.

I have heard this singular phenomenon accounted for by a supposed difference of race between village and village. In the case of the celebrated strip of country, about forty miles by seven, which is usually accounted the 'worst' in England, race might possibly operate; but I am fairly certain that it was not so in either the Freight or C—— Street. It was not a matter of position either that gave them their peculiar similarities, since one lies well in the marsh, and the other is high on the ridge – one is composed of rather squalid modern brick cottages, the other of quite decent little old houses, so that it was hardly to be set down to insanitary surroundings; nor yet could it be laid to the charge of overcrowding, since in neither village is there more than one family to be found in any cottage, nor has any one family more than three children. I am personally inclined to put it down to the absence of a clergyman in either parish.

For – and being no churchman, I may say it without fear – the influence of a clergyman in a village may be very potent for good in the cleanliness, the sobriety, and, above all, in the treatment of the children. He acts to some extent as a former of public opinion. He is frequently narrow, bigoted, and short-sighted; he is almost invariably quite out of touch with the mental and spiritual needs of his parishioners, and, as a rule, he is regarded by them with either suspicion or good-natured tolerance; but one does notice a distinct deterioration in parishes where the clergyman is lazy or dishonest. And the deterioration is not in morals alone, but in the feeling of solidarity in the parish itself. Where he does not keep the accounts of the club, administer the charities, take part in the parish meetings – where, in fact, he does not do his best to be the centre and to organise *some* sort of social life, social life seems to die out altogether. But the really good parson – the man who does his best after his own lights or after the simple traditions expected of him, that man may do an almost infinite amount towards making his parishioners hold together. The mere fact that he establishes and keeps going little clubs and organisations – silly as they may be from any high intellectual standpoint – brings the men and women of the cottages out from their homes. A Cottage Garden Show Society is a small thing, but it will need two or three 'officers' of sorts, and these officers will come together on a ground just slightly different from that of the churchyard corner or the potato field. It enables the men to meet each other under newer and slightly wider aspects.

In a sense the clergyman is the only organiser that a village is certain to possess. There *may* be men of ability among the cottagers, but they will have to fight for any position of authority. The clergyman has it already; and, given a certain tact and a certain goodness of heart, he may go to the grave with a good deal of affection and leave an easy task to his successor, however incapable. On the other hand, a really dishonest clergyman may do an infinite deal of mischief; for the parson is almost always regarded with suspicion by very keen eyes, and once a clergyman runs, say, into debt, flagrantly and without the excuse of a poor stipend or a large family, an angel from God would find it an almost impossible task to persuade the inhabitants of that parish that there is ever any good in the clergy – or in human nature at all. And that effect will outlast the efforts of generations of his successors.

From the point of view of faith, I believe that the Church of England is absolutely out of touch with the field labourer in Southern England. Its creed is unknown, its ritual meaningless, and the language of its services so antiquated as to be almost incomprehensible. I had in my service a girl from a very decent labourer's family – a girl of very much more than the average quickness of natural intelligence. Our vicar heard that she had not been confirmed, and after having given her what he deemed the necessary instruction, he presented her at the next confirmation. A week afterwards I happened to ask her if she would care to go abroad with the family. She declined very resolutely, and upon my asking her why, she said, 'Because if the ship sank the fishes would eat my soul.' And upon going through the confirmation manual that she had got by heart I discovered that she understood hardly seventy-five per cent of its words. Thus, in such a sentence as, 'Here the priest shall approach the altar', she understood only the words 'here', 'the', and 'shall'.

My dear friend Meary once brought me a Bible that another cottager wished me to value for her. She said: 'I don't believe it can be real old, because it's got the New Testament in it.'

The other day I heard a very intelligent gravedigger say: 'I wonder Jesus Christ made so many damp places whilst He was making the earth.' He was also the parish clerk, and the words were said quite reverently.

Talking to me in my garden one day, W——n said to me –

'I don't blame the parsons for what they tell us. They're taught by the folks above them when they're young – just as that tree there was crook'd when *it* were young.' But he did not see how he could be called to believe that three Gods are one, or that if he were made in God's own image he could be troubled with toothaches as he was. And if so be God did make man in His own image, then the man's as good as his master.

I am not, of course, indicting the creed of the Church, but I am convinced, as far as my own observation will convince me, that that creed is very little brought home and very little explained to the field labourer. He needs something extremely simple, something extremely comforting and something taught in the plainest language. It is in very few parishes that he gets it. And, upon the whole, I should say that the chapels are nearly as far out of touch with the field labourer as the churches. Thus, with his long hours for introspection, his frequent readings of the Bible, and the fragments of church or chapel language that he has been able to make his own, the field labourer moves across the acres, half heathen, and patching together religions, superstitions, and cosmogonies, each man very much for himself. I remember hearing the reply of a priest abroad to a poor woman who said that she found it very difficult to believe in the doctrine of Papal Infallibility. He said, 'That is a matter for the theologians. Try, my child, to believe as much of it as you can.'

And for the English field labourer, most of the articles of the Christian faith are matters for the theologians; and the theologian is as much outside his world as is the classical scholar or the spiritualist. The spiritualist would indeed be nearer the needs and creeds of the field labourer if he had any means of reaching him, since beliefs in manifestations of that particular kind of other-worldliness die very hard in the rural districts. In fact, I doubt if they decrease at all except in so far as the populations decrease. I have never myself taken much interest in these particular phenomena, but I am personally acquainted with two witches, and I can hardly think of a wood or a farmyard which has not its ghost, if one will take the trouble to search for it. At times in country districts one will run up against odd reluctances on the part of the peasantry. Thus, I have found it impossible to get an errand done for me along a certain road, or a man has for no obvious reason been more than reluctant to dig a certain patch of ground, to cut down a certain tree, or to doctor one of his cows. And, by going tactfully into the matter, I have discovered that a headless horseman rides down that road, an evil fate overtakes the digger in that ground, the tree is one in whose branches there lives the spirit of a suicide, or the cow had been overlooked.

These things do not play much visible part in the life of the heart of the countryside; but there they are. They exist; they are factors of the daily round; they are as much part of the field labourer's life as are, say, the stars, the rain that follows on the sound of the sea heard inland, the legends of creation, or the price of crops. They are part of the nature of things – nay, they are even more, since he regards them as an ultimate resource. When his doctor, his vet, his parson, or his prayers have failed, he may always discover where there dwells a white witch or a wise man who for five sixpences placed on a table in the form of a cross will do him a world of good, or tell him at least whether his cow or his old woman will get through this time. I met last Saturday (and shall meet next) a young, dull-looking farm-labourer who has achieved some remarkable cures where doctors have been given up; and, for the matter of that, I know where to go to procure a piece of written paper that, worn round the neck, will prove a most potent love philtre.

The field labourer is tacit in front of these things. There they are; you may use them or laugh at them till you need to use them; but you do not much question them. Why should you? Parson tells you one thing, and papers and people who don't like parsons tell you something else. Your problem is how best to keep all on going till you drop. Different men differ a lot – from Portuguese to Members of Parliament and men from the Shires. It takes all sorts to make a world, and some men must needs know more than others. Have not all of us seen old Ned Post, who has been in the Indies and learnt how to keep his head in a basin of water for ten minutes without being a farthing the worse, which is more than you or I or old Squire Williams could do? And old Ned Post is nothing to look at. So the field labourer keeps an open mind.

Dyspepsia is a scourge of the cottagers, and most men have had long periods of hunger that cloud the thinking faculties a little. I have been soundly taken to task by a critic of a former book of mine for quoting the words of a doctor. He said that the town street-arab had a stronger grip on life than the field labourer. But although I am not sure, I think that the doctor was right. For, as far as I have seen, the field labourer dies very easily once he is ill. His diet is atrocious; it is atrociously cooked: his cottage, as a rule, is insanitary, draughty, damp, and too small. His work is too hard, his opportunities for mental relaxation pitifully too restricted. Except for his open-air life – which causes a great deal of over-exposure – he has very little to keep him in either mental or bodily health. And I do not really see why he should want to live.

I was much impressed the other day by the death of a man who had worked on a certain farm all his life. He was stalwart, bearded, hook-nosed, and his figure, with a broad felt hat which he always wore tied on with a handkerchief round crown and chin, had been to me always a familiar feature of that country-side. One saw him

pottering about among the sheep of distant fields or stamping across
the mixen in the heavy rains. His face was fresh-coloured, and he
had a sort of saturnine humour, a taciturnity of his own. One day
we heard, 'N—— is taken ill.'

I went to see him. It was odd, his brown face and grizzled beard
peeping out from the white bed-clothes, and he said, grimly, 'Well,
mister, I'm going to die.'

His wife set up a wail from the scullery – 'He's going to die! He's
going to die!'

There was absolutely nothing the matter with him save for a
touch of chill to the liver. But, standing beside him, I felt really that
there was no reason why he should make an effort to get better.
The rain fell dismally outside, yellow damson leaves stuck themselves on to his window-panes with each gust of wind, the hills
were grey, the road was grey. What exact reason could I give him
for getting up and facing the eight months of cold, wet, and toil
that must be his? I did, of course, my best to induce him to make
an effort; but you cannot make bricks without straw. He was dead
within the week.

I have here done my best to render my particular impression of
the field labourer, because it seems to me that he is the basis, the
bedrock upon which the social fabric of our country-sides must
rest. If there be a heart of the country, he is the heart of the heart.
He is the stuff from which we have all developed, and to him, no
doubt, we shall all return sooner or later. He seems to me to be, in
fact, just much of a make with his fellows, not much better and
certainly not at all worse than his neighbours of whatever class. Of
course every one of us will meet with field labourers who are nearly
brutes; I have met many. But the general impression left after much
dealing with him is not that of association with a low type. Rather
it is that of pleasure and of admiration. For such virtues as he has,
he has in spite of his environment; his vices are nearly all the product
of his hard life. You cannot expect much more than a decent friend-
liness, sobriety and openness of mind from a man whose function
in life is no more than to keep on going; and the wonder is how
he does it. Yesterday I had a man in to do some weeding for me,
and whilst he worked I talked with him. He was a Yorkshireman
who had been a stonemason of the higher class, one of those men
who make good money by imitating mediaeval work for the
restorations in old churches. But the stone-dust had injured his
lungs, and he had come south to find a better climate and purely

out-of-door work. Going about among the field labourers, he said, made him think precisely that, he could not make out how they did it. He never went near a public-house, he never bought himself any new clothes, he lived with the utmost frugality, like a canny Yorkshireman, yet he could not make both ends meet. Yet these fellows always seemed to have twopence for a glass of beer, though they had wives and families. He uttered his opinion with a rather unctuous and odious tone, as a condemnation of the beer-drinking that he was above. But the tribute was, to my mind, none the less striking.

And there, for me, the agricultural labourer stands. He is, after all, Everyman, this final pillar of the state, this back-bowed creature who supports king, soldier, priest, merchant and the rest. And if I desire to have a good idea of my kind, *une fière idée de l'homme*, I think of him. He is the raw material from which we draw, the mud from which our finer clays are baked. It takes all sorts to make a world, and in the cottages, precisely, you find all the sorts that are necessary. You will find unlettered men who have in them the makings of kings, of priests, of merchants, and of soldiers. They seem as it were to be resting there beneath the thatches, on the clay floors, to be waiting for the call of Destiny, for the odd flick from the finger nail of Fate that shall send them, in the persons of their seed, up the ladders to the highest ranges. And to these cottages there shall descend in good time the children of our rulers, the seed of our mighty ones; just as today, driving carriers' carts, speeding the plough, carrying buckets to pig-styes, you will find men bearing the great names; Fiennes, Talbots, Howards, Spencers, Darcys, all are there, all came from there, and shall no doubt once more go out thence into the world.

For the real heart of the country is the cottage, the image being not far-fetched but exact, since in this dwelling the sons of men learn temperance, endurance, caution, tolerance, since here they are hardened, strengthened, tempered and rendered tough. The cottage is, as it were, positively the heart, since it sends forth the aspiring drops of blood that go to make up the body politic, since it receives them always again at last, purifies them always once more, and always once more sends them forth upon the eternal round of ups and downs that is the history or the families of mankind.

CHAPTER V

Utopias

'D——D is the farm of T.W. L——n, the sportsman and financier.

'It consists of 800 acres of made land... Though of comparatively small acreage... for perfection of equipment it is approached by no farm on the earth; its livestock is the best that experts can select and money can buy. The D——d stables contain the best trotting-bred sires in the world, the champion large harness-horse and champion small harness-horse, the champion saddle-horse and the champion pony. Its herd of Jersey cattle is headed by the best Jersey bull in existence; its kennels of English bulldogs, Blenheim, Prince Charles, and Ruby spaniels are equal, if not superior, to any in the world...

'D——d represents the outlay of £400,000 spent, and it is run at an annual outlay of £40,000 over receipts... It is lighted by electricity, the lights, by the way, being specially worthy of notice from the manner of their hanging – they are attached to the trunks of the trees, and the wires leading to the lights are hidden under a profusion of ivy and roses... The grounds are piped for water under high pressure, and the ugly stand-pipe has been elaborated into a picturesque look-out tower with a peal of bells that strike the hours and play the Westminster chimes at sunrise and sunset. The buildings are heated throughout by hot water, the stables have ceiling coils that give a temperature of 50° in the coldest weather. The roads are macadamised and are lighted by electric lamps at intervals of 200 feet... That the scale of D——d may truly be called grand is apparent from the next building, the riding-school, 200 feet x 130 feet, or larger than the Agricultural Hall at Islington, England... The stable for farm horses is 200 feet long and contains a carpenter's shop...'

This castle is not in Spain, nor is it the dream of some farmer worried to death with the problem of making both ends meet where everything that goes off his farm walks upon its own legs; nor yet is it the ideal work-house of the one field-labourer who has had leisure for ideals. But perhaps it *is* what we are coming to.

I copy these passages – they are not the most profuse – from one of the more respectable of our country journals, where D——d is cited as a model of what things should be if Great Britain were an agricultural Utopia.

And of course, except for the superlatives, the 'no farm on earth', 'the best that money can buy', and so on, the description of any one of these marvels might come from some English valley or parkland. Lord B——'s famous breed of Wensleydales might be as sumptuously housed; Mr C——'s prize Berkshires might have floors to their sties of marble as costly; or the cow-stalls of the Duchess of W——'s shorthorns may be as well warmed as those of D——d. But at D——d there are all these things together; and there is everything else as well; and D——d and the electric lights, and the trees, and the flowers (Mr L——n, the owner, was the proprietor of the world-shaking L——n carnation, which sold for $30,000) – all these things, all this fairy palace, sprang up in a barren land in three years' time. It was a leisure creation of Mr T.W. L——n, whose real work is 'captaining the fight against the S—— Trust, the greatest combination of capital the world has seen'.

Of course it is really only the old story over again. All over England, all over Europe, there are the great and mellow houses. They confront the evening skies from hill tops, or in sleepy valelands they take the luxurious rays of the sun. And most of them rose in the same way, Blenheim having been built as a leisure work whilst Marlborough was 'captaining the fight' in the Low Countries against 'the greatest combination' of chicanery and of troops the world had seen. And whether gained by the sword of knights or the reed pens of diplomatists, whether the growth of ages in the hands of dominant families, or whether they sprang up at the biddings of single geniuses of one kind and another, our cis-Atlantic castles and houses are not intimate products of the soil. They were not based on fortunes made by the plough and crook; they were bought with money made on the battle-field or the back stairs of palaces, with money earned at sea or in the plains of the Punjab. It is this fact that makes D——d, which of course is in Massachusetts, so profoundly uninteresting. It is not a new creation; it is not showing the way to anything; it is simply imitation by a man who has money enough for *anything*. Mr T.W. L——n might just as well have spent his gold upon having made for himself a crown of radium.

On the other hand, so vast is the problem of the country, so deep do its ramifications go that it is really only the spirit of Mr L———n's enterprise that one can cavil at – the spirit that prompts an 'annual outlay of £40,000 over receipts'. For what is the use of this expenditure? It is on a par with that of a Roman emperor who might feed his horses on gilded corn. As well give his cows marble baths; no knowledge is gained. Yet the problem of the best stabling for cows is intimately interesting to the social reformer, since it must have a bearing upon the whole question of land tenure. If you cannot afford the best sort of stable for a cow out of a smallholding, you must rule cow-keeping out of the profitable pursuits of the smallholder, and to that extent you must discount the possibility that the smallholding will prove the basis of your agricultural Utopia. Or again, a princely expenditure upon electric apparatus may undoubtedly have its uses as leading a forlorn hope. For certain thinkers hold that the whole problem of the fight between the stock-breeder and the butcher might be solved by giving cold-storage into the hands of the farmer. In that case the stock-breeder could fatten his beasts just when and how he would, according to his district, his climate, the nature of his soil, the state of his seed crops, and so on. And having his fatted beast he could slaughter it when it suited him and store his carcases in his refrigerator, selling his meat to a chastened and humbled butcher. In that way the farmer would secure the bulk of the price that the consumer pays for his meat, and the middleman would be brought to his knees.

That, at least, is the contention of the cold-storage theorist. Yet how is it to be tested unless *some* farmer capitalist make the experiment and actually finds out whether the idea is financially as sound as it is alluring? It is for these reasons that, in face of a rural question as saddening as it is bewildering, one regrets the belauding of displays like that of Mr T.W. L———n. It is as if one should, in the days when Arthur Young was trying to improve farming, hold up the Trianon châlets as models to an admiring world of agriculturists. Heaven forbid, at the same time, that I should seem to decry the expenditure of the millionaire who built D———d in three years. For perhaps D———d itself *is* the solution to the problem.

Perhaps it is to be the fate of the country – of the English country at least – to become just one large playground for millionaires. In essentials, large stretches of England have for many years past been little else than that. And it is perhaps the inversion of that feeling that has given to land-owning its power to confer social precedence; for in essence the political strength of county families has been the fact that their rents from broad acres lifted them above the necessity of making a living by the commercialism that our legislature exists to control. They could, as it were, erect great town houses, because they drew their resources from the country, just as the county families that perpetually succeeded theirs could build great country houses out of town revenues.

Perhaps that tendency is on the wane; perhaps – and D——d might be evidence of the fact – it is on the increase. I imagine, however, that it remains really much the same – that when one of us, one of the ordinary half-town, half-country mortals that most of us are – when one of us shuts his eyes and builds his castle in the air, in his particular image of where and how he would live if he became really rich, some sort of D——d would arise, some sort of great house, not so vulgar, not so shining, lacking the electric-light wires that are trained to climb up trees and shine out amongst the astonished sparrows in their nests. We should have, no doubt, our town asylum; but substantially there would be large, tall or low rooms, with high, clear or leaded windows, looking out upon a lake with water lilies, upon a sunny Italian garden, upon urns, statues of fauns, upon a paved courtyard, or upon the misty distances of lawns, the still forms, the branch-like antlers of tranquil deer.

We might or might not have our tall and quiet libraries; we should have our long, still galleries of old pictures; we should have our gun-rooms, our saddle-rooms, our boot-rooms, our still-rooms. We should have our great ranges of stables, our kennels, perhaps, and possibly our neat, pleasant home-farm. We should almost certainly have our immense and well-stocked coverts (with perhaps a litter or two of netted fox cubs); we should perhaps be too lazy to aspire to anything more than a very honorary mastership of our local Pytchley; or we might, whilst building our castle, imagine ourselves endowed with the gift of hard riding, and enough of nerve and of energy. We might have our thatched pavilion, our smooth lawns, on which, each summer, our underkeepers, our stable-men, and our local curates should meet wandering teams of cricketers. Our outer architecture might be all stone or all black-and-white; our fireplaces all Italian marble or all British oak. But if we are wise in our imaginings, though our halls gleam with marble, our argosies, as in the days of Bacchylides, will still be laden with

Egyptian bales. I mean that, for our revenues, we shall still depend on investments other than those in land. We shall have acres enough to play with, acres enough to give us consequence in the neighbourhood, but never one that would give us anxiety.

And there is D——d again, a little more mellow, a little less spick-and-span, without the champion heavy harness stallion that there would really be no fun in purchasing ready-made; but substantially there would be D——d, and the problem of what is to become of the real land as far away as ever. It will be objected that in my castle of Spain I have taken into account only the most material things – I have left out the soul. But our climate, our dear green turf, our good roads, our excellent railways, but above all our climate, are responsible for that. It was, I think, Charles II who said that, upon the whole, the British weather was the best weather in the world, for in the whole year there is no day, either for its inclemency or its heat, so unpleasant that a man may not go abroad.

Our English great houses are out-of-door houses; our English country life is an out-of-door life. You do not, with all the expenditure, find concert rooms, theatres, or studios as part of the English house design. A small German prince would solace himself in the winters and summers with an indoor and an outdoor orchestra. An ordinary Russian landed proprietor would have a number of his house serfs trained as actors. But we do not choose our servants on those lines. After all these years, the old Norse spirit survives in us – the spirit that dictated the lines depicting how a man should feel after a hard day:

> Who heedeth weariness
> That hath been day-long on the mountain in the winter
> weather's stress
> And now stands in the lighted doorway and seeth the wives
> draw nigh,
> And heareth men dighting the banquet and the bed whereon
> he shall lie?

If you substitute the coverts or the grouse moors or the saddle for 'the mountain' of the second line, you have there the feeling of the whole of the really Utopian country-sides – the feelings to lead up to which the whole of wealthy rural England really exists. Fox-hunting, perhaps, has gone. It is said to be too expensive all round; it costs, say, two thousand pounds to keep a two-days-a-week pack now where it used to cost one thousand pounds; and with the present system of keeping the great shoots back, it is almost impossible to draw the best coverts till after Christmas; the foxes, preserved within wire enclosures, are too plentiful, and show no sport. Partridge shooting is no longer what it was, and the annual pheasant slaughter is a matter of two gorgeous days a year, instead of affording moderate occupation all the winter through. A pheasant costs a pound apiece to shoot, a partridge ten shillings, a salmon twenty-seven shillings per pound to the rod; and, so the old-fashioned sportsmen will tell you, all these things have gone to the deuce, because of the specialisation in all sports. Nevertheless the spirit – that of the lighted doorway after the winter day – remains the dominant factor of our country life in its wealthier aspects, whether we rush down to it for three days out of the year in which we shoot into a sort of dark milky-way of pheasants, or whether we still have the heavenly luck to hunt five days a week

It has, of course, its æsthetic and poetic sides too; without them it would probably not appeal to the Englishman, who is at bottom always at least a potential poet. In the long rides back do not we all remember the dying swirls of sunset in the winter skies, the still darkness of the Scotch firs, the gleam of light upon the laurels in the drive, and that sweetest of all sounds, the robin's song, from the dark bushes? Do not we all really remember the gleam of the bedroom candles as we lounge before our private and particular fire, too lazy, too luxuriating, too pleasantly reminiscent not to let the near clamour of the gong, reverberating along the great corridor, startle us before we have even begun to think of dressing? And, indeed, in a sense, the æsthetic satisfaction will remain to one through dinner-time, with its show of candles on women's shoulders, and through the long, lounging hour or two before the smoking-room fire. The body, as it were, being beaten and purified by the long day, the mind has the power to be appreciative, and we are as lazily attentive to effects of light and shade as to the smoke-room stories, or to the 'shop' of the sport in which we may have sought this Nirvana.

It *is* a good life; but how very much an out-of-door life! Think of what an English country-house party is on a really torrential day – on a day on which even an English country lady will not go into the open. Think of the intolerable boredom of it. There is absolutely *nothing* to be done. In the dim, tall library a hunting-crop and a flask lie on the writing-desk, and you are not in the mood for a folio edition of Drydale's *Monastikon*; you are not in the mood for a mechanical piano's rendering of the Seventh Symphony in the great drawing-room; you are not in the mood for flirting in the little drawing-room; you have written all the letters you can possibly write before breakfast – and the rain pours down. At last something really exciting occurs. Two self-sacrificing persons, the son of the house and his *fiancée*, having in desperation put on shiny mackintoshes and sou'westers, stand, wind-blown and laughing figures, putting at clock-golf on the lawn just beneath the billiard-room window. And for as long as they will keep it up beneath the furious showers, you may stand with all the rest of the house party, watching them, and betting as to whether his skill – or his admiration for her pretty, wet, blonde cheeks – will make him win or lose the next five puts. When they are tired of it you may go to the stable and talk to your man as to how he is to get to the next house on your programme. There is nothing else for it.

The point is – of course one must qualify all these generalisations with 'as a rule' – there will be absolutely no resources in the house for any organised and general indoor occupation. As for building a concert-room or a theatre, the English territorial magnate would rather consider seriously the idea of erecting a covered tennis-court, since tennis is a game that a man may play till he is fifty, and improve all the time. Of course, the court, with its grilles and pent-houses, will cost a little more than a music-room, but then it will be of more social value. And, indeed, since there are so few days of an English year on which one cannot go out-of-doors, it is hardly of much value to make, in the arrangements of our everyday great houses, too much allowance for indoor occupations, which must inevitably be of an intellectual nature.[1]

---

1   I do not wish to be taken as sneering at the intellectual faculties of the country gentleman, or to insinuate that no great noble has taken an interest in music or the fine arts, or that no house party has ever organised private theatricals, or occupied itself on rainy days in playing card-games. In how many country houses have we not been overwhelmed by the splendours of Raphaels, of Holbeins, of Snyders, of Vandykes, or even of Correggios? There is, of course, no land like the English country for them. And in how many noble libraries have we not longed to spend long hours? And no doubt, across the counties, one might still find scholars as fastidious or *dilettanti*, as keen as those who gathered together these dear and priceless things or erected those long and august corridors. Nevertheless the 'note' of modern English country-life, in its social aspects, *does* seem to me to remain an out-of-door one; and on their social sides the great English land owners do seem more and more to be directing their energies towards giving their friends that particular physico-sensuous feeling of wellbeing after stress of weather. So that, if one wanted to imagine a country Utopia, one would picture it, not as a land where it was always summer and always afternoon, but as a land where the year turned always between

Such, no doubt, and more or less, is the usual psychology of the really wealthy life as it is lived in the English counties. Naturally it is always in a state of fluescence; the motor car may be affecting it; one card game or another may be rising to fashion or falling into desuetude; hunting may be becoming impossible, or shooting merely a means of organised boredom. But in the large that kind of life is very much alive, is very much 'lived'. Considered Utopianly, as an ideal, as a region where one may build castles in the air, it is not more really inspiring than any other. And if it draws its revenues from outside the land, it is merely D——d over again; it is not, as a social phenomenon, more interesting than a life lived, say, in a gorgeous and uninspired palace of the Riviera.

But the moment that we can think of such a life as a growth of the soil, the moment we can think of the great house as being supported almost absolutely by the acres that surround it, we reach a different level of social interest. For then it is at least real and significant. It becomes even poignant; for I have frequently felt aroused to interest when, in such a great house, I have been able to remember that, whilst the rest of the house-party were having as much of a 'good time' as, to each one after his kind, the gods, his liver or his temperament, would vouchsafe – whilst all the rest were talking in knots, looking out of windows, running laughing along the corridors, there was, somewhere in some lower room, deep in the background of the great pile of buildings, in a sort of den hung round with maps and estate plans, in some office of one sort or other, a man with knitted brows engaged in getting out of the land the wherewithal to keep in motion all that light-hearted and pleasant life – the real landowner.

One knows very well that nowadays his is no very easy task. It is a desperate process of making two ends meet, and the tendency of this particular two ends is to get further and further apart; the wire of the circle as it were contracts and contracts between his hands that strive to draw them together. For whilst his rent-roll grows steadily less, his standard of living – which, if he is to lead his countryside, needs must vie with the standard set by townsmen – his standard of living grows more and more costly. He is hampered by the wastefulness of his ancestors, with acres of Italian gardens laid out by the second earl, with a mile of stone terraces planned

---

October and February, and where it was nearly always half-past six – when, naturally, it is too dark to look at pictures, and one feels too healthy to want to read books.

by the eleventh marquis, or with a whole town of stables. All these things must be kept up, whilst rents are falling and whilst the hereditary pack costs two pounds for every one that it cost when rents were at their highest.

Of course the acres of garden should be turned into lawns, the gardeners sent to the right about, the stables pulled down, the stone balustrades allowed to crumble in the winter frosts; the hounds even should be once more sent back to their trenchers. It is the day of desperate remedies; but these things are comprehensibly bitter.

Naturally the keynote of the symphony is struck by a very different phrase. I was talking to one of the largest and most progressive landowners in the country, and he said –

'Well, you see, landowning as a business simply doesn't pay any longer.' I doubt myself whether, 'as a business', it ever really *did* pay on that particular scale. As a rule the Italian gardens, the stone terraces, the stable towns were built originally by 'spenders' or by men who had made money outside the land. They represent either trees cut down or successful manipulations of the funds; either sales of outlying farms or grants from a grateful nation; either newly-discovered coal-pits or the growth of manufacturing towns upon estates in another county. And the great land fortunes of today are regulated by all sorts of odd improvidences on the part of distant ancestors. Thus today the Earl of B—— is starving in his castle with his thousands of acres, because in 1840 his grandfather was powerful enough to prevent the passage of a railway within seven miles of his estate. And Lord L—— is a millionaire twice over because *his* grandfather could not prevent that railway's trespass, and now the descendant owns two pottery towns which have covered the green grass. And there are, of course, instances of that sort of ill-luck or good to be heard everywhere for the asking.

But, as a rule, landowning as a business simply does not pay any longer. It would be premature to assert that it never will. Perhaps, owing to some unforeseen revolution of the wheel of fortune, owing, say, to the new fashion of week-ending, the landowner who has been forced to let his mansion to a financier will really see the end of his rainy days, will really come into his own again, and return once more to the sound of welcoming church-bells. Perhaps, in fact, the old system will simply come back again to its lusty growth. It is not, of course, by any means dead yet; you may discover throughout the length and breadth of the land hundreds of estates that pay very well; the old spirit of land-owning, its exclusiveness, its belief that the possession of secular title-deeds is ample atonement for the lack of good looks, good humour, wit, intellect, talent, or any other human quality. It is still, socially, nearly as good a thing as ever it was to be one of the Shropshire Thwaites and nothing else. But, upon the whole, it is not as good a 'business'.

And the real fight for existence will come not so much from the great landowner. The ownership of 40,000 acres and a castle is not so poignant a thing as to own 2,000 and an old house. The great man is, as a rule, much further from his fields and his trees. But the small one knows, sometimes, each blade of grass, and has for years debated with his father or his brother whether the view from the drawing room would or would not be improved by cutting down three old elms that stand two hundred yards away at the top of a rise. He will have pondered for years in his mind whether the day has come to give up the time of his estate carpenter to opening out the twelve windows that were blocked up at the time of the window-tax. He is, after all, the man who will fight bitterly for the retention of the present system. And all his retainers, his brothers, his sisters, even his old uncles, will fight with him.

For I do not know anything *quite* like standing on ground that one's ancestors have owned for a century or so. You have heard of garden paths, of coppices, of cow-stalls, of deer-licks; you have heard your people speak of them all your life. You will see in the house-diary just when your grandfather determined to make that fish-pond at the bottom of the lawn; in the same old books you will see when the high timber in the home-woods was last cut, and you will discover why that very old oak in the centre of the wood was spared then. It was because it reminded your great-grand-mother of a tree under which *her* mother had sat two days before she died.

The struggle, with these smaller holders, is not so much to make both ends meet. It is not a matter of putting Italian gardens down to grass, or one of putting down ten or a dozen horses, of letting a castle here or there, and retaining still a princely income. One may say of Lord So-and-So that he is the luckiest man in the peerage, since, when his Towers was burnt down, he lost at once the necessity of keeping up an enormous house erected by generations of 'spenders' and received insurance indemnities amounting to a quarter-of-a-million pounds. But if the manor-house of Squire William burns he will receive little enough by way of insurance, and his rentals, when everything is deducted, will not bring him in seven hundred a-year on which to bring up five children and to maintain some sort of traditional splendour. And it will be the squire rather than the lord who will be cut to the heart at the thought of parting with his estate at a 'times' price or for more. And it will be the squire, with his family, large in number and filled with the love of the family house, the trees, the fish-ponds and the paddocks – it will be all the great class of Shropshire Thwaites who will the most bitterly oppose any system of reform of land tenures. With those people, as with the others, landowning as a business has ceased as a rule to 'be profitable'. But they would rather pay for their sentiment, they would rather live on their seven hundred a-year than see their particular beloved holdings broken up into three or four hundred small plots and sold for a price that might make them for ever independent of the land. No doubt their sentiments are the right sentiments, and no doubt it is better for such men to wait with an anxious eye upon the markets in the hope that once again they may be able to ask from his farmers rents such as will enable him to send *all* his sons to Sandhurst.

The step from such a man to the farmer who owns his own farm and from that farmer to the owner of two or three acres of accommodation land is not very far; but it is far enough. Yet, with them and the agricultural labourer, the whole of the community that lives directly out of the land is exhausted. There remains that curious middleman, the tenant farmer.

The really large tenant farmer, the man with sufficient energy and sufficient capital to manage fifteen hundred acres or so, is a business man for whom one may have a respect. He is a great employer of labour, an organiser, a man with special knowledge and with possibilities of self-adaptation. But I am inclined to see in the smaller tenant farmer the real weak spot of our rural system, the real inefficient third wheel that is cracking beneath the weight of this particular cart. Our present triple-stranded rope is made up of landlord, tenant, and labourer. It has been laid down over and over again, and I suppose it is true, that the land today will not show three profits, that one of this trio must go. It cannot very well be the agricultural labourer; it certainly will not be the landlord. It must then be the small tenant farmer.

The really large farmer, whether he 'runs' a district of the Cotswolds on the ranche system, or really farms great plain-lands on the downs, pays a rent proportionately so small that he is, financially at least, in as good a position as his landlord, since what he loses in rent he gains by not having the fancy that he must maintain a feudal position. He *must* employ good workmen, since his supervision cannot be very meticulous; he must farm well, since his stake is so large that he cannot afford to change his tenancy once he is settled. And, his stake being so large, he has great power over his landlord. The small tenant farmer has neither these advantages nor these incentives. It pays him to cheat his hands, to neglect his hedges, to starve his land, to take scratch crops, to indulge in the hundred-and-one meannesses by which a hundred-and-one small profits may be gained.

I offer these views, of course, only for what they are worth, and as a purely personal contribution to a puzzling subject in which I profess to see no more clearly than five hundred of my neighbours. And were I in a position to initiate legislation I am not sure that I should do so upon the lines of a drastic abolition of this third wheel. I see the matter in this light, but I am by no means sure that it is not merely because of a 'kink' in my own eyes. For I must confess that the small tenant farmer as a class does not interest me nearly as much as either the farm-labourer or the landowner. I am far less at home at the ordinary of a market-day than at the fireside of a ridge alehouse; I feel myself more likely to come in contact with ignorant prejudice and self-conceit uttered in loud voices, and it has always seemed to me that, as a class, the tenant-farmer is just a tradesman like any other. He goes somewhat more into the open-air, but there the difference seems to end. He sells the produce of other men's handiwork, and he sells it very badly. If it be claimed for him that he directs that production, it must be conceded that he directs it very badly. I have had it said to me, by a friend who knows tenant-farmers as well as I may claim to know the field-labourer, that the best farmers had, in his experience, almost always been something else. The most successful farmer he ever knew had been a linen-draper who had found the long hours of his trade too trying for his health. And, on the whole, my own observation would lead me to confirm the views of this particular friend, for the two most prosperous 300-acre tenant-farmers that I have known began life, the one as a country grocer, the other as a Wesleyan minister.

I ought, however, to add that one of the very worst farmers I know is also a country grocer and draper, a man who is singularly adept at all the tricks of farm-starving. He does certainly contrive to make his farm pay, and even pays his reduced rent very regularly;

but the state of his hedges and of his farm-buildings makes me sigh whenever I think of them, and I should not like to be the tenant who will succeed him.

Nevertheless, the general moral of this seems to be merely that the farmer gains by having had at one period of his career some outside interest, some experience of a larger world, or at least some training in keeping accounts. For in these hard days and years farming, like everything else, has become a competitive business, and needs for success a thoroughly awakened man with an eye to public events, and perhaps, before all things, a power of combination. This the farmer never seems to have possessed; he is not, in the councils of the nation, any better represented than is the field labourer. He is, for instance, hopelessly penalised by his railways, yet he never even thinks of combining to force down freight rates. He might not be successful even if he tried; but he has never tried.

I write of him with some harshness; but I am not blind to the pathos of his case. It will wring my heart when I think of the hopeless struggle made by many small men; of the tired look in their eyes, of their thin beards, of their weary struggles with that most capricious of all the flails of Fate, the weather. But in spite of the pathos of it, this class of wearied and haggard men seems to me to be just precisely the wrong men in the wrong places. They have been on their farms for generations without getting any 'forrader', and in this bitter struggle the man who stands still must for ever be left behind.

I do not mean to say that there is no place for the small farmer, but I should like to see his particular farm regarded as being merely one stage in a definite career. Let me sketch perfunctorily my ideal parish, my particular Utopia of the present land system. For, at least under the present system, what seems to me to be sapping the land of its population, and sapping the population of its energies, is the fact that there is no chance, no *ignis fatuus* chance even of a career. If you are an agricultural labourer you have no chance of rising, you *cannot* take a smallholding because there are none to take; if you are a smallholder you have no chance of getting a larger farm, and you have no chance of rising from farm to farm. Humanity being romantic, this means that no rural Dick Whittington will ever turn on any hill-top to listen to his chime of bells. What could the bells say to him? 'Turn again, Whittington – and end in the workhouse.' Now, if I had, say, 50,000 acres of mixed down, hill-side, woodland and marsh to play with, I should like to experiment with the holdings in some such arrangement as the following. I would have, say –

400 holdings of between 1 and 10 acres apiece,					
	averaging 5			=	2,000 acres
50 holdings of		20	acres apiece	=	1,000
10	"	150	"	=	1,500
5	"	300	"	=	1,500
4	"	500	"	=	2,000
3	"	1,000	"	=	4,000
2	"	5,000	"	=	10,000
1	"	10,000	"	=	20,000

This would account for 42,000 acres, and the remaining 8,000 I would leave available for the pleasure-grounds of large houses, for villa residences, for week-end cottages, and for what not.

Here we should have, as it were, the manœuvring-ground for an army of 10,000 souls. So many thousand – the privates – would be the men and the families of the field labourers, men too young, too indolent, too dissipated, or too merely slow-brained ever to rise or to have risen. But such a man might save enough money to acquire a holding of from one to ten acres; or he might show enough intelligence to satisfy an agricultural bank that he could be trusted with money enough to be aided in the acquirement of such a holding. Then he would be, as it were, promoted to the rank of corporal or lance-corporal. He would have a holding not large enough to render himself quite self-supporting, and he would be there ready to be employed by the larger farmers at times when there was need for extra labour. And from that stage, either by proofs of saving or of being aided by the banks, he might be promoted to the rank, as it were, of a sergeant in this army – he might acquire a holding of twenty acres; and so given luck or genius, he might go upwards until he or his sons might take one of the large mixed farms of five thousand, or one of the downland ranche farms of ten thousand acres.

Here there is a practicable scheme – practicable enough to a syndicate with a million of pounds to experiment with, and one needing nothing like special legislation to put it in force. I do not, of course, go into any detail, such as the planting of woodlands, which, in the winters, would provide so much and such attractive work to the poorer labourers; nor yet such details as the providing of amusements, easy means of transit, or social centres. For these, after all, necessary as they are, are not so much of an attraction to keen men as is the chance of making a career. But here, at least, is a scheme, Utopian in a sense, but in a sense, too, founded on the eternal necessity of mankind to struggle upwards. It would be a Utopia, but not one of those bright, cast-iron schemes in which all provision for development, for flux and reflux, all chances of change, are left out. And it would be practical, inasmuch as it would give a chance to keen men of entering the lowest ranks and of striving up to the highest. That, I think, is really what is wanted. It would give a chance, too, to the field labourer; it would be a means of tapping all that substratum which, as I have tried to prove in a previous chapter, contains *every* possibility. There are in the present-day cottages men and the children of men fitted to fill every position in such a community – men fitted to be workers, to be overseers, to be wood-reeves, to be farmers, and to be accountants. Modern education is excellent in its way, because it really does give some commencements of a wider outlook. And children so educated would be excellent recruits in such a land army, excellent raw material for such apprenticeships.

But if no such chances of a 'career' be given, or if no such chances arise, there seems to me to be very little use in starting farm colonies, or bringing town labourers back to smallholdings. Possibly the present generation, disillusioned as to the conditions of town life, might remain in the glebes and closes, but their children would inevitably recommence the process of going into the towns. The gain would be merely temporary.

I labour the point of the 'career', because I have not anywhere seen it put as clearly as I should wish, and because it seems to me the most valuable contribution that I personally can make to this old-standing and intolerable problem. Once that could be settled, many other vexed points, such as that of housing, that of rentals, that of tenures, of land registration and transfer – even the really burning question of transport – would settle themselves. For such a community would be so powerful, and composed of units so bound together by common interests, that it would be able to make its voice heard and its power felt by all the railway-companies and the other vested interests that now so hamper the isolated 'farmer'.

The question of land-tenure, as I have said, would settle itself upon the lines most profitable to all concerned. I am by no means certain that an individual possession of smallholdings or of large farms would be really as free from objection as the ownership of the land by a public-spirited individual or a broadly-constituted syndicate, or that it would be as free from objection as the state ownership of the land. But I do think that the opening of an office – whether state, estate, or syndicate – where every man who wished it, and could produce, say, a voter's qualification, where, in fact, every voter of a district could purchase on the lowest reasonable terms the right to a certain occupation of a certain minimum extent of land for a certain limit of time – where a man could ask to have an interest in the land as freely as he now can purchase postage-stamps – the provision of such an office is one of the first duties of experimentalists in land reform.

No doubt we want, before all things, 'data'; but the collection of statistics is an endless task, and the reading of meanings into these collections is little more than pleasant occupation for persons who have never had any dealings with the land. And at present the broad tendency of the real countryman is to say, 'Leave things alone to right themselves.' The townsman meanwhile is crying out, 'We must force the masses back to the land because we are on the eve of physical deterioration. We must send the old people back to form new and healthy blood with which in the future we once more may be recruited.'

For, upon the whole, the townsman, aware that the country interests have been neglected for the last sixty years so that the towns may grow, is itching to apply town methods of legislation to the country; and upon the whole, the country says, 'Having neglected us for half a century, neglect us yet a little more so that we may work out our own ruin or salvation along the lines of supply and demand.'

And the problems set before the reforming townsman are bewildering enough. The young and confident cry out – 'The whole thing will be solved by the provision of cheap cottages.'

'*I*,' says my friend the great Liberal landowner, 'have just built 400 cottages at £200 apiece,' and he plumes himself upon his public spirit.

'But,' cries out a new section of the young and confident, 'the truck system must not apply. No employer, no landowner must build cottages for his own labourers, since that will mean that the labourer will take his rent in kind.'

'Then how in the world is the trick to be done?' a good Tory of the old school growls sardonically. 'I must build cottages on my neighbour's land, and the other fellow must build cottages on mine, I suppose?'

A young friend of mine, having no personal views, sober, quiet and essentially a listener, told me that one night, having tired himself for many months with collecting 'data' and listening to 'views', he fell asleep. He had formed no views of his own, perhaps he was incapable of an original effort. But he dreamt that he was on a certain terrace overlooking the Thames. At first he sat alone in a cane arm-chair, and he was saying dreamily –

'Something *ought* to be done for the land.'

'Something is going to be done,' said a voice at his elbow, and he saw that he had been joined by one of a Party that was coming into power then. 'We are going to tax land-values. We are going to make landowning such an expensive business that no one will *want* to own land. We need new sources of revenue.'

'How will that help the farmer?' another voice said. A man from Lincolnshire had come upon the terrace, and many other figures were pouring desultorily into the open air from the tall windows of the grey buildings. 'What we need is intelligent labour. Give lessons in potato-planting at the Board Schools and do away with arithmetic.'

'No, no!' cried a Northerner. 'Make your Board School education even more literary than it is, but re-establish the living-in system on farms. It was when the boys learned their work on the farms and in them that the best labourers were bred.'

'No. Away with the living-in system altogether,' muttered an American Londoner. 'It hinders the increase of population. Labourers who live in do not marry until they are old. We need all the children that we can beget or the country will be absolutely solitary.'

'Something *ought* to be done,' my friend murmured in his dream, but his murmur was a little less confident.

'We are going to tax all the large estates with a graduated tax so that the smallholder will be encouraged,' a working-man member fulminated. 'We are going to drive out the Yankee millionaire who is turning the whole country into pleasure parks.'

'That would be absolutely wrong,' said one political economist. 'That would drive money out of the country. The man who erects a D——d is spending more money on his pleasures than any farmer can. And pleasure is a commodity that a land may produce, just as much a commodity as corn is.'

'But,' said another political economist, 'the point is whether five thousand planters on five thousand acres of land will not produce more of some other commodity than will be produced in pleasure by one man with 5,000 acres of deer park.'

'Oh, that's all nonsense!' said an ironical Conservative. And he proceeded to tell an anecdote of a lady of title who had disforested her deer-moors at the demand of her crofters. The crofters, at the year's end, had found that their rates went up to 27s in the pound because the moors no longer paid deer-forest rates. The crofters had clamoured for the deer again.

'I'm rather in agreement with the deer-park man,' said an Advanced Thinker, a little surprised to find himself in the same boat with the Conservative. 'The real problem of today is *not* the re-population of the country, but the evolution of an ideal town. So, at least, it has always seemed to us who are the scientific sociologists. But still, since the subject is on the *tapis*, it should be an easy matter to evolve a really Utopian agricultural community. The really ideal ———'

'If you will excuse me,' said a Director, 'I should wish to point out to you that a city which is at once the ideal town and the home of the ideal agricultural community is already under construction. Our prospectus says, "This company has not been formed with the view of entering into a land speculation, its primary object being to promote a great social improvement, and to deal at once with the two vital questions of *overcrowding* in towns and *depopulation* of rural districts. The land comprised in the estate ———"'

'I have read your prospectus,' a Mathematician interrupted the lecture, 'and it occurs to me that if your city were extended upon its present scale the whole country would be taken up before the whole population of the country was accommodated.'

'Besides,' a Political Historian took up the objections, 'history teaches us that great industrial cities have always been caused to arise by natural features, such as rivers, sea-ports or, as is the case of Lancashire and its cotton cities, by a combination of seaports, rivers and atmospheric conditions. Now your city possesses *no* natural advantages except that it is within easy railway journey of the capital. It will therefore differ from no other suburb, will solve no problem, and will depend for its existence on the fact that the problem of housing in the capital has not yet been solved.'

'Let me remind you that you are getting far away from the problems of agriculture,' the Advanced Thinker once more took up his parable. '*I* stand for the future; therefore I surely before all others have the right here to be heard.'

The terrace by this time was entirely filled by disputants. They obscured the view for my friend whose dream had caused them to arise. He was surrounded and overwhelmed by their forms and by their voices. But giving way, as all crowds will do, to the disputant who made the most confident claim to a hearing, they fell silent and paid attention to the Advanced Thinker. He lay back in his armchair, facing that of my friend who had dreamed him; he cleared his throat and, with the level intonation of one used to making long speeches and thinking long thoughts, he began, after having swallowed a jujube –

'The matter divides itself into several heads. In the first place it is open to doubt whether all reasons for the existence of the field labourer have not vanished with the advance of the applied sciences. We are now – or we are upon the point of being – able to reconstruct out of common clay, coal-tar products, and natural mineral oils, all the food-stuffs that are necessary for human sustenance. Let me, however, concede for the sake of argument that it would be possible to cultivate one staple commodity – say wheat – at a cheaper rate than its constituents could be evolved from coal-tar and reconstructed so as to be digestible and nutritive. Then we have constructed engines that, with the expenditure of the care of merely one man, will be able to scratch up, rake, furrow, roll, and cover practically unlimited acreages of land in the shortest of spaces of time.'

'How about my heavy clays?' cried a Norfolk farmer from the background.

'How about my light sands?' cried another. 'I've had to give up steam-ploughs and return to horses!'

'Details – details,' said the Advanced Thinker unconcernedly. 'I think I have proved to my hearers that even for purposes of cultivation the need for *men* upon the land has vanished.'

'You need a man with a d——d good head-piece to drive one of my engines,' said a steam-plough proprietor.

'Precisely – precisely,' the Advanced Thinker retorted. 'What we need is not men with a knowledge of soils, but skilful mechanics. *Any* soil, light or heavy, can be handled and clean ploughed by the *right* type of engine. But let me resume my train of thought. It seems to me, as to many of my friends who have spoken or not spoken, that the ultimate and the real function of the land is to become one vast pleasure park. We shall be rid, then, of the poor, warped, gnarled, unintelligent farm labourers, farmers, smallholders, and the rest. We shall be rid once for all of the steam, the mire, and the grime of Mother Earth. We shall be able to breed a clean, straight-backed race of men, fit to meet and to solve the real problems that lie before humanity.'

Loud cries of derision, of rage, and of mockery came from all the idealists of the now great assembly. Our friend the dreamer caught fragments of phrases: 'Return to the earth', 'Mother Nature', 'The good, free air', 'The health-giving, brown soil', 'The truth of the broad heavens', and 'The dignity of labour'.

But the tumult stilled as dream tumults will still themselves, and the Advanced Thinker proceeded –

'Oh, well, since you *will* have mud-grubbers, let me sketch a really modern rural Utopia…'

There were to be in the centre of this town or village great light and airy schools – these before all. Then there should be a library, communal cook and bake-houses, a vast communal eating-room where all meals should be taken in common, communal thrashing-barns and cold-storage barns, communal engine-sheds, communal theatres, concert-rooms, debating halls, and a place of free worship, communal barracks for communal domestic servants who should at convenient hours make the beds, dust, sweep, or decorate the individual cottages. These, small, white, beautiful in design, and not too close together, should cluster in a ring round one of the communal buildings, and from each cluster, radiating as the spokes of a wheel, there should run over the plain, cinder tracks along which the men should cycle to their holdings… Here at least men might live the lives of men and find food for the mind along with a measure of health-giving labour…

Stirred by this attractive vision of a white-walled township studded with a ring of trees, the spires of its communal buildings rising like tall poplars above the red roofs, the white walls, and the green plain like a great shallow bowl beneath a plain blue sky dotted with balloon-like pink and woolly clouds, itching to be nearer the realisation of this smiling and radiant vision, impatient for some one who should take the first step towards it, my dreaming friend moved in his cane armchair and uttered his unfailing formula –

'Something must be done!'

And immediately the whole assembly began to cry out in a babel of tongues; a vast multitude of white faces, each with intent eyes, and opened, shouting mouths; a weird and tremendous crowd, like that in the gigantic imaginings of a great mediaeval painter of a Last

Judgment; thousands and thousands and millions and millions of voices, in all the tongues of the world, in all imaginable accents, with all the possible tones of assurance, began to cry out panaceas, all the first steps towards the solution of this problem. And each man of all the millions (the thing was apparent to the dream consciousness of my friend) – each man had a panacea that differed from that of his neighbour.

A cold chill, a weariness of nightmare, oppressed the dreamer, he half started from his chair, and found himself lying alone upon his own veranda in his own cane lounge. A suddenly arisen great gust of wind was rushing through the dark forms of the pines and poplars across the way, and against the full white face of the moon the form of a bat silhouetted itself for a minute.

'Certainly *something* must be done,' my friend said to himself.

The wind fell, and the poplars reached, tall, motionless, and black, towards the heavens.

'By Order of the Trustees...'

OUT on the field before the house, in serrated rows that dwindle from the height of clothes-presses to the small clusters of jam jars showing above the tufts of already wintering grass, there lie all the paraphernalia with which a man throughout his life has attempted to stave off the bare terror of the four walls of his rooms. There is the old armchair in which he throned it for so long as the central figure of the small cluster of beings that went with him to the edge of the last descent that he should ever make. There, a mere bundle of brown pieces of wood, of sacking, of cordage and of screws, is the bed on which he passed so many nights; it confronts at last the grey sky from which during so many hours of darkness he hid; and ludicrous, pathetic or merely sordid, confronted as they are by the eternal truths of wind, weather, light and earth, from which they too hid so long, lie all the essential verities of a man's life.

Near the field-gate stands the thin blue figure of the policeman, a symbol of the law, with the pale light glinting on his silvered buttons; near him, fat, bearded and assured, stands the auctioneer, a symbol of the commerce that continues, though all men die; plastered upon the gate-post, its bold black letters odd and pathetically frail, contrasted as they are with the aged spines of the high-road hedges, there shines the white placard whose first words read –

'By order of the Trustees of So-and-so, deceased.'

Far down in the meadow, huddled together in dull amazement, is the flock of sheep, the rightful tenantry of this October grass; and entering the field, in knots or singly, desultorily, shyly, as sheep themselves enter an unaccustomed pasture, there come the buyers, who, gradually growing emboldened, saunter down the rows of 'things'; finger the worn curtains that once shut out the light; sit warily in chairs that, meant for hard floors, sink ominously into the damp turf; or turn round to the skies pictures of men in hunting coats who bear golden-headed children upon their shoulders.

A small nimble pony, frightened by an arriving motorcar, breaks away from the knot of traps tethered at the further gate-way. With its little dog-cart behind it, it runs round and round in the field as if it were performing some circus feat upon the soft tan of the turf. Men with their knees bent and their hands stretched out and downwards, narrow the circle around it. When at length it stops and allows itself to be caught, the occupants of the motor-car enter the field as if they were the masquers of *Henry VIII*, distinguished strangers from another planet. The auctioneer, having drunk from a case bottle and brushed some crumbs from his grey beard, mounts a kitchen chair; the crowd, sure now of a legitimate centre, close round him with faces already on the grin; an old saucepan is held above the heads of the crowd. The auctioneer says –

'Now here's a very valuable...'

You do not hear the last word because already the laugh goes up. The sale has begun.

And, wandering among the least considered trifles of how many poor friends of mine (they will never be poor any more), I have often thought that that first laugh of the auction crowd marks the last stage in the dissolution of So-and-so. Never before, however poor or however despised he were, could his meanest household utensil be really laughed at. If it were only an old kettle, its holes stopped up with soap, so long as its owner kept it in use it would have about it some of the sanctity of the house itself, and some of the sanctity of a tool. And we never laugh at tools; the more old, the more battered, the more makeshift they may be, the more we admire its owner, since with them he performs feats of increasing difficulty. Nor, for the same reason perhaps, do we ever laugh at a poverty-stricken house, since that too is an implement, and, gazing at broken roofs, broken doors, gaping walls or apertured windows, we must needs wonder how a man, much such a one as we are, can in it and by its aid perform that most desperate feat of all, the feat of living.

As long as poor So-and-so kept things going with all these poor makeshifts, as long as the small bundle of odd bed-wrenches, broken chisels, disused clock keys and rusty pony-clippers formed a portion of his worldly goods that now forms 'Lot 7' – as long as he lay still in an upper room, as long even as he retained a sort of corporate identity by means of the 'Trustees of So-and-so' who have ordered this sale, for so long these poor things were still sharers of that reverence that we must pay to a man however despised. I remember being present when some farm-hands, from beneath a bed of rotting straw in an out-house corner, raked out old pipes, old boxes of matches, mouldy crusts of bread, mouldy rinds of gnawed cheese, and a battered tobacco-box. They were the horde of the village idiot who on that bed in that barn corner had six months before yielded up his soul to the clutches of a rigid frost. He had been dead six months, but in the face of these scraps of his we felt him suddenly to rise once more; he had been the last man to touch them; he had so ordered their lying there. And until they were kicked pell-mell out into the mixen before the door, his presence seemed still to stand in the corner of the barn. We called him 'Poor Old Ben…', remembered him, and to that extent paid to him the tribute that each man pays to the majesty of humanity in its units.

But the auctioneer is the ironist speaking from beneath the august shadow of the eternal passing of life. He has taken the place of the gravediggers of *Hamlet*, and since a man's skull is so much less than his snuff-box a part of the man that we know, the auctioneer's broad, coarse or bitterly jocular comments are more winged than were ever those of the digger of graves. For the grave is inevitable and we accept it without protest; but no man's Chippendale bureau set out on the grass need say inevitably, 'To this favour we must all come.' Every man must die; but it seems always a little pitiful that any man should die so unbefriended that he has no one who will treasure up for his dead sake these most intimate of his associates, these his implicitly faithful vassals.

Yet in the end to these favours almost everything that is lasting must come. Heirlooms, descending as it were stage by stage in a funnel-shaped progress, must almost inevitably reach an outlet which is this of the auction. To the oldest of families there always comes a last member, and to that last member always his trustees. It is that at the best, since it is always good to be dead; at the worst the trustees may be those 'In Bankruptcy'. Then selling is at its bitterest and each of the intermediate kinds of sellings means change, and every change is a thing that humanity must a little fear. Thus in that open field, beneath that grey sky, round the public jester upon his kitchen chair, the laughter of each man and woman rings a thought falsely. For who among us can be quite certain that it will not be his turn next to die untreasured, to fail miserably, or to leave that countryside?

Countrymen rise and fall; the auctioneer is always at the flood of his eloquence. He is the one man of the rural world who is assured of prosperity, the one man certain to flourish all the more because of widespread ruin. It is always a little depressing to me to open my country paper about Michaelmas. There, in place of the familiar and uninteresting local notes of the central pages, I find, year after year, four immense sheets, an area almost as large as the mainsail of a yacht, given up to the announcements in small, broken print of forthcoming sales by auction. Glimpses of how many farms will not flash before one's eyes if one have really the heart to go through all those little poignant notices of failure, of decay, and of change. Here is Ruffian's Hill farm, with its great stone kitchen that one remembers best lit by one tiny candle flame; here is Penny Farthing farm with the great barns. Well, Higgins has gone; old Hooker has failed. Here is the Brook farm that stood so high, with the two twisted poplars, like plumes, on each side of it against the sky. Here are Coldharbour and the Court Lodge that Files ran. Well, rum-shrub is said to have caused *that* display of 210 sheep, so many drawing-room chairs, and so much live and dead farming stock beneath the inclement sky. Here too is Dog's Hill. Mrs Hackinge has had to sell. We all knew she would ever since her husband hanged himself in the cart-lodge because hops fell below thirty shillings. Hackinge was always a wild-cat man, going in for poultry and apple farming, and selling feathers for mattresses and the Lord knows what.

Thus most of us shiver a little when we meet the auctioneer in his dog-cart briskly quartering the roads like a game-dog. It is as if on the hard road the shoes of his horse rapped out, 'Change, change, change-ty-change'; it is as if his bright eyes saw the smut on how many fair fields of wheat, the foot-rot in how many flocks. And 'change, change, change', is the note of all countrysides. Yet it is astonishing how little the change is in evidence once the changes are made. You put a corrugated iron roof in place of the thatch on the great barn, and in two years' time you have forgotten that the covering was ever dun-coloured and soft. You put James Harper into Penny Farthing in place of old Hooker, and, if you do not forget old Hooker, you wonder a little, when you think how well James Harper, who started as a weazened and niggardly innovator, has been bronzed, beaten and worried by weather till he fits into his place for all the world as well as old Hooker ever did. And one forgets, somehow, that old Hooker died before the telegraph office was opened at the Corner. One forgets even that he was there before the new tenants came to the Hall, and it startles one to hear them say that they do not even remember old Hooker's mother, who trotted about on two sticks for a year-and-a-half after old Hooker died. These people at the Hall do not even remember Miss Wilton, the post-mistress, though, when one comes to think of it, it does not seem possible that the hills can look quite the same without her to tear a hole in one's brown-paper parcels so that she might see what one's friends sent for Christmas.

Yet in spite of all these impossibilities there is the place, our heart of the country, very much the same. It is even more the same, since to all the original new impressions that it once made upon us there is superadded this cloud of little memories, these films of dust, these makings of histories. For in a sense it is just the deaths that go to make up the restfulnesses, the old associations, the glamours of each heart of the country. At each change we cry out, each death we lament, each bankrupt we shake by the hand and assure him that after his failure the place can never seem the same. Yet each of these changes hallows for us some spot; each of them renders some corner of a corner more sacred, more intimately our own by right of memories. We do not, as it were, discover the Fountain of Youth that we set out to seek; but we do find out, little by little, the secret of growing old mellowly and with reverence. We discover suddenly that we are one of the few who can remember when Penny Farthing tithe-barn was thatched, who can remember an old fellow called Hooker. He used to break in a team of black oxen to the plough every year, and, wild as you may think the idea, it paid him very well. If he had call to use them for any press of plough-work, there they were; if not, he fattened them off just like any other bullock, and nothing lost save the small pains he had been at. And, sitting by the fire one winter night when it is too wild to get out and too wild for a friend to come in, one will surprise oneself by trying to remember how the place looked when first, by birth or by imagination, we opened our eyes upon it. And we shall surprise ourselves by saying: 'Why, it *isn't* the same place at all.' For so gradually will the change have come that we shall never have heeded it in the large, the spirit of the place will seem to remain utterly the same. It is that sort of feeling that prompted the direction that I once received in a strange countryside –

'You go down the lane till you come to the place where Farmer Banks's old barn used to stand when he kept six cows in it.'

In the imagination of the speaker, the barn and even the cows existed hazily, but not more hazily than did the now cleared field; the field was there cleared, but not more real than the barns of some years ago. This detritus of the dead, this dust left, as it were, in a film, is like the 'patina' that gives value to old bronzes, like the age and yellowness that give tone to old ivories. We see our country-sides through this veil, and the trees, the hillocks, and the smithies seem to speak to us with human voices. In other lands, in lands to which we can attach no associations, a hill is just a hill, a river a river. Without at least a fictitious crop of historic facts no scenery would hold us. The plains of France to us may be fair; but if we cannot at least invent for ourselves some sort of scheme of all the dead who have ploughed them up, fertilised them with their blood, or ridden over them towards love or death, without some cloud of human ghosts to people them, we shall not settle down amidst the hedges of Brittany. California has its brilliant hues, its great gorges, its vast prospects, but they will not really hold us; neither will the lakes, the swards, the green trees of those most beautiful of islands, New Zealand. Work might keep us there, the chance of profit, or even the hope of healing a damaged lung; but no spirit of the place calls us. Many of us may love solitude; we may hate the sight of living man; but few can dispense with the invisible presence of the dead – of the dead that the auctioneer with his croaking jokes long has since doomed to oblivion.*

Changes may worry us dreadfully – the cutting down of familiar avenues, the setting up of wire fences in place of old hedgerows; but as long as the changes are real in the sense of being called for by the spirit of the age we shall at last accept them and make them a part of our spirit of the place. It is only when, as in the case of that most odious of all things, the restoration of old churches and old buildings – it is only when the changes are out of touch with modernity – when, in fact, the changes are 'fakes', that they will remain for ever eyesores, that they will for ever strike false notes. A landowner that I knew has erected some brick pigsties in a lovely old orchard. At first I hated them; but little by little I have grown accustomed to the sight of the buildings and the 'feeling' of the pigs. I have grown to feel that the pigs were more or less necessary,

---

* It is in passages like these on pp. 223–5, that Ford's writing is most evocative of Hardy's vision of the English countryside. Look particularly at *The Woodlanders* (Penguin, 1985, p. 172) for a comparison.

and that the sties, because they are suited for their purpose, are neither distasteful nor vulgar. But every time that I pass our old church, now, alas! picked clean and white as dry bones are clean and white, I shudder a little, and every time I enter our fine old Hall that has been spoiled by the addition of a new wing in a style limply aping the mediaeval.

These latter changes are imitative and are meaningless; but the others we accept. If it be the fate of the country to be turned into one vast territory of pleasure parks eventually, we shall accept the pleasure park as the standard, just as now, upon the whole, we accept the small farm; if it be the fate of the country to be cut up into squares for smallholders, sooner or later we or our children will accept the fact that every view over dales and valleys will appear like a never-ending draught-board. The eye will accept its freedom to travel over miles and miles, just as nowadays it welcomes its imprisonment by hedgerow after hedgerow, and the flat sweep of cultivated territory will be as much the country as is today the closed-in maze that we love. In the region of change that is the country, change is, in short, the very breath of life, the sole thing that we have to comment on, the sole basis of the news that keeps us all going.

And it all goes so very slowly. Last year I took a late October walk down a long valley. It had been one of those days that one loves and lingers through, as if they must be our last on a pleasant earth. The valley was broad, the grass covered with a bluish haze, the sunshine was very red, the river ran sluggishly between high banks. The year was dying away, so that each minute of sunlight seemed a precious gift, and the day died so fast that hardly could one resist the attempt to hold it, physically, by some gesture of the hands, by some effort of the will. It was one of those days that, one is acutely aware, can never return. Other days pass, and are no doubt reckoned; this will live for ever in the memory. Winter was coming, night, sleep – and who knows whether or not death itself?

But suddenly, on changing the direction at the turn of the river, there before us, close at hand in the absolutely still air, all warmed with the wash of light from the low sun, was the little range of hills that bound the valley. And everything on them had a quaint distinctness. Below was the golden roof of a farm that might have been a roof in Caxton's day; just before it was a rush-thatched hut, its background small, green, foreshortened fields like squares in a pattern, and all flat. And appearing so exactly above the hut that it seemed as if they must fall down the smoking brick chimneys were a ploughman and his team moving swiftly – two black horses and two white, a boy with a harrow following, and to one side a man with a seed-trough slung round him, sowing with both hands. Even at that distance one could see the light haze of the flying seeds. It might have been a coloured picture in a child's book of today; it might, without the change of a visible detail, have been a picture in a missal. Just over the bank was the great high-road along which the motor-cars screamed; just beyond that, over the hill and out of sight, was a great, broad, hedgeless 'scientific' farm. But, standing there that afternoon, and walking back in the dying day for miles along that bank, we might, for all the eye could see, have been there this afternoon or half a millennium ago, so slowly does always moving Change move in the heart of the country. If there we do not find the Fountain of Youth, there at least we may learn to grow old without perceiving it, to fuse into the tide of humanity that individually matters so little – the tide of humanity that in its course across the earth has smoothed and rounded so many hill-tops, has altered the lines of so many fields, has bound down so many rivers to their courses, has held back the sea from so many wildernesses of marsh and fen, has fought so bravely, with so little glory, so long a fight against the irresistible forces of Nature.

Nature is, indeed, at once the auctioneer and the trustee of us men who walk the furrows in the heart of the country – the trustee rather than the auctioneer, since the price of labour that we pay goes into no pocket other than ours. Men, so long ago, scraped and furrowed the ridges that terrace the dun faces of the great slopes, and Nature hands them down to us who have forgotten even what those old householders looked like. We have forgotten them, just as we have forgotten how that dead man looked who sat, years ago, in the armchair that we bought off the grass – in the armchair in which now one of us thrones it, the king of a tiny clan, the leader of a little caravan-load of mortals – the leader for a short moment across the smallholding of time that shall still be ours.

The End

The Spirit of the People

AN ANALYSIS OF THE ENGLISH MIND

Omnes ordines sub signis ducam, legiones meas,
Avi sinistra, auspicio liquido, atque ex sententia.
Confidentia est inimicos meas me posse perdere.
Pseudolus, Act ii scene 4

To the Most English of All

Author's Advertisement

THIS is the final instalment of a book which the author began to publish three years ago. It occurred to him very much earlier that to attempt to realise for himself these prolific, fertile, and populous islands would be a pleasurable task – to realise them, that is to say, in so far as they had presented themselves to himself and to no other person. It has been a pleasurable task, and inasmuch as, in the form of books, the results attained appear to have given pleasure to quite a number of people, it would be false modesty to pretend to apologise for publishing these results of pleasurable moments.

The author has put into them no kind of study of documents; they are as purely autobiographical products as are the work of Pepys or Montaigne. Setting for himself certain limits – as one might say, certain rules of the game – he very definitely observed those rules and set out – to play.

England rather more than any other land divides itself into two portions – the Town and Country; for, roughly speaking, no other land has towns so crowded or countrysides so sparsely populated; no other nation has a country type of life so well organised or so characteristic; few peoples have towns so loosely planned or so wanting in self-consciousness.

It is human to think first of the body and then of the soul. And, since Town and Country form together as it were the body of a nation, so the People is the soul inhabiting them. Hence the plan of this book in three volumes, to which – having evolved it several years ago, and observed it as the rule of his particular game – the author has rigidly adhered.

In the first place he gave to his readers a projection of a great English town as he had known it; in the second he provided his personal image of the English countryside. The one volume was *The Soul of London*, the other, *The Heart of the Country*.

In *The Spirit of the People* an attack is made on a rendering of the peculiar psychology of the Englishman – on that odd mixture of every kind of foreigner that is called the Anglo-Saxon race.

The reader is probably familiar with what is called a composite photograph. A great number of photographs of individuals is taken, and one image being set upon another, a sort of common denominator results, one face blending into another, lending salient points, toning down exaggerations. And, when one speaks of the 'Englishman' or the 'Frenchman', one refers to a mental composite photograph of all the thousands and thousands of English or French that one has met, seen, conversed with, liked, disliked, ill-used, or beaten at chess.

It is this image as it remains in his own mind – it is this particular 'Englishman' – that the author analyses in the present volume. If he differs – this Englishman – from the Englishmen rendered by or known to others, that is only because the author's experience has differed from the experience of others. For the author has, for the purposes of this book, read no other books and studied no statistics. He has lived such a life as he chose or as Fate directed, and has noted such things as accident has brought in his way in the streets or between the hedgerows.

He has dwelt, for instance, very much on the fact that his 'Englishman' has appeared to have the characteristics of a poet; he has not dwelt at all on the Englishman as, say, a drinker of strong liquors. That may be because he has been attracted to the contemplative, pleasant, kindly, romantic, active – but quite unreflective – individuals of this nation. And probably he has given drunkards a wide berth.

Both these things he has done unconsciously, if he has done so at all; but the fact remains that he has met thousands of Englishmen who appeared to him to be poets, and hardly tens who have been drunk. Celts who claim to be the only poets, or temperance reformers who wish to see a world reeling towards hugely-crammed workhouses, will have a different vision. The author can only claim to be a quite ordinary man, with the common tastes and that mixture in about equal parts of English, Celtic, and Teutonic bloods that goes to make up the usual Anglo-Saxon of these islands.

The author's original plan – and he has adhered to it rigidly, sternly, and in spite of many temptations – was to write about only such things as interested him. He might, that is to say, have aimed at producing a work of reference. He might have written of the influence on the Englishman of, say, the motor-car, the Greek drama, vegetarianism, or Marxian Socialism. But he has left out these and many other subjects. Distrusting his powers, he has limited himself to attempting to produce an image of the world he has lived in, reflected in his own personality. He has tried, in short, to produce a work of art.

It would, however, be too great insincerity in the author to say that he does not regard a work of art as of as great a usefulness to the republic as a work of reference. Primarily it should give enjoyment. Secondarily – and that is its social value – it should awaken thought. This a work of reference – a serious, statistical, Blue, or unimaginative work – will seldom do. The artist, however, should be an exact scientist. (This is not a paradox.) His province is to render things exactly as he sees them in such a way that his rendering will strike the imagination of the reader, and induce him to continue an awakened train of thought.

It is all one whether the artist be right or wrong as to his facts; his business is to render rightly the appearance of things. It is all one whether he convince his reader or cause to arise a violent opposition. For the artist's views are of no importance whatever. Who cares whether Dante believed the Guelphs to be villains or saviours? Who cares whether Aristophanes believed that the temple of Asclepius at Tricca was a better sort of Lourdes than that at Epidaurus? The point is that one and the other have given us things to enjoy and things to think about.

Perhaps it is, or perhaps it is not, good that we should enjoy ourselves: that will always remain an open question in a nation where joy is almost invariably regarded as a waste of time and very frequently as a vulgarity. So that it is better, no doubt, to fall back upon that secondary province of the work of art – the awakening of thought, the promotion of discussion…

This, however, is not a defence of the present book, but a defence of all books that aim at renderings rather than statements; for that, in essence, is the difference between the work of art and the work of reference. Is not it Machiavelli who says, 'It is not in my power to offer you a greater gift than that of enabling you to understand in the shortest possible time all those things which in the course of many years I have learned through danger and suffering'? And if the author has not passed through so many years or dangers as the author of *Il Principe*, neither, presumably, has any reader today as much need of instruction as Lorenzo the Magnificent.

F.M.H.
Winchelsea
January 27th, 1906 – August 3rd, 1907

CHAPTER I

The People from the Outside

THREE years ago I was talking to a Professor of Literature near the city of Münster, which is in Westphalia. At a certain point in our discussion my interlocutor said: 'But then, the Spirit of your People has always been so bloodthirsty. One becomes almost ill in reading your history, with its records of murders and beheadings.'

That this should have been uttered where it was rendered it the more bewildering to one prone to form impressionists' views upon general subjects. For the remark was made upon a level plain, within sight of a city whose every ancient stone must once at least have been bathed in blood. Those levels, vast and sandy or vast and green, stretching out towards the Low Countries, must in the secular wars of Europe have been traversed again and again by the feet of those licensed murderers that are soldiery. The very church towers of Münster are pointed out to the tourist as characteristic: they are square, because the spires that once crowned them were overturned by Anabaptists in their last desperate stand against the Prince Bishop – a last desperate stand after a siege in which fire, famine, cannibalism and rapine played a part unparalleled in the history of the world. The arcades of Münster witnessed murders of the most terrible: the church towers of Münster are square because, so the legend has it, the Anabaptists set their cannon upon the platforms left after the spires had fallen. And the very outline of the city is dominated still by the pinnacles of the Friedensaal – or hall erected to commemorate the Treaty of Münster, – to commemorate that Peace of Westphalia ending a war that had outlasted generations. Yet, with the glittering city beneath his eyes, with all these reminders of ancient bloodshed plain to the view in the clear air, in the peaceful summer weather, this student of literature could give it, as his particular impression of the English race, that its history in the reading made him ill.

This remark impressed me so singularly that ever since that day, three years ago, I have hardly passed any single twenty-four hours without giving at least some speculation to the psychology of the curiously mixed and mingled populations of the partner predominant in the history and fortunes of these islands. Incidentally, of course, I have speculated upon the history of that other, still more curiously mingled, and still more predominant, branch of the race that inhabits a western half-continent. As the result of these speculations I have offered to the world two volumes of impressions – the one of this people very much compressed into a great town, the other of this same people amidst the green acres of a restricted island. In the present volume I propose to myself to record a view of this people's corporate activities, of its manifestations as a nation. With the completion of this volume I shall have achieved the task that set itself to me during the night after the aforementioned student of literature made his singular remark.

The person who sets himself such a task should, if he is to perform it at all ideally, possess certain qualities and the negation of certain qualities. He should be attached by very strong ties to the race of which he writes, or he will write without sympathy. He should, if possible, be attached to as many other races as may be by ties equally strong, or he will, lacking comprehension of other national manifestations, be unable to draw impartial comparisons. He must be possessed of a mind of some aptness to interest itself in almost every department of human thought, or his view will be tinged with that saddest of all human wrong-headedness – specialisation. He must look upon the world with the eyes neither of a social reformer nor of an engineer, neither with the eyes of a composer of operas nor of a carpenter. He must, as well as it is possible for a single man to compass it, be an all-round man. He must, in fact, be an amateur – a lover of his kind and all its works. At the same time he must be sufficiently a literary artist to be able to draw moving pictures; for his work, if it fails to interest, loses its very cause for existence. To what extent I who write these words possess these qualifications, I must leave to my biographers to decide.

★ ★ ★

Let me now attempt to put before the reader the reasons for the frame of mind of my excellent friend, the student of literature. It must be remembered that he is not English: he has not the reasons that the Englishman has for drawing morals from, or for accepting, our historic sequences. He is aware that his own land is steeped, is rendered fertile, by the blood of man in ages past. He sees however in these matters, domestic to him, the pressure of immense necessities, the hand of an august if inscrutable Providence. But, never having been so much as momentarily moved by our national middle-class poet's dogma that English history is a matter of precedent broadening down to precedent, he cannot see that English state executions are part of an immense design. He sees instead a succession of sanguinary incidents. For let it be remembered that of the first twenty-six sovereigns who reigned in England since the Conquest no less than ten died deaths of violence; that, in addition to this, several Queens Consort, one Queen of Scotland, many rightful heirs to the throne, and innumerable statesmen of prominence died by the hands of the headsman or the secret murderer. And what great names, what picturesque and romantic figures has that roll not included!

There is a vivid French historical monograph that puts all history as a matter of catchwords, as misleading as you will – so that Henri IV and his period are typified by the '*poule au pot*', the Second Empire by '*l'Empire c'est la paix*'. And there are millions of observers of our present epoch who see the whole world of today menaced by a cloud bearing the ominous words '*l'ennemi c'est le Prussien!*' In a similar way the Romantic movement, still dominating Europe in a manner extraordinary enough, has made, for continental eyes, the whole of English history appear to be one vast, brown canvas, in which, out of the shadows, appears the block. Shadowy executioners hover in the half-lights behind brilliant queens or dark and melancholy kings – queens Flemish in looks, queens French, queens Spanish – but queens that are generally Mary Stuarts, or kings that are always Charles Stuarts, or children that are always the Princes in the Tower.

It is perhaps precisely because these dead kings of England do represent principles that they stand out so clearly in the historical imaginings of Europe, and it is perhaps because they themselves stand out so clearly, that the principles they merely represented are lost in the light of their brilliant fates. Speaking generally, we may say that in the large scheme of things the fall of Mary Stuart was a mere episode in the great downward trend of revealed religion; that in the large scheme of things the fall of Charles Stuart was but an episode in the great rise of popular dominion, or that the murder of the Princes in the Tower represented a step forward in the great theory of the English kingly history – that theory that still makes the English kingship elective. But, just because these episodes were so admirably adapted for the handling of the Humanists, who were the romantic artists and poets – for that reason the executions were the things that counted. The doomed principles that Mary or Charles or the infant Edward so picturesquely 'died for' – those doomed principles of Catholicism, aristocracy or 'tail male' – served to make Charles, Mary and the infant Edward sympathetic figures in the eyes of a sentimentalising Europe. For, if you die for a principle you will become an attractive figure; what the principle may be does not very much matter.

But England has very largely outgrown the influence of the Romantic movement, and, living in the centre of a crowd that is generally humane beyond belief, the Englishman sees his history as a matter of a good-humoured broadening down of precedent to precedent, a broad and tranquil stream of popular advance to power in which a few negligible individuals have lost upon the block their forgotten heads. Who in England remembers that more than one in three of England's earlier kings died deaths of violence?

For, upon the whole the English crowd has grown humane beyond belief.[1] The other day a large dog took it into its head to lie down and fall asleep in the centre of the roadway in one of our largest and busiest thoroughfares. And it effectually blocked the way. Cabs avoided it: large motor omnibuses drove carefully round it: a great block was caused by the deflected traffic, and a great deal of time was lost. Yet the dog itself was absolutely valueless and unpresentable. And, curiously enough, I happened on the next day to witness in South London an episode almost exactly similar. A sheep, one of a flock on the way to Smithfield, had wedged itself firmly into the mechanism of an electric tram. It remained there for three-quarters of an hour, and I counted twenty-two trams all kept waiting whilst the officials of the first car endeavoured to save the life of an animal that in any case was doomed to death within the day.

These seemed to me to be singular instances of humanity on the part of a race that, at any rate in that part of its land, is remarkably

---

1 I do not wish to be taken as implying that the English crowd is polished, or gentle, or considerate. I have before me a newspaper article which enumerates twenty-nine distinct causes for offence given by one Bank Holiday crowd to one individual. And the estimate does not appear to be excessive.

in a hurry. They effaced for me much of the impression of underlying ferocity in the people – the impression that had been caused
by some small sufferings at the hands of hostile mobs during a period
of strife some years ago. For, upon the whole, the ferocities and
barbarities of the English crowds during the Boer War might have
been matched in any part of Europe. One suffered as much, being
English upon the Continent, as one suffered for being pro-Boer in
this country. But I cannot well imagine in any continental city a
crowd of a couple of thousand people watching with intense
sympathy (or even suffering with good humour considerable
inconvenience for the sake of) a sheep that was shortly to die. It is
true that in any English street one may see a broken-legged horse
stand for hours waiting to be put out of its agony. But that is a manifestation of official stupidity, and is upon the whole a spectacle
repugnant to the feelings of the onlookers, any one of whom would
approve or applaud the instant slaughtering of a poor animal.

I do not assume that these instances of humanity in English
crowds distinguish the Anglo-Saxon from all his human brothers.
But just because almost every Englishman will recognise the truth
in them, and just because almost every Englishman will applaud the
action of these tram-conductors or cab-drivers, it does seem to me
to be arguable that, upon the whole, much of the ferocity that was
a part of the spirit of the people has died out.

Since witnessing these two events, I have 'put' them to several
foreigners. It has been noticeable to me that each of these foreigners
has taken the humanitarian standard of his own country to be, as it
were, the normal and proper level from which to regard the brute
creation – this although practically none of them was what we
should call patriotic. But each of them agreed that the instance of
the sheep betrayed what they called 'sentimentality'; each of them,
indeed, used this very word. Even a Hindu said that if the sheep
were to be slaughtered within the hour it mattered very little
whether its end came at the hands of a butcher or beneath the
wheels of a tramcar; and a Frenchman, a German, and a Russian
lady agreed in saying that it was absurd that so much inconvenience
to human beings should have been incurred merely to save the life
of a dog. No doubt, if he were asked to judge the matter in the
light of pure reason, every Englishman would have agreed with
them; but I think that there is little doubt that such an Englishman,
if he had stood upon the kerb-stone and watched these two small
dramas, would have voted life to the dog and the sheep, or would

at least have applauded these forbearances.

It happened that one of the persons to whom I put these cases was the very German student of literature to whom I referred in my first words. He, for his part, was by no means ready to admit that the English were more the friends of beasts than the inhabitants of Westphalia. He cited, for instance, the case of his brother, a landowner who possessed a favourite but very troublesome horse. This animal refused to stand in harness, with the result that every member of his brother's family who desired to take a drive was forced to spring into the cart whilst the animal was going at a sharp trot. This they had borne with for many years. And, indeed, I myself have met with instances of foreign family coachmen who resented as autocratically as any Englishman the keeping waiting of their horses. But my German friend, whilst unwilling to admit that his compatriots fell behind our own in *reasonable* humanity, stigmatised the sparing of the dog and the sheep as part of the quite unreasonable 'sentimentality' with which he credited the Anglo-Saxon race. He is my friend, by way of being Professor of English Literature in a German university, and as such he is at present engaged in writing a history of Sentimentality in England. This, he seems to see, begins (at least as far as the sentimental attitude towards the brute creation is concerned) with the *Sentimental Journey* of Laurence Sterne. In this will be found the celebrated sentimentalising over the dead ass, or the still more flagrant instance of the caged starling that cried incessantly, 'I can't get out!' Bishop Law, the author of the 'Devout Call', was another of these sentimentalisers, inasmuch as he was unable to pass a caged bird without an attempt to purchase it and to set it at liberty.

Nothing, indeed, could be more interesting than to discover just when this humanitarian movement did really originate in the English people. For however right my German friend may be in dating the commencement of the sentimental movement in its other aspects he has certainly very much post-dated this particular strain in its birth. For Sterne, it must be remembered, called himself Yorick. And if he had a sentimental attitude, he got it by imitation very largely of another creature of the creator of the Prince of Denmark. For most of the meditations of the 'Sentimental Journey' are in the 'vein' of the melancholy Jacques, and if we read through the *rôle* of that character it is not long before we come upon the tale of the

> Poor sequestered stag
> That from the hunter's aim had taken a hurt
> And came to languish...
> Thus the hairy fool,
> Much markèd of the melancholy Jacques,
> Stood on the extremest verge of the swift brook
> Augmenting it with tears...
> 'Poor deer,' quoth he, 'thou mak'st a testament
> As worldlings do, giving thy sum of more
> To that which hath too much.'
> ''Tis right,' quoth he, 'thus misery doth part
> The flux of company.'
> 'Sweep on, ye fat and greasy citizens;
> 'Tis just the fashion; wherefore do ye look
> Upon that poor and broken bankrupt there?'

Here is, indeed, the 'note' of that sentimentalism which Sterne afterwards and so ably exploited. Another department of English sentimentalism – that which the German, with some wonder and some contempt, is apt to call the Englishman's *Natur-Schwaermerei*; his mad infatuation for nature – my friend was equally prone to find in eighteenth-century English poets. Gray's letters from Switzerland are, for instance, distinguished by rhapsodical passages of veneration for the spirit of the Alps. He finds, too, in Horace Walpole's coquettings with the Gothic on Strawberry Hill the first indications of the modern Englishman's veneration for tradition in writings and in tone of mind. He finds, in fact, in that remarkable and only half appreciated eighteenth century of ours the first shoots of nearly all our present-day failings.

But, to anyone in touch with these tendencies, to anyone who has felt the almost sublime forgetfulness of self that the Anglo-Saxon will feel when looking at animals, at flower-filled woods, or even at old buildings or ancient ceremonials, – any Englishman, looking back through his literature will find himself stirred by echoes of the things that now stir him. He will feel that curious and indefinable flutter of sentimentalism in reading the balladists, in Herrick, in Shakespeare, in Chaucer, or right back in Orme, who wrote a bestiary in the twelfth century. And, indeed, I am inclined to see that these things are inherent to the British Isles; that, born of the climate, the soil, and the creatures of the earth, they have arisen sooner or later in each of the races which have come to be dominant in these islands of continually changing masters.

One theory is, of course, little better than another; but for me, my private and particular image of the course of English history in these matters is one of waving lines. I see tendencies rise to the surface of the people, I see them fall again and rise again. The particular love for beasts, flowers, and even for old buildings that the German calls in the Englishman sentimentality, appears to me to be part of an anthropomorphism, that has always been particularly characteristic, at sufficiently separated intervals, of the English inhabitant.

If the Englishman today loves animals it is because he sees, to some extent, in every beast a little replica of himself. Other peoples may see in a field-mouse a scientific phenomenon, or in a horse an implement meant to be used. But the Englishman sees in the little creature with beady eyes a tiny replica of himself; he 'subjectivises' the field-mouse; he imagines himself tiny, filled with fears, confronted by a giant. In flowers even, to some extent, he sees symbols of his own, or his womenfolk's, chastity, boldness, and endurance, and in old buildings he recognises a quality of faithfulness, old service, and stability that he himself aspires to possess. On this account the modern Englishman feels towards these things very definite and quite real affections.

Of all this we are sensible in English expressions of thought as they crop up down the ages. Robert Burns 'subjectivised' precisely field-mice and daisies. Herrick wrote 'To Daffodils' and 'To Meadows', attributing to them a share of his own feelings. Shakespeare wrote of the deer what I have quoted, and he wrote:

The moon, methinks, looks with a watery eye,
And when she weeps, weeps every little flower
Lamenting an enforced chastity.

And a similar anthropomorphism may be found, peering up, like the crests of waves at various periods right back into the days of Beowulf and the early Anglo-Saxon poets.

I am far indeed from saying that no other poets than the English ever loved nature. The German minnesingers came as near the spirit of ecstatic delight in a life out of doors as did even Chaucer or the man who wrote *As You Like It*. But in essence, although Walther von der Vogelweide could write such a ballad as *Tandaradei*, even the minnesingers treated of nature as a collection of things that they observed – as phenomena in fact, not as part of themselves. If the effect of a green world is conveyed, the spirit which is supposed to inhabit leaves, fowls and fishes is a different one. And, roughly speaking, even this measure of delight in nature seems to have deserted the spirit of the other Germanic peoples with the minnesingers' disappearance. Nothing indeed is more interesting than to travel across a really typical English countryside in spring, with really typical German and really typical English companions. The shorn woodlands are decked with improbable bouquets of primroses; in the fields amongst the young lambs the daffodils shake in the young winds; along the moist roadsides, beneath the quicken hedges, there will be a diaphanous shimmer of cuckoo-flowers. And, as the coach rolls along there will be from the English little outcries of delight. They cast off even their manners: they say: 'Oh, *look!*' The Germans in the meantime stiffen a little with astonishment, a little with contempt. For the Englishmen a thousand words are singing in their ears. They are in the presence of things that *really* matter: in presence of some of the few things in which it is really legitimate to be sensuously and entirely delighted. *All* the warrants of *all* their poets are on their side. Words, words, words, tingle in their ears. All sorts of phrases – from the Bible, from Shakespeare, from Wordsworth, from Herrick – 'The flowers appear on the earth; the time of the singing of birds is come'; 'They flash upon that inward eye which is the bliss of solitude'; 'When ladysmocks all silver white do tint the meadows with delight.' A thousand quotations – and the Englishman is *the* man in the world who knows his poets, *the* man of this world who is compact of quotations – a thousand quotations are implied in his 'Oh, *look!*' The Germans in the meanwhile sit a little stolid, a little sardonic, a little uncomfortable even, as I myself have felt when I have driven with Germans along a broad *chaussée* and they have burst into some folk-song. For the German has not any German quotations behind him; he hardly knows the German for daffodil, since the daffodil in German is confounded with all the other *narcissi*: he only knows that he is confronted with a foreign manifestation: with a manifestation of that *Natur-Schwaermerei* which to a German is as odd and confusing a thing as to an Englishman is the Teutonic habit of bursting into part-songs, or the Latin foolishness of male embraces.

The Latins themselves face this particular English emotionalism with a different complexion. If they have not the English quotations to help them they have not the German's self-consciousness to hinder them. Emotional themselves, they are pleased to witness emotions, they are even anxious to understand the nature of this new emotional resource, since here is perhaps a new emotion in which they themselves may revel – so that I have myself had my own quotation caught up and repeated by a gentleman of Latin origin. He eyed my daffodils – they grew in a green bank given over to poultry, and had in consequence been fenced round with wire netting for protection – he eyed my daffodils with some non-comprehension, and then, catching my words, echoed quite enthusiastically:

'Oh! yes; yes that come "before the swallow dares, and take the winds of March with beauty".'

We may, indeed, take it that the English and the German are akin in their respect for authority. If it were possible to imagine a German scientific pronouncement in favour of daffodils, considered, say, from a military or a commercial point of view – if it were theoretically possible to imagine so improbable a thing – we might well see the German, too, burst out enthusiastically over the grey-green clumps with their golden, dancing fountains of flowers. But, whilst the German calls out for an authoritative or a scientific pronouncement, the Englishman craves a weighty phrase, a Biblical line, a something suited for 'treatment' in the noble blank verse of his romantic and singular, poetic dialect. For the Englishman is very wonderfully under the domination of the 'mighty line'. The German might quite conceivably rhapsodise over a factory chimney: the Englishman will never see its wonderful poetic value until some poet has died after having put factory life into a new epic glorious in sound. That day may, however, never come – for who, nowadays, can hope really to compete with the English Bible, or the lyrics of Suckling? – and until something can be 'quoted' in favour of the factory chimney, it is likely that the factory chimney will remain despised or openheartedly ignored. The subjection of the Englishman to the spoken word is indeed very remarkable. The German, speaking of an opponent, will use language very terrible; but once he comes to action his deeds will fall short, upon the whole, on the side of humanity. The Frenchman, on the other hand, adjusts his actions to his threats with some nicety. With the Englishman his deeds are apt to be more weighty than his words. Thus, I remember lying, on a hot and sultry day, upon a beach beside three very excellent and humane City merchants. The sea lapped the strand, the sky was very blue, and one of them (it was during the South African war) read out from his paper the announcement that the Boer women were arriving to fight beside their husbands. The second commented, almost beneath his breath, as if it were a dismal and obscene secret:

'Oh! well; if they do that we shall have to shoot back at them.'

The third said:

'Oh! yes; we shall have to treat them like the men: but we mustn't *say* so!' And all three agreed that we must not *say* so.

I return to the subject of the late war because it is the last evidence that we have of any really public ferocity latent in the English people. During that rather disagreeable period I made one or two speeches in the interests neither of Boer nor of Englishman, but of the African natives. To them it seemed to me – and it still seems so – the African continent belongs. I received on that account a certain amount of mishandling from either party. By the pro-Boers I was contemptuously silenced as an impracticable sentimentalist; by the Imperialists my clothes were torn. I witnessed, too, on the occasion of the Queen's Hall pro-Boer meeting, a certain amount of mob violence. The attitude of the crowd appeared, upon the whole, to be expressed somewhat as follows: 'Here are a lot of foreigners conspiring in our very midst to do something against our Queen and country. Here are policemen protecting them. It's a very mysterious business. Let's knock down any person in a soft hat.' And they did so.

But it must be remembered that here were people acting in a great crowd, and it must be remembered that great crowds are liable to contagious madnesses. And, indeed, abroad, where I passed for an Englishman, I witnessed and suffered from more ferocity during that period than I did in England, where I passed for a pro-Boer. And upon the whole, lamentable as the patriotic excesses of crowds during that time appear nowadays to every Englishman, I am inclined to think that, by comparison with the actions of foreign crowds during similar periods, the English crowd may be called singularly lacking in ferocity.

I am anxious to guard myself from appearing to write with too great a complacency of a nationality that is more or less my own; therefore I use the words 'lacking in ferocity' after having pondered over them for some time. For, from one very tenable point of view, ferocity is an attribute very proper to a crowd, since in a crowd all the human attributes, whether of humanity or of cruelty, are wrought up to their highest expression. A crowd *ought* to express itself by means of excesses; it turns its thumbs either up or down;

it does not stay to reflect. Therefore we may say that a crowd of only moderate ferocity must be made up of individuals each of whom is relatively emasculated.

I am inclined therefore to think that the idea of a resort to physical violence in any extreme whatever has almost died out of the English race in the large. For, supposing that the British peoples really did believe in the justice of their cause, the pro-Boers, the foreign, uncouth, un-English traitors to the nation, ought, in the general scale of these things, to have been visited with extreme punishment. Yet I hardly think that one organ of opinion seriously proposed that even Colonel Lynch – who was actually and in sober earnest a traitor – that even this notable rebel should be put to death. It is true that a number of British traitors, taken with arms in their hands amongst the Boer prisoners, were summarily shot in South Africa. But these episodes passed almost in secret: I imagine that the fact is hardly known even now to the majority of Englishmen; and I imagine that even during the war hardly a single Englishman would in cold blood have sanctioned those military executions.

Upon the whole, then, I should be inclined to repeat that ferocity may have passed away from the spirit of the people. We cannot, I should say, any longer seriously imagine the British people condemning its ruler to death: we cannot well picture it clamouring for the death of an unpopular Minister of the Crown. We cannot imagine these things in England, whereas in almost every continental nation some sort of physical violence is a quite conceivable resort in political differences, either on the part of peoples or of rulers. Of rulers on the Continent almost without exception, it is to be said that they will use the drawn sword to repress trifling disorders. I have myself twice seen the sword used in France and once in Germany for the mere clearing of a public place. Upon to how great an extent lethal weapons are the instruments of government in Russia it is hardly necessary to dilate.

It is in fact, for any one really acquainted with the temper of the English crowd, difficult to imagine it really violent in action, and it is almost equally difficult to imagine its rulers violent in repression. One can, of course, never be certain that circumstances may not tomorrow arise in which over some perfectly trivial cause blood may be shed in the streets of London. But that at least is the 'impression' that is left upon me after much mixing with English crowds. That a residuum of brutish violence may remain, in pockets as it were, in crannies of the slums or in police barracks, no one will care to deny who has seen London policemen make some arrests, or who has seen that most disagreeable of all sights, a South or East London crowd attempting to rescue a prisoner from the police. Nothing, indeed, can be more disagreeable to witness than either of these manifestations of street violence. The kick on the shins or the hard nudge in the ribs that a tall policeman will give to some wretched loafer seems to be skilfully and impassively designed to inflict more pain than almost any human action that one cares to figure to oneself; whilst the spectacle of the blue figure with its intent face, hemmed in shoulder high in a knot, in a drab, straight street, is, in its own particular way, as hideous and suggestive a nightmare as one cares to figure for one's unpleasant imaginings. But in a sense both these things are excusable. Who gave the first blow in the miserable struggle that always wages between the police and the unhappy poor, it is impossible to determine. The original contest or its rights and wrongs are hidden in the impenetrable mists of an unchronicled history. Perhaps it was the first guardian of the peace who gave the first unnecessary nudge in the ribs to the first loafer; or perhaps in the first built of London courts the first loafer slipped beneath a glimmering lamp round a corner to bonnet the first policeman. Be that as it may the obscure blood feud remains – the blood feud between these lowest fringes of the public and its controllers. Probably this, too, will die away. Occasionally, as things are at present constituted, for some obscure reason, having its rise in some too virile tradition, a wave of senseless violence will rise from these depths; will rise to be called hooliganism, or something of the sort. That the great public will hear of and will fight with as best it may, till it dies as mysteriously as it arose. Occasionally, too, some inspector will set a tradition, a standard, of brutality to the men under his charge. Of that, as a rule, the great public will never hear, but the groans that arise from the crowded and narrow courts will eventually reach the ears of the higher authorities, and the evil be mitigated by a removal or a promotion.[1]

---

1   I am aware that my remarks upon the police force may be open to misinterpretation because I have had occasion to dwell upon brutalities. I may state that in the course of my ordinary vocations I have five times witnessed acts of what appeared to me unnecessary violence on the part of policemen. One of these latter I subsequently questioned, and he assured me that his violence was *not* unnecessary, and I believe he was right. I have twice seen policemen rather seriously mishandled by small crowds, and I have known rather well at least one quite decent 'rough' whose *idée fixe* was to murder a certain member of the T division. These facts appear to me to constitute a reasonably intelligible *casus belli*, a sufficient complement and supplement.

And indeed these things, regarded from the broad point of view of national manifestations, matter very little. For it is just in the organised forces of authority that traditions of violence must necessarily be longest preserved; and it is just to the poorest, least fed, and worst housed of the community, it is just into the darkest and deepest crannies of the body politic that the light of humanitarianism will last penetrate. Even as one can hardly imagine that the British soldiery will ever use their lethal weapons against an English crowd, so one imagines that hardly any English criminal would nowadays do anything more than say to an arresting policeman: 'Oh, I'll come quietly!' One imagines, I mean, that any British ministry would give in its demission rather than incur the responsibility of ordering soldiery to fire into an English crowd, just as one imagines that almost every English criminal is sufficiently educated to refrain from vindictively attempting – without chance of escape – to mutilate the mere instrument of justice. It would be a silly performance: it would be like biting the handcuffs.

I have pursued this train of thought with some tenacity, not because it was accidentally suggested to me by my friend the German student of literature, but because it seems to me to be the most important aspect of English national life. For it must be remembered that what humanity has most to thank the English race for is not the foundation of a vast empire; the establishment of a tradition of seamanship; the leading the way into the realms of mechanical advance. It is not even for its poets that England must be thanked; it is certainly not for its love of the fine arts or its philosophies. It is for its evolution of a rule of thumb system by which men may live together in large masses. It has shown to all the world how great and teeming populations may inhabit a small island with a minimum of discomfort, a minimum of friction, preserving a decent measure of individual independence of thought and character, and enjoying a comparatively level standard of material comfort and sanitary precaution. There have been empires as great as the British; there have perhaps been naval captains as great as Nelson – though this I am inclined to doubt, since as a private confession I may set it down that for me Nelson is the one artist that England has produced. There have certainly been writers as great as Shakespeare, and musicians, painters, architects, generals, ironworkers, chemists, and even possibly mathematicians, galore greater than any that have been produced within our Seven Seas. A nation each of whose individuals is apt to be brought to a standstill in any train of thought by the magic of a 'quotation' can hardly hope to be a nation of artists, since, in the great sense, the supreme art is the supreme expression of common sense. But – in the great sense, too – life is a thing so abounding in contradictions and bewilderments that a great sense of logic is of little service to a nation whose main problem is how to live. For that purpose a mind well stored with quotations is a much better tool, and the more sounding and the more self-contradictory those quotations may be the better will be the tool.

For, upon the whole we may say that a universally used 'quotation' has the weight of a proverb, and if a proverbial philosophy have little in its favour as an instrument of intellectual investigation, it is yet a very excellent aid to bearing with patience the eccentricities of our neighbours, the trials of the weather, and the tricks of fate. In dealing with his neighbour, in fact, the Englishman is singularly apt to be lacking in that imagination which is insight – and I can imagine few worse places than England in which to suffer from any mental distress, since, with the best will in the world, the Englishman is curiously unable to deal with individual cases, and every case of mental distress differs from every other. On the other hand, there are few better places in which to suffer from financial or material troubles. These the Englishman can deal with, since they are subject, as a rule, to one or other of his maxims. He will say: *'Bis dat qui cito dat*: Heaven loves a cheerful giver'; or, 'Better love can no man show than that he lay down his life for his friend.' And he will do it. But for mental distress he has only: 'Therein the patient must minister to himself'; or that most soul-wounding of all maxims: 'There are hundreds worse off than you, my friend!'

In a sort of mathematical progression this almost ferocious lack of imagination has made, in the English race, for an almost imaginative lack of ferocity. You may set down the formula as this: i. I do not enquire into my neighbour's psychology; ii. I do not know my neighbour's opinions; iii. I give him credit for having much such opinions as my own; iv. I tolerate myself; v. I tolerate him. And so, in these fortunate islands we all live very comfortably together.

CHAPTER II

The Road to the West

ENGLAND, almost more than any other, is the land that has been ruled by foreigners, yet the Englishman, almost more than any other man, will resent or will ignore the fact that his country has ever been subjected. Confronted with this proposition, he will at once produce his quotation from Shakespeare:

> This England never did nor never shall
> Lie at the proud foot of a conqueror...

And he will believe it; and in the fact, and in its being ignored, may be found the true sources of English greatness. Almost every continental race – and at least one Asiatic race – can take a kindly interest in English territory, because almost every continental race of importance can say: 'At one time we conquered England.' French, Latin, German, Dutch, Scot, Welshman – all can say it. Even the Spaniards can say, 'Once a King of Spain was King of England.' But if you put these facts to an Englishman, he may confess to their truth in the letter. Nevertheless, he will say that, in the spirit, these allegations are untrue, unfair, un-English, in short; and 'the letter', he will quote, 'killeth'. Approaching the matter more nearly he will say: 'All these fellows *are* "ourselves". We, being English, have swallowed them up. We have digested them. It is, as it were, true that they conquered us; but they conquered us not because they were foreigners, but because they were predestined to become Englishmen.' The facts concerning the component factors of the Englishman's greatness are so bizarre and so varied, that only that one generalisation can embrace them all. Thus the greatest of all Englishmen was of Danish extraction: the most singular, the most popular and most diversely gifted – the most appealing of all England's real rulers during the nineteenth century was a Jew. These facts are such truisms that it seems hardly pertinent to bring them into a serious page; the Englishman blinks them with his formula, 'All these fellows *are* ourselves.' Yet these facts are so important to a comprehension of the Spirit of this People, of its greatnesses and its weaknesses, that no knot in a handkerchief could ever be sufficiently large to keep them in our memories. It is not merely for the achievements of those men, important though they were, that these facts should be remembered in this conjunction. It is for the hold that Nelson and Disraeli had over the popular imagination. And it is part of the same train of thought that brings one to the consideration of the reverse of the medal. For, if the attraction of a foreign figure is really enormous for the Englishman, the attraction of England and the English spirit for the foreigner is almost as startling. Once he becomes, by means of papers, a British subject, your Chinaman, Russian, or Portuguese is, more than any Englishman, ready and anxious to asseverate, 'I am an Englishman.' I have seldom been more embarrassed than when travelling in foreign countries with such persons; their unwillingness to conform to continental habits; their recalcitrance in the face of ticket collectors, waiters, guides to monuments, and all the other constituted authorities is singular and troublesome; and, in the other department of life, I can imagine few agonies of injured innocence quite equal to that of a boy of foreign extraction at an English school. At times he will get called 'Frenchy' or 'dirty German'. This will not happen very often, perhaps, because the English boy, like the English man, is ready to accept for his particular small republic the services of all and sundry. I remember being at school with an African prince, who was a fast bowler of formidable efficiency. With enormous arms and the delivery of a windmill he sent down a ball that, to myself usually keeping the wickets, was for the five minutes or so of an over a thing to be almost deprecated. It was power for our side, but embarrassing for myself.

In the last match that he played in he took seven of the wickets for thirty-two runs, and in the second innings six for twenty. Our victory was signal. But I never forgot the injured innocence of our side when we were faced with the remonstrance that it was not sporting to have the aid of a 'foreigner'. I remember very well saying: 'He's been to our school. It isn't even as if he were a Frenchy or a Dutchman.'

The singularity of my own racial position brought me at that moment to a standstill. But the rest of my team took up the parable for me. We felt intensely English. There was our sunshine, our 'whites', our golden wickets, our green turf. And we *felt*, too, that

Stuart, the pure-blooded Dahomeyan, with the dark tan shining upon his massive and muscular chest, was as English as our pink-and-white or sun-browned cheeks could make us. It may have been this feeling only, a spirit of loyalty to one of our team. But I think it was deeper than this. It was a part of the teachings engendered in us by the teachings of the history of the British Islands: it was a part of the very spirit of the people. We could not put it more articulately into words than, 'He's been to *our* school.' But I am almost certain that we felt that that training, that contact with our traditions, was sufficient to turn any child of the sun into a very excellent Englishman. In our history, as we had confronted its spirit, a touch of English soil was sufficient to do as much for William the Norman, who, though we call him a Conqueror, seems to most English boys eminently more English than the Anglo-Saxon who was weak enough to get shot in the eye. Similarly, for the English boy, the French Plantagenets, the Welsh Tudors, the Scotch Stuarts, the Hanoverian Guelphs, and even Dutch William – all these kings became 'English' the moment they ruled in England. I know very well that that was the 'impression' that the study of English history left upon the mind of the English boy of my date.

Looking back upon the remarkable process now, it is a little difficult for me to reconstitute the gradual development of this singular, but none the less veracious, Historic Spirit. When I read the erudite and almost puzzling *Child's History of England* that one of my own daughters reads for her private delectation, I am apt to be a little puzzled to pick up the string. In this particular work – its circulation is almost incredible – I see groups of facts, groups of maps, groups of engravings, but I do not see anywhere a trace of the great English Theory. Here are facts about the conditions of serfs under the great abbeys; maps of England under the Angevin kings; admirable engravings of rose-nobles; of pre-Reformation church ornaments, even of Gothic homesteads. But I do not quite see how my own children, who by blood are more English than myself, are to become so violently English as was I myself in spirit at the age of, let us say, sixteen. That they will do so, I do not much doubt; and I do not much doubt that they will do so along much the same road as that taken by myself and my comrades.

Our serious impressions of English history began, of course, with the Conquest – began, I should imagine for most of us, with the excellent 'Mrs Markham', of which I remember only the name. Without doubt, before the Conquest there was, for most of us, too, 'little Arthur', of which I can remember only a shadowy form of small books in yellow, shiny linen covers, that curled backwards in the fingers. 'Little Arthur', I imagine, most of us confused with the small prince, son of Geoffrey Plantagenet, who died a pathetic, anecdotal death. 'Little Arthur' *had* made us dimly acquainted with the fact that there had been in England, before the dark wall of the Conquest, some sort of fairy-tale population of the British Isles. There had been, for instance, a King Alfred who burned cakes. But he and his contemporaries were, for us, precisely figures of fairy-tales, perhaps because his adventure with the cakes formed one of those anecdotes that we heard along with the tales of Giant Blunderbore and the other engrossing projections of English nursery life. These died away as soon as we went to 'school'.

History began with 1066. And the Normans being the first rulers of England that we heard of became for us the first Englishmen. That territorial fact did perhaps have the greatest influence over our minds. These things took place in England; this was a history of England; therefore it was a history of Englishmen. So the Normans were the first Anglo-Saxons we became acquainted with. They were the first to be successful: to conquer against great odds – they were the first to show the true genius of the race. (I fancy that that remains the 'note' of adult England of the present day. I put the question to a very typical Englishman with whom I entered into conversation yesterday during a prolonged railway journey. He said: 'Well, of course, the Anglo-Saxons were a sort of German, weren't they?') And, indeed, when later we came at school to learn that there were English before 1066, we really did regard these Anglo-Saxons as a sort of German – not a modern, efficient, Prussianised German, but a pale, disorganised, ineffectual population. They were always being harried by the Danes; they had not really 'settled' the Danes' war when, just before the battle of Hastings, Harold defeated Harold Harfager at Stamford Bridge. And I fancy that most of us regarded the Romans as being infinitely more 'English' than the Britons, in spite of Cassivellaunus and Boadicea, who being a woman did not really count. For, after all, Caesar did the sort of thing that every English boy imagines himself doing.

The really tragic incident of my youngest days was a Homeric battle which I fought on a piece of waste ground. It was really tragic because it made me acquainted with the fact that, even in England, fate was unjust: fate was on the side of the big battalions. There was at my small school a red-haired, hard-headed Irish boy called R——

—, with a freckled nose. We had been learning history: we heard how Julius Caesar had invaded Britain. The snow lay on the ground. So that when playtime came we divided into two sections, the less fortunate boys being the Britons. (There was, after all, something un-English about these Britons: perhaps that is why, though few Englishmen resent being called Britishers by their cousins across the water, every Englishman dislikes being lumped, along with Scots, Irish, Welsh, and the inhabitants of the town of Berwick-on-Tweed, as 'British'. For the British were beaten, the English never have been.) Now R—— insisted that I should be Caractacus: I was equally determined to be Caesar. We fought: I was beaten – and I *was* Caractacus. So far so good. But the battle continued for three whole months. At the end of that time I beat R——. It was then my turn to be Caesar. But alas! R—— called in to his aid his brother – his big brother from another school.

I fought him on that waste ground. I feel to this day the passionate distention of my chest; and to this day, at moments of stress, when fate has played me some evil trick, my eyes wander round upon the passionless and inscrutable surfaces of the material world, and I feel the hot rage that then I felt to be lurking at the backs of grim and unfinished houses. I stood up, I was knocked down: I stood up, I was knocked down. I lay in bed for a whole week afterwards. It was not because of my injuries, but because of my passionate rebellion against fate. For I was doomed to remain a Briton, as it seemed, to the end of my days. That at least was the promise – the dreadful oath – extracted from me by the big brother of R——, an Irishman, a Celt, descendant, no doubt, of Caractacus; but one who aspired to be, for the remainder of *his* days, a Roman. I had not fought for so long because I expected to win by mere force: I was not rebellious against fate because the boy who slogged into my poor chest and poor jaws was so much bigger. Being English one expects to fight against odds. But, being English too, one expects Providence to intervene for one. Providence, after all, always ought to intervene for the English. And, gazing round upon that black and desolate waste ground, I had, I know, been expecting in some sort of dim way that night, that Blucher, or Minerva, or an earthquake – one of the miraculous aids by which Providence manifests itself, one of the providential assistants that an Englishman has a right to expect – that *something* would come to the aid of me, an Englishman who had not more than a few drops of really English blood in my veins…

Our more protracted studies of history may perhaps a little have blurred the figures of our mental puppet plays. But the principle remained undimmed in its radiant effulgence. The Jews remained Englishmen: was not Jehovah for them? Did they not smite Egyptians, Assyrians, Philistines – all the Gentiles who were really French or Germans? The Conqueror remained English too – and the Normans. But *Ivanhoe* changed the aspect of the case: we read it all together with a fury of enthusiasm for the 'English' of that book. But somehow the Normans, Front de Bœuf and the rest, were not *the* Normans. The Providence of the Romancer was not on their side: the mysterious current, the elixir, the fluid, the guiding light which makes all blows strike home, all arrows pierce the casque – *that* was on the side of the Disinherited Knight and all his followers. *They* were the English in spirit. Even Rebecca was English.

And so we went our way through English history. If we lost the French dominions it was because it was providentially designed. Joan of Arc beat us in order that our kings might pay more attention to domestic matters – and, after all, Joan of Arc, that splendid, shining and original figure, was, in spirit, an Englishwoman. And the Stuarts, Dutch William, and the Hanoverian sovereigns, were they not predestined to become English? It is true that they were born in foreign lands – but that only made the principle the more singularly demonstrable. Was it not, too, providential that England lost the North American colonies when she did? Was not even Washington an Englishman? And Lafayette? I am sure that each of us boys would have answered each of these questions with a sparkling and unanimous 'Yes!'

And the influence of such teaching, of such a careful and deeply-penetrating system of thought, upon the opening minds of a generation – or of how many generations? – must have been inestimable and far-reaching beyond conception. Personally I look at the world with different eyes nowadays – but at the back of those eyes the old feeling remains. Still for me William, who landed at Pevensey in the year of our Lord 1066, was the first Englishman to touch British soil since Julius Caesar's day. And still, for me, the loss of the North American colonies is the crowning mercy. No doubt, too, for the vast majority of those who were at school in my days – for the great majority of the English people – the history of these islands presents itself in that light still. To what extent the modern, comparatively scientific breath of thought that has crept over England since the days of Darwin may have modified these preconceptions, or may have altered the methods of approaching the English race problem as it affects the teaching of history to children, I can hardly tell. But the other day I travelled along a branch line: in my carriage were six members of a grammar school fifteen going to play a proprietary school in a neighbouring town. Their frequent reference to one of their masters as 'Chaucer' – (he was the father of two boys who had written verses in the school magazine) – led me to question one or two of them. They were 'doing' the Angevin kings for some examination. And there were all my old beliefs brought back to me in a flood. It was not so much the fact that a spectacled boy in a muddy cap told me that the possession of French dominions by the kings of England 'exercised a deleterious influence' upon domestic affairs – so that it was a jolly good job we lost them.

I asked: 'Were not the first Angevin kings English?' and got the answer that they jolly well were. I asked: 'Did they become, more or less, English when French was not their language any longer?' and I got the answer: They were jolly well English when they came, they supposed, and they were jolly well English when they learned to speak English. Anyhow, the French they spoke was an English French, not a French French. That was what you jolly well meant by the French of Stratford-atte-Bow. As for the subject race – the scientist's real Anglo-Saxons – the people who had been there before the Angevins, they were English too. They were *all* English.

A rather silent boy, who had been cutting his initials on the door of the carriage, volunteered the following sentences for the enlightenment of my excessive dullness:

'It was like this. You and the lady with you were in the train at B——. Well: you were third-class passengers on this silly line. We six got in at A——. Well: now we're all third-class passengers together on the rotten line, and I wish we could jolly well get somewhere where they sell ginger-beer.'

The sentence seems to prove that the old spirit has not died out of the English schoolboy people; and, inasmuch as the people seldom troubles to revise its schoolboy judgments once it has passed adolescence, it may be taken for granted that that spirit remains to most of the people at the present day. It seems to me, that sentence, to sum up very admirably the attitude of our population towards itself. It is not – the whole of Anglo-Saxondom – a matter of race but one, quite simply, of place – of place and of spirit, the spirit

being born of the environment. We are not Teutons; we are not
Latins; we are not Celts or Anglo-Saxons in the sense of being
descendants of Jutes or Angles. We are all passengers together,
carving or not carving our initials on the doors of our carriage, and
we all vaguely hope as a nation to jolly well get somewhere. How
we look at our line, whether we style it a rotten line or a good one,
depends very much upon the immediate state of our national self-
consciousness. But, in a dim way too, we do hope that we shall
jolly well get somewhere where they sell ginger-beer.

I am inclined to doubt that the Englishman – whether we
consider him nationally or in that sort of composite photograph
that for us is the typical individual – to doubt that the Englishman,
as far as these matters are concerned, ever gets much beyond the
schoolboy's point of view. I have used already the word anthropomorphic in regard to the Englishman's attitude towards the brute
creation; I am inclined to repeat it in regard to his way of looking
at other races. He regards himself as the one proper man, but,
possessed of a sense of modesty, he cannot rule all the other races
out of the human category. An ordinary foreigner is, of course,
hardly a man; but as soon as a people does something fine, the
Englishman is inclined to hold out to it the hand of kinship. I am
sure, for instance, that the English of the middle nineteenth century
regarded Garibaldi as an Englishman.

At the risk of being thought paradoxical, I will venture to say
that this attitude of the Englishman is not only philosophically true,
but is even historically correct, for in the case of a people so mixed
in its origins as is the race inhabiting the most fertile, the most
opulent, and the most pleasant parts of these islands – in the case of
a people descended from Romans, from Britons, from Anglo-
Saxons, from Danes, from Normans, from Poitevins, from Scotch,
from Huguenots, from Irish, from Gaels, from modern Germans,
and from Jews, a people so mixed that there is in it hardly a man
who can point to seven generations of purely English blood, it is
almost absurd to use the almost obsolescent word 'race'. These
fellows are all ourselves to such an extent that in almost every
English family, by some trick of atavism, one son will be dark,
broad-headed, and small, another blonde, and huge in all his
members; one daughter will be small and dark, with ruddy glints
in her hair when the sun shines, with taking 'ways', and another
indeed a daughter of the gods, tall and divinely fair. There is possibly
a west of London population of these giants, but there is also an

east of London population – (let us at least say so for the sake of
argument, in order to frame some sort of theory with which we
may agree or from which we may differ); there is an east of London
population which is small, dark, vigorous and gentle. In the natural
course of things this eastern population will rise in the scale, will
cross London, will besiege the palaces, will sit in the chairs and will
attain to the very frames of mind of these tranquil giants. We cannot
nowadays say of what race are either the giants or the small dark
men, still less will the sociologist of the future be able to pronounce
upon the origins of that mixed dominant race that shall be. The
Englishman is then uttering a philosophical truism, a historical
platitude, when he says his 'All these fellows are ourselves'; and he
is uttering other platitudes and truisms when he says that Joshua the
son of Nun, or Garibaldi, were Englishmen. For what he means,
more precisely stated, is that circumstances, environment, the hand
of destiny if you will, have given him a share of the spirit of those
apparently unrelated and irreconcilable peoples. For if there be no
Anglo-Saxon race, there is in the population of these islands a
certain spirit, a spirit of human fallibility, of optimism, of humanity,
of self-deception, a spirit of a thousand finenesses, of a thousand
energies, of some meannesses, and of many wrong-headednesses –
a spirit which I am very willing to call English, but which I am
more than loth to style Anglo-Saxon.

So many things have gone to these makings – the fertility of the
land, the pleasantness of the climate, the richness of its minerals, the
spirit of security given to it by its encircling seas. For invaders of
England have seemed to see in the land not only communities that
they may sack, but a stronghold in which they may maintain themselves, their goods, and their sovereignties. And this dream of theirs
seems, indeed, well warranted, since the Norman invaders held
England but lost Normandy, the Angevins held England but lost
Anjou, and even the Hanoverian Guelphs hold England still whilst
Hanover has been wrested from their house by a formidable and
predatory race. But it seems to me that almost more its position
than its desirability has made England what it is. If in the eyes of
the Englishman England be a home, in the eyes of the whole world
England is almost more, a goodly inn, a harbourage upon a
westward road. Just as you will find upon one of the shores from
which birds of passage take their flight advanced islets, rocks, or
shingle-banks, where for the moment swallows and finches will rest
in their thousands, so you may see England a little island lying off

the mainland. And upon it the hordes of European mankind have rested during their secular flights westward in search of the Islands of the Blest. If they have succeeded only in founding a 'race' more mingled, more ungraspable, a race that is a sort of pluperfect English race, a race to whom no doubt the future belongs; if, instead of finding a classical ideal, they have only founded a very modern and very inscrutable problem, that fact must be regarded rather as a comment upon the proneness of humanity to fall short of its ideals than as a refutation of the convenient image that England is a road, a means to an end, not an end in itself.

For it is, I think, a fact that even the most hardened Anglo-morphist, the English schoolboy with the very largest race appetite, will not dare to regard the American people as in any sense English. The great northern half-continent cannot, even by a vast figure of speech, be regarded as a morsel too large to chew. It is simply a sphere so great that the most distended jaw cannot begin to bite upon it. Whatever we may think that Napoleon Buonaparte *ought* to have been, we do not even commence to imagine that General Grant was an Englishman. Perhaps Stonewall Jackson may have been.

The American in his turn well returns that compliment. There is no American Historic Theory to make the Duke of Wellington appear to be a 'Yankee'. I doubt whether, much though American histories belaud him, Governor Spottiswoode can be regarded as an American. For, upon the whole, the spirit of the American Historic Theory is as exclusive as is that breathed in our island schools. But a certain parallel between these theories is observable. Thus, on the east of the Anglo-Saxon ocean history begins suddenly at 1066: on the west it begins with the shots fired at Bunker's Hill. On the east, before the dawn there was a night in which there moved pale Anglo-Saxons: on the west there was a crepuscular period in which there lived the colonists. And just as, before the Anglo-Saxons there had been the Romans who were really English, so before the colonial days there had been a truly American race – the Pilgrim Fathers. But there, upon the whole, the parallel ceases.

For the English, having a distinguished history of their own, find it most agreeable to regard the history of the United States as a thing practically non-existent. The Englishman will tell you that he never really had much to do with 'America'; the American, on the other hand, will tell you that he flogged the Englishman.

On the one hand, the United States have a singular kinship with

England of the Spirit. Its peaceful invaders, coming in their millions to seek castles in Spain, become almost more violently American than naturalised English become English; but, on the other hand, they do not seem to acquire, once they are fused into the body of the people, the English faculty of considering themselves one with foreign nations. Upon the whole, the American is insular 'all through': the Englishman is insular only in regard to his clothes, his eatables, and his furniture. There is, of course, an excellent reason for this: the English people is very well aware that it is, along its own lines, as nearly perfect as a people can be; I mean that it breeds true to type. Thus there is, in a corner of Kent and Sussex, a certain stretch of marsh-land. Here all the sheep are Kent sheep; good, heavy, serviceable, not very fine-bred animals. Now, if you introduce upon this stretch of territory sheep of other breeds – Southdowns, Wensleydales, Blackfaces, or what you will – you may be certain that, as the years go on, in a few generations the progeny of these sheep will so assimilate themselves to the Kent sheep, that they will become Kent sheep. Thus the problem before the Kent and Sussex breeder is not to keep his flocks pure, but rather to attempt to modify them by the introduction of foreign blood.

Speaking psychologically, that problem is before the English people. It does not need, in its own view, to trouble its head to keep the race pure. The climate, the tradition, the school, will do that. The children of any Wallachian will become as English as the children of any Lincolnshire farmer, so that, at times, an uneasy wave passes across the English people. A few years ago, for instance, the whole country was crying out for the Prussianisation of our schools, our armies, our laboratories, because 'we are a nation of amateurs'. But the problem before the United States, the problem present always in the consciousness of the American nation, is precisely that of producing a pure type. Without any secular traditions, without any homogeneity of climate, of soil, or of occupation, the American has not yet been able to strike any national average. Upon the whole, the Englishman of today is very much akin to the Englishman of early Victorian days; but the American, *Consule* Roosevelt, is almost a different animal from the American who sought, say, to impeach President Johnson; and certainly the American of today is unrecognisable as a descendant of those who were caricatured by Charles Dickens.

We seem to arrive here at two contradictory facts. It would appear that, on the one hand, the island upon the west of Europe existed solely as a half-way house towards the western continent. Yet, in face of this, it breeds, this island, a population whose sons come singularly true to type. But, contradictory as these facts may seem, it will appear, as soon as they are examined closely, that they are facts belonging to two different planes of thought – that, as it were, to say that the ball is round does not contradict the statement that the ball is white. And these seeming contradictions may be drawn in a hundred different and startling ways. Thus nowhere in the world, so much as in England, do you find the spirit of the home of ancient peace; nowhere in the occidental world will you find turf that so invites you to lie down and muse, sunshine so mellow and innocuous, shade so deep or rooks so tranquil in their voices. You will find nowhere a *mise-en-scène* so suggestive of the ancient and the enduring as in an English rose-garden, walled in and stone pathed, if it be not in an English cathedral close. Yet these very permanent manifestations of restfulness were founded by the restless units of European races, and these English rose-gardens and cathedral closes breed a race whose mission is, after all, to be the eternal frontiersmen of the world.

These paradoxes reconcile themselves immediately at the touch of one simile or another. We may, that is to say, reconcile ourselves to the dictum of the Chinese Commission that lately visited our shores: they stated that we had grown too slumbrous, too slow, too conservative, to be safely imitated by a renascent Oriental Empire. But, if we put it that these rose-gardens and cathedral closes are, as it were, the manifestations of the pleasantness and fullness that attend the digestion of a very sufficient meal, these dark places become plain. Assuredly, the various individuals who took these great dinners had huge appetites – and, equally assuredly, those huge appetites will remain to their descendants once the phase of digestion is over. The English nation, that is to say, cannot have been made up of all the 'bad eggs' of Europe since the dark ages without retaining the bad-egg tendency in a degree more marked than is observable in any continental nation.

For, philosophically regarded, that is one of the two great lessons of English history. Like the Romans, the English are not a race: they are the populations descended from the rogues of a Sanctuary – of a Sanctuary that arose not so much because it was holy, as because it was safe or because it was conquerable. All through the ages it has attracted precisely the restless, the adventurous, or the outcast. The outcast were precisely those who did not get on well with their folk at home; the adventurous were those who were not satisfied with the chances offered to them at home; the restless were the men who could never settle down. The descendants of these last have, perhaps many of them, passed already further west. They may be the eternally unquiet gold-diggers of South America, the beachcombers of the South Seas, the hoboes of the United States, the Jameson raiders, or the mere casuals of our workhouses. But the children of the adventurous and the outcast remain with us: they are you, I, and our friends – young Carruthers, the parson's son, who was no good at home and died, shot through the head, at Krugersdorp; or our other friend, Murray, who suddenly threw up his good post of land-steward to go out, heaven knows why! to Argentina. He will, they say now, die dictator of the whole South American Pacific railway system.

If we go impressionistically through the history of South Britain, we see how true, impressionistically speaking still, is this particular view. We might almost stretch the theory further, and say that England is the direct product of successive periods of unrest in the continental peoples. For want of a better terminology we may adopt the language of the Race Theorist, and say that we know practically nothing of the aboriginal inhabitants of Britain. We cannot nowadays trace in England any type corresponding to the Digger Indians of North America – corresponding to those unfortunate cave-dwelling, mud-eating beings who are said to have been driven into their holes and fastnesses by the triumphant Iroquois or their rival races. Interested observers – observers, that is, who are interested in race theories – will, however, tell you that in various parts of England, most notably in Wiltshire around Stonehenge, they find a dark-haired, dark-eyelashed, mysterious, romantic child, who, in their view, represents the new outcropping of a never extinct, aboriginal race. Now, they say, that at last the English race has become an admixture, comparatively stable, of the continentals, the aboriginal, non-continental race is about to assert its permanence; it will gradually increase by force of atavism until it have swallowed up all us descendants of blonde, red, dark or tawny peoples. But that is still very much stuff of dreams and visions; even yet we cannot say what visaged children of men made the great escarpments on the side of Whitesheet Hill. We cannot say what manner of men were our aborigines whom, by so many relays, we have displaced.

Even the original displacers, Gauls, Gaels, Goidels, Celts, or what you will, are legendary to us; we know neither whence they came, nor whither really they wended. In a vague way we know that a horde of barbarians, dominated more or less by a myth styled 'Brennus', issued, innumerable, wild, and desolating, from the gloomy forests of Central Europe. They sacked, doubtless, Rome; they passed perhaps into Spain; it is said that they overran Hellas and despoiled the temple of the Pythic oracle. They found a home, permanent enough, in the very east of the mainland, and other homes, permanent enough, in the western parts of our islands. But across England they were fated to go, if with delaying footsteps. They found, in fact, no home, but an hotel; and though we cannot any more tell what particular kind of unrest it was that drove them forth from their hiding-place, we may be very certain that it was some kind of psychological or material pressure that forced out from the Central European forests these, the adventurous, the outcast, or the restless of an immense people. It was, again, a national unrest that sent hither the first Caesar and his troops. They in their day were the troublesome populations of a Rome that was in a state of ferment, constitutional and psychological. It is well not to drive a theory too far, so that we may refrain from taking the view that the governors that Rome sent to Britain during the stable Imperial era were men of unrest whom the Emperors wished to send to the ends of the earth. Indeed, we might well draw a contrary moral from the story of the Roman occupancy of these islands, for it was perhaps precisely because the Romans who held Britain were more or less conscripted soldiers, that the Roman period of dominance left so little trace upon the English peoples. But it remains a fact, observable enough today, that a colony administered by men who are sent, has very little chance of permanence in comparison with one founded by men who choose to go. In that fact we may perhaps see the secret of the British Empire: it is certainly the secret of 'England'.

The Angles, in turn, were men of unrest and of adventure; the Danes, who harried them, were even so, and the Northmen, who finally conquered them, were the offscourings, the adventurous overmen of those very Scandinavians whose unrest had peopled the northern parts of France. And, roughly speaking, we may say as much of the Angevins, and the Stuarts with their hordes of Scots. It is, of course, less true of the Dutch that came with William III, or of the Hanoverian kings.

The tide of armed invasion did actually stop with the Angevins, and by the time of Shakespeare, England might well, to a poetic imagination, present the appearance of an island whose foot spurns back the ocean's rolling tide that coops from other lands her islanders. At that date England had very victoriously passed through a phase of alarums and excursions; she might well boast of being throned inviolable in the west; she had survived all the projects for invasion of the reign of Henry VIII, projects founded in all Europe during fifty years, to culminate in the crowning defeat of the Armada. But that very period of the Elizabethans was in itself a time of Continental unrest that brought to English shores a new tide of invasion; it brought to us all those bad eggs who, beginning with the Anabaptists from Münster – the city from which my friend, the Professor of Literature, surveyed our race – culminated with the Huguenots, who have meant so much for England.

England, indeed, that seemed so stable a nest to the past of the race, was already beginning to assume more definitely the aspect of a hospice on the long road to a western Atlantis. And it is significant that, a few years after the writing of the phrase 'coops from other lands her islanders', England herself, approaching a period of unrest, exported to the other shores of the Sea of the British Empire, her first shiploads of 'bad eggs'. For it was not a generation before the Pilgrim Fathers set sail.

From that time onwards England assumed more or less definitely her character of a road to the ultimate west. Thus, in any history of the United States, we may read that such and such a state was founded by the restless people of France, who, having tried Flanders for a home, tried England, and finding no home in England, sailed westward.

CHAPTER III

The Melting Pot

IN my two previous chapters I have drawn attention to two facts – or, let me put it more exactly, to two aspects that most have struck me in the corporate manifestations of the history of the population of England. Let me now add a third strand to the plait of theories that I offer to my reader. In my first chapter I put the proposition that the chief value of England to the world was that it had shown the nations how mankind, composed as it is of differing individualities, might, with a sort of rule-of-thumb agreeableness, live together in great congeries. And this indeed – if one may be pardoned for drawing morals from one's own projections – is the moral that I should draw from my previous book, the first of this series. In my second chapter I have attempted to make plain a view of England as a resting-place of humanity in its road westward. And this, indeed, if I am allowed to draw a further moral from a further projection, is the one that I should draw from the second work of this series. For in that, if any generalisation stands out for me, it is: that the English field-labourer is throwing down his tools and abandoning his master's acres. What has hitherto been regarded as the staple of the population, the stable units of all peoples, appears to me to be reverting once more to the order of restless people.[1] This, of course, is no very new cry, nor is it a very modern phenomenon. It was to be observed, for instance, in the time of Henry VIII, just before the disestablishment of the monasteries. Such a displacement of the population has always been attended by great changes in the psychology of the people; but for

---

1 I wish again, and very emphatically, to draw attention to the fact that these pages embody only my personal views, founded upon facts that have come under my personal acquaintanceship. This facet of the rural cramping, this phenomenon of depopulation of the country districts was, for instance, denied *in toto* by a writer in the 'Academy', who cited against me the fact that Major Poore's smallholdings at Winterslow were attracting many settlers.

the moment it is not convenient to enter minutely into the question of whether the change in the psychology is caused by the movement of the population. Nor, for the moment, is it my purpose to attempt to settle, even in my own view, whether this change in the basis of population is for good or for evil in the future of the people. The general opinion is that it makes for what is called degeneration; but it behoves every thinking man to question the general opinion. In my book upon a town I have pointed out that the one problem before the people is the evolution of a healthy town type. In the second book of this series I have laid stress upon the fact that the other problem of the people is the retaining, or the attracting, of a sufficient population upon the land. But in this thorny and difficult question it is as easy to find consolation as to grow depressed. It depends largely upon one's temperamental or temporary obsessions.

To the man whose ideal is a dense rural population the gradual shifting of countrymen to towns, and thence to other lands, is a race nightmare. Population, he will say, tends invariably to decrease in the towns: philoprogenitiveness decays in the cities. Nevertheless he may find comfort in the thought that the present type of a city life is not necessarily permanent. A townsman may very conceivably be evolved ready to increase and multiply. I was in a country inn the other day and a commercial traveller came in to lunch. He was so worried with these questions (he 'travelled in' a kind of lace that is used principally for decorating infants' clothes) that, finding me disinclined to talk, he must needs utter his terrors to the waiter, who stood fidgeting with the dish-cover in his hand. Said the commercial traveller:

'Have you read what Roosevelt says?'

The waiter said: 'No, sir.'

'Well, what I say is this' (the traveller punctuated his words with heaps of cabbage): 'what we want is alliance with America. What's the good of the *entente cordiale*? We haven't any use for learning the ways of Frenchmen whose birth-rate is declining.'

The waiter uttered 'No, sir', shuffled his feet in his pumps, and, pretending to hear a call from the bar, whisked from the door.

'Here am I unmarried,' the traveller fixed me. 'Now why?' And, after a pause in which I said nothing, he continued: 'Because the birth-rate's low! How can I afford a wife?'

I suggested that, in that way, he too contributed to lower the birth-rate.

'There you have it,' he said. 'Now the interest that I represent employs some of the best men in the country. You'd be astonished if you knew the brain that there is in the fine white linen trade. Well, *they* can't afford to marry either. So there you have the straight tip. The best men can't afford to marry because the birth-rate's low, and the birth-rate's low because the best men can't afford to marry, and so old England's going to rack and ruin!' He went on to revile Malthus.

But, without going to the full length of the commercial traveller, we may, for the sake of argument, set it down that some sort of depopulation is taking place, and that this depopulation is bad for the English people. Let me, against this picture of gloom, hasten to set down a counterbalancing theory of a more cheerful kind.

I lately tried to have made for my private guidance composite likenesses of the leading spirits of several English centuries. The attempt failed because of the great difficulty I had in finding assimilable portraits of the ages that had preceded the era of photography. But what I wished to prove to my private satisfaction was this:

It may be granted for the sake of argument, that the psychology of the civilised world changes – that the dominant types of the world alter with changing, if mysterious, alternations in the economic or social conditions of the races. I have had it put to me that the modern world began with the discovery of methods of working metal in great quantities – that, in fact, the machine has rescued us from the dark ages. That is a view like another. If for the moment we adopt it, it will then become obvious that the nation that will best survive the struggle for existence is the nation that shall contain the largest number of individuals fitted to administer, to manufacture and to develop machines – that that nation will eventually control, for the time being, the resources of the world. My own personal view – which is no doubt as idiosyncratic as that of my friend who favoured me with his view of a machine age – or my own personal preference has led me to see that the modern world began with the discovery of the balance of power as an international factor. Others, again, will say that the modern world is the product of the printing press, or of the fore-and-aft rig in ships – a very powerful factor. And yet another view will have it that the real modern world began only with the evolution of the theory of the survival of the fittest, or with the discovery of the commercial value of by-products. All these things are merely convenient systems of thought by which a man may arrange in his mind his mental image of the mundane cosmogony – or they may be systems of thought by which he is able to claim for his particular calling, craft or art, the status of the really important factor in life. Whether we style our present age, or any previous age, the Machine, the Balance of Power, the Schooner, the By-product or the Press Age is immaterial enough – the fact arising out of this mist of conflicting ideals is that in the history of the world as among man there have always been psychological ages.

It remains then one other platitude, which I hasten to repeat, that in any given age the nation having the largest number of individuals most fitted to deal with the peculiar circumstances of that age – that nation will be the one on the top of the market. In an Ice Age, in fact, Esquimaux will have an immense advantage. There is one profound truth that the English people has always taken for granted – along with that other truth that Providence is upon our side. In periods of trial and national stress we have always the comfortable conviction that somehow we shall muddle through. And somehow we do, in a way that almost invariably works for our material advantage. If, in fact, an Ice Age did supervene, we might be pretty certain that the Esquimaux would have a great immediate advantage. England would be horribly discomposed; all sorts of reputations would be hopelessly marred. But somehow, one man, coming probably from the very bottom of our particular basket, would arise among us; would teach us how to set a glass roof all over England—how to turn the land into a vast hothouse. Incidentally, too, he would probably give us the chance of roofing in, say, half Sweden or the whole of Africa, so that either as investors or as a nation, we should profit very materially. Wherever, in short, the sun did set, its last rays would shine upon a roof of glass, that upon the map could be comfortably coloured with red amidst the white of those polar nights, engulfing the other nations. We might have begun pretty badly; we should be certain to end more than moderately well.

This, of course, is a fanciful projection, but it does figure a national characteristic. It means that we believe that somewhere in the back of our people, in the great middle class, in the aristocracy, or in the submerged tenth, there are to be found men – the one man – fitted to deal with any emergency. And, if we consider our history and our composition as a people, we may find comforting assurance that this view is at least reasonably to be justified.

We begin our campaigns, military, economic or moral, always

rather badly. The other nation, our adversary, is almost invariably
in a stronger position. The age will be either a French, a German,
a Spanish or a Portuguese Age; and the other nation being truer to
type will, in the immediate present, be able to overwhelm us. We
shall have to go through a number of domestic revolutions before
we shall be fitted even to begin to face the problem, whatever it
may be. We are, for reasons to which I will refer later, the nation
of vested interests and of established reputations, so that before we
can really get to work we have to shake off always an immense
number of ancient generals, admirals, agriculturists or textile manufacturers who have grown into a rut. But *the* man among us, seeing
his opportunity, hearing his call, will eventually burst through, and,
being quick to follow a lead, we shall acclaim him, learn from him,
reward him, and then let him and his tradition become an incubus
on us in face of some rising age in which, for a time, some new
nation will take the lead.

In order to escape the charge of glorifying a people to which, at
least partially, I belong, let me hasten to say that we should do all
this precisely because of the men that that nation will have given
us. If eventually – and no doubt we shall – we beat the Germans
in the great war of by-products, it will probably be because of the
German strain that is in us already; if eventually we did beat the
Flemings at wool-weaving, it was because Philippa of Hainault
introduced into England many large colonies of Flemish weavers;
if eventually we took the finer textile trades from the French it was
because France sent us the Huguenots.

In the larger matter of political manœuvres it has always seemed
to me that this characteristic was particularly observable. England's
greatness as an international factor in Europe began incidentally
with the birth of the modern world.[1] And, for me, as I have said,
the modern world was born with the discovery of the political
theory of the balance of the Powers in Europe. That this discovery
was in any particular sense modern, I am not inclined to assert. Julius
Caesar, for instance, as a boy ridded the Eastern Mediterranean

---

1 Let me here very particularly impress upon the reader that these remarks are intended as
a purely personal view. They are matters to promote argument; they are views, not statements of fact, spoken with any *ex cathedra* weight. They are intended to arouse discussion,
not to instruct; they are part of a scheme according to which one thinker arranges his
ideas. If, in short, any other thinker would present us with a scheme as workable for his
particular temperament, I should be perfectly willing to make the attempt to arrange my
ideas according to that scheme.

of pirates by skilfully taking advantage of the fact that he was an isolated third party in a naval warfare between freebooters. And, no doubt, that very able and very wonderful man, King John of England, used and felt the effects of a nice adjustment of international forces. But, upon the whole – speaking impressionistically – we may say that the mediaeval history of Western Europe before the fifteenth century, and the history of England in particular during that period, leaves upon the mind the impression of being a matter, or a long series of matters, decided by sword blows. Before that date, as a rule, the king was a man who smote his opponent over the head with a heavy mace and set upon his own brows the circlet that he found in a thorn bush. In this mode of international contact England did little more than hold its own. Its fleets at times held the seas, at times were driven from them. If England had its Black Princes, France had its Du Guesclins and its Joans of Arc. The Plantagenets were the great and haughty race of their age, the fine flower of combatant royalty. But the Plantagenets were Frenchmen. And, if we took France, we were driven out of France. We ended up, upon the whole, all square. Many factors, no doubt, conduced to this end – internal warfares, pestilences, the awakening of the dominant type in these islands. But, upon the whole, at the end of the fourteenth century, at the death of Henry VII and during the early years of Henry VIII, England counted for practically nothing in the comity of European nations.

I am aware that this statement of the case is a thought contrary to the general impression. But upon the whole it is historically true, since the general impression takes little account of such abortive attempts at invasion of France as that made by Henry VIII in the first year of his reign. He sent, that is to say, a great expedition of horse and foot into Spain with the intention that, with the aid of the Spaniards, they should take France and divide it. But every kind of failure and ignominy awaited this attempt, and, great though the effort was, we have forgotten it.

We may, however, reconsider it for the moment; it is, that is to say, significant that it was not a direct frontal attack upon France. The expedition was intended to make its way through the country, and with the aid of a friendly nation. In that sense it was what I may call modern in spirit. It was, at the same time, conceived in the older spirit, since it was a haphazard, unprepared blow, struck without much preliminary negotiation. It was, in short, a conception akin to the old one of a word and a blow; there was not any particular manœuvring to obtain a diplomatic advantage; there was not any particularly patient waiting for an advantageous moment to strike. It was, moreover, practically the last attempt of an English king to assert by force of arms his theoretic right to the throne of France. It seems to mark, this futile, disastrous sortie, the end of the old era.

In a former book, when comparing the works of Dürer with those of Holbein, I had occasion to say that the life which Dürer's art seems to chronicle was at its close. It had been essentially an out-of-door life. Dürer's lords rode hunting in full steel from small castles in rugged rocks; the flesh of his figures is hardened, dried and tanned by exposure to the air. But Holbein's lords no longer rode hunting. The change had set in fully by 1530 or so, when Holbein chronicled the English court. His lords were precisely indoor statesmen; they dealt in intrigues; they inhabited palaces, not castles; their flesh was rounded, their limbs at rest, their eyes sceptical. And, indeed, the composite photograph that I have had made from the portraits left by Holbein does portray a definite type – a definite type that rather curiously coincides with Holbein's sketches of the typical Englishman of that day. This was a heavy, dark, bearded, bull-necked animal, sagacious, smiling, but with devious and twinkling eyes – a type that nowadays is generally found in the English rural districts. If it is not too topical or too personal, I should say that he reminds me, this typical Englishman, most of all of Dr W.G. Grace, the cricketer.

And, indeed, a sort of peasant cunning did – let me add again the qualifying 'to my mind' – distinguish the international dealings of the whole world at that date. Roughly speaking, the ideals of the chivalric age were altruistic; roughly speaking, the ideals of the age that succeeded it were individualist-opportunist. It was not, of course, England that was first in the field, since Italy produced Machiavelli. But Italy, which produced Machiavelli, failed utterly to profit by him. England, on the other hand, had to wait many years before falling into line with the spirit of its age. It had, as it were, to wait until most of the vested interest of the middle ages were got rid of – until practically the last of the great barons were brought to the ground. It had to wait until a man could climb from the very lowest stage of the body politic into the very highest chair that the republic could offer. But then it profited exceedingly, so that the England which, at the opening of Henry VIII's reign, had been the laughing-stock, became, towards the close of that reign, the arbiter of Europe.

But it *did* produce from its depths, from amidst its bewildering cross currents of mingled races, *the* great man of its age; and, along with him, it produced a number of men similar in type, and strong enough to found a tradition. The man, of course, was Thomas Cromwell, who welded England into one formidable whole, and his followers in the tradition were the tenacious, pettifogging, cunning, utterly unscrupulous and very wonderful statesmen who supported the devious policy of Queen Elizabeth – the Cecils, the Woottons, the Bacons and all the others of England's golden age.

This splendid and efficient dominant type had, of course, its apogee, its crest of the wave and its decline. It fell a little low with the second of the Stuart Kings and, as far as international expression was concerned, its place was taken by the new, Puritan type. This type, efficient if not very splendid, is interesting, because it shows so very immediately a foreign origin. You have only to go back a generation or so to find its introduction into England. In Ben Jonson's day the Puritan was still being laughed at for a sanctimonious and nefarious Low Country sniffler in black; within a generation the strain was ruling England. It was, too, dictating terms to France, just as it had laid the foundations of a New England. If the suddenness of its uprising and the violence of its manifestations caused it to fall into temporary discredit in this country – for the Restoration was the product of a mere reaction – it recuperated itself soon enough in the final expulsion of the Stuarts.

For we may put it that James II was the last representative of the statesmanship which, founded by Machiavelli, reached its highest point with Thomas Cromwell, the Cecils, Strafford, Laud, and Richelieu, and declined with Mazzini towards the obstinate impracticability of the last Stuart king. Speaking very generally, we may say that mediaeval England was ruled by French-Norman; renaissance England and the England of the Stuarts by Italian-Celtic dominant types. And, speaking very generally, we may say that both those types were dominant also in the occidental Europe of that day. The great rebellion of the Cromwellians, the revolution of William III and the whole Georgian era, were a calling out of the Germanic forces of the nation.

In my private picture of these great national waves I see the dominant type of the centuries preceding Henry VIII as rufous, reddish tanned, with dusky-red complexions; the dominant type of the Tudor-Stuart ages presents itself to me as dark, bearded and shrewd; the years following the fall of James Stuart seem to me to show the gradual growth of a dominant type that was fair-haired; ingenuous perhaps, unimaginative perhaps, but 'sentimental'. I do not wish to imply that the pre-Tudor psychology was childish, but it seems to me that pre-Tudor history appeals more directly to the boy in us. That is probably because its history was largely a matter of wars for the acquisition of territory or upon the point of honour. And, upon the whole, save for the episodes of Smithfield burnings, of the Armada and the pirating on the Spanish Main, of Drake and his rivals, the Tudor-Stuart periods of dominance interest the boy in us very little. They were, that is to say, periods of tortuous intrigues, upon no settled basis of principle. Neither the quasi-religious manœuvres of Henry VIII, nor the matrimonial manœuvres of that king and Queen Elizabeth interest either the man or the boyhood of the nation very much. I am far, indeed, from wishing to be taken as implying that these things in themselves are uninteresting; but the case may be put very fairly that for one person who will know anything of Cardinal Pole's crusade against his sovereign, ten thousand will be found remembering the comparatively unimportant exploits of Richard of the Lion Heart. And, for one person who remembers the great works of Thomas Cromwell, twenty thousand will be found to grow condemnatory or enthusiastic over the actions, relatively unimportant, of his great-nephew.

For, the pre-Tudor times appeal, by their actions, to the schoolboy that is in us all; the post-Stuart times appeal, for their principles, to the amateur moralist that is in us all. But the Tudor-Stuart era is interesting merely for its exhibitions of human greed, heroism, bigotry, martyrdom or savagery. It is, as it were, a projection of realism between two widely differing but romantic movements. I am aware that in thus writing down the Puritan age as romantic I lay myself open to the disagreeable charge of writing paradoxes. But I write in all sincerity, using, perhaps, only half appropriate words. For in essentials, the Stuarts' cause was picturesque; the Cromwellian cause was a matter of principle. Now a picturesque cause may make a very strong and poetic appeal, but it is, after all, a principle that sweeps people away. For poetry is the sublime of common sense; principle is wrong-headedness wrought up to the sublime pitch – and that, in essentials, is romance.

I possess the diary of my English grandfather, a romantic of the romantics, a man who never survived his early Byronism. In its faded bluish pages, stained with a faded and rusting ink, he records

the minutiæ of a strenuous, a heroic and a very romantic struggle
with a world unsympathetic enough. At the end of one of his very
hard days he had sat down to read, I should say, Macaulay. He had
been in the winter air painting a shawl which was sadly needed
indoors by his patient wife. In pursuance of his principle of
recording the smallest details, he had frozen his hands so that he
could no longer hold a brush that night. And there, suddenly, in a
sprawled and sputtering handwriting, in great letters appears the
portentous announcement – the result of his winter night's reading:
'I love Dutch William!'

I confess that, at the first, being confronted with this point of
view – with this national outburst – I rubbed my eyes. For one
cannot imagine any Romantic writing the words in sober, or in
romantic earnest. It seems as difficult, at first sight, to love William
III as to love Queen Anne or George II. No one is more unpic-
turesque. But no one is more of a principle typified. It is difficult
to call up any personage of recorded English history who is less of
a figure than William III; it is, indeed, difficult to call him up at all.
One remembers neither his features nor the cut of his hair; neither
his clothes nor whether he stood six feet high. Nevertheless, this
vacant space stands for principles the most vital to the evolution of
modern England – of the whole modern, Germanised world. If, in
fact, William III was no figure, he was very assuredly the figure-
head of a very portentous vessel.

And no doubt inspired by the Victorian canons, by principles of
Protestantism, commercial stability, political economies, Carlylism,
individualism and liberty – provided, too, with details of feature,
dress, and stature, no doubt my grandfather could evolve a picture
of a strong, silent, hard-featured, dominant personality. Rising hot-
headed from his romantic perusal he inscribed, before putting out
his light, the words: 'I love Dutch William.'

Be that as it may – and I think the diagnosis is in this case a just
one – my personal impression of the three more or less distinct
phases of the English court – the pre-Tudor, the Tudor-Stuart and
the post-Stuart – remains that of fair quasi-Communist, dark
Socialist-Tory, and blonde Germanic-Protestant-individualist
dominant types. Incidentally I may note that that entry in my grandfather's diary does, to some extent, substantiate my theory, that the
post-Stuart period most interests the adults among us, the pre-
Tudor making an appeal to the young who have not yet formed
themselves. It is true that in my own later years at school we were

confronted – I am bound to say, appalled – by a text-book which was called, I think, a *Short History of the English People*, which sought to push the theocratic period much further back than the Tudors. But I well remember the rage and indignation which its substitution for our other manuals excited. In our particular class the really brilliant boys sank to the lowest places, and I sank with them. And the pained look upon our headmaster's face – a mild, bearded, dark, rather excitable face, with spectacles that gleamingly half hid a slight cast in the black eyes – the disappointment and the trouble, I remember very well after many years. He was a man who took a pride in, who had an affection for, his best boys. And they failed rather lamentably to follow, or to remember, history as it was put by the Short Historian. They had been brilliant to seize the points, the incidents, the adventures of kings and generals. Facts were vivid in their minds; the onus of a gradual and ordered growth of a democratic people, puzzled and confused them. They could get, I mean, some sort of idea of life from the facts; they could add something of themselves to the recital. But they could only memorise the pages of the *Short History of the English People*, and, in consequence, it was what Mr E—— called his parrot boys that came to the top. I fancy that it was for this reason, as much as any, that Mr E——, who was an artist in teaching, who delighted to feel himself in sympathy with awakened intelligence and disliked forcing pages of sound theory into dull memories; who, in fact, was an educator and not an instructor – that it was for this reason that Mr E—— shortly afterwards resigned his headmastership. I remember very well his standing on high by his table, his ragged gown flapping behind him, his mild dark eyes bent upon a tormentor, who was the top boy. A——s, a small, spectacled automaton with a slight impediment in his speech, had completed without a hitch a long sentence beginning: 'The evolution of the English peasant was never more strikingly exemplified...'

Mr E—— said impatiently, 'Very well, A——s, but what does it mean?'

A——s fingered the top button of his coat:

'It means,' he said, '"that the evolution of the English peasant was never" ——'

Mr E—— stopped him with a 'tut-tut!' 'What does it *mean*?' he asked, his voice rising.

A——s stuttered very badly:

'It–t–t means that the evolution of–of ——'

Mr E—— sat down exasperatedly and rapped the table for three or four seconds. His dark head hung down dejectedly.

'Ah well,' he said at last, 'you'll be an immense credit to the school, A——s, in the examination room!'

He bade us write an essay on the 'Statute of Uses and its effect upon the psychology of the Reformation', and, whilst we sighed in silence at this impossible task, even A——s not having committed these pages to memory, Mr E—— himself began to write. It was, I believe, his letter of resignation to the governors that he was composing. At any rate, all the school knew next morning that Mr E—— was going. During his tenure of the head-mastership, the school had dwindled in numbers to the extent of 150 boys. Mr E——, in fact, could not be brought to regard himself as a crammer, and under him we gained only four scholarships.

I do not wish to draw from this the moral that Mr Green's History is ill-adapted for its special purpose; but I do seem to see in this particular scene evidence that the theory of evolution, as applied to English history, is little fitted to the boyish apprehension. It is, it seems to me, ill-fitted because it calls upon a boy to be acquainted with modern trains of thought; to be acquainted, in fact, with modern conditions of life, and to read into mediaeval history the lessons that only years of experience or years of reading the leaders in newspapers and the works of the Victorian writers could have taught him.

It is easy, in fact, to say that the turning of the agricultural districts to wool farming led inevitably to the evolution of the Puritan spirit, when you know that the Puritan spirit succeeded to the quasi-Catholic-quasi-Pagan phase of English mediaeval life. But you will only see that when you have learned the doctrine that the sole purpose of English mediaeval strivings was to produce the Protestant, individualist, free speech, free thought, free trade, political economics of the Victorian era. This doctrine, this group of doctrines, this once tremendous frame of mind was so riveted on the people of the nineteenth century, that its theories might well be accepted as unquestionable fact. There stood all these things, from Protestantism to freedom, firm, unquestionable, unshakeable, – and thus, in the psychology of the man, divine intervention in favour of the nineteenth century was as deducible from his study of history, as in the boy was the theory that Providence was on the side of the Englishman. I remember once putting it tremblingly to a very liberal relative of the pre-Home Rule days – putting it that, according to his theory of the gradual growth of liberty in the English race, the cataclysmic abolition of the monasteries was a mistake. He regarded me from above a foam–flecked, blonde beard of an imposing venerability.

'Of course,' he said, 'the monasteries were not abolished gradually. It wasn't evolution that did away with them. They were swept away because they were in the way of a gentle evolution.'

I said, in absolute good faith:

'Then the law of a gradual evolution was not invariable?'

He made a great and irritable gesture with his plump white hands.

'You irritate me with your casuistry,' he said. 'I have just explained the matter. The monasteries had to go because they cumbered the ground; it was inevitable. Besides, if they had not gone how should we have reached our Paradise – or the Puritan spirit? That's the backbone of England.'

It was, I suppose, this sort of reading of history that the adult Victorian sought to impose upon the Victorian schoolboy. I think that it probably grated, since I am sure that it inspired my classmates with an invincible dislike for, say, Sir Robert Walpole. But it certainly induced our grandfathers to love Dutch William, and to believe that the Puritan spirit is the backbone of England. Perhaps it is.

In a sense I am, I am aware, running counter to an accepted idea, when I say that the modern Puritanism of English life began, not with the Cromwellians, but with the coming of William III. The Cromwellians, in fact, seem to me to have left little enough mark in England. The Revolution, since it led the way for Walpole and the National Debt, still holds us in its clutches. It did away with personal Royalty; it did away with priesthood; it did away very emphatically with the arts, or rather, with the artistic spirit as a factor in life. And it began the process of doing away with the county interest. Philosophically speaking, too, it began that divorce of principle from life which, carried as far as it has been carried in England, has earned for the English the title of a nation of hypocrites. It did this, of course, because it riveted Protestantism for good and evil upon the nation's dominant types. For, speaking very broadly, we may say that Catholicism, which is a religion of action and of frames of mind, is a religion that men can live up to. Protestantism no man can live up to, since it is a religion of ideals and of reason. (I am far from wishing to adumbrate to which religion I give my preference; for I think it will remain to the end a matter for dispute whether a practicable or an ideal code be the more beneficial to humanity.) But, by voting once and for all for Protestantism, by casting out from us the possibilities of dominance of that pagan half of humanity which is fitted for Catholicism, the Revolution doomed England to be the land of impracticable ideals. Before that date a man could live without his finger upon his moral pulse: since then it has grown gradually more and more impossible.

And inasmuch as, by the lusty sort of health and appetite that it brings, a country life does in essence tend to produce pagans, the Revolution did tend towards producing a dominant type that could no longer inhabit the country. And, inasmuch as it is in the nature of man to desire to rise to eminence, we may say that the Revolution did conduce towards the present building up of the great towns. That we are now tending towards a reaction against these tendencies seems to me to be arguable, and in a subsequent chapter I shall endeavour to put that case. But for the present let me return to my main argument – that of the successive dominant types that the land has produced. It is not my purpose to do more than slightly allude to such of these as suit my purpose.[1]

It may be taken for granted as a general impression that the immediate effect of the Revolution was to do away with loyalty to the personal king. It produced in its stead a loyalty to the throne; and the throne meant an institution whose main purpose was to conserve certain definite interests – those mainly of Protestantism and the money-making classes. It did away with Clarendon, who was more royalist than the king; it produced John Churchill, Duke of Marlborough, and his wife, who was more royal than his sovereign; it did away with the irresponsible enjoyment of life, and rendered possible the sentimental movement; it did away with the true Toryism which is Socialism, and rendered possible Individualism, which today we call the upholding of the right to free competition; it gave us, in fact, liberty by gradually removing responsibility from the state – and it gave us two centuries of enmity to France and of growing subjection to German ideals.

So that, if indeed it be true that the enemy is Prussianism – that the world is gradually coming to a state of mind in which it shall be most important to a nation to produce the more essentially

---

1 I do this without scruple – because, obviously, my desire is to produce an argument that may or may not be controverted, and not to lay down with a high hand any law that is to be regarded as immutable or incontrovertible.

Germanic type, we may well hope to produce the man. We may well hope, in fact, to muddle through. We have, in the composition of our complex republic, Germans enough to select from. And it must be re-affirmed that the Germans who have come to England, like the Scots, the Danes, the French, the Poles, the Huguenots or the Doukhobors, are precisely the bad eggs, the adventurous, the restless, the energetic of their several nations. And these adventurers, these restless, these energetic units are, precisely too, the best breeders for a fighting race. We may, in fact, very well produce yet another dominant type that shall help England to retain its own, and to gain just that little bit of material advantage that, except in the great struggle with the English superman across the Atlantic, England has always had. Just as in a world attuned to Plantagenet ideas, England produced the Plantagenets; just as in a world attuned to Machiavelli, England produced Thomas Cromwell; just as in a world that was opening up to adventurers, England produced the Drakes and the Raleighs; just as in a world fitted for parades of troops and tortuous intrigues with a Roi Soleil, England produced a William III and a Marlborough – so England may well hope to produce a man fitted to contend, in the end with the kaiser or professor who is to set the tune for the next generation. We might even produce a plenty of the best Slav blood to lead us against Slavs. We might produce anybody to lead us against anything. Given, in fact, its proper breathing space in which the man may arise, England may yet muddle through, since England is not a nation, not the home of a race, but a small epitome of the whole world, attracted to a fertile island by the hope of great gain, or by the faith that there a man may find freedom. The other day I was down at the docks, watching the incoming of a ship that brought many Jews from Odessa. As man after man crossed the gangway he knelt down and kissed the muddy coping of the wharf. That was because still, as for the Anabaptists and the Huguenots, England appears to the bad eggs of the nations to be the land of freedom. And it is not impossible that one of the children of one of these adventurers may be, like another Disraeli, the man who will help England to muddle through.

CHAPTER IV

Faiths

I WAS asked some time ago, on the banks of a great foreign river, by a fair-haired foreign girl, for the name of an English book to read. She seemed to be conversant with the whole of the Tauchnitz collection; she knew the names at least of all the English novelists, essayists and romancers with whom one could be acquainted; she knew, certainly, the names of many English writers that I had never heard of. She spoke English idiomatically; she was sufficiently akin to the English in sentiment to be able to appreciate a certain work, so parochially English that it dealt with the amenities of middle-class child-life in the topography of Kensington Gardens. That, she had found ravishing. I suggested to her the name of the one English work of importance that she had not read, because she risked certain considerable penalties in the perusal. I told her that although, from reading the eminent secular novelists and the less eminent novelists whose works are merely commercial in value, she would doubtless acquire, or had already acquired, a considerable insight into the psychology of the various classes portrayed by novelists, essayists or romancers, she could not claim even a nodding acquaintance with the real bases of the Spirit of the People until she had assimilated this particular book. A month or so later she said to me:

'I have finished reading it; it is *horrible*.'

Upon the whole you could not have said that she was not English to look at her – only in her enunciation of the word that meant '*horrible*' there was a sincerity that was entirely un-English. Because, of course, no typical Englishwoman of her class would be allowed, or would allow herself, to come in contact with anything that is really 'horrible'. An Englishwoman, after all, must not be moved; if she suffers it she is not English. But the blue eyes of Miss G—— were really rigid with horror at the remembrance of what she had read. The book was *horrible*.

That a girl should be so moved by the reading of the English

Bible did not strike me as peculiar upon reflection, though for the moment I had to cast about in my mind for a reason. The point of view was new to me. Of course the Bible is forbidden reading to the great majority of Christians – but that is for reasons purely doctrinal, purely arbitrary, purely of priestcraft. One accepts the fact, not as a judgment of the Bible, as poetry, or as a projection of life; it is merely because it is inconvenient to the priesthood of a certain Church that their special interpretation of passages should be called in question. It is part of a game, of a system; it reflects no discredit on the Bible as a projection of a frame of mind. But Miss G——'s emotion was a direct censure of Biblical morality. It said: 'Here is a book, horrible for its ferocity, for the bloodthirsty incidents that it realistically portrays, horrible for its rendering of sexual necessities, horrible for its spirit.' Miss G——, in fact, regarded it with the new candour of a reader confronted with a terrifying French piece of realism: it was as if she had been reading of the gigantic metal automaton in Flaubert's *Salammbô* – the metal automaton that into its blazing jaws lifted the bodies of living children to be incinerated.

Thinking about the matter, I remembered a certain evening service at which I had been present. There is a country church which I attend somewhat frequently. It is ancient Norman in character, on a tranquil knoll in the pleasant English south. You cannot figure for your private satisfaction anything more delightful, anything more soothing, than to sit out a service in the little pews of one of the aisles. Through the small windows the trees are seen to spread tranquil boughs; the organ drones; the choir boys sing in tune, and the wonderful English of the church service awakens all the singular and very blissful remembrances of one's boyhood between white stone walls. And, upon the whole, there is nothing in life that I more rejoice in than that, as a boy, I went regularly to English church services. It is a thing that a nation may be devoutly thankful for: it canonifies, it blesses, a whole side of one's life. It is not, of course, everything – but it is the most tranquil thing in life as it today is lived.

But, as I sat that evening in the little church at I——, in the quiet of the sunset, great rays of light fell across the chancel. The choristers sat still, the cry of sheep came in through the opened doors, a swallow flitted round among the square pillars, and the priest read the first lesson. I listened attentively – and suddenly the whole tone of what was being read seemed appalling. And all that service, from psalms to offertory, seemed overwhelming. I looked round me to see if no one else noticed it; but there was no sign. An old man with a shaven chin looked with weary eyes at the palms of his hands; a little boy, with a callous, shaven head, was cutting his initials on a corner of the pew; the great tenant-farmer of the parish had his head cocked back and gazed at the panes above the reredos with eyes that saw nothing. But the first lesson was, precisely, horrible. It described how a king, incited by priests and the Almighty, sent his soldiers to surround a church, to massacre the worshippers and to behead them. It made you see the soldiery returning with hands sticky with blood, to cast baskets of palm-leaves, each one filled with a head, at the feet of the king as he sat in his courtyard.

I am not, of course, quarrelling with the conception of a deity; it is to me nothing that Jehovah should claim his tens of thousands or Torquemada his thousands. These things are the necessary concomitants of certain phases of human thought; they exist, and cannot be questioned. But the second lesson was about damnation; the psalms were gloomily minatory. Even the sermon was tinged with a black, predestinarian pessimism, and dealt rather intelligently with the mental horrors that must be endured for all eternity by the outcast of the next world. But this, as I have said, was acceptable enough: if you sin against the Omnipotent you must take the wages of sin. I will however confess that the whole thing filled me with gloom; it was so tremendously well projected that, for the moment, the view of life, such as it was, seemed irrefutable. The statements were so definite, the language so tremendous and so inspired. It was, precisely, horrible – since horror was the feeling that the whole service caused to arise.

Receding from these particular emotions I do not, of course, feel the same horror. I am filled instead with a sort of wonder that for so long I could have basked in the tranquillity of these services. For I will repeat, that there are in the church service certain moments which are unsurpassable in this life. There is, for instance, the wonderful pause at the very end. The priest has uttered the beautiful sentence which begins: 'The peace of God which passeth all understanding keep your hearts...' And then an absolute silence falls – a silence that seems to last a lifetime, an utter abandonment, a suspension of life. Then someone sighs, someone stirs, a great rustle commences, and, a little sobered, one is again ready to face the material world. I can imagine nothing quite like this; the silence of the canon of the mass is profoundly exciting and disturbing; even

the silence of a Quakers' meeting in one of the bare Friends' Houses
is a tension, not a restfulness; but this silence is a slight footnote, a
momentary suggestion of that peace which passeth all understanding. I am anxious to emphasise my partaking in this feeling,
because in other places it is my purpose to write in cold blood of
this very wonderful product of the national frame of mind. Having
done it, let me return to my analysis of the horror of the actual
tenets.

For the calmness of the assistants at this terrible drama seems to
me to be extraordinarily characteristic of the singularly English
faculty – the faculty of ignoring the most terrible of facts; the faculty,
in short, which makes us the nation of official optimists. For the
singular congregation of that church – and of all our churches –
was kindly minded to a high degree. It would have been appalled
at the idea of the slaughter, nowadays, of ten thousand sheep, it
would have blanched dreadfully at the thought of the slaughter of
ten thousand men, even of ten thousand enemies of the British God
of Battles. But most of them listened to the details of this sacrifice
to Jehovah, who was their own God – sat and listened unmoved,
not inattentively, but probably in the same frame of mind as that
of children listening to fairy tales. They half-believed, half-
disbelieved; it all took place so very long ago. If the same set of
circumstances should arise, no doubt Jehovah would exact of the
English king that he should make the same sacrifice – but, fortu-
nately, in these days of pleasant Sunday clothes, of the tranquillity
of an English Sabbath, of the faint smell of prayer-book leather and
glove leather – in these days no such set of circumstances could
thinkably arise. People don't any longer do such things; probably
there no longer exist such inscrutably noxious heathens; Baal, in
fact, is dead – so this wonderful and happy people has no call to
think about these slaughters. We owe still the cock to Æsculapius
– but he would never think of exacting it.

It is, in fact, one of the things that it is unfair to mention. And
really it is unfair. I have frequently been struck with that aspect of
the case when I have listened to one of the Atheist orators in the
London parks. In some strange way the Englishman has digested
the early ferocity of his creed just as he has assimilated all his early
conquerors; and, just as he will say, 'these fellows are ourselves', so
he will feel that his God, who now gives a peace which passes all
understanding, has assimilated the Jehovah of Joshua the son of
Nun. It isn't, that is to say, his business to see life steadily or to see

it whole. The audience of the London park atheist never puts the matter coldbloodedly that the remorseless follower of cause is effect, whether you call effect Jehovah or indigestion; it never puts to the atheist the fact that if you eat your cake you cannot have it, that if you enjoy yourself you must pay for it, whether you call your Baal the pursuit of pleasure or your Jehovah race deterioration. I question, indeed, whether the Englishman – that typical, composite photograph that, for his convenience, each one of us carries, and labels 'my countryman' – whether the Englishman really believes these things.

The English Church allows of no Purgatory between Heaven and Hell. The English official deity is a just God. But I think that, for the Englishman, this just God is just in the sense only that he rewards the good. The evil he lets slip by him, as the Englishman, remarking 'poor devil', would let most impotent sinners escape punishment. So that, if the modern Englishman dispenses with Purgatory, it is because he hardly believes in Hell. He will repeat to his children a hundred times in the caresses of childhood the familiar proverb: if questioned, held to it, and, unfairly pressed, he will acknowledge the truth of it; but he will never believe with the instinctive faith that is part of all our lives, that you cannot eat your cake and have it.

Two alternatives present themselves to us in the consideration of this phenomenon. Perhaps he is actually right in his belief; perhaps there is a third term between cause and effect; or perhaps, in the alternative, it is only that he does right to believe this fallacy. It is, perhaps, that alone which makes him keep all on doing things. For it must be remembered that, according to his creed and to the creed of his fathers more especially, we are, all humanity, miserable sinners. We act always wrongly, but somehow we muddle through. And, upon the whole, we hope to do this in the face of the Almighty, as we hope to do it in the face of all the nations arrayed for our downfall. It is, I think, an English town frame of mind, this of muddling through; perhaps it is a town and maritime frame of mind; for the seaman faces appalling elements with his little machines of sticks and strings, so disproportionately tiny that they seem an absurd challenge to the force of the waters. Yet somehow he reaches his port. And the townsman has to fight with the millions of his fellow townsmen and survive in the business he makes his career. His watchword, his catchword, is that something will turn up. He trusts to a fortuitous rise in the bank rate to give him, finally, a competence; he trusts to the miraculous properties of some widely-advertised pill to save him from the effects of an irrational mode of life. Or, perhaps, it is only that the hurry and rush of what we call modern life – which is a city product – perhaps it is only that that allows him to forget the eternal verities.

But the countryman is perpetually faced by them; he battles with things that have been the same since the world began – with rain, with frosts, with the too great heat of the sun in droughty weather. He does not, taken as a whole, have much hope of attaining to an ultimate reward greater than his deserts. He does not keep on doing things in the hope that something may turn up trumps. He keeps, as I have said before, 'all on gooing', without much hope of a better state. He reads his Bible more closely, in fact. Jehovah still exists for him; the sinner is still the sinner – not the poor devil who will scrape through when God, applauded by all the good-natured, momentarily averts his face. And, indeed, it is in the country – it is at least in the provincial frame of mind – that one will still discover the stern, old fashion of Protestantism. Perhaps that is only to say that the countryman is, precisely, old-fashioned.

One will find, of course, centres of Protestantism dispersed in all the towns; one will find bigotry, narrow-mindedness, genuine faith, or simple, heavy earnestness. And, perhaps, the heart of the nation is, in that sense, still sound. But in essence the note of the great towns is that of tolerance; a town is a great, loose, easy-going place, where a man may do pretty well what he pleases – may break away from chapel, church, or conventicle, and disappear for ever in some next street. So that, speaking broadly, we may say that the simple faith, the simple, earnest intolerance of small or large knots of allied worshippers – the Protestant-Puritan spirit, is precisely 'provincial'. I do not write the word in any sneering spirit, but simply state the fact that Puritanism is out of fashion in the towns. It is no longer for the moment in the swim; but very possibly – if we remember the phenomena of our past history, we should say very probably – it will return again. It must be remembered, for instance, that in the seventeenth century the town frame of mind was that of dilettante atheism; any kind of religious belief was quite hopelessly not in the swim. And following immediately upon this came the great wave of Methodism, with its miraculous calling to life of a religious spirit throughout town and country alike. Tomorrow, in fact, there may be a revival.

It would be hardly possible for there not to be a revival if the conditions of the nation had not altered very materially since the days of Wesley. But it must be remembered, again, that in the days of Wesley the preponderance of the population was still in the country, and that Methodism was a country reaction. Nowadays the preponderance of the townsman is so huge that it is difficult to imagine a movement in the rural districts that should seriously affect the towns. And, nowadays, even the spirit of the very rural districts seems to have been breathed upon by a new kind of thought. There is a certain country chapel which I pass every day. It is a new, red-brick, expensive structure. Round the corner is a little old barn which John Wesley himself built, in which Wesley himself preached, which this red and yellow structure has replaced. The new chapel has windows in imitation of stained glass; these windows portray scenes in the life of the Virgin, culminating with her coronation in Heaven at the hands of her Divine Son.

This surprises in itself, but it might have been an accident, due to the fact that the German commercial traveller who brought round samples of his transfers came from the neighbourhood of Cologne. Yet, when I put the matter to the Wesleyan in authority in the village, he was not at all perturbed. He answered simply: 'Well, I don't see why they should not have crowned the Virgin in Heaven. She deserved it.'

He was perfectly sincere; and no doubt he was perfectly right. Nevertheless, his frame of mind does seem to betray a singular loss of touch with the theological[1] history of his creed. He was much more sound in his secular history, for once when I walked up with him from the station, he said to me – with a very great sincerity too – 'I suppose that if the Papists came into power again they would burn us all!' And I do not question that Mr W—— would cheerfully go to the stake in defence of the tradition whose tenets he had so tolerantly forgotten.

Probably this, too, is only a symptom of that general good nature that has spread through England; most Wesleyans are as much inclined to deprecate the sterner manifestations of their earlier years as are the Anglicans who deprecate the earlier sternness of the agents of Jehovah. And the Wesleyan who is prepared to go to the stake

---

1   It should be remarked that the theological notions of this gentleman were very bizarre. The cook of a family in our village being much perturbed to account for the fact that the mistress allowed no currants in the kitchen went to Mr W——, who was her spiritual guide. He said: 'Oh, Mrs —— is a Mahometan, and it is part of her creed not to eat currants!'

thinks that contingency as unlikely to arise as does the Anglican who would be prepared to carry out the dictates of a New Jehovah. In a similar way Unitarians, Congregationalists or Quakers will deprecate the earlier phases of their creed. Of course, the revival may be yet to come.

But upon the whole it may be doubted whether the revival in the nation will come soon. The signs of the times, in the town and country, are against it. Speaking impressionistically – and I hope not offensively – I should say that what distinguishes the worshippers belonging to the Established Church is a frame of mind and not a religion – a frame of mind in which, though the ethical basis of Christianity is more or less excellently preserved, the theological conditions remain in a very fragmentary condition. I do not mean to say that the higher criticism has led to this cleavage – but that the general sense of the congregations has rendered any literal acceptance of, say, the Athanasian Creed, almost a thing of the past. (I wish again to guard myself from seeming to imply that it may not be a thing of the future.) But the whole psychology of the immediate present is a thing of such minutiæ; our attention is charmed by such an infinity of small things, that close thinking – which theological logic demands – is for the moment almost impossible, save to the specialist. Thus the devout and carefully practising churchman is apt to awaken and find the state of his mind to be singularly chaotic. I remember walking home from the service of which I have spoken with a singularly earnest churchman, for whom I had and still cherish a very great affection. We discussed the immortality of the soul, and my friend, who was a man of sixty, made, as it were, then and there the discovery that he no longer believed in a future state. Nevertheless a belief in a just – and even in an avenging Deity – remained almost unshaken in his mind, and, along with it, his unwavering attachment to the Church.

He seemed, however, gradually to have dropped the other belief; it had vanished, fading away, little by little; it had been hardly missed in the passage through a very strenuous middle life. In much the same way, while we walked in the shadow of tall elms along the white road that still retained the heat of the day, the last vestige of rosy light had faded from the sky. The land lay about us, still visible, with its long valleys, its tranquil hollows, its blue sea-horizon. But the last tinge of red had gone from the shadows.

For my particular friend, the stress of a too complex life had done this – a stress that eventually broke him down, the more easily, perhaps, in that he had lost the stay of that belief. So it may be for many people. But for many others, too, the same complexity of modern life, with so many of its inner depths, with so many of its privacies laid bare for our daily inspection – the mere number of things that we have to think about in order to remain at all in contact with our fellow men, has sapped much of our power for sustained thought.

I move principally among men of a certain type – men, that is to say, who 'specialise' in one or other of the departments of thought. But it is rather seldom that I ever have time for any sustained discussion of any specialised department of thought – simply because the daily topic claims so much attention. With a clergyman one will find oneself discussing the surest method of obtaining novels from a lending library; with a mathematician, the latest murder; with a scientific agriculturist one begins to talk of the politics of the day, or a bishop will tell one of the latest idiosyncrasies of the admiral commanding the Channel Squadron. These idiosyncrasies will have been revealed in an interview with the admiral's lady and published in an illustrated service magazine. It is true that in the country this characteristic grows less rapidly, yet it is growing, and the newspapers facilitate the process daily. It is true, too, that in solitary chambers throughout the land, thinkers of the old school may be found. Without doubt, in Cambridge, say, by applying to one of the dons, one might come across men in book-lined cells pursuing some glorious and abstruse train of thought of all the trains started by Hume, pursuing it with that half-artistic, half-ironic fervour that has distinguished the English schools of thought of the past.

But, even amongst such thinkers, there is a tendency to turn their machinery of thought upon topics of the day. And I am not sure that such a process is not very valuable: the utterances of a mind trained in one or the other of the schools of preciser thinking – upon a *cause célèbre* in the divorce courts, or the ultimate ramifications of a Tibetan mission, may have a very material value, and, in the ultimate future, the evolution of a trained and slightly negative school of observers upon life as it is lived may well atone for the loss of several commentaries. Of that, one may well be uncertain; but it is hardly possible to doubt that the influence of the world upon the Churches is eminently destructive of the letter of laws.

It leaves, probably, the same capacity for faith – but for a faith of a vague and a humanitarian nature. It is, I mean, almost impossible for a man to believe that he and his comparatively small sect of the elect are the sole peoples that shall prosper upon the earth; it is almost impossible for a man to believe that when, say, the Japanese are sinking European fleets and prospering exceedingly. It is, in short, possible to say that the Japanese are Englishmen in all but name, but it is impossible to believe that their success is due to the fact that they are, say, New Connexion Methodists with nominal differences.

Yet, until quite lately, it *was* possible to look at the world in that light. The prospering powers were invariably Christian, and almost always Protestant. French, Italian and Spaniards were, with a suffi- cient frequency to give support to the point of view, beaten by the Lion of the North, by the Protestant Hero, or by ourselves. The rising of the United States was a Protestant ascendancy. Even the Franco-Prussian War could be pressed into the service – for all Germans were Protestants, as all Frenchmen were atheists. These, in fact, were victories by people who, if they weren't Anglican, Low Church, Nonconformist, might by Anglican, Low Churchman or Nonconformist be considered almost of one faith with themselves. The Germans, for instance, are all Lutherans in the general view, and a High Churchman knows that Lutherans are very high; a Low Churchman knows they are very broad; a Nonconformist knows that they do not form a part of the Church of England as by law established. But the coming of the daily press has in several directions shaken this world theory. The enlighten- ment that the daily press has wrought has proved to us not only that German Lutherans are practically atheists and certainly not Bible Christians: has proved to us not only that the majority of the German people are actually papists: it has proved to us that even the heathen have faiths respectable and venerable. I am not merely referring to the Japanese victories. For consider the possibility that some Indian prince of sacred rank should find it desirable to travel to England without setting foot upon any soil other than that of the land that saw the birth of Buddha, without victuals cooked in the waters of the Indus, and hourly ablutions in those of the Ganges.

The whole English world – or nearly the whole of it – would follow with respectful sympathy, or with a sporting interest – the building of a special vessel made of iron all mined in India, the conveying of tons of soil on to the decks, the construction of the special holds that should contain a sufficient supply of the waters of the holy stream. We should read, we should see drawings, of the almost miraculous tricks by which the journey was performed. In innumerable photographs we should see the sacred man himself, handsome, melancholy, austere, aloof. His journey safely accomplished, his return engineered, we should, when he set foot once more upon his secular and sacred ground, heave a national sigh of relief. And assuredly, for a moment, we should feel that this man did, indeed, possess some of the sacredness to which he laid claim – to which he had a prescriptive right conferred on him by the faith of many millions of the infinitely patient and the very wise in faiths. We should find it difficult then to go back to our services and imagine *all* the heathen as furiously raging. In that way one little corner-stone of our doctrinal faith might be shaken. But we should not the less believe that God is good.

We have grown rather, to see that God, the giver of life, is very wonderful. Wonderful he is, in short, because he is so very complex – and faith, that of old was a matter of pondering upon a few simple certainties, tends more and more in this modern world of ours to become merely a frame of mind, religious, without doubt – fatalistic, very probably – with which a man may confront the changing aspects of his changing day. For it is very certain that, for the vast mass of the people, if the spread of knowledge of a sort have in these latter days dealt a shrewd blow to faith of a doctrinaire kind, it has killed atheism.

Nothing, in fact, is more striking in the modern world than this change of attitude in face of knowledgeable things. In the days of Darwin – which are surely not so long ago – the anti-Darwinians cried: 'This is anathema!' The Darwinians cried: 'This is the end of God!' But in these years we read yesterday, and we shall read tomorrow – in the enormous type – in the loose phraseology of the papers: 'Discovery of the secret of life.' And the statement being in print, we believe it as we believe in the discovery of a new cure for consumption. But it hardly shakes our position towards the eternal verities. We have, in the language of the newspapers, annihilated space so long ago, that there is no reason why we should not destroy, sooner or later, the other attribute. We may, in fact, get rid of time, or achieve a physical immortality. But, though we may destroy the one half of the prophet's saying, we are faced with the other so long as man continues to be born of woman. We may, that is to say, become of many days: we have still to face sorrow. It is there that God comes in.

For the function of God, after all, is to teach us so to live that our strength may be as our days; that is the end to which the man with the religious frame of mind sets out. For, if he cease to believe in a personal immortality, a man becomes more filled with the desire for an immortality in his seed: for the consummation of a sane and healthy humanity. And it is there that the idea of God, again, comes in. We search the Scriptures still, to find that Jehovah is effect, Baal cause...

That is, upon the whole, the impression that much converse with our fellows will leave upon most men, and, vaguely and indefinitely, he feels something akin to those feelings. But the calls of modern life are so insistent, the idea that a prosperous race is a race fertile of children has rendered competition so clamant upon our attentions that most men in England, as opposed to women, have little time to ponder upon these things at all. One sees, however, vaguely shadowed in the future, a day when the dictum: '*Taceat mulier in Ecclesiâ*' shall have found its earthly close.

It is naturally to America, that land of the future, that one must go to find the first manifestation of a cutting loose from this particular tradition. In America, of course, one will find everything: there a man may see the Mormon Church, in which woman, more than anywhere else in Christendom, has been trampled under foot. For it must be remembered that monogamy is the one powerful, the one universal, law that woman has given us. There, also, one will find – according to the newspapers – the 'first cathedral raised to a woman'. The newspapers of course forget the temple of Diana, or the several cathedrals of the Blessed Virgin that may be found in both Old World and New. But, in the sense that the mother church of the Christian Scientists is the first manifestation in stone of a cult founded by a woman and administered largely by women, we may accept this headline as being as true as headlines can, in the nature of things, be expected to be. For Joanna Southcott, the false Joan of Arc, Elizabeth Burton, or Selina, Countess of Huntingdon, may be forgotten.

But, roughly speaking, we may say that the Church founded by Mrs Eddy is the first modern faith to be evolved by a woman. It is interesting, then, to examine this phenomenon as coldly as we have examined the more ancient creeds established by men. We find at once, as we might have expected, that the chief activity of the Church is almost purely material: it deals with the attainment to a sane mind by the evolution of a perfected body. I stayed for some time of a lately-passed summer in an oddly heterogeneous colony that had filled all the huts and hovels of a tract of sand dunes across the water. Here the tone was almost entirely set by the women. They came from all parts of the world – from New York, from Sweden, from New Zealand, from the Transvaal, and, naturally, many came from Hampstead. Beneath the tall pines the men of these women seemed to stand in loose-limbed, incongruous knots. They were artists, men from government offices, merchants, brewers, social reformers, schoolmasters or singers. They gave the impression of being careless, except as to the weather, which was rather execrable, heavy shafts of rain piercing the blue shields of foliage and digging minute pits in the white sand... But they seemed, all these men, to be at very loose ends; their knots were small and isolated; they seemed to have lost the power of combination.

The women, on the other hand, appeared to form great and very voluble gatherings of fifties in the hollows. Their dresses were gay, flouting, many-coloured, or sad, close-cut and self-coloured. They were infinitely articulate – and an infinite number of children seemed to run in and out between their skirts, intent, as children will be, upon a world of their own. It was a scene eminently rejoicing to the eye and pleasant for the consideration. Here – and that was the dominant note – was man absolutely dethroned.

It is true that these were the holidays. The artists might make cartoons on brown paper to decorate the bare walls of barns: the musicians might accompany or might sing in the choirs. But they did this rather as helots, and the merchants, government officials and schoolmasters seemed to make up, as helots, too, the numbers of the congregation. They were, all of these men, good workers in their particular 'lines'; they stood a little out of the common run, as being heavy and solid thinkers. But, beyond that, as general thinkers they were not, I should say, particularly gifted. You had, in short, to get them on their own grounds before they shone. And they were united by a common air: it was that of men returning from distant regions of work to find their households running riot. It was as if Ulysses had come back from long wanderings to find Penelope surrounded, not by suitors, but by professors of strange learning.

And thus, on their social sides at least, the cults of the morrow seem to be foreshadowed. The man must more and more specialise in his vocation: he must apply to his daily task his whole intellect and all his better parts. Returning from these depths of thought to the light of the world he must be dim-eyed and inarticulate. That the effects of this are felt in all departments of the arts every practitioner of them must know. It takes various forms, but the end is always the same. Thus every novelist knows that the only readers are the women: the distinctively man's writer appeals only to a very small public. Every journalist knows, too, that the papers now are written with an eye that more often than not is turned to the women. In one quite serious paper that was newly started it was proposed to have an agricultural page once a week. The proposal was, however, negatived by the editor-in-chief, who substituted a woman's page. 'All the other papers have it,' he said. I was travelling, quite unwillingly, the other day in a railway carriage into which there introduced themselves, hurriedly at the last moment, a pleasant, well-dressed couple, obviously upon their honeymoon. At the next stopping station the gentleman leaned out of the window and purchased, apparently at random, a couple of daily papers. One of these, a substantial sheet of Conservative tendencies, he offered to his companion. She made a little *moue* and did not wish to take it. He substituted the other, remarking, 'Oh, of course. The ——— is the lady's paper, isn't it?' and, leaning back gracefully, she began to read the magazine page with what contentment my presence allowed her. The ——— was the paper with the largest circulation in the world.

In one of the other arts this tendency reacts in a manner quite dissimilar. I was asking a very intimate friend what the ladies had talked about in the drawing-room after a certain dinner.

'Well,' she said, 'all the married women were lamenting the type of play they were forced to go to.' They would have preferred, all these martyrs said, to go and hear something 'really vital'; something serious, harrowing or merely problematic. Instead of that, every one of them was forced to go to musical comedies. This was because their husbands came home from business too tired for serious entertainment. One of the ladies said she had been six times to *The Geisha*. All the time she had been yearning to see *Ghosts*.

The arts, of course, are not taken very seriously in England; but it should be remembered that, as society is at present constituted, it is to the arts alone that the English people can go for any knowledge of life. And it must be remembered, too, that from one's knowledge of life alone can a religion be compounded. We seem, then, to be driven to the conclusion that the religions of the immediate future must be founded upon kinds of art that appeal to women alone. And, since women alone have time to think or to feel, women, it would seem, must found the religions of the future. That this tendency is the more pronounced in the United States than even in the islands of the East Atlantic makes the prospect somewhat less dubious.

So that we seem to be faced by an ultimate return to those distinctively Alemannic conditions that, according to some sociologists, was the state from which the Teutonic races sprung. Here the basis of the household was, no doubt, 'he to the plough' – but, to the pulpit, she. The system was once matriarchal: that it may once more become. That, no doubt, is very right and proper: it is, at any rate, all in the day's journey for humanity that, in its course through such a part of eternity as may belong to it, may well pass many times from woman's dominion to man's, and back again. But constructive or projective sociology is no part of my immediate purpose, which is that of constructing an image of my present day as it impresses me. Nevertheless, as an illustration, as an exaggeration, of tendencies now observable, the prophecy of feminine dominion is not without its illuminative uses. For, looking at things by its particular light, many things present themselves to us.

It is obviously begging the question to say that the result of the regiment of women at the present day is to belittle – to belittle in particular the press, Christianity, and the science of healing. For the littleness of today is so very certainly the greatness of tomorrow that, from any aloof point of view, the theory is hardly worth combating. The press today is turning gradually along certain lines: it is converting itself into an organ for conveying, not sustained 'articles' in one trend of thought, but an infinite number of small and interesting facts. This is a principle like another, and the object of the press being to attract attention by awakening interest, the principle is a very valid one. It should indeed be remembered that the principle is a very ancient one, too; for I suppose that two of the most attractive books in the English language are Boswell's *Life of Johnson* and Florio's *Montaigne*. And both of these works are, in essence, collections of 'snippets'. That they are well written tells in no wise against the contention, for there is nothing to prevent the small announcements of the daily press from being well put or even from being reasonably accurate.

It might indeed be said that the domination of the press by women has led simply to a greater honesty – that, for all the centuries during which man has been the public of the newspapers man has consented to be bored for the sake of a principle. Man, according to this theory, which I have heard gravely asserted, has thought that he ought to read informative matter; it is only woman that has had the common sense to say: 'Now that we read the newspapers we will have what we like.' And man has very gladly taken her gifts. In a similar way, when she approaches the matter of constructing a religion, woman, according to this theory, has decided to have what she wants.

What she wants is most decidedly not theology. And it is, very decidedly, a healthy race. She takes accordingly from the Scriptures what best suits her, and from the science of healing what best suits her, and of the two she constructs her faith and her rules of conduct. From the man-made religion that she has found ready to her hand she has taken the figure of the Second Person of the Trinity: from medicine, the principle that for a person to be cured he must be '*bonæ voluntatis*'. For it must be remembered that the chief social function of woman – the one which causes her the greatest pleasure and the greatest pain – is the keeping healthy of her children. A religion which does not in some sort ensure this is not a religion that can very intimately appeal to her. In Catholic countries or communities this element of satisfaction is to be found in the intercession of the saints or of the Virgin. I remember being present at an adult baptism in Paris, and of the touching ceremony the most touching feature to me was the number of kneeling women in the rear of the little church. As soon as the baptism was completed – as soon, that is, as the convert was purged of all past sin, and able in consequence to plead weightily before the throne of grace, these women approached him and begged him to intercede for their sick children. And this possibility must have formed for them a very strong tie with their church – a motive for adhesion which is lacking in these islands. But indeed it is hardly necessary to emphasise the fact that Catholicism maintains a very close hold over its women communicants – that its chief hold on the peoples comes from them. It is only necessary to state the case of Poland, where with the men, forced by the necessities of the day to enlist in the public services, and to abandon alike their national characteristics and their faith, the women with a splendid perseverance keep alive the old traditions.

Catholicism – with its female saints, with its female religious, with its feminine element in the Divine Concord – has its chief safeguard in its women. But in these islands, which have discarded alike female saints, female religious, and the Mother of God as an object of worship, a comparative lukewarmness in attachment to established forms of worship has resulted. I am aware, of course, that the lukewarmness is only comparative, and that in England as, say, in France, the women form the substantial bulk of the congregation; nevertheless it is in England more easy to conceive of a woman's changing her religion to fall in with the views of her husband than would be the case in France.

We may set this down to the fact that Protestantism is of a nobler intellectual growth than is Catholicism, which is an evolution almost entirely of the sentiments and the weaknesses of humanity. Protestantism in getting rid of the least credible of the Christian tenets, sacrificed – nobly enough – a great deal of the appeal of the Church; it availed itself of reason at the expense of intuition. It said, to all intents and purposes: 'Here are the holy writings; we will use them as a basis for our reasonings; we will allow of no corollary however attractive.' By so doing it sacrificed a great part of its appeal and a great part of its authority. It sacrificed, too, it seems to me, a great part of its theological traditions and of its popular comprehensibility.

The other day one of my little daughters returned from her convent with a rather badly scratched hand. I said that it must have hurt her a great deal, and she turned her small face up to whisper to me: 'God suffered much more than that.'

The phraseology struck me very forcibly: it aroused in me all that was Protestant in my early training. An English child might have said: 'Jesus suffered much more'; or it would, more likely, have used some proverbial expression, or have contented itself with saying that it did hurt. But that an English child should have attributed to God – to all the persons of the Trinity – a possibility of physical suffering is, I take it, almost an impossibility. Of course, were the proposition put to the child grown a man he might, after reflection, agree that the sufferings of Christ, being of one substance with the Father, would be communicated to all the persons of the Godhead. But I am inclined to believe that no Englishman really feels these matters in that way.

Judging from my own early predispositions and from English conversations on this point, I am fairly certain that most Englishmen regard the Saviour as an adult, fairhaired male, distinct altogether from God the Father, and not very easily or conceivably blended into the mysterious and ineffable Three in One. Christ remains the visible sign of the Trinity: it is not legal to attempt to visualise God the Father: it is impossible utterly to attempt to form an idea of the Holy Ghost.

It is difficult to conceive of Jesus even as a child – it is, at least, not usual to do so. It may be remembered that towards the middle of last century there were certain painters called pre-Raphaelites. One of these painted a picture showing the Saviour as a child subject to his parents. This picture raised a storm: it was considered blasphemous, simply because for many centuries it had been the custom in England to regard the Saviour as a grown man, aloof from most of the trials, privations and subjections of humanity. That he should be shown obeying Joseph and Mary – that he should be shown kissing his mother – these things seemed to be anathema. In fact, in the course of the centuries that had succeeded the sixteenth, there had grown up in England a cult which was almost solely that of Christ. This began without doubt as a protest against Mariolatry and the worship of the saints. But the seed fell upon soil very fertile: it became a part of the tradition of this great and useful nation.

For England is the country of *Christism* simply because this human figure of the Saviour appeals so very strongly to a nation whose human contacts are always its first consideration. To the modern Englishman the actions or the nature of the Father are comparatively unknown: they appeal to him perhaps at moments: he is the God of Battles, precisely, and in England's military moods he is appealed to. But Christ is always with us – Christ and his eleventh commandment. We hardly know what are the attributes of the Holy Ghost, yet every word of Christ Jesus, every action, every parable we have, all, by heart.

In a Continental city, at the end of an old market square, there will stand a church with its doors wide open. In the intervals of selling her goods the market woman will go up the steps of the church, will, before a shimmering altar, tell her beads, mutter a prayer or two, perform some act of faith. She will return to her chaffering; she may have prayed to St Servatius, St Eloi, or the Virgin, and her whole mind will be a matter of her cult, little fragments of religion interpenetrating the whole fabric of her inner self, little acts of faith filling in the interstices of her outer life. In this way the whole being of great continental nations is imbued with a sense of the supernatural side of religion.

In that sense the Englishman is hardly religious at all, since it is not so much the supernatural as the human side of the deity that has a daily significance for him. His main worship is paid in no church builded by mortal hands. His service, which is not an act of faith, but the payment of a tribute, is something apart from his life, part only of a special day, which is singled out from all the others, and dedicated to what consideration he gives to the supernatural deity.

Yet if he is not religious he is assuredly devout, since we may consider the measure of his devotion to be his desire to act in the spirit of the Master. For this tradition of Christ is a very singular and very fine manifestation, and the Englishman, instead of asking himself: 'How may I best propitiate St Servatius?' – asks in any given contingency: 'How would Christ have acted here?' He takes, in fact, the Saviour for his master and his model, and I have been very much struck upon occasions by the virulence with which even professing unbelievers in England will defend to the last word, to the utmost comma of the English New Testament, the teachings and the person of Christ.

And herein lies at once a very great strength and a very great danger to revealed religion in England. For whilst utterly unwilling to acknowledge that a personage so perfect as Christ can have been of other than miraculous origin, can have been other than a God, the Englishman troubles himself very little about the other sides of his theology. With him, indeed, his religion – Christism – is almost entirely a standard of manners. His problem, much more than the saying of 'Holy, holy, holy', is that of how he shall do as he would be done by. Other Christians may hope for temporal advance and ultimate escape from divine wrath, because they have set to their account a great number of those small acts of faith. They try, in short, to do things acceptable to the hosts of saints and the enthroned deities. But the Englishman's hopes of profit and salvation are based upon the fact that he shall be able to say he had followed his Master's teaching, who bade him be good to his fellow man.

This is, I think, the keynote of the Englishman: fierce and singular idiosyncrasies. It is the 'note' of the matter. It explains the singular anthropomorphism – the singular lack of sympathetic imagination that distinguishes the Englishman. His motto is: 'Do as you would be done by.' That does not mean: 'Examine into the other man's nature and see how he would be done by.' But it does mean that, in England, upon the whole, one will find more well-intentioned and tolerant consideration than in many countries more religious. And it explains, I think, why the chief function of the English in the comity of the nations has been to show how men, in an easy, a rule-of-thumb and a bearable manner, in great numbers, scattered across the acres at home or across the seas, tolerantly and pleasantly may live together.

CHAPTER V

Conduct

THERE is a passage in the diary of Samuel Pepys in which he quotes some speaker whose name I have forgotten. I am unable, too, to find again the passage itself. But it is to the effect that the function of the law is not to avenge but to restore. And, upon the whole, we may say that nowadays and, in the large, the function of the English law is successfully fulfilled. The English law as it stands upon the statute-books is more fitted to prevent crime than to avenge it: the English national temperament *vis-à-vis* of, say, a thief is scarcely an avenging one. If, that is to say, a thief has failed to come off with his booty, or if he has surrendered it before or after his capture, the Englishman as a rule will be contented with, or will applaud a light sentence. But it must be a sentence that will deter other criminals.

This 'note', I think, permeates the whole fabric of English society. I was talking to a sheepshearer this morning. Whilst he knelt in the hot sunshine above the hot fleeces of a panting ram he told me that the day before a casual labourer, employed during the pressure of lamb-shearing, had taken three shillings from his coat when it hung in the wool barn. I asked him if he had told the police, and he answered:

'No, nor I don't suppose I shall. At any rate, I'll give the chap a fair start. After all, he wasn't of these parts, so nobody will take him for an example.'

And yesterday, lying upon the sea beach, I asked a member of our administrative class what would be done to the fellaheen of an Egyptian village. They had risen in a body and murdered some officers of the English army shooting in the Nile fields.

'Oh,' he said, 'they'll deport a whole lot of them to the Soudan. It is a beastly thing to do with them, poor beggars, and probably no one here will know of it. But it must be done or there would be no end of these murders. You see Englishmen are walking about the villages there all day long unarmed'...

At the same time, the Englishman views with equanimity the fact that the law does sanction the most appallingly vindictive sentences for crimes of the most insignificant. If you put it to a lay Englishman that it *is* appalling that a man should be sentenced to six months' hard labour for stealing a pair of shoes, he will say: 'Oh well, it is the law.' And, in a similar spirit, he will comment upon the fine of ten shillings upon a man who just fails to murder his wife.

In this the English legal courts differ from those of almost all other nations, since the spirit of nearly all foreign legal systems is the rendering of justice. In England the judge administers the law. He must administer the law in face of his notions of equity, of right; he must do violence to his most intimate feelings and to the spirit and sympathies of all people, if the law so demands it. I had a friend who was tried for a certain misdemeanour before a judge, whose whole private life was devoted to combating a side issue of that misdemeanour. It was, that particular crime, founded upon atheism, though it was not exactly a manifestation of disbelief in the existence of a Deity – and, indeed, the words were never mentioned in the Court, though Mr Justice ——, it was notorious, had a hatred of atheists that in one or two instances had bidden fair to prejudice his career. Nevertheless, although my friend was found guilty, technically, of his misdemeanour, Mr Justice —— passed upon him a sentence that was practically one of acquittal – the payment of the plaintiff's costs. This, of course, is a commonplace record; but my friend, sitting in the court, was well aware of the personal hatred that the judge felt towards him. He said that it felt like being in a cage with some tremendous, malevolent-eyed, wild beast prowling round the exterior and trying bar after bar by which he might enter and devour. And happening to meet Mr Justice ——, a venerable if bad-tempered old gentleman, at a friend's table shortly afterwards, I had the gratification to hear him interrupt a discourse upon the Etruscan vases which were the chief delight of his private existence, by a violent diatribe against my friend the misdemeanant. According to him he was, my friend, a dangerous scoundrel whom, if the law were satisfactory, he would have sentenced to penal servitude for a long term of years. But he had, of course, to administer the law.

There is no lesson to derive from this save that the average Englishman would say that Mr Justice —— was in the right. But I

fancy that, in pure reason, he was in the wrong to have inflicted a
sentence so moderate when his instincts and desires – and the
practice of the Courts – would have justified him in inflicting a
penalty certainly more severe than the mere payment of the
plaintiff's costs. I went indeed so far as to question his lordship, who
happened to be a distant connection of my own, not as to this
particular instance – I had indeed allowed the topic to recede far
enough into the past of the conversation to allow it to pass from
his mind – but as to how, in general cases, he allowed his predilec-
tions to affect his judgments. I put my question in a sufficiently
deferential form, and he answered good-naturedly:

'Well, you see, there are in every judge two gentlemen rolled
into one, as some one said. Now, in the case of that fellow ——'
– and his mind *had* reverted to the case of my friend – 'I dare say
you weren't acquainted with the particulars. But it was so-and-
so…'; and, leaning back in his chair and taking a sip of the barley
water that his health forced him to drink even at dinner, he
proceeded to sketch the case of my friend. It was instructive to see
that though he was virulently unfair to the motives and the person
of my friend, he stated the legal aspect of the case with an extreme
temperateness. 'Now,' he continued, 'when you have to pass
judgment in such a case you have to consider not only what the
criminal deserves, but what were the legal risks he ran. Indeed, I
personally make it a practice to cast a general average in my mind
of other judgments on that sort of case, if I don't – which I do very
often – take the opinion of my fellow judges. The law, you know,
is not any respecter of persons.'

So that we seem to arrive at the fact that in the English lawyer
there is not only a personal conscience, which may or may not sway
his judgment, but there is also a legal conscience, a special casting
of the average of what may be the legal public opinion of the day.
And this last does undoubtedly sway our judges most considerably
of all. There are, of course, cases of outrageous judgments; just as,
obviously enough, there are persons who, owing to a fortunate
manner in the witness-box, or to some subtle influence that it is
hard to analyse, do get themselves respected. But, upon the whole,
and speaking impressionistically, the spirit of the law as it is administered in England today is, both actually and psychologically,
wonderfully level in its manifestations.

The law, then, is no respecter of persons in England, and that is
as much as to say that English law, like the typical Englishman, is

singularly unimaginative, is essentially lacking in constructive sympathy. That there is one law for the rich and the poor may or may not be reasonable to the bulk of humanity in the world; but that there should be one law for doctor, man of letters or linen-draper, is a proposition that most other nations will deny. Thus, in France bankruptcy for a tradesman is a crippling and terrible cata-strophe, involving loss of civil rights and other disabilities. For the French lawgiver argues (I am not concerned to say whether he is right or wrong) that the business of the tradesman being money-making, the tradesman who fails to keep his money accounts straight is a member detrimental to society. The professional man or the artist, on the other hand, according to him, devotes his chief endeavours not to the making of money, but to the advancement of his science or art, a thing beneficial to the Republic, outside the accidents of its marketability. And thus the French judge attempts to administer, not a law which respects no persons, but a law which aims at rendering an individual justice. The apparently irrational but psychologically justifiable verdicts of French juries are so many confirmations of this theory. And it is, no doubt, owing to the consciousness of this that French lawyers in practice assume the guilt of an accused citizen, calling upon him to establish his innocence; just as it is no doubt owing to the consciousness that the law never can render an ideal justice, that the English law assumes the innocence of an accused subject. It is as if the Englishman had said in the past:

'Oh, well, the law is wonderfully capricious in the way it affects people; let us make it affect as few people as it decently need.' And so we have that wonderful phrase: 'The benefit of the doubt', and this tranquil, unreasoning belief in the rightness of all legal decisions, which casts so singular, so steady a light upon English character. For I think that there is nothing in the world more wonderful as a national expression than the tranquillity which falls upon England after the decision of a great case. For days, for weeks, nay, even for months, we may have been following a trial with a nearly breath-less attention. We discuss the evidence in every club corner, over every restaurant table, or across the fields where the footpaths lead us. We form our private judgments; we say, 'He is guilty', or 'We don't believe they did it'. And, when the blow falls, when the doom is pronounced, we really hold our breaths for a moment. I remember walking along the Strand not so long ago with a companion, and suddenly there flashed across the crowded, hurrying, dizzying street the announcements, in yellow, in pink, in white papers – 'Result of the —— case'.

It did, quite literally, call a halt to that tide. For a long time we had followed the fortunes of the thin, bold, military-looking, tired-looking prisoner in the dock. If we had not identified ourselves with his fortunes, we had felt for them the interest that one feels for a long-unsolved riddle. And I think every one of us in the Strand felt convinced that the man was innocent, in that he was too mad to be sentenced. At the block in the corner of Wellington Street we were able to stop to buy a paper from behind the pink-lettered apron of a newsvendor, who had, I remember, a black hat absolutely dun-coloured with age. As he took the penny he muttered hoarsely:

'He's got five years!'

There was not any doubt about who the He was – though that was a fame, when one comes to think of it, almost breathless: to be He for the whole crowded Strand. I looked in my companion's eyes: I know I felt some physical shock, a catch in the throat, perhaps, or a minute difficulty in standing. I said: *Five years!* and my companion looked back at me and said: 'Five years!' And for an appreciable moment things really seemed to stand still, till we could take up a definite mental position with regard to this new factor in the world. And in that moment I could see the figure of a traffic policeman as he leaned back his head to call to an omnibus driver: 'He's got five years!' We opened our damp broadsheet in the street and looked, to make certain. Then my companion said: 'He was guilty, then!'

That was the view at which she had arrived during her pause. And that is the point that I wish to make – that in the whole of the Strand there were all these people taking up that same point of view. 'He *was* guilty, then!' It was not, I mean, in any of us to doubt the rightness of the verdict, and few people doubted the justice of the sentence. And, without giving voice to it, we framed in our minds the corollary: 'He's had more than a fair trial: he has had the benefit of all the possible doubts, and therefore he *is* guilty.'

And that frame of mind is a great tribute from the nation to the administrators of its laws – but it is also a very singular national symptom. For it is obvious that this benefit of the doubt, if it is beneficent to criminals at times, acts rather hardly upon the innocent accused, since he would obviously have stood the test more unflinchingly if he had come out acquitted from an ordeal in which no possible doubt existed. And for that reason, in many cases, it is nearly as much of a calamity to have been tried and acquitted as to have been tried and found guilty. I have known more than one man whose whole careers have been blasted by prosecutions that, as the phrase is, had not a leg to stand on. Still, when one meets them where men congregate one seems to hear behind their backs the whisper of: 'The Recorder said that the plaintiffs had failed to make out their case.' I do not indeed know whether, to thinking men, the continental system of leaving it to the accused to 'make out their cases' is not psychologically preferable. Abroad, in a sense, the law strains all its faculties to ensure a condemnation, but the human feelings of the jury have full play, and, probably, in the result, the general averages of justice or injustice are about equal in England or on the Continent.

There can, however, be no doubt that to men who feel – as opposed to men who are cold-blooded enough to think – the English system is infinitely the more desirable as an ideal. And we must remember, too, that the English state of things is the product of what is practically the oldest system of justice in the world. For, from French law, which is an evolution of the Code Napoléon, to Dutch law, which was founded comparatively lately upon the Roman, there is not a law to be found that is so much the product of an ancient and gradual growth of national necessities. The enactment that makes it penal to own a Bank of Engraving note is the most striking instance of the odd adaptability of English penal law to changing circumstances. There were, that is to say, after the '45 certain Jacobites who were still desirous of spreading confusion amongst the lieges of George II. They hit upon the stratagem of the Hanover Jack. This was a gilt coin that had upon its face the head of the reigning king – but upon its back there was shown, not St George and the Dragon, but the Devil flying away with George II. It was an imitation near enough to pass, with other coins, for a half-guinea, and a great number of these medals were put into circulation. When prosecutions ensued it was found that, although it was treason to counterfeit, or to pass counterfeits of, the coin of the realm, this was no counterfeit, inasmuch as the reverse differed from that of the guinea. The accused were acquitted. The legislature then passed an Act making it penal to pass medals that were colourable imitations of the king's coinage. The Jacobites replied by selling the Hanover Jacks in the street at so much a dozen. This, again, was not criminal, since it was merely selling for value, a thing entirely differing in kind from passing, which implies an attempt to deceive. Parliament accordingly passed a law making it penal even to possess a colourable imitation of current paper or coinage. And it is this eighteenth-century statute that still makes us bound, if by misfortune we come into possession of the staple commodity of the confidence-trick man, to hand it at once to the police, or to destroy it as best we may.

This instance is striking, not only because it shows how a very old law may suffice for modern purposes, but because it shows how innate in English legal procedure is the tendency to give the prisoner the benefit of something – if not of the doubt, then of flaws in the indictment. For there can be no doubt that if, in each of these cases, the Jacobite humourists did not contravene the letter of the law, they very notoriously sinned against its spirit.

It is true that England never had a legal theory that called upon the accused or the defendant to make good his case; nevertheless, though the practice of the law might forbid this, and though, in principle, ever since the days say of Henry VIII, the spirit of the penal law was merely deterrent and that of the civil law merely restorative, there can be little doubt that the spirit of the legislature was vindictive. It met its opponents in the administration. This is strikingly shown in the case of that other 'benefit' – that of clergy. Until the Reformation this was to all intents and purposes merely an ecclesiastical privilege. The Church, that is to say, contained at first all those who could read and write; later it instructed all readers and writers, and these became its special *protégés*. And these it subtracted from the felons or misdemeanants who were liable to feel the powers of the secular law.

The English Reformation – that singular movement which was only partly a manifestation of public opinion – did away, at the bidding of the cowed legislature, with the ecclesiastical courts altogether – in so far, at least, as they affected offences against the secular authorities or against lay subjects. But, although the legislature could affect them, and although the legislature could pass the savagely vindictive penal laws of Henry VIII and Elizabeth, it was unable, in face of the spirit of the whole people, to do away with this particular benefit – a benefit which in essence was entirely foreign to the practice of the secular law. Then there ensued a long struggle between the legislature and the public conscience – a struggle which lasted for three centuries and ended, to all intents and purposes, only with the complete surrender of the legislature.

At the beginning of this period benefit of clergy was extended to all offences save those of treason. Men who had stolen eggs or men who had committed murder could alike go free when they had signed their names and read a passage from the Psalms. And, indeed, in this particular manifestation at the commencement we may see something of that French spirit, that makes doctors and men of the arts comparatively free of the laws of debt because of their extraneously benefiting the Republic. For, in the sixteenth century, the man who could read and write had still a certain special value. But gradually the struggle assumed the aspect of a stubborn determination on the part of judges and juries to extend to poor devils a means of escape from hatefully vindictive penalties. As the legislature continued to extend the number of crimes that were punishable by death, so the judges continued to make proof of benefit more easy, until at last any man who had the capacity to remember certain pothooks and get by heart any verse of the Bible which he could pretend to read, could plead his clergy. The legislature − which came of a class more intent on the protection of property than sympathetic to the opinions or feelings of the people − replied, after several women had escaped death for stealing loaves, by gradually limiting the crimes to which benefit of clergy could extend. As against that, the administrators of the law invented the 'flaw in the indictment', giving criminals the benefit of slips of the pen to atone for the loss of the other benefit. Until at last the legislature abandoned a contest grown unequal and, as it were, with one stroke of the pen abolished the capital punishment for all crimes save wilful murder, high treason and the burning of arsenals or dockyards.[1]

In this way we have arrived, by the influence of a public opinion acting upon legal practitioners, at a legal practice that is eminently humane; that, in a rule-of-thumb way, works eminently well, and at a legal practice that is singularly relied upon. Litigants may nowadays find the costs of lawsuits inconveniently high, but it is to be argued that no pay can be too high that ensures the cleanhand-

---

1   I may set down here in counter to the objection that I have here treated of criminal laws alone, the contention that our civil law has always followed the practice of the criminal − with the sole difference that, since no human life or limb is at stake, the various 'benefits' have not been so marked. Nevertheless, the fact remains that, in general, the onus of proof remains upon the plaintiff, the defendant being, with the necessary modifications and the general principle that the province of the law is not to revenge but to restore, in the position of a prisoner. And, indeed, we might regard the Statute of Limitations as a special extra benefit not enjoyed by any criminals save deserters from the army.

edness of national officials. And, upon the whole, no large class of public opinion could today be found to endorse the words of a character in an early Victorian novel. The law, in those days, appeared to be a 'Hass', because it was in a transitional stage because, in fact, the effects of the long struggle between legislature and people had not yet worn off. But nowadays we can feel to the full the influence of the simplifying and nationalising work that was done upon the body of the law during the lifetime of, say, Chancellor Lord Lyndhurst.

It is to the judges of England, influenced as they were from below and not from above, that we owe this fact, that today England enjoys a law that is so eminently a national expression. Like every national expression it is, thus far, full of theoretic unreason; but, like every national expression, it remains a monument of excellent practice. 'It works out well', to use words that are so eminently characteristic of the English nation. It is, in fact, even as is the English Constitution itself, like an easy cloak, like an easy piece of footwear that gives pleasure to its wearer by dint of many patchings. That it has its disadvantages is obvious – that it has its unreasons is obvious, too. For we might say that the earlier stage of the law, in which crimes against property were punishable by death, was a more logical expression of the nation to whom the attainment and retaining of property more than all else is the ideal of life; to whom still, a crime against the person is one of so relatively little importance that, if a man strike another and just miss killing him, he will escape with a tiny fine, whereas if he strike just a hairsbreadth deeper he will be hanged – the moral offence in both cases being precisely similar. I remember coming across a case in a country police-court, that brought these aspects of the law out in a singular light of absurdity. A man called Chapman had just missed killing his wife with a curious and valuable stick that he had brought from India. A month before, a labourer called Noakes was left waiting in Chapman's hall, having brought a message from a neighbouring farmer. Noakes, who was a silly, but generally honest, boy, stole the stick, which appealed to his fancy, not as an object of worth but as a curiosity. Chapman, who had just failed of manslaughter with this very stick that had just been returned to him, was fined forty shillings at the petty sessions succeeding those at which Noakes was sent to six months' hard labour for stealing the stick.

And, indeed, it is one of the disadvantages of such a legal system as that of England, that the profound respect which the Englishman has for the practice of his law, blinds him to such anomalies as that which I have related above. That is one of the very cases that I had in my mind when I said that the Englishman will answer always: 'Oh, well, it's the law!' to any recital of a hard case. For during the ensuing year I put this particular case of Noakes and Chapman (it had shocked me because I liked Noakes, a simple, rather vacuous youth with a great love for birds, whose nests he protected with sedulous care); I put this particular case to at least twenty Englishmen. I received almost invariably that particular answer.

It hampers – this particular answer – the righting of several wrongs that do earnestly need righting; it engenders a tranquil and optimistic state of mind in which the Englishman, confident in the excellence of his judge-made legal practice, forgets that today, as always, there are laws that are too strong for judges, just as there occur at times judges who will warp the law into allowing them to inflict penalties that are cruel and oppressive. The Englishman, in fact, is apt to forget that the excellence of his law resides in the men who administer it – forgets, that is to say, that it is the judges, rather than the law itself, that have inherited a very great tradition. And this is in very truth what we call official optimism.

It would, indeed, be too much to say that this official optimism is produced by the excellence of the English legal system. It is, rather, this rare and valuable attribute, the product of the national characteristic reacting upon itself. English public opinion – the broad, tolerant, humanitarian, practical optimistic thing which in these islands is public opinion – has produced an excellent thing – two excellent things; since it has produced the body of the law and the spirit of the constitution. And these two excellent things filling very much the mind's eye of the public, the public is very apt to say that all is well with everything because we have always those things to fall back upon. It is, of course, difficult in this matter to disconnect cause from effect; it is, that is to say, difficult to say whether it is because we are a nation singularly hard to rouse to discontent, that we are pleased with our state, or because our state is upon the whole so excellent that we are not easily roused to discontent.

But certain manifestations of the English spirit are really amazing. I remember going through a dense fog to a London station, to catch a train that, officially, should have left the platform at twenty-five minutes past one. At twenty-five minutes past one there was not a single train in all the sidings of the great terminus. At the almost invisible barrier the dimly-seen officials had no knowledge of when any train would leave any platform for anywhere. As the hour of train after train arrived crowd after crowd filled the station more and more densely. And, for hour after hour nothing happened. The fog deepened; the crowds grew more dense – but nothing happened. No single person proposed even to make a hostile demonstration before the booking-office; no one hooted, no one groaned. We stood there, our arms filled with parcels, string bags – it was Christmas time – rubbing against our calves. And still – nothing. At last, at a quarter-past four, a string of unlit carriages pushed its way almost soundlessly between the thick piles of humanity.

And the crowd raised a cheer – humorous, cynical – but still, a cheer. I do not think that in any conceivable world-centre this would be possible – one could not, I mean, if one were a fanciful person, figure for one's private delectation, an imaginary planet where human beings would be so longsuffering. Yet in London, year in, year out, we endure this crippling strain upon our civic efficiency without the slightest perceptible effort to change a law that renders so farcical a service possible and permanent. It was, after all, the law that we should wait there; it is, after all, the law that permits the ceaseless recurrence of such events. And this characteristic acts balefully upon our national spirit in two distinct directions. It renders us patient in the face of this abuse; it causes us to be patient in our attitude towards every abuse; and, in the still more deleterious direction, it renders our officials nonchalant and wanting in enterprise. I will admit that it is difficult to deal with a fog, just as it is difficult for our Foreign Office to deal with, let us say, Leopold II, King of the Belgians. The one and the other are mephitic phenomena – baffling, protean. Yet, assuredly, were the national spirit at all easy to raise, we should insist that our railway officials should search among the inventors until some system were devised by which all trains at all times could be worked by blind-folded men. Yet we suffer our bodies to be wearied, our trade to be harassed, our time to be lost, and our spirits to be vexed, year in, year out, at odd moments, at hurried seasons of the year. We let our officials grow slack, our inventors lack that incentive of reward and encouragement that is so necessary to our national energy. We are fond of taking refuge in the soothing consideration that we, the English race, have been so much the pioneers of the railway system that nowadays we have to suffer for inconveniences that were unforeseeable by the early inventors. In this case, too, we say, 'Ah, well, it's the law.' It is, that is to say, the law that pioneers work roughly, and contented with having so early led the van, we do not harass the officials who have inherited the merits of the long-dead pioneers. We have still the belief that, if it were absolutely necessary, something would be done. Someone, probably, will turn up from somewhere, and do it for us. Competition will force it or an eventual decrease in the use of soft coal.

And, just as we hinder our national and material welfare by this official optimism, so we jeopardise our national soul by allowing our Foreign Office to remain impotent in the face of a dismal potentate, the organiser of a band of callous scoundrels. I was looking yesterday at a photograph; it showed, seated against the light, a sculpturesque nude form. A bearded, wonderfully moulded man sat, his knees nearly up to his mournful face, gazing inscrutably and without expression at two small objects. These were the hand and foot of his child. And the child, a little girl, had been eaten by men, and the men were the soldiery of a Christian monarch whom we, as a nation, had helped to set in power over the regions in which the photograph was taken; a monarch whom we still maintain in this authority. Every voter in this country is directly responsible for the mournful gaze of that negro.

It was open, that is to say, to every voter of the United Kingdom to be aware of this fact; it was equally open to him to exact from the parliamentary candidate for whom he voted a definite pledge that Great Britain would do its uttermost to put an end to the reign of Leopold II, absolute monarch of the Congo Free State. That the task would be a difficult one for our officials I am not set to deny. The late Foreign Minister when privately urged to move in the matter, said that his hands were tied by the fact that abuses of natives as great in degree as those to be witnessed in the Congo were to be witnessed in a certain portion of the British Dominions. In consequence his hands were tied; the Belgians responsible having threatened to raise against him a *tu quoque* terrible enough. But, within reason, it should be possible for the British nation either to reform the offending colony or to save its reputation and regain its freedom of criticism by cutting the colony in question adrift from the assuredly glorious traditions of the British Empire.[1]

---

1 I do not mean to say that the Queensland question was the only difficulty that faced Lord Lansdowne and, unbacked as he was by any strong public feeling, the complicated inter-

This, of course, is no very important matter; no doubt a negro child or two must suffer that the world may march triumphantly towards Occidental civilisation. I do not raise it with any propagandist motive, but merely to illustrate a national characteristic, just as I have suffered much, and shall probably continue to suffer much, from the erratic train services of several lines without attempting to cure them with my pen. It is, in short, not my affair at all to attempt to better the world as I see it, but merely to attempt to render, to account for, the defects of the singular and very high qualities of the nation that gives me shelter.

The defects of the Englishman's qualities are strange in practice, but obvious enough when we consider the root fact from which they spring. And that root fact is simply that the Englishman feels very deeply and reasons very little. It might be argued, superficially, that because he has done little to remedy the state of things on the Congo, that he is lacking in feeling. But, as a matter of fact, it is really because he is aware – subconsciously if you will – of the depth of his capacity to feel, that the Englishman takes refuge in his particular official optimism. He hides from himself the fact that there are in the world greed, poverty, hunger, lust or evil passions, simply because he knows that if he comes to think of them at all they will move him beyond bearing. He prefers, therefore, to say – and to hypnotise himself into believing – that the world is a very good – an all-good – place. He would prefer to believe that such people as the officials of the Congo Free State do not really exist in the modern world. People, he will say, do not do such things.

As quite a boy I was very intimate with a family that I should say was very typically English of the middle class. I spent a great part of my summer holidays with them and most of my week-ends from school. Lady C——, a practical, comfortable, spectacled lady, was accustomed to call herself my second mother, and, indeed, at odd moments, she mothered me very kindly, so that I owe to her the recollection of many pleasant, slumbrous and long summer days, such as now the world no longer seems to contain. One day I rowed one of the daughters up a little stream from the sea, and halting under the shade of a bridge where the waters lapped deliciously,

---

national questions aroused by the peculiarly guaranteed position of Leopold II were sufficient to warrant the government in taking very little action upon the report of their official. But this fact is not the more creditable to us as a nation, though it may be taken as largely absolving the government which exists to put in force the national will.

and swallows flitted so low as to brush our heads, I began to talk to the fair, large, somnolent girl of some problem or other – I think of poor umbrella tassel menders or sweated industries that at that time interested me a great deal. Miss C—— was interested or not interested in my discourse; I don't know. In her white frock she lay back among the cushions and dabbled her hands in the water, looking fair and cool, and saying very little. But next morning Lady C—— took me into the rose garden, and, having qualified her remarks with: 'Look here. You're a very good boy, and I like you very much,' forbade me peremptorily to talk to Beatrice about 'things'.

It bewildered me a little at the time because, I suppose, not being to the English manner born, I did not know just what 'things' were. And it harassed me a little for the future, because I did not know at the time, so it appeared to me, what else to talk about but 'things'. Nowadays I know very well what 'things' are; they include, in fact, religious topics, questions of the relations of the sexes, the conditions of poverty-stricken districts – every subject from which one can digress into anything moving. That, in fact, is the crux, the Rubicon that one must never cross. And that is what makes English conversation so profoundly, so portentously, troublesome to maintain. It is a question of a very fine game, the rules of which you must observe. It is as if one were set on making oneself interesting with the left hand tied behind one's back. And, if one protests against the inconveniences attendant upon the performance of this prime conjuring trick, one is met by the universal: 'Oh, well; it's the law!'

The ramifications of this characteristic are so infinite that it would be hopeless to attempt to exhaust them. And the looking out for them leads one into situations of the most bizarre. Thus, I was talking about a certain book that was hardly more than mildly 'shocking' to a man whose conversation among men is singularly salacious, and whose life is notoriously not clean. Yet of this particular book he said, in a manner that was genuinely pained:

'It's a thing that the law ought to have powers to suppress.' There was no doubt that he meant what he said. Yet he could recount with approval and with gusto incidents that rendered pale and ineffectual the naive passions depicted in the work in question. But Mr N——'s position was plainly enough defined and sufficiently comprehensible; it said in effect: 'These things are natural processes which must exist. But it is indelicate to mention them.' And you

may set it down that 'delicacy' is the note of the English character
– a delicacy that is almost the only really ferocious note that remains
in the gamut. It is retained at the risk of honour and self-sacrifice,
at the cost of sufferings that may be life-long; so that we are
presented with the spectacle of a whole nation bearing every
appearance of being extraordinarily tongue-tied, and extraordinarily unable to repress its emotions.

I have assisted at two scenes that in my life have most profoundly
impressed me with those characteristics of my countrymen. In the
one case I was at a railway station awaiting the arrival of a train of
troops from the front. I happened to see upon the platform an old
man, a member of my club, a retired major. He, too, was awaiting
the train; it was bringing back to him his son, a young man who
had gone out to the war as of extraordinary promise. He had, the
son, fulfilled this promise in an extraordinary degree; he was an only
child, and the sole hope for the perpetuation of an ancient family
– a family of whose traditions old Major H—— was singularly
aware and singularly fond. At the attack upon a kopje of ill-fated
memory, the young man, by the explosion of some shell, had had
an arm, one leg, and one side of his face completely blown away.
Yet, upon that railway platform I and the old man chatted away
very pleasantly. We talked of the weather, of the crops, of the
lateness of the train, and kept, as it were, both our minds studiously
averted from the subject that continuously was present in both our
minds. And, when at last the crippled form of the son let itself down
from the train, all that happened was the odd, unembarrassing
clutch of left hand to extended right – a hurried, shuffling shake,
and Major H—— said:

'Hullo, Bob!' his son: 'Hullo, Governor!' – And nothing more.
It was a thing that must have happened, day in day out, all over
these wonderful islands; but that a race should have trained itself to
such a Spartan repression is none the less worthy of wonder.

I stayed, too, at the house of a married couple one summer.
Husband and wife were both extremely nice people – 'good
people', as the English phrase is. There was also living in the house
a young girl, the ward of the husband, and between him and her –
in another of those singularly expressive phrases – an attachment
had grown up. P—— had not only never 'spoken to' his ward; his
ward, I fancy, had spoken to Mrs P——. At any rate, the situation
had grown impossible, and it was arranged that Miss W—— should
take a trip round the world in company with some friends who

were making that excursion. It was all done with the nicest tranquillity. Miss W——'s luggage had been sent on in advance; P—— was to drive her to the station himself in the dogcart. The only betrayal of any kind of suspicion that things were not of their ordinary train was that the night before the parting P—— had said to me: 'I wish you'd drive to the station with us tomorrow morning.' He was, in short, afraid of a 'scene'.

Nevertheless, I think he need have feared nothing. We drove the seven miles in the clear weather, I sitting in the little, uncomfortable, hind seat of the dogcart. They talked in ordinary voices – of the places she would see, of how long the posts took, of where were the foreign banks at which she had credits. He flicked his whip with the finest show of unconcern – pointed at the church steeple on the horizon, said that it would be a long time before she would see that again – and then gulped hastily and said that Fanny ought to have gone to be shod that day, only she always ran a little lame in new shoes, so he had kept her back because Miss W—— liked to ride behind Fanny.

I won't say that I felt very emotional myself, for what of the spectacle I could see from my back seat was too interesting. But the parting at the station was too surprising, too really superhuman not to give one, as the saying is, the jumps. For P—— never even shook her by the hand; touching the flap of his cloth cap sufficed for leave-taking. Probably he was choking too badly to say even 'Goodbye' – and she did not seem to ask it. And, indeed, as the train drew out of the station P—— turned suddenly on his heels, went through the booking-office to pick up a parcel of fish that was needed for lunch, got into his trap and drove off. He had forgotten me – but he had kept his end up.

Now, in its particular way, this was a very fine achievement; it was playing the game to the bitter end. It was, indeed, very much the bitter end, since Miss W—— died at Brindisi on the voyage out, and P—— spent the next three years at various places on the Continent where nerve cures are attempted. That I think proved that they 'cared' – but what was most impressive in the otherwise commonplace affair, was the silence of the parting. I am not concerned to discuss the essential ethics of such positions, but it seems to me that at that moment of separation a word or two might have saved the girl's life and the man's misery without infringing eternal verities. It may have been desirable, in the face of the eternal verities – the verities that bind together all nations and all creeds –

that the parting should have been complete and decently arranged. But a silence so utter, a so demonstrative lack of tenderness, seems to me to be a manifestation of a national characteristic that is almost appalling.*

Nevertheless, to quote another of the English sayings, hard cases make bad law, and the especial province of the English nation is the evolution of a standard of manners. For that is what it comes to when one says that the province of the Englishman is to solve the problem of how men may live together. And that, upon the whole, they are on the road to the solution of that problem few people would care to deny. I was talking in Germany last year to a much-travelled American, and he said to me that it might be taken for granted that English manners were the best in the world. In Turks, in Greeks, in Americans, in Germans, in French, or in Redskins certain differing points were considered to distinguish the respective aristocracies – regard for truth, quiet cordiality, softness of voice, independence of opinion and readiness of quiet apprehension – each of these things were found in one or the other nations separately and were regarded as the height of manners. And all these things were to be found united in the Englishman.

Personally, I think that the American was right; but I do not wish to elevate the theory into a dogma. And against it, if it be acknowledged, we must set the fact that to the attaining of this standard the Englishman has sacrificed the arts – which are concerned with expression of emotions – and his knowledge of life, which cannot be attained by a man who sees the world as all good; and much of his motive-power as a world force which can only be attained by a people ready to employ to its uttermost the human-divine quality of discontent.

It is true that in repressing its emotions this people, so adventurous and so restless, has discovered the secret of living. For not the railway stations alone, these scenes of so many tragedies of meeting and parting, but every street and every office would be uninhabitable to a people could they see the tragedies that underlie life and voice the full of their emotions. Therefore, this people which has so high a mission in the world has invented a saving phrase which, upon all occasions, unuttered and perhaps

---

* The tale told by Ford in these pages is the germ that becomes *The Good Soldier*, and specifically the characters of Edward and Leonora Ashburnham and their ward Nancy. The play on the word 'good' is central to the novel, and repression is an important theme.

unthought, dominates the situation. For, if in England we seldom think it and still more seldom say it, we nevertheless feel very intimately as a set rule of conduct, whenever we meet a man, whenever we talk with a woman: 'You will play the game.' That an observer, ready and even eager to set down the worst defects of the qualities in a people, should have this to say of them is a singular and precious thing – for that observer at least. It means that he is able to go about the world in the confidence that he can return to a restful place where, if the best is still to be attained, the worst is nevertheless known – where, if you cannot expect the next man in the street to possess that dispassionate, that critical, that steady view of life that in other peoples is at times so salutary, so exhilarating and so absolutely necessary, he may be sure that his neighbour, temperamentally and, to all human intents, will respect the law that is written and try very conscientiously to behave in accordance with that more vital law which is called Good Conduct. It means that there is in the world a place to which to return.

L'Envoi

I TOOK my doctor – one of my, alas! too many doctors – to the play some time ago. He was, this Doctor K——, a typical Englishman. It is nothing to the point that he was born in Glasgow and had a Spanish mother. For he was fair, firm in the jaw, with a drooping moustache, keen, rather reflecting grey eyes that quailed before no glance, a devout respect for tradition and a devout, ironic contempt for what he called 'the Radicals', though no one by disposition and in his own life could be more Radical. The play was one of those relatively good but positively bad pieces of false sentiment that occasionally make a success in London. It turned upon the elopement of a married woman from a husband who was impossibly bad, with a lover who was impossibly good, in the company, and under the chaperonage of an aunt who was altogether impossible. The chief actress had one property – a worried look, and she had nothing else, except, of course, a certain bodily charm. She used her worried look and nothing else for every possible occasion, gazing always into a great distance and absently brushing a curl from her forehead. This performance grew monotonous to me and, at about the twenty-fifth 'scene between husband and wife', I leant back in my chair and said to my companion:

'She is very bad.'

Still leaning forward, intent, he turned his head towards me and uttered, irritated, shocked and distracted by my callousness:

'But think of her temptations.'

I was thinking of how the actress performed – he of how he would have had his sister – or possibly the woman he was in love with – behave if her husband treated her as badly as the stage-husband treated his wife. And that is how, it seems to me, the typical Englishman behaves at all plays – or at this spectacle which is life. He thinks so much about how he would have himself behave – or his sister, or the woman he loves – that he loses, once and for ever, the critic in the sympathiser. And that is the main note of English life – that the Englishman is always a poet, he is almost never a critic.

For the poet is the man who acts as far as in him may be in accord with a certain high and aloof standard of morals. He views life, not as it is, but as it should be if, in some golden age, he himself were not driven to play the mean part that, almost invariably, he does play. If he idealises himself it is because he has ideals, it is because he sees himself, to the bitter and disillusionising end, as a hero. For, if you catch an Englishman, or if, which is more often the case, he catches himself, in an act of meanness, he will feel angry, irritated – he will feel above all a sense of the flagrant unfairness of Fate. He will protest, and it will be true: 'This is not the real I; this is not the normal I; I am, really, a man of high standards. This is an accident that, set against my whole record, does not really count.'

In this he differs very radically from the men of one other nation, who will shrug their shoulders and say: 'What would you have? Man is a mean beast at bottom'; or from the man of yet another nation, who will say : 'I did this because I wished it; *everything* that I wish is right!' For he will admit, your Englishman, that he ought to have played the game, and he will believe that, really, the game is a perfectly practicable one. Only a cursed piece of bad luck has, in this instance, forced him to lift his voice or do whatever else it is that circumstance has coerced him into doing. The number of living Englishmen who have never told a lie to gain a material advantage must be incredible; the number of living Englishmen who would never, save at the cost of a shrinking like that from a touch upon a sore place, tell a lie to get out of a scrape must be almost equally large. And this is not only because of the incessant clamour of the meanest of all proverbs – it is because the Englishman believes that his neighbour does not tell lies, and he hates to think himself a meaner man than his neighbour. That honesty is the best policy he may or may not believe, but his official optimism makes him believe that people do not tell lies. Nothing, I think, wounds an Englishman more than to discover his child in its first lie; consternation, agony, a half glimpse of all the tragedy that life may hold, beset him at once, and, after a moment devoted to a sort of inarticulate prayer, he sets to with a will to force upon his child's mind the fact that a lie is the one unpardonable offence. He tells his son that he will forgive him any sin so long as it is at once owned to; he subjects himself to the possibility of any annoyance if only he may make his child truth-telling. He enjoins these things upon all his nurses, upon all his servants, upon all his educators. For, for instance, he will send his son to no school where the masters do not profess to act upon this principle. He will, that is to say, certainly send his son to no school where the ushers are allowed to be spies upon the boys. In that way he fosters in his children a belief that the universe is run upon those lines – that the world will pardon, the Almighty favour beyond his deserts, the man who is ready to confess to his faults when he is asked about them.

The defects of this policy are twofold. For, in the first place, the teaching is too soft, too optimistic, and, in the second, a man finds out that there are in life many sins that he can commit without ever being asked about them by any other man. Thus a hedonistic cult is apt, more particularly in after life, to lead a man to disaster. I do not say that, as a system, this discipline of truth-telling is worse or better than, say, the French system of spying plus confession to a priest. It is only different, and, if it is probably worse for the individual, it is almost certainly better for his neighbours. In the result, the Frenchman believes in honour, which is a curious cross between great achievements and not being found out; the Englishman believes in probity which is a cross, equally curious, between behaving justly and having undue allowance made for his faults. Probably, if we were all to check exactly the ethical results we should find that the moral balance of English and French individuals worked out exactly equal, the Frenchman gaining and losing more, the Englishman less.

This characteristic of the Englishman is the more remarkable in that he knows very well that the truth is an impracticable thing, a thing to make life a weariness, since, hard pressed, he will acknowledge that life itself – unless we console ourselves with illusions – is an illusion. He has come far enough away from his Elizabethans, yet he is still so saturated with their quotations that he is singularly open to convictions of the transience, of the shadow-nature, of life itself. For no one is so open as the Englishman to being impressed, say, by the mottoes upon dials. He will read: 'For our time is a very shadow that passeth away' – and though he will put the conviction from him as fast as he may, he will, nevertheless, feel it for the moment, very intimately. The fact is – and it is one of the irritating qualities of this singular nation – that, whatever the Englishman may be called, he cannot be styled a materialist. For the materialist looks things in the face; the idealist never does, but weaves around them instead a veil of values that are purely relative. If you ask an Englishman why the truth is valuable, he will say: because it is the truth. If you press him still further he will say, as like as not: 'Magna est veritas et prevalebit' – and, as likely as not, it will be because of this sounding phrase that he really sets truth upon a pedestal.

If he would open his eyes – or with his eyes closed – he might see a thousand instances in which truth has not prevailed. He might, that is to say, see instances enough to make him question his dogma. But he will take refuge in his quotation, and there, for him, is the end of the matter. He will never carry his analysis of life sufficiently far to allow him to say that a society is conceivable the basis of whose relationship is a lie; that, in fact, it is really because the truth is upon the whole a convenience, a simplification of relationships, that truth-telling communities prosper. If you put it before him that the truth is convenient as a standard simply because it saves time, he will agree. He will agree, too, that a market in which all the vendors tell the truth is a market that will save so much time that it will be able to handle a greater number of goods than a market in which the buyer must test every handful of peas. In this dim way he has discovered the practical value, as he has discovered so many of the other practical values, of altruism. But, not content with that, he must needs look out for a special and mystical value – a moral value that, precisely, will prevail because of the greatness of the principle.

The Englishman, in fact, *is* the poet. He is not the poet because in this use of truth he is alone among the nations. But he unites in himself the practical virtues of all the nations: he has assimilated *all* the quotations. Upon a pedestal as high as truth he puts, for instance, cleanliness. Now cleanliness is of the greatest practical value in a man, and it is obvious that a nation that washes will have a great advantage over a nation less stringent in its ablutions, simply because that nation will contain a greater percentage of healthy individuals with alert brains. The Englishman accordingly elevates this characteristic into a mystical virtue, and says that cleanliness is next to godliness – putting a purely material factor into the same range of ideas as a purely spiritual virtue. He carries, naturally, this idea into practice – so that, for an Englishman, a hero has no value if his face be not minutely clean. For how many times in the course of one's social career will one not hear: 'Oh, one couldn't know S——. He doesn't look as if he ever washed.' Yet S—— is the greatest living metaphysician. Very similarly, the Englishman attaches a mystical value to things that have no immediate or obvious value at all. For how often, again, has one not heard it said of So-and-So that he is a 'thorough sportsman'. And to these words attaches a special significance that no one who is not an Englishman can at all comprehend. For to it we attach the corollary that So-and-So is trustworthy, socially possible, truthful, sober, cleanly, sane and generous. So-and-So, in fact, may be trusted to be a good fellow. And in so trusting him we are in the right, since the thorough sportsman – as apart from the man who merely excels, say, at steeplechase riding – on account of the fact that he 'plays the game' and lives in the open air a fairly abstemious life, is pretty certain to be 'straight' and is pretty certain to have a sufficient stock of technical and entertaining anecdotes, to be pretty good company. He will breed sound children; he will vote according to his conscience; he will be loyal to the plot of earth that bore him. In consequence, he is a valuable citizen; so we assign to the sport that he follows a mystical value.

And, as another corollary, with an almost invariable wrongheadedness, we set about ruining the sport of the moment by 'specialising' it. So that cricket, which has a national value of the very highest kind, and a mystical value too, since 'playing cricket' is synonymous with pursuing honourable courses – cricket has been practically ruined and reduced to mathematical displays of tactics so scientific that no mere amateur very much cares any longer to take part in a game. And, similarly, we have ruined football, croquet, hunting, pheasant-shooting – and we are ruining Bridge and have long since ruined the great game of racing.

Nevertheless, what the Englishman pursues in all these things – in truth-telling, cleanliness, or games – is a personal record. And there, again, he is the poet. For he desires never to have told a lie, never to have been unclean, never to have infringed a rule in any game. And he does these things, he has these aspirations to satisfy a certain inward sense. He does not do them for glory alone, not for health alone, and not alone to escape punishment, but as it were to preserve a sort of virginity in a fine wrong-headedness – just as now and then you will still come across a countryman of great age cherishing an invincible pride in never having been in a railway train.

And here again is another great strength of the Englishman, since there are many nations that revel in sport, in truth-telling, or in the mania of personal ablutions; but in no other nation are so many of the civic and the practical virtues so worked into the mystical code of life. The Frenchman loves sport as practically as the Englishman; the German loves truth as unreasoningly; the Japanese excels all Occidental nations in the number of times that he submits his cuticle to the influence of hot water. But the man of these islands, as it were avid after proverbs, takes them from the German, the French, the Spaniard, the Swedes, and even from the Irish, and out of them builds up the typical Englishman.

It is for this reason that one may, with some confidence, set down the fact that the English is the type of the future. For, being born of the best types of so many other races, the English unite nowadays in themselves all the virtues of a special sort – all the perpetuating virtues of the Occidental nations. That they accept the world and do not grumble at the rules of the game – that they have nothing in them of the negational, and little of the questioning, frame of mind, only make the forecast the more probable. For a person who accepts the rules of, say, Bridge, and does not question the justice of giving a person thirty marks merely because he holds three aces, whether he employ them well or ill – the person who plays the game without being troubled by introspection, will obviously consider the game better worth playing and will play it better. That is what one calls unimaginativeness, and there is little doubt that to be unimaginative is to be unhandicapped for the practical business of life.

So that, just as the English language, on account of its romantic traditions, its utter unreason, and its slipshod practicability is probably destined to be the language of the future, so the English frame of mind, which unites all these characteristics, is almost logically destined to be the frame of mind of the world man of the future. I do not say that this prospect does not appal me – I merely state the fact. And perhaps one may be even optimistic in face of it. For, just as the English language is so vague and unconnected an instrument that one may turn it to the uses of a clear Latin frame of mind – of a long-drawn-out and tenacious Germanic, or a misty and 'locally-coloured' Celtic verse-prose, it is possible, without going outside of England, to find men to suit one's mood whatever it may be. I do not mean to say actually that there are so many Russians, Prussians, Hindus or Chinese in England that it is possible to live all one's personal life amidst these foreigners; what I mean is, that the Englishman himself, if one digs into him, if one presses one's arguments home sufficiently, is able, romantically if you will, to assimilate almost any point of view, since probably in his ancestry he unites the most widely-differing individuals. It is not, in fact, in his mind that he is true to type, but solely in his national manifestations. He will receive the culture of any nation; he will even, given the chance, feel all sorts of their national patriotisms. And if he says that Garibaldi or David King of the Jews were really Englishmen, this signifies actually that the Englishman is able to appreciate to the full the heroism, the spirit of national endeavour of Italians as of Hebrews. When, in fact, the Englishman says, 'These fellows are Englishmen', he means, 'We are at least, in part, Italians', or Greeks, or Lost Tribes. He never attains to this scientific statement of the case simply because he is a poet – and the poet states deep truths in the phrases of imagery. He is, in fact, the poet through and through in his preference for the fine phrase, in his self-centring, in his anthropomorphism, in his idealism, and, above all, in his want of sympathy. For the poet's business is constructive; it is not analytical. He has to frame a world – a portion of a world – for himself. Especially he is not analytical – and no person can be sympathetic who is wanting in the faculty of analysis. He may be kind, he may be genial, he may be the pleasantest of company constructively; but he will not have the gift of sympathy. I have at the present moment a cook with a perfect mania for rescuing fledglings that have fallen from the nests. She keeps these little things with their enormous mouths in a number of baskets near the stove. She feeds them sedulously, all of them, from larks to thrushes, from robins to chaffinches, upon a mixture of bread sopped in water and crushed hemp seed. Some of them live to pass their days in cages; many of them die. But she never stays to enquire whether a diet of bread and hemp seed may suit, say, a lark, as it will suit a sparrow. It has for her, this diet, a mystic, a poetic significance. And she never stays to enquire whether Nature, that gives fallen nestlings over to the swift death of cold or at the hands of rodents, is not more kind; for she has a poet's love of the pretty creatures. I have another friend with a mania for sending all the fallen to Canada. He persuades them there, he opens his purse to send them there: tramps, prostitutes, discontented postmen, consumptives, broken-down men of letters or incipient barristers; he dodges them past the medical inspectors in the Liverpool gangways. Some of them prosper, some of them die, and many, no doubt, go to hell. But, to my friend it is all one, since to him Canada appears to offer a paradise of golden grain fields, and it is in these that a man finds health and high thoughts.

And that, too, is the Englishman in his national manifestations. He takes the subject races – Maltese, Hindus, Malays, Bengalis, Zulus, Irishmen, Burmese – he feeds them on the sopped bread of English constitutional lines, he educates them with the crushed hempseed of English codes, Christism and the rules of the game. Some of them live, some of them die, many of them go to hell. And so there has arisen the great tradition of the British Raj. That nature is more kindly, that allows the Hindu to starve in his own way, is a proposition – whether it be right or wrong – that never occurs to him. Immense, tolerant, wise in its views, assimilative up to a point but intensely timid intellectually, intensely afraid to probe things to the depths, the English nation slowly makes its way towards becoming the home of every man. Its intellectual timidity, its very want of sympathy, arises from the Englishman's necessity to have something fixed, to have some standard, some model. So that just as the Englishman accepts an Anglicised Christ Jesus for his personal model, so he accepts the British Constitution and the British frame of mind as the standard according to which he must deal with the undying Celt. If he fails it is because of his very virtues which are miasma to certain peoples.

For the Englishman is so much a creature of the game that he is intensely wearied if he is told that the game of life has no rules. He is worried, because he is intellectually lost directly an accepted belief is destroyed. It is not that he loves the accepted belief because it is a truth, since he loves it only as a standard. He hates the iconoclast because the iconoclast gives him the trouble of finding a new proverb to elevate into a divine dogma. In the great drink question, for instance, he has accepted, upon the whole, the principle of the restriction of licences. Yet it is certainly open to question whether, for a hundred psychological reasons, the unrestricted sale of drink might not conserve better the interests of temperance. Or, if he could once accept that the unrestricted sale of drink were the millennial state, he would find it equally difficult to allow for a moment that the restricted licence might find something to be said for it. For, what he dreads above all things is a world in a fluid state; what he suspects above all things is the open mind. He wants, above all things intellectual, that 'something settled' which will allow him to make new practical plans.

These, in short, are the defects of his qualities – the great defect being his want of sympathetic imagination. It is this that has got him his reputation for hypocrisy – a reputation that is singularly undeserved. The fall of an idealist seems to be greater than the fall of a cynic, because he maintains that the world is perfectible. Yet, actually, idealist and cynic are of one flesh, and the temptation that brings down the one is none the less great for the other. And for the rest, the Englishman is singularly human.

He is this because of his hopefulness, his optimism and his eternal childishness, his unreason, things all which make him good to live with. Speaking for myself, a man of no race and few ties – or of many races and many ties – I know perhaps one Englishman and perhaps two Englishwomen that are absolutely and to the end sympathetic to me. I know twenty foreigners that I could put up with for long periods. I know just one corner of these green and fertile islands that I really love with all my heart, and one English city. But I know a dozen foreign districts where, too, I could dwell in comfort for a long time. But I know very well where the pull lies. I know very well that, when the key of the street is given to me, it is that one English city, it is that one corner of England, it is that one Englishman and those one or two Englishwomen that will call me back in the end.

I may well say in my pride: there is no reason why I should dwell in any one spot. But in my heart I have proved that this boast is a vain one. Heaven knows why this is so; but I remember being 'abroad' for a long space of time, amongst people the most sympathetic, the most benevolent, the most instructed, the most enlightened, speaking languages that, logically, were better adapted to express thoughts than is this amorphous and fragmentary language that I now write. There was no reason why I should not have set up my home, deepened my associations, taken up again old ties of blood in that foreign land. There was no reason at all.

Yet somehow, at nights, there rose up before my eyes a cottage, black against the wintry sky, the stars being between the black and velvety lines of bare elms in this place where now I write. And by day, in the green and sunlit valleys, by the borders of a great lake, I was obsessed always with an intense longing to see once more the sails of ships above the sea wall, the wide stretch of land, the church spire of Lydd breaking the distant horizon – and I longed, ah! beyond bearing, to hear English spoken again; I longed, beyond bearing, to be in the mists, the lamplight, the smell of asphalt, of horsedung and of humanity that so distinguish the English capital. And more than anything I longed to see again those one or two Englishmen and women...

Of course, habit may have done much to create these feelings – early associations, early readings, the passage of time, the mere fact of having lived longer in these places than in others. But I think that England, more than any other land, has the power to exercise this attraction simply because in England it is so easy to form ties, because life is so easy to live, because the issues of life are so simple. It is obviously England that has made the English; it is the climate, the shapes of the land, the moisture that covers walls with lichens, the rain upon the fertile soils, the great valley in a river basin set towards the East. It is these things that have engendered the tranquil state of mind, the optimism, the contentment, the belief – illusion if you will – that life is worth living. It is because, in fact, his climate and his fertile fields give to him this belief, or this illusion, that the Englishman really does make such a pleasant thing of life whether in the cities or in the country. We imagine perhaps signs of change in the national psychology. And I am quite prepared to have it said that these pages – if they get at any spirit at all – get only at a national spirit that is already on the wane. We are, it will be said, getting Germanised or Americanised or automobilised or electrified. But I think that whilst England remains England, with its climate and its greenery, these new tendencies will do little more than be assimilated and converted as it were into a new language expressing always the old thought. For, if this people be not the chosen people, this land will be always one that every race would choose for its birthings and its buryings until the last Aaron shall lead the last of the conquering legions across the world.

Finis

APPENDIX

Author's Note

From *England and the English: An Interpretation* (New York: McLure, Phillips and Co.), 1907

I WAS walking today in St James's Park and I was wondering about two things: Why is New York so unlike London? – and, why should a Londoner feel so at home in New York? – The two statements from which the two questions arise – their promises – seem to be so mutually contradictory that, as it were, there appeared to be no answer to either. For New York is unlike London – and the Londoner – the *true* Londoner – does feel at home in New York. I think he feels there more at home than in Manchester: I am certain that there he feels more at home than in Boston or Philadelphia.

Yet Boston – particularly in the streets below the old State House and in the streets around the Custom House, in Washington Street (which is more like the Strand than is Broadway, New York), or even in Tremont Street, which is, remotely, like Knightsbridge – or, in the Boston habit of mind which so intimately represents the habit of mind of Hampstead – Boston or Philadelphia are infinitely more like parts of London than is New York in any of its parts or as a whole. Yet in Boston or Philadelphia one feels foreign: in New York one feels as if one ought at least to pass unnoticed.

And with those words one adumbrates at once the reason: Philadelphia and Boston are small enough, old enough – crystallised enough – to be provincial. New York is big enough, new enough – easy-going enough – to be Metropolitan. For a Metropolis, though it may contain a fragment of building set up by Julius Caesar, is always young: a truly provincial city though it may have been founded only yesterday is always old. It is old because it has lived long enough to have learned all the lessons it is going to learn and has evolved the sort of man it is always going to evolve. In this sense London, though it has been where it is for a couple of thousand years, is infinitely younger than Philadelphia, and so is New York, though New York is, say three, and Philadelphia only two, hundred years old.

And there you have it – for the Londoner walking along his beloved streets can't for a moment be sure of the type of the next man he will meet. The New Yorker being drawn along in his trolley car can't either. The Londoner can't ever be certain that his most familiar landmark is not going to be pulled down to make room for something much taller: neither can the citizen of New York. The Hotel Cecil might have to go tomorrow to make room for some new tendency: so might the Flatiron building. It is that – it is that sense of being in a world where things change in tune with the change of the Spirit of the Age – it is that fine and exciting sense that unites New York and London. It is the feeling that Boston or Manchester, England, have solidified that differentiates them. For there is a Bostonian: there is very decidedly a Manchester man – but there is not any Londoner or any New Yorker.

Boston suggests a bit of Hampstead set side by side with a fragment of the City. But London is not the City and not Hampstead: it is a whole world of other little districts. It is Peckham; it is the Tower Hamlets; it is West Ham; it is Kensington; it is Highgate; it is Greenwich; it is Richmond. It represents almost every Occidental frame of mind that you can imagine. And each frame of mind is represented almost daily in such different proportions that you cannot ever say which is the dominant note. A little time ago the German element made itself so powerfully in evidence here that we were all, in London, crying out that we were being Germanised. Yesterday we were saying that 'American methods' were swamping us: today it is the turn of the '*entente cordiale*'.

And the inhabitant of New York must be familiar with a similar feeling. In a spirit of enquiry I asked, upon a transatlantic liner, various statistical questions of various fellow-travellers like myself approaching New York. One told me that there were in the great city three and a half million Jews. Another said that there were two million Germans; another, one and a half million Slavs; another two million Italians and half a million Frenchmen. So that, if I had accepted these figures as statistics, I should have had in my mind's eye the image of a city containing nine and a half millions of 'foreigners' of various kinds and perhaps a million and a half of 'Americans' – a city of, say eleven millions, mostly of inferior races.

But I wasn't, among my New York fellow-travellers, looking for exact statistics. I was trying to get at their frames of mind. And their frames of mind were very similar to those that would be found in any body of my own fellow-townsmen hurrying homewards. Most Londoners are of course aware that the population of their city is seven millions – they are in that more exact or more informed than most New Yorkers. But every Londoner is aware that he lives amongst an immense body of foreigners – of Jews, Germans, Slavs, Italians, French, and what not. I suppose we, as Londoners, exaggerate in these matters more than do most New Yorkers. My own personal impression leads me, personally, vastly to exaggerate. I know whole districts of London where all the signs in the shop windows are incomprehensible to me; just as, walking down Broadway, I was overwhelmed by the fact that *every* shop sign appeared to bear a name ending in Baum or Stein. (And, indeed, at this moment as I write in a room of a London club – in a room which is supposed to be blessed with silence, – in a club whose members are all supposed to be British born – two German Jews are talking in loud voices, one Frenchman is reading the *Patrie*; one Irish member is reading the *Times*; a solitary Englishman is reading a novel translated from the Russian; and a person of singularly mixed origin – German, Scotch, Welsh, and English – sits writing words that will be read only in America.) I introduce these biographical facts because they seem to me to be typical of the spiritual kinship of the two great world cities that nowadays really count. They show that, in both, a man of good-will may rejoice in being in touch with a spirit of cosmopolitanism; may feel that he is in a place where he is in touch with the ends of the earth. They are the great clearing-houses of humanity; in them a man has no need to fear that he will become insensibly hardened into a 'type'. He cannot, because as long as London and New York remain alive there never can be a London or a New York type. In each city humanity is forever in a state of flux; in each – as if each were a gigantic sounding-board – the echoes of the frames of mind of all humanity are forever reverberating.

But, when it comes to the question of why New York is so unlike London, I confess to a feeling of hesitation. It is obvious to say that New York lacks the augustness of size – though actually, to a Londoner, New York feels tiny – feels tinier than it ought in decency to do. It will I know seem difficult to a New Yorker to appreciate this: it may seem an outrageous boast. Nevertheless the

Londoner, standing in, say, Times Square does not feel the same sense – the sense of having vast distances of crowd, passing all round him as he feels, say, at Piccadilly Circus. It is no distance to speak of from Forty-third Street to the Battery – and there New York ends; it is no distance in particular to Claremont – and there is not much of the city left there, it isn't far in the crosstown trolleys to either river; it is nothing so very unreasonable either to the pretty little settlements on the road nearly to Manhattan Beach or to the squalid and dismal regions above the Palisades on the other shore.

But think of Piccadilly! The miles and miles and miles of streets through the city, through the Mile End Road, the East End, the Docks; think of the miles and miles of streets through Knightsbridge; through Kensington; through Hammersmith, Chiswick, Kew, Richmond – who knows where it ends. And right down to Limpsfield and right up to Hendon! The American won't know these vastnesses; he won't ever – and perhaps he's to be congratulated – know just the feel of it, the pressure, all round him, of endless miles of humanity; something of which he is only subconsciously aware as he is of the pressure of the atmosphere.

Perhaps it is only a silly insensibility in the Londoner not to feel it in New York, too – for New York is large enough for any reasonable needs. But many things go to make up the feeling of smallness; the very newspapers do it. When one looks at a London paper one feels – as I shall later have occasion to point out – that no one in London matters very much to London, because it is so big. But when one looks in the New York papers one sees a never ceasing blur of portraits. There are portraits – endless portraits – of politicians; of trolleymen; of pharmacists; of shop-girls who refuse to marry; of bachelors who can't get any one to marry them; of women who throw peanuts at policemen; of people who do nothing in particular. And somehow one gets the impression that all these people – the trolleyman; the pharmacist and the shop-girl *do* matter to New York. (The impression is probably wrong but it is irresistible.) And the Londoner says: 'Ah, London is too big for *that*!' Perhaps it isn't; perhaps really – and if our newspaper proprietors knew their business – the Londoner, too, cries aloud for portraits of its distinguished tram-car conductors.

But the sense of the greater largeness of London does remain and does overpower one. It may be only a product of the greater darkness of the atmosphere. At the moment of my writing a cheery November sun is shining; there is a small, white mist over the

Thames; the harnesses of the cab-horses on the Embankment glitter as they hurry along. But the prevailing feeling of London is one of darkness – of a comfortable darkness. The Londoner never sees very far; his vistas are cloudy, tenebrous, opacitic. This makes all his distances seem very great. To look from Hampstead across London is to seem to look across a continent of shadows, of glooms, of shafts of light. But from the top of the great buildings near the post-office in New York you can see with the naked eye the details of the tall, white, slender and beautiful building that makes a wedge between Broadway and Fifth Avenue on Twenty-third Street. I don't know how far, exactly, it is from the City Hall to Madison Square – but again and again it has taken me three-quarters of an hour to walk it. I can walk from the British Museum to the National Gallery in ten minutes, yet I have the impression that it is much further from Great Russell Street to Trafalgar Square than it is along the stretch of Broadway that I have named – and I cannot, from the top of Museum Mansions, see any detail of Nelson upon his column. He remains a faint grey silhouette.

Perhaps I am wrong in saying that in London one seems so much further from Nature than in the centre of New York – for that is what this feeling of vastness amounts to. Perhaps I am wrong – but I think that I am right. And how to account for the adumbration of an impression, struck me this afternoon in St James's Park. St James's Park in London is a beautiful little oasis, sacred to the after lunch digestional of innumerable clubmen; to innumerable children and to innumerable birds and bird lovers. But today, the little green lake had been drained – I imagine to give an opportunity for the bottom to be cleared of mud and the detritus of autumnal leaves. There were small pools of water in the dry, shallow, bottom and, towards the Whitehall end, near the little island, like monuments of boredom, white, dejected and immense, upon high grey pedestals, at whose base there squatted whole crowds of meaner birds, stood the poor pelicans that so many Londoners much love. But the pelicans did not, for the moment, count much to me. What counted were the rocks upon which they stood.

One had been used to seeing the flat tops of these rocks just above the water, decorated with a pelican or two. One saw them now, these whitey grey masses, about man high and a little more. But, alas! – they stood revealed – not rocks, but mere masses of Portland cement. And the truth forced itself upon me; there are no rocks in London. To find, in one's mind, rocks, one would have to let the thoughts travel so immensely far. There isn't a real rock for miles from St James's Park.

But, in New York, there are real rocks. There are rocks even in Central Park. And I remembered one memorable afternoon in New York. We had sought the Zoological Gardens which are in the Bronx Park; we had thought that 'the Bronx' was an epithet sufficiently protracted. We had emerged from the subway at 135th Street and had taken a crosstown car, for miles and miles as it appeared, through the clear weather, the broad suburban streets, between the great piles of tenement buildings and of factories. 'The Bronx' had revealed itself not as a Park containing the finest menagerie in the world – but as a clean, rather empty, industrial quarter. We reached eventually the Zoo.

But what had impressed me of the afternoon's adventure was to see rocks – real, blue, broad, lichenless rocks, cropping through the soil all over the district, right in among the tenements and in the very lawns of the few old, good houses that remained from a former period. I don't know how it may be for a New York child – but, for a Londoner, a rock is a romantic, a symbolical, object. It represents all sorts of wildnesses; it represents Nature in her most untouched mood. So that, to that extent, New York seems infinitely nearer to Nature than London does – for, for the Londoner to find rocks – those symbols of a past undisturbed by man and his necessities – he has the impression that he must go at least out of England. He feels that he must go to Scotland. Of course he need not, for he will find them in Derbyshire; he will find them even as near at hand as Folkestone or Tunbridge Wells. But he has that feeling – whereas in New York one has always the feeling that one can find a solid, virgin rock at any time, in twenty minutes. And the feeling is just enough. For London is surrounded by flat, green fields – fields that have felt the touch of Man for centuries and centuries. But round the City of New York there stretch wastes untouched enough – swamps, even; hungry fields through which there crop up those undeniable rocks. So that, in London, one has an impression of the youth of Man hastening to its work amidst age-settled circumstances; in New York one feels all the youth of Man hurrying amidst circumstances that have not even begun to settle. This impression is probably inaccurate enough according to actual figures; for I imagine that, if the alterations that are daily taking place in Kingsway, in the Strand, in Regents Street, in Oxford Street, in Piccadilly, in Knightsbridge, in the High Street,

Kensington – all over London – if the actual bricks, tons of mortar, miles of iron girders and wooden joists that are being used at this moment were totted up and tabled against those used in the rebuildings in Madison Square, in Riverside Drive, on Broadway, on Fifth Avenue, on Amsterdam Avenue and the rest – it would be found that London was being actually more made over, rebuilt and transmogrified than is New York itself. Nevertheless, there the feeling is: any average man would say that New York is being much more rejuvenated than is ever the case with its large rival across the water. At the same time am I not well acquainted with the saying of the New Yorker: 'Little old New York is good enough for me!'

I offer these remarks not for any substantial value that they may have. They probably haven't any and the resident of New York who lives say where Thirty-eighth Street crosses Eleventh Avenue, might say that they were all nonsense. But they do, these analyses of feeling, indicate: They're a sample of the sort of matter that in this book I offer to the American reader. For what I offer is not a statement of facts: it is precisely a set of analyses of feelings. The American visiting our Islands has had offered to him a great number of very excellent guides to things in London or the English country. I expect that many American visitors to London have seen many more of our 'sights' than ever I have; I am pretty certain that most American visitors have 'seen' more castles, abbeys, manors, and British places than ever I shall do in the English country. Returning the other day from New York I found in the barber's-shop of the vessel a stack of a little publication called, I think, *London in Three Days*. I have spent much part of the thirty years in London – but I computed that if, in his three days, the American visitor followed out exactly the course mapped out for him in this excellent six-pennyworth he would have seen exactly three times as many of the sights of London as I. But I don't think he would understand London as well as I do.

And, in this book, I have tried to make him understand as well as I could the Spirit of England – of the English people; of the English great town; of the English countryside. If I have done this, I may claim to have done him some service – to have done him a very great service. For the value of a visit to a place is not measured by the number of sights a man may have seen. It is to be measured, precisely, by the amount of enjoyment that has accrued to a visitor. And you can't have enjoyment without sympathy; and you can't attain to sympathy without some sort of 'pointer'; without some sort of indication of the values of the people, of their desires, their hopes, their fears. In order, in fact, to understand and enjoy a country, you must have some sort of appreciation of the Spirit of the Place. It is materials for forming some such appreciation that in this book about England, I have attempted to supply. It divides itself naturally into three parts. In the first I treat of the People brought together into that most modern of all products – the Great City. In the second it treats of the People left much more in contact with their past – for, just as the roots of Ararat are deeper than those of Rome – so the Heart of the Country – must be a thing of older growth than that of any London. The third book attempts to analyse the Spirit of the English People – of that great, migratory people who in the course of centuries have taken root in some small islands and produced, in Town and Country alike, that subtle and difficult thing, a national spirit. For the Country was before the Town; but, before either, mounting the hills of the one and shaping the streets of the other, was the People itself.

Most of us love places very much as we may love what, for us, are the distinguished men of our social lives. Paying a visit to such a man we give, in one form or another, our impressions to our friends: since it is human to desire to leave some memorial that shall record our view of the man at the stage he has reached. We describe his manners, his shape, his utterances; we moralise a little about his associates, his ethics, the cut of his clothes; we relate gossip about his past before we knew him, or we predict his future when we shall be no more with him. We are, all of us who are Londoners, paying visits of greater or less duration to a Personality that, whether we love it or very cordially hate it, fascinates us all. And, paying my visit, I have desired to give some such record.

I have tried to make it anything rather than encyclopaedic, topographical, or archaeological. To use a phrase of literary slang I have tried to 'get the atmosphere' of modern London – of the town in which I have passed so many days; of the immense place that has been the background for so many momentous happenings to so many of my fellows.

A really ideal book of the kind would not contain 'writing about' a town: it would throw a personal image of the place onto the paper. It would not contain such a sentence as: 'There are in the city of —— 720 firms of hat manufacturers employing 19,000 operatives.'

Instead there would be a picture of one, or two, or three hat factories, peopled with human beings, where slow and clinging veils of steam waver over vats and over the warm felt on cutters' slabs. And there would be conveyed the idea that all these human beings melt, as it were, into the tide of humanity as all these vapours melt into the overcast skies.

Similarly, in touching upon moral ideas, a book about places must be passionate in its attempt after truth of rendering; it must be passionless in the deductions that it draws. It must let neither pity for the poor nor liking for established reputations and clean floors, warp its presentations where they bear, say, upon the Housing Question. Its business is to give a picture of the place as its author sees it; its reader must seek in other books, statistics, emotional views, or facts handy for political propaganda.

This author's treatment of historic matters must again be 'presentations'; and he must select only such broad tendencies, or such minute historic characters as bear straight upon some aspect of his subject. The historic facts must illustrate, must cast a light upon modern London, if that is what is being presented. There must be no writing about Dr Johnson's chair in a certain tavern merely because it appeals to the author. The reader will find details of all such things in other books – this author's endeavour should be to make the Past, the sense of all the dead Londons that have gone to the producing of this child of all the ages, like a constant ground-bass beneath the higher notes of the Present. In that way the book might, after a fashion, forecast even the Future and contain prophecies. It should, in fact, be instinct with the Historic sense which will afford apt illustrations, rather than the annalist's industry, or the love of the picturesque.

That sense of the picturesque will, however, be both a salvation and a most dangerous stumbling-block. In a turning off an opulent High Street, there is a court[1] with the exterior aspect of which I am very familiar. It is close to a large freestone Town Hall and to a very tall red-brick Fire Station. It is entered by a square archway through which you get a glimpse of dazzlingly white cottages that, very obviously, were once thatched, but that now have pretty red tiles. It is flagged with very large, old stones. It is as picturesque as you can imagine; it is a 'good thing' for descriptive writing, it might

---

1   Alas: even as I finished writing these words, I see that the housebreakers are at work upon this very court. Its place is to be taken by a Carnegie Library!

be legitimate to use it. But the trouble is that it is old – and, if the book were all old things, deluding by a love for the picturesque of antiquity, it would give a very false and a very sentimental rendering of London.

But the author might desire to illustrate the tendency of parasitic humanity to lurk in the shadow of wealthy High Streets – this court would be an excellent illustration: it is peopled with 'bad characters', male and female. Or he might desire to illustrate the economic proposition that letting small houses to bad characters is more profitable than selling the land for the erection of flats – here, again, the court would be an illustration; its extreme cleanliness, neatness and good repair would go to prove how careful that landlord was to prevent the condemnation of his rookery on sanitary grounds.

The author then must be careful not to sentimentalise over the picturesque. His business is to render the actual. His heart may be – it ought to be – torn at the sight of great hoardings, raised for the housebreakers, round narrow courts, old streets, famous houses. He ought to be alive to the glamour of old associations, of all the old associations in all their human aspects – but he ought to be equally inspired with satisfaction because work is being done; because dark spots are being cleared away; because new haunts are being formed for new people around whom will congregate new associations. And he ought to see that these new associations will in their turn grow old, tender, romantic, glamorous enough. He should, in fact, when he presumes to draw morals, be prepared to draw all the morals – he must not only sniff at the 'suburbs' as a place of small houses and dreary lives; he must remember that in each of these houses dwells a strongly individualised human being with romantic hopes, romantic fear, and at the end, an always tragic death. He must remember that the thatched, mud-hovels that crowded round the Tower of original London, were just as dull, just as ordinary, just as commonplace even as were the first huts that the first settlers set up near the Battery End of New York, or the first wooden houses on the island of Squidunk; that men in them lived lives, according to their scale, just as squalid and just as unromantic – or just as alert and just as tragic. This author – this ideal author – then, must be passionately alive to all aspects of life. What picturesqueness there is in his work must arise from contrasts – but actual contrasts vividly presented. This is what gives interest to a work of art; and such a work must, before all things, be interesting.

F.M.H.

THE FORD MADOX FORD SOCIETY

Ford c. 1915   **©Alfred Cohen, 2000**   **Registered Charity No. 1084040**

This international society was founded in 1997 to promote knowledge of and interest in Ford. Honorary Members include Julian Barnes, A.S. Byatt, Samuel Hynes, Alan Judd, Sir Frank Kermode, Ruth Rendell, Michael Schmidt, John Sutherland, and Gore Vidal. There are currently over one hundred members, from more than ten countries. The Society organizes an active programme of events. Besides regular meetings in Britain, it has held major international conferences in Italy, Germany, and the U.S.A. In 2002 it launched the annual series, International Ford Madox Ford Studies, which is distributed free to members. If you are an admirer, an enthusiast, a reader, a scholar, or a student of anything Fordian, then this Society wants to hear from you, and welcomes your participation in its activities.

The Society aims to organise at least two events each year, and to publish one or two Newsletters. It has also inaugurated a series of Ford Lectures, which have been given by Martin Stannard, Alan Judd, David Crane, Sergio Perosa, and Oliver Soskice.
  To join, please send your name and address (including an e-mail address if possible), and a cheque made payable to 'The Ford Madox Ford Society', to:
  Sara Haslam, Department of Literature, Open University, Walton Hall, Milton Keynes, MK7 6AA.

Annual rates: **Pounds sterling:** Individuals: £12; Concessions £6;
                                  Member Organisations £25
              US Dollars: Any category: $25

For further information, either contact Sara Haslam (Treasurer) at the above address, or Max Saunders (Chairman) on e-mail at: **max.saunders@kcl.ac.uk**
The Society's Website is at: **www.rialto.com/fordmadoxford_society**